Urban Revolutions

Historical Materialism Book Series

The Historical Materialism Book Series is a major publishing initiative of the radical left. The capitalist crisis of the twenty-first century has been met by a resurgence of interest in critical Marxist theory. At the same time, the publishing institutions committed to Marxism have contracted markedly since the high point of the 1970s. The Historical Materialism Book Series is dedicated to addressing this situation by making available important works of Marxist theory. The aim of the series is to publish important theoretical contributions as the basis for vigorous intellectual debate and exchange on the left.

The peer-reviewed series publishes original monographs, translated texts, and reprints of classics across the bounds of academic disciplinary agendas and across the divisions of the left. The series is particularly concerned to encourage the internationalization of Marxist debate and aims to translate significant studies from beyond the English-speaking world.

For a full list of titles in the Historical Materialism Book Series available in paperback from Haymarket Books, visit: www.haymarketbooks.org/series_collections/1-historical-materialism.

Urban Revolutions

Urbanisation and (Neo-)Colonialism in Transatlantic Context

Stefan Kipfer

Haymarket Books
Chicago, IL

First published in 2022 by Brill Academic Publishers, The Netherlands
© 2022 Koninklijke Brill NV, Leiden, The Netherlands

Published in paperback in 2023 by
Haymarket Books
P.O. Box 180165
Chicago, IL 60618
773-583-7884
www.haymarketbooks.org

ISBN: 978-1-64259-995-4

Distributed to the trade in the US through Consortium Book Sales and
Distribution (www.cbsd.com) and internationally through Ingram
Publisher Services International (www.ingramcontent.com).

This book was published with the generous support of Lannan
Foundation and Wallace Action Fund.

Special discounts are available for bulk purchases by organizations and
institutions. Please call 773-583-7884 or email info@haymarketbooks.org
for more information.

Cover art and design by David Mabb. Cover art is a detail of *Long Live
the New! Painting 7, Kazimir Malevich drawing on William Morris, Indian,*
paint and wallpaper on canvas (2016).

Printed in the United States.

10 9 8 7 6 5 4 3 2 1

Library of Congress Cataloging-in-Publication data is available.

Contents

Acknowledgements

The texts assembled in this book were written and researched mostly in Toronto and Paris, roughly between 2002 and 2019. They draw on select themes from my PhD dissertation and benefited greatly from subsequent insights gathered and discussions I had in other places, during workshops, conferences, public events, travels and site visits and informal meetings. Among these: Martinique, Tunis, Algiers, Marseille, Bordeaux, Caen, Zurich, Geneva, Lausanne, Vaumarcus, Ottawa, Montreal, Vancouver, Winnipeg, Saskatoon, Batoche, North Battleford, The Pas, Timiskaming, Iroquois Falls, Rouyin-Noranda, Québec City, Gaspé, London, Liverpool, Denver, Seattle, Casa Grande, Los Angeles, Chicago, New York City, Washington D.C., Hong Kong, Ramallah, and Istanbul. Inevitably, then, the texts are products of translation, in the specific sense of working across different languages (English, French, German in my case) and in the more general sense of transporting (and thus recasting and modifying) the meaning of texts, situations and experiences from one historical and geographical context to another.

The people and organizations that had a direct or indirect role in making the production and publication of this book possible are too numerous to recall. Among them, I would like to highlight Karen Wirsig, my life partner with whom I have been privileged to share many of the political experiences and intellectual exchanges that were crucial for the creation of these texts; my parents Stefi and Ernst Kipfer, who always insisted that I question common sense; and Chantal Kipfer and Felix Wirsig, my daughter and son who challenge my thinking and sensibilities continuously. I would also like to express my deep thanks to my immediate co-producers, Kanishka Goonewardena (who gave me permission to adapt and re-use the text for Chapter 1 and with whom I discussed many themes in this book since the early 2000s) as well as Mustafa Dikeç, Mike Ekers, Gillian Hart, Alex Loftus, Parastou Saberi, and Christian Schmid (who have shaped my outlook in various ways as we worked on different but inevitably related projects and materials since the late 2000s).

This book would not have seen the light of day without the initiative of Sebastian Budgen and the editors of the Historical Materialism Book Series and Brill Publishers. In Paris, I benefited from the inestimable support of the comrades at *Période* and *Contretemps*, and the *Parti des Indigènes de la République* (notably Stella Magliani-Belkacem, Félix Boggio Ewanjé-Epée, Sadri Khiari, Selim Nadi) and *Eterotopia France* (Cosimo Lisi, Duccio Scotini, Tiziana Villani) as well as university colleagues in Geography at Paris-Est Marne-la-Vallée (Anne Clerval, Claire Hancock), Political Science at Paris VIII (Sylvie Tissot), and the *Centre des études européennes* at Sciences Po (Patrick Le Galès). In Toronto, elements of my work have been supported institutionally and intellectually by friends, comrades and colleagues at York University (Environmental Studies, Political Science, Geography), the University of Toronto (Geography and Planning), Historical Materialism Toronto, the Greater Workers' Assembly and the Socialist Project.

In these and other places, I would like to thank the following people for answers, comments, questions, and critiques over the last 15 years: Greg Albo, Himani Bannerji, Houria Bouteldja, Neil Brenner, Sebastian Budgen, Christine Chivallon, Raphaël Confiant, Glen Coulthard, Chayma Drira, David Featherstone, Honor Ford-Smith, Kyle Gibson, Liette Gilbert, Derek Gregory, Shubhra Gururani, Oded Haas, Laam Hae, Jin Haritaworn, Flora Hergon, David Hugill, Pablo Idahosa, Ilan Kapoor, Alia Karim, Ken Kawashima, Roger Keil, Ute Lehrer, David McNally, Louis Joseph Maugée, Radhika Mongia, Karen Murray, Ayyaz Mallick, Ugo Palheta, Linda Peake, Justin Podur, Mohamed Ragoubi, Norma Rantisi, Matthieu Renault, Sue Ruddick, Ted Rutland, Cate Sandilands, Ato Sekyi-Otu, Nicola Short, Rachel Vernisse, Audra Simpson, Łukasz Stanek, Wing-Shing Tang, Kasim Tirmizey, Dale Tomich and Anna Zalik.

I gratefully acknowledge the publishers of Eterotopia for giving me permission to use, in significantly extended and reworked ways, *Le temps et l'espace de la (dé)colonisation: Dialogue entre Frantz Fanon and Henri Lefebvre* (Paris, 2019) for Chapters 1 to 5 of this volume. These chapters also borrow passages, insights and arguments from the following English-language publications. Chapter 1 is a modified and expanded version of Stefan Kipfer and Kanishka Goonewardena, 'Urban Marxism and the Post-colonial Question: Henri Lefebvre and "Colonisation"', *Historical Materialism*, 21, no. 2 (2013): 76–117. Chapter 2 is a revised, much expanded and updated version of a text that was published in abridged form as Stefan Kipfer, 'The Times and Spaces of (De-)Colonisation: Fanon's Counter-Colonialism, Then and Now' in *Living Fanon*, ed. Nigel Gibson (New York: Palgrave, 2011), pp. 93–104. Chapter 3 contains fragments and preliminary arguments from Stefan Kipfer, 'Worldwide Urbanisation and Neocolonial Fractures', in *Implosions/Explosions*, ed. Neil Brenner, (Berlin: Jovis, 2014), pp. 288–305. Chapter 4 is a modified, much expanded and updated version of an original submission ultimately published as 'Pushing the Limits of Urban Research: Urbanisation, Pipelines and Counter-Colonial Politics', *Environment and Planning D: Society and Space*, 36, no. 3 (2018): 474–93. Chapter 5 is an updated, expanded and modified version of Stefan Kipfer, 'Démolition et contre-révolution: la rénovation urbaine dans la région parisienne', *Période*, revueperiode.net (5 October 2015), which itself is a longer, unabridged version of the article submitted to *Antipode* and published there under the title 'Neo-

Colonial Urbanism? *La Rénovation urbaine* in Paris', *Antipode*, 48, no. 3 (2016): 603–25. Finally, the conclusion borrows a few insights and facts from a longer interview with Cosimo Lisi and Duccio Scotini about the COVID-19 pandemic published as 'Espace urbain et distanciation sociale' in *acta.zone* (4 June 2020).

Marxism, Anti-Colonialism and Urban Research

This book is about Marxism, anti-colonialism and urban questions. It demonstrates that urban research can mediate effective encounters between Marxist and anti-colonial intellectual currents. In turn, it shows that these encounters can sharpen our understanding of the (neo-)colonial aspects of capitalist urbanisation today. Theoretically, the book's centre of gravity rests in the works of Henri Lefebvre and Frantz Fanon and the Marxist and anti-colonial traditions within which each of these *oeuvres* are located. From there, it radiates to the creole intellectual current based in the French-dominated Antilles, radical Indigenous theories on Turtle Island/North America and political anti-racist traditions in mainland France. The book connects various urban centres (Paris, Algiers, Fort-de-France, Toronto, Winnipeg, Vancouver) and travels through the manifold networks that connect these urban regions to each other and to other parts of the world. In so doing, the book relates the aforementioned intellectual currents to a range of political situations that are each mediated by comparatively distinct, capitalist, imperial, and (settler-)colonial histories of city, countryside and urbanisation as well as the urban strategies and spatial imaginaries that are tied up with these histories.

1   Starting Points

The following pages deal with two basic assumptions made in this book and unpacks these in relationship to the intellectual sources that generated them. In the first instance, I assume that a project of re-covering and developing resonances between Marxist and anti-colonial lineages is both possible and desirable. Desirable because Marxist anti-capitalisms that abstract from the role of imperial and (neo-)colonial realities in shaping capitalist development are as abstractly utopian (or dystopian) as anti-colonialisms and anti-racisms that are blind to the specific dynamics of capitalist development, including the capitalist dimensions of modern racism, colonialism and imperialism. Even in our world, where imperialism often (but, as several chapters of this book underline, not always) operates without direct colonial control, both currents are vital to understand how space is produced by colonial and capitalist relations and, in part, through the territorial relations that cut across dynamics of urbanisation. They are also both crucial to further any project that wants to recast spatial relations, challenge dynamics of space production, and make life on this planet worth living against the mortal threats of climate change and social barbarism (including fascism). Linking Marxism and anti-colonialism is possible because points of fruitful contact between Marxist and anti-colonial lineages have been numerous. Of course, it goes without saying that to develop such lineages requires ongoing work. All chapters insist, for example, that Marxist approaches to politics, social life and spatial organisation be stretched and reformulated once more in relationship to anti-colonial traditions.

1.1   Marxism, Anti-Colonialism and the Problem of Eurocentrism

> The theses that I have developed on global history never seemed to me to require the abandonment of Marxism.[1]

The first assumption is based upon anti-racist, feminist and Marxist currents that have refused to uphold schisms between materialist concerns and considerations of subjectivity, language, and ideology; between political economy and cultural theory; and between class and other social questions such as race, gender and sexuality (which have been grouped too frequently and simply under the rubric of identity).[2]

In English-speaking intellectual circles, these schisms emerged as a result of the postmodern and deconstructive turns of the mid-1980s and some unnecessarily defensive (also Marxist) responses to these turns. Since then, these turns have lost much of their steam. Yet, as contemporary Anglo-American debates about intersectionality, whiteness, anti-Black racism or (post-)coloniality show, earlier schisms have not disappeared. Instead, they have been recast, unnecessarily, as many sharp observers have highlighted.[3] My starting point is to suggest that thinking through the tension-fraught links between non-identical aspects of life – political or theoretical orientation, belonging (identification and identity), experience and social position in and across multiple social relations – is indeed a vital task. The best way to do so is not, however, to abandon socialist and Marxist orientations but to mobilise intellectual sources that have worked to articulate Marxist, anti-racist, anti-colonial, feminist and queer traditions of liberation.

---

1   Amin 2011, p. 9.
2   Bannerji 1995, Sekyi-Otu 1996, McNally 2001.
3   Bannerji 2014, 2015; Taylor 2016, 2019; Boggio Ewanjé-Epée, Magliani-Belkacem, Merteuil, and Monferrand 2017; Bhattacharya 2017; McNally 2017; Sekyi-Otu 2019; Gordon 2018; Haider 2018a, 2018b; Moran 2018; Gandesha 2019; Aouragh 2019; Bakan and Dua 2014; Bakan 2014; Olaloku-Teriba 2018; Thomas 2018a; Ekers 2013; Rebucini 2017; Sears 2017.

In research fields concerned with (neo-)colonialism, past and present, schisms between materialist and cultural approaches have had the unfortunate effect of throwing the baby (Marxism and associated critiques of capitalism) out with the bathwater (Eurocentrism). One effect of such divides is to enable those who want to dismiss past and present attempts to forge anti-colonial Marxisms or Marxist anti-colonialisms by overlooking once more the historical fact that Marxism has long ceased to be the property of 'Europe', thanks to long decades of tricontinental networking, national liberation struggles and revolutionary practices in what we now call the global South.[4] Another effect of these schisms has been a tendency to transpose critiques of Eurocentrism onto a cultural-civilisational plane, one characterised by ontologies steeped in the distinction between tradition and modernity, sometimes echoing familiar civilisational tropes on the political right from Spengler to Huntington.[5] Exemplified by debates generated by the postcolonial turn in subaltern studies and some Marxist critiques of this turn,[6] such a transposition has made it easier for critics of postcolonial theory to minimise the weight of colonial and imperial history, while pushing those with the laudable intent to 'provincialise Europe' (and thus undo the temporality of 'not-yet', the state of being condemned to play catch-up in perpetuity)[7] to hypostatise 'Europe' and its 'others' as overly coherent figures. This procedure has lent rather too much credibility to Euro-American property claims to reason, science, democracy, secularism, universality, modernity, and other such goodies.[8, 9]

Eurocentrism is of course a most serious matter. As Samir Amin suggested,[10] Eurocentrism is no mere ethnocentric parochialism, although often it is this, too. It represents a central ideological component of the modern culture that emerged in and through the rise of capitalism and its colonial and imperial foundations.[11] Following Amin, who also builds on Martin Bernal and Edward

---

4   Prashad 2007; Bouamama 2014, 2016.
5   Bannerji 2011; Harootunian 2005.
6   Chakrabarty 2000; Chibber 2013.
7   Chakrabarty 2000.
8   Sarkar 2000; Kaiwar 2013; Cooper 2005; Boggio Ewanjé-Epée and Renault 2013; Brennan 2014; Harootunian 2000, 2015; Matin 2011.
9   The problems with this tendency to inflate 'Europe' into a philosophically and epistemologically coherent figure are not unique to the postcolonial turn in subaltern studies. They have also been debated within and in relationship to Latin American decolonial theory, often with reference to the pitfalls of Occidentalism (Dussel 1993; Coronil 1996, 1997, pp. 14–15; Ahiska 2008; De Sousa Santos 2009).
10   Amin 1989; Amin 2011, pp. 153–6.
11   See also Lazarus and Rashmi Varma 2008, pp. 314–16; Lazarus 2002.

Said,[12] Eurocentrism refers to the habit of treating the world as a normative or analytical projection of an 'eternal Europe'. This conception of Europe as a coherent, self-sufficient, and historically invariant civilisation is predicated on two intellectual procedures: (1) an annexation of non- or not-just European influences (Hellenism and Christianity) to Europe (leading in some cases to a veritable European confiscation of philosophy per se), combined with (2) an insulation of Europe from others with the help of cultural and biological forms of racism, Orientalism included.[13] Eurocentrism is deeply ideological in the precise sense of falsely universalising particular realities that cannot be so universalised. While our originally Eurocentric capitalist world order harbours universalising tendencies, these cannot be fully realised for two reasons: the necessarily unequal, imperial structure of world capitalism and the squarely anti-universalist culturalist ontology of Eurocentrism. Dividing the world into homogenous civilisational blocs, the latter blinds us to the world-wide interdependencies that made the constructions and self-projections of Europe and its others, the Occident and the Orient, possible in the first place.

What to do about Eurocentrism? Amin makes it clear that any attempt to tackle Eurocentrism without challenging its material basis (imperial world order) and its ideological core (reified ideas of 'eternal Europe') is bound to fail. In response, Amin proposes two paths, one political and socio-economic, the other intellectual and theoretical. Most broadly, Eurocentrism can only wither away if its foundation, the imperial world order, also falls. Revolutionary strategies of de-linking from the capitalist world system are required to create a polycentric and non-capitalist world. On such new foundations,[14] it may be possible to develop a truly universal constellation of socialist cultures that ap-

---

12   Bernal 1987; Said 1979. In hindsight, Amin's bridge to Said may have been an early indication of what Said himself pointed out more firmly later in his life: the importance of steering clear of civilisational ontologies (Said 2000, pp. 198–215; Said 2003; Lazarus 2011, pp. 183–203; Traboulsi 2008). Following Mahmood Mamdani's terminology, it points to the urgency of circumnavigating the 'culture talk' promoted by Samuel Huntington's civilisational *raison d'état* and the war on terror (2004, pp. 17–62).

13   Amin 1989, pp. 90–103. On the European property claims to philosophy that may follow from the procedure of retroactively Europeanising ancient Greece, see Gordon 2008, pp. 1–18.

14   Needless to say, Amin's socialist vision of polycentricity is not to be confused with the multipolar but still capitalist and imperialist world Radhika Desai anticipated, against the basic tenets of world-systems theory (2013). Aspirations for such a capitalist multi-polarity sometimes come with their own state-sponsored claims to alternative modernities, as Arif Dirlik has argued for some time, also in relationship to a resurgent neo-Confucian Chinese nationalism (1996; 2007, p. 79), and thus years before the consolidation of Modi's India and Erdogan's Turkey.

propriate elements from the status quo to build a radically new order.[15] For this purpose, theoretical efforts to liberate Marxist traditions from all Eurocentric straightjackets are both possible and necessary.[16] Such efforts to 'strengthen the universalist dimension of historical materialism'[17] must include notions of time and space that defy both diffusionist approaches to historical development and culturally homogenising notions of the world and its components. How? By stressing cross-civilisational connections in capitalist and pre-capitalist, also tributary formations, thus illustrating the internal incoherences and external dependencies of 'Europe'; and by showing the role of unequal development (spatial unevenness) and historical discontinuity (temporal disjuncture) in the formation and eventual transformation of capitalism.[18]

Amin is one among several authors who have tried to reconstruct historical geographical materialism on a decisively anti-Eurocentric basis in order to defy, as Fernando Coronil had it, 'imperial geo-histories' that treat the formation of capitalism and European expansion in a smoothly linear and unidirectional fashion, often on the basis of Occidentalism, the assumption of European historical self-sufficiency.[19] Along with his partners in world-systems theory, Amin informed the so-called spatial turn in social theory, to which we will turn shortly. When it comes to matters of history, time and temporality, Amin remains a reference point for all those committed to replacing linear-progressivist conceptions of history with robust alternatives. On this point, other recent efforts have recast arguments about multi-temporal or multi-rhythmic conceptions of history in the early and late Karl Marx, José Carlos Mariátegui's analysis of the Peruvian situation, Antonio Gramsci's peculiar historicism, Walter Benjamin's conception of modernity as a temporal dialectic of experience, Ernst Bloch's treatment of tradition and discordance, Tosaka Jun and Henri Lefebvre's respective notions of everyday life, Leon Trotsky's theory of combined and uneven development, the articulation of modes of production debates, and relational contributions to comparative method.[20] In this

---

15   Amin 1989, pp. 137–52.
16   Amin 1989, pp. 118–23.
17   Amin 1989, p. xiii.
18   Amin 1989, pp. 79–88. See also Kolja Lindner (2010) and Thierry Drapeau (2019) on the necessity and possibility of reengaging with Marx and Engels themselves along these temporally nuanced lines in light of debates in postcolonial studies.
19   Coronil 1996.
20   Hall 1996, 2003; Bensaïd 2002; Banaji 2011; Tombazos 2014; Mariátegui 1971; Harootunian 2000, 2015; Anievas and Nisancioglu 2015; Tomba 2013; Menozzi 2019; Coulthard 2014; McMichael 1999; Goswami 2002; Hart 2006, 2018a; Thomas 2017; Morfino and Thomas 2017.

book, we will encounter a number of these debates in a spirit of developing non-Eurocentric political and theoretical orientations.

With his call for a genuinely universal, post-imperial and post-capitalist culture, Amin rejoins others for whom a radicalised universalism represents a necessity, an unavoidable theoretical and political response to objective, if incomplete and contradictory universalising tendencies unfolding within the constraints of a deeply fractured and uneven capitalist world.[21] Similar to Immanuel Wallerstein,[22] Amin navigates between a broad sketch of world historical development and theoretical interventions pitched at a high level of generality. To this tableau, one can add other universal/ising arguments, including those that pay particular attention to subjective and ethico-political mediations between the universal and the particular. Particularly important for me have been Ato Sekyi-Otu's conceptions of partisan and vernacular universalism, which avoid one-sided particularisms and unilateral universalisms all at once. With the former, Ato Sekyi-Otu describes a seemingly paradoxical relationship between situated critique and universal commitment that is rendered possible through the kind of 'dialectic of experience' Frantz Fanon captured in his rendering of the Algerian liberation struggle.[23] With the latter, Sekyi-Otu pushes us to consider the universal not only as the result of the political economy of capitalism or the experience of revolutionary struggle but also as an argumentative, ethical and political starting point embedded within everyday life, including the daily lives of colonised peoples.[24] These dynamic and dialectical conceptions of the relationship between the universal and the particular open up productive dialogues between Marxist and anti-colonial traditions because they decisively eschew the false universalisms generated by imperial and Eurocentric frameworks. In the eyes of Sekyi-Otu, such encounters offer the possibility of one among multiple possible paths to communism.[25]

This brief review should help clarify my terminological choice to deploy the adjectives anti- or counter-colonial rather than post- or decolonial to describe the traditions mobilised in the book. This choice results principally from the fact that I have been most energised by writers who have rethought colonial questions in ways that are not confined to postcolonial or decolonial discourses, including the deconstructive, genealogical, and cultural-civilisational

---

21   See also Lazarus et al. 1995.
22   Wallerstein 1997.
23   Sekyi-Otu 1996.
24   Sekyi-Otu 2019.
25   Sekyi-Otu 2019, p. 133. Sekyi-Otu draws on Ayi Kwei Armah's conclusions (1984, pp. 39–40).

frameworks and sensibilities that have dominated these debates.[26] As a result of these contributions, some have broadened the meaning of postcolonial studies to include specifically Marxist approaches.[27] This seems to underscore a point that some theorists and militants have been making for some time: that one can refer to postcolonial approaches in a theoretically and politically ecumenical fashion.[28] But still today, the post- and decolonial are not mere descriptors of historical realities (after-colonial realities still informed by colonial legacies) or political strategies in and against these realities. They often continue to function as codes for the deconstructive, genealogical or cultural-civilisational currents that make up the postmodern turn, which developed at a distance from or in opposition to Marxism. As will become obvious in various parts of this book, I do not systematically reject insights from these currents. However, I follow Priyamvada Gopal's advice[29] and prioritise the terms anti- or counter-colonialism for the sake of precision and to signal the actuality of dialectical and materialist traditions of liberation.

1.2   Spatial Organisation and Urbanisation: Strategic Questions

Thunder Bay has always been a city of two faces. The Port Arthur side is the White face and the Fort William is the red face.[30]

The second basic assumption I make in this book is that spatial organisation – and processes of producing space more generally – matter to how we understand the world and intervene in it, and that strategies to study and transform the production of space should not therefore be the exclusive purview of spatial specialists, be they architects, planners, designers, or even geographers. This twin starting point has two immediate consequences. For critical theorists, radicals and revolutionaries to take the spatial organisation of life and politics seriously means that they should avoid treating it as an epiphenomenon without explanatory or strategic weight, a habit that tends to take mainstream, bourgeois conceptions and practices of space for granted. In turn, challenging the

---

26   Sekyi-Otu 1996, 2019; Coulthard 2014; Bartolovich and Lazarus 2002; Lazarus 2004, 2011; Majumdar 2007; Sarkar 2002; Gopal 2005, 2019; Bannerji, Mojab and Whitehead 2001; Bannerji, 2011; Hallward 2001; Brennan 2006, 1997; Cooper 2005; Harootunian 2000, 2015; Ahmad 1992; Hart 2006, 2018; Goswami 2004, Gallissot 2006; Bouamama 2016, 2014; Ortiz-Dunbar 2015; Kulchysky 2013.

27   Bartolovich and Lazarus 2002; Lazarus and Varma 2008; Lazarus 2011; Murphy 2007.

28   Young 2001.

29   Gopal 2019, pp. 5–6.

30   Talaga 2017, p. 3.

monopoly of specialists over the production of space requires that one undo a *déformation professionelle* one often finds in the applied spatial sciences: spatial determinism, or the idea that space or the environment (and, thus, spatial intervention) determines social life unilaterally.

Amin's attempt to relate the rise (and fall) of the ideology of Eurocentrism to the formation (and demise) of the capitalist world order makes a powerful case to take to heart the weight of spatial (dis)organisation in politics and social life. Amin's more specific point – that Eurocentrism is unthinkable without the idea of an 'eternal', internally coherent, externally demarcated and historically invariant Europe, and that this idea depends on the selective annexation of cross-civilisational historical lineages – can also be made at the scales of the nation and the city. The confiscation of Hellenism by advocates of an eternal Europe has parallels in the re-Hellenisation of Greece in its modern national form. Since the nineteenth century, independence from the Ottoman Empire made room for attempts to recreate a commercially profitable, tourist-focused and nationalist historical continuity between modern Athens and ancient Greece. As Alexander Clapp has pointed out,[31] a combination of ethnic cleansing and urban strategies (many of which were financed from abroad, Germany, Britain, the USA) to recentre Athens around the excavated ruins of antiquity made it possible to socially and symbolically demarcate Greece from the East, that is, the Ottoman Empire and Turkey, in order to assimilate it to the West. Internally, this demarcation meant covering up, literally, the signs that would remind us of the centuries of social, physical, linguistic and cultural discontinuity between ancient and post-Ottoman Greece.

One crucial reason why space should be taken seriously is thus related to urban questions. These far exceed planning and architecture in places called cities, however. During the modern industrial revolutions and the rise of the Anthropocene,[32] urbanisation has played a crucial, qualitatively new role, generating a veritable 'metropocene'.[33] According to conventional measures that relate urbanisation to the relative demographic weight of settlement forms described as urban, the world's degree of urbanisation has increased from a few

---

31   Clapp 2018, pp. 23–43, 69–73. In effect, Clapp's ruminations about Athens raise serious questions about the integrity of the idea of the European city and remind us of the methodological problems with attempts to typologise cities in cultural-civilisational terms. On the equivalent methodological problems with the idea of the Islamic city, see Janet Abu-Lughod (1987).

32   For debates on the character of the Capitalocene and its racialised dimensions, see Malm 2015, Moore 2017, and Vergès 2017.

33   Whitehead 2014, p. 100.

percentage points in 1800 to more than fifty percent in the first decade of the twenty-first century.[34] This quantitative explosion (measured in the conventional terms of urbanisation) points to qualitative transformations that cannot be grasped if urban questions are reduced to thing-like, place-bound, even local matters: a collection of physical structures (the built environment) or a geographical concentration of activities as defined by population size and density. For some time now, urban researchers have adjusted their focus to keep pace with the shape-shifting, boundary-destroying dynamics of capitalist urbanisation. They now shed light not only on spatial concentrations (towns, cities, metropoles, agglomerations, conurbations) but also on extensive networks that connect and cut across these spatial nodes (transportation, infrastructure, migration, institutions of state and capital). The dual and multi-scalar character of urbanisation has long been recognised in various corners of urban research, not only by the Lefebvre-inspired approaches that will be an important reference point in this book.[35] Accordingly, metropoles and cities studied here such as Paris or Fort-de-France embody a wider set of socio-natural relations,[36] in part through the spatial networks that traverse them and connect them to each other and other places.

    The main source for these spatial and urban starting points is a field of fields that has played an important role in the so-called spatial turn in the English-speaking social sciences: radical geography.[37] Shaped by the multiple radicalisms that shaped the world-wide explosion that was '1968', radical geography developed approaches through comprehensive critiques of the mainstream spatial sciences that reigned at the time: the Chicago school (in urban sociology), modernisation theory (in development studies) and neoclassical economics (in regional science). In the 1970s and 1980s, radical geography was always multiple, but remained strongly shaped by Marxist, feminist, anarchist, anti-racist, and anti-colonial versions of materialist social theory. As we will see in Chapter 1, Marxist-influenced theories of space and urbanisation

---

34   United Nations 2018.
35   Lefebvre 2003a; Kipfer 2009a; Brenner and Schmid 2015.
36   Massey 1991; Hart 2018b.
37   For crucial access points, see Dear and Scott 1981; Gregory and Urry 1985; Wolch and Dear 1989; Barnes and Sheppard 2019; Antipode Editorial Collective 2019. I should note that radical geography is not a mere wing of the discipline called geography. Authors contributing to the diverse body of knowledge cited here have had various 'homes' in and beyond geography and other sub- or multidisciplines with spatial qualifiers such as urban sociology, rural sociology, urban studies, environmental studies, planning, and architecture. In fact, radical geography represents a particular condensation of a wider 'spatial turn' in the human sciences. For more on this turn, see Soja 1980, 1989; Warf and Arias 2009.

developed into two overlapping fields: metropolitan formulations of urban Marxism oriented towards understanding developments in Euro-America; and global formulations focused on studying urbanisation at a world scale and in the Third World. Instead of entrenching the more recent divide between postcolonial and Marxist spatial and urban theory, which would wrongly confine urban Marxism to Euro-America while cleansing historical-materialist currents of urban research on colonial matters, I am interested in reconnecting and recasting these global and metropolitan formulations on capitalist and (neo-)colonial urbanism. This is why I spend much time establishing relations between Euro-American urban Marxism (from Lefebvre to theories of gentrification) and anti-colonial traditions (from Fanon to Indigenous resurgence).

While emerging out of a particular historical conjuncture, radical geography also picked up on earlier traditions, including Marxian traditions broadly conceived. Marx and Engels's own contributions (as well as those of some of their anarchist contemporaries) tended to treat urban questions in relationship to people's daily lives and larger patterns such as the division between city and country in the history of capitalism (in the *German Ideology*, the *Communist Manifesto, Capital*) and the 'place' of particular spatial and urban questions (land rent, housing, biophysical metabolism, enclosure) in the accumulation of capital, original or otherwise (in various parts of *Capital* and the *Housing Question*). While these early contributions proved vital for current debates (for example, on urban political ecology, accumulation by dispossession, the built environment, the rent gap in gentrification and suburbanisation),[38] Marx and Engels's works also indicate that urban questions are not static or historically uniform but subject to a radical redefinition in and through the dynamics of capitalist development. Engels's *Conditions of the Working Class in England* set the tone early on by observing the production of entirely new landscapes (beyond historically constituted forms of city and country) and stressing the role of spatial segregation, transportation, and commodity culture in class formation and the experience of modernity. With Engels, and Marx's analysis of Bonapartism and the Commune (in the *18th Brumaire* and *Civil War in France*), city-country relations provide the key to grasping state-formation, revolutionary strategy and the exercise of political rule. As a result, urban questions cease to be of only local and particular interest.

The era of (counter-)revolution that ushered a new era in the history of Marxism added much ammunition to the repertoires of radical geography.

---

38   Harvey 2001a, 2001b, 2003a, 2003b; Walker 1981; Smith 1996; Heynen, Kaika and Swynge-douw 2006.

The radical political strategies that emerged in the course of these revolutions (Trotsky's Permanent Revolution, Lenin's and Gramsci's versions of the United Front, Mao's conceptions of the peasant revolution, Che's *foco* approach to guerrilla warfare) had decisive impacts on later intellectual developments, from debates about *Uneven Development* (Neil Smith) to investigations about *The Country and the City* (Raymond Williams) as imaginaries and practices tied to both empire and peasant revolution, cross-cutting dynamics of urbanisation notwithstanding.[39] '1917', '1949' and '1959' (and other proto-revolutionary moments in between) also rattled the worlds of spatial expertise. The ruptures promised and generated by revolution forced new questions onto the agenda: what is the relationship between spatial organisation and social revolution, and, more specifically, what is the role, if any, for specialists (and other avant-gardes) in the spatial reorganisation of life during revolutionary change? These questions informed not only contemporary debates (about modernist urbanism, national spatial planning, appropriate or dialectical technologies, to speak in Cuban terms). They also came to inform English-speaking radical geographical and urban circles, sometimes by way of various other places, including Brazil (Milton Santos),[40] France (Anatole Kopp, Manuel Castells, Jean-Pierre Garnier, Henri Lefebvre),[41] or Italy (Manfredo Tafuri, Toni Negri).[42]

Radical geographers have learned from revolution also negatively, by having to come to terms with the ways in which spatial strategies may underwrite counter-revolution or help exhaust revolutionary efforts. In this respect, they have once again walked partly in their predecessors' footsteps. In the 1920s and 1930s, Victor Serge chronicled the historical proximity of revolution and counter-revolution in the Soviet Union in part by tracing their respective spatial manifestations.[43] In the same period, Walter Benjamin, who himself observed this proximity when visiting Moscow in 1926 and 1927, placed 'Haussmann' in an explosive mix together with the Commune, fascism and the daily life of the commodity (thus transfiguring Engels's critique of the Baron into modernist form).[44] Others continued to shed light on the counter-revolutionary character of urbanism by highlighting the role of planning and architecture in the rise of Americanism and Fordism (Antonio Gramsci),[45]

---

39   Smith 1984; Williams 1973.
40   Santos 1971, 1974, 1975, 1977.
41   Kopp 1970; Garnier 1973; Castells 1977; Guilbaud, Lefebvre, and Renaudie 2009.
42   Tafuri 1976; Negri 2017.
43   Morton 2018.
44   Benjamin 1982, 1980.
45   Gramsci 1971, pp. 280–318.

the practice of separation (Guy Debord),[46] racialised compartmentalisation
(W.E.B. Du Bois, Frantz Fanon, John Rex, George Lipsitz, Carl Nightingale)[47]
and mass utopia (Susan Buck-Morss, Owen Hatherley)[48] in various postwar
orders, capitalist, (neo-)colonial or state socialist. Cutting across these efforts
have been feminist analyses of counter-revolution, including Dolores Hayden's
comparison of US Fordism (as the domestication of life through spatial decentralisation, the generalisation of the property form and household debt, and a
patriarchal and technocratic administration of interior design) to Alexandra
Kollontai's communist vision of women's liberation: a socialisation of domestic
work/space, a reorganisation of sexuality, and a restructuring of gendered divisions of labour, all aimed at an ultimate withering away of the patriarchal family.[49]

1.3   Form, a Minimal Unity of Urban Life in the Modern World?

Even if only briefly sketched here, radical geographical debates and their predecessors make it clear that the dynamics of spatio-temporal rupture and
unevenness of the modern world undermine any attempt to hold onto linear-
progressive conceptions of (urban) history and geography. This has made it
possible for more recent authors to develop explicit alternatives to Eurocentric
schemata. Jennifer Robinson, for example, has mobilised Walter Benjamin's
writings on Moscow and Naples as bridges between his writings about modernity in Paris and Berlin, on the one hand, and debates about modernity in
the Zambian copperbelt, on the other.[50] In this comparative constellation, Benjamin's notion of modernity as a spatialised experience of time (now-time,
a jarring juxtaposition of past and present) throws wrenches in the empty-
homogenous notion of time that is produced by capitalist clock-time, which
one finds also in the evolutionary, progressive conceptions of the relationship between modernity and tradition so central to classical sociology, and
its offshoot, the Chicago school of urban sociology. Instead of splitting apart
European modernity from alternative modernities, a comparatively stretched
Benjaminian notion of modernity as spatially mediated temporal experience
makes us see each comparative situation (from Lusaka to Marseille) as a qual-

---

46   Debord 1977.
47   Du Bois 1967; Rex 1973; Lipsitz 2010; Nightingale 2012. For Fanon, see Chapter 2.
48   Buck-Morss 2002; Hatherley 2015.
49   Hayden 1981. For more recent insights about Kollontai, the promises of her Marxist femin-
      ism as well as the limits of her perspective in relationship to the Russian colonies, gender
      relations and heteronormativity, see Renault 2017b and Adamczak 2017.
50   Robinson 2006, pp. 28–56.

itatively distinct articulation of past and present, a *sui generis* window into the modern world that allows us to see 'the intertwining of now and then' as well as 'here and there'.[51] Just as it is not a simple counterpoint to tradition, this modern world is not a product of linear progression from one place to the next, for example from the rural to the urban (town or city); in fact, it often reconfigures, recreates, or incorporates in tension-ridden form the relationship between town and country understood as socio-natural spaces or imaginaries.[52]

Benjamin's jives well with other recipes against Eurocentrism, as Harry Harootunian's work reminds us. Connecting Benjamin to Henri Lefebvre, Tosaka Jun and debates about everyday life in interwar Japan, Harootunian mobilises resources against another couplet that embodies Eurocentric conceptions of temporal progression and comparative difference: modernisation theory and area studies.[53] He, too, develops a form analysis of modernity as a dialectical structure of time, a tension-fraught combination of past and present. This analysis opens up to a coeval conception of modernity where each comparative situation is contemporaneous with all others, but always through a specific articulation with path-dependent historical geographies. Understood as a temporal structure open to a potentially infinite number of situated constellations of past and present, modernity represents a 'minimal unity' of the world at the level of everyday life.[54] Debates about modern everyday life in imperial Japan are thus not to be understood as a 'latecoming' (and thus forever delayed) result of Europeanisation.[55] As incomplete as all other modern experiences of time, it expresses the contradictory ways in which novelty and history were articulated through Japanese modernisation strategies, imperial projects, and fascistic experiments. Harootunian offers us tools to genuinely provincialise (not hypostatise) Europe while also 'deprovincialising Marxism'[56] by confronting Marxian insights with various comparative realities and the political struggles and intellectual currents these have produced.

---

51   Robinson 2013, p. 662.

52   Ibid. For more on the Zambian debates in African context, see also Ferguson 1999; Freund 2007, pp. 82–137.

53   Harootunian 2000.

54   Ibid., pp. 18, 62. Harootunian's argument resonates with Dirlik's notion of global modernity as a singular *and* fractured form adequate to capitalist and colonial world order (2007, p. 90).

55   Ibid., p. 112.

56   While Harootunian used the term deprovincialising Marxism in relationship to Tosaka Jun (2012), one may also use it to describe the various Marxian strategies he mobilises to understand the formal of subsumption of labour comparatively (2015).

Harootunian's Japanese and Robinson's African inflections of modernity as spatialised time, a contemporary fusion of past and present, can be brought to bear more fully on Henri Lefebvre's own modular conception of the urban as form. In his exploratory *Rhythmanalysis*, Lefebvre himself decided to further temporalise and spatialise the critique of everyday life. He suggested that urban life represents a tension-filled confluence of multiple rhythms, cyclical and linear. With his comparative notes on Atlantic and Mediterranean cities in Europe, Lefebvre stressed that that particular combination of these rhythms are comparatively distinct. Geographically uneven, urban life as a confluence of temporalities thus expresses in temporal fashion the contradiction between use-value and exchange-value of capital and the commodity form.[57] Lefebvre's rhythmanalysis puts into comparative and explicitly urban terms an earlier concern in his critique of everyday life: the search for 'moments', flash-like elements of cyclical time to be found in the gaps left within the inexorable sequence of 'instants' through which human bodies become absorbed into the reified, linear forms of repetition characteristic of capitalist space-time.[58] These fragment-like moments are part of the reservoir of possibility that can become, under specific circumstances, collective moments of political interruption through which subaltern capacities and aspirations condense and concentrate.[59] Through the mediation of political organisation, such collective moments can energise revolutionary strategy and help transform actually existing differences into a different social world.

Lefebvre's temporal understanding of urban life as a confluence of daily rhythms added a crucial aspect to his then already developed twin conception of the urban as form and mediating level.[60] Concentrated in the *Right to the City* (1968) and *The Urban Revolution* (1970), this conception grew out of more than a decade of observations about spatial transformations in the postwar era (collected in *Du Rural à l'Urbain*, 1970).[61] These observations ushered in a dialectical critique of functionalist planning and architecture and a conviction that urban questions 'put in sharp relief' the social structure as a whole. Urban questions had thus become an 'indispensable' 'aspect' and 'chain-link' of

---

57   Lefebvre 1992.
58   Ibid., pp. 13–30, 71–6; Lefebvre 2002b, pp. 340–58; Lefebvre 1973, pp. 312–13.
59   Lefebvre 1991a, p. 56.
60   The formulations in the following three paragraphs draw from Kipfer 2002; 2004, pp. 147–61; 2008; Kipfer and Goonewardena 2007, section 3, and Kipfer, Saberi and Wieditz 2013, pp. 4–6. For a closely related reading, see Schmid 2012, Goonewardena 2011.
61   Lefebvre 1996, 2003f., 1970; on Lefebvre's labour process of urban research from the 1950s onwards, see also Stanek 2011, 2014.

(but, of course, not a substitute for) the socialist revolution.[62] They had ceased to be reducible to particular human settlements and their relationship to non-urban spaces. They needed to be framed more broadly, first, as a *level* of the social totality mediating between everyday life and the large forces of the social order; and second, as *a form* of centrality through which a range of differences encounter each other in various ways, physically (in the built environment), socially and economically (through dynamics of agglomeration) or politically (by means of a convergence of political forces).

One can see how the idea of the right to the city emerges from this conception of the urban as form and mediating level. Understood as a concept within Lefebvre's broader work, the right to the city refers not only and not strictly speaking to struggles by inhabitants for given physical forms (towns, neighbourhoods, public space) and the right of these inhabitants to determine them in various ways, through daily use and political decision-making. Instead, the right to the city refers most centrally to particular kinds of encounters through which centralities are produced. What Lefebvre has in mind here are struggles waged by a multiplicity of forces that generate complex combinations of geographical centrality (a spatial convergence of struggles) and political centrality (a condensation of power expressed in the state and its capacity to centralise the social surplus). It is through this dual centrality that social struggles for political power and the social surplus may create collective and political moments, moments through which different movements and the multiple differences they express meet and transform each other in a dynamic search for a different world, one that promises to radically restructure both everyday life and the institutions of the social order at large.

Two clarifications need to be added here. As we discuss further in Chapter 1 and then throughout the book, Lefebvre related the urban as form to social content. He insisted that the urban, that couplet of centrality/difference, is traversed by territorial relations through which dominant and dominated social groups relate to each other spatially. In contrast to liberal-pluralist conceptions of urban life as density and diversity, the right to the city is a struggle concept; its meaning depends on the aspirations of a multiplicity of subaltern forces who often find themselves in a state of geographical dispersal and social peripheralisation and transform each other and themselves in part thanks to the encounters rendered possible in the process of converging mobilisations. In this way, the concept of the right to the city is a contribution to the arsenal of revolutionary theories at our disposal. In fact, the radical, even revolution-

---

62   Lefebvre 1970a, pp. 218–19.

ary implications of Lefebvre's approach to urban questions can also be seen in relationship to the question of scale, as we will see again in Chapters 3 and 4. The right to the city (to centrality/difference) is not reducible to city politics, to struggles in and for urban regions, central cities, or (sub/ex/urban) municipalities. Centralities understood politically can emerge at any point in the uneven tapestry that is urbanisation, whether in urban concentrations (towns, urban regions, conurbations) or from within the tentacles of extended urbanisation (bundled infrastructural networks, extractive zones, or agroindustrial complexes).[63] These political centralities may affirm and appropriate, and sometimes reject the urban as a normative horizon.[64] In all cases, political revolution and structural spatial transformation, the two meanings of urban revolution, are related; they both escape the confines of particular, notably local or regional scales.[65]

It is not difficult to detect the contemporary and comparative pertinence of Lefebvre's conception of the urban. The phrase 'right of the city' has travelled across the globe over the last generation. Often a slogan rather than a concept, it has done so in many different, reformist and radical, state-bound and autonomous ways. This has happened usually without explicit reference to Lefebvre or French politics, but often on the basis of initiatives in the global South, most prominently Brazil and other parts of Latin America.[66] In this context, the idea of the right to the city as political convergence, a medium to conjoin multiple social movements in comparatively specific contexts does sometimes emerge, be that in organisational or academic registers.[67] The world-wide presence of the Commune (as one revolutionary form combining uprising with generalised self-management) is another way through which Lefebvrean conceptions of the urban have travelled, albeit in an even more subterranean fashion. Next to the urban revolts and guerrilla movements in the Americas in the late 1960s,

---

63 On extended and concentrated urbanisation, see Brenner and Schmid 2015; Kanai 2014. For more elaborate discussions, see Chapters 3 and 4.
64 Lesutis 2020.
65 Kipfer 2009a.
66 Samara, He and Chen 2013; Duarte 2016; Fernandes 2007; Friendly 2013; Wainstein and Ren Galonnier 2012; Cassano 2013; Kuymulu 2013; Pithouse 2010; Mayer 2012; Liss 2012.
67 The *Global Platform for the Right to the City* (2019) convened by Habitat International Coalition (2019) mobilises the term right to the city to produce a nodal point within transnational networks of NGOs, movements and local authorities. Thanks to Lorena Zárate for pointing me to these recent sources. Meanwhile, social movement researchers have pointed out that centrality remains critical to understanding the urban dynamics of collective action, whether these are understood as uprisings, social movements or revolutions (Bayat 2017, pp. 120–9; Thörn, Mayer, and Thörn 2017, p. 28).

the Paris Commune of 1871 and May 1968 in Paris were the key inspirations for Lefebvre, who reinterpreted these two moments as *urban revolutions* before and right after Lefebvre's tome on the right to the city.[68] Commune-like political phenomena thus constitute a condition of possibility for the right to the city to travel in unexpected directions. The appearance of the Commune form in China and Mexico, for example, invites careful comparative reflection precisely because it did not appear there as a French export product but through qualitatively distinct, national or regional histories of struggle that relate to other revolutionary centres, Paris included, in horizontal or indirect fashion.[69]

For a formal conception of the urban (as centrality/difference) to function as a 'minimal unity' of the urban/ising world in non-Eurocentric fashion, it is not sufficient, however, to ascertain whether or not Lefebvrean conceptions travel. It is to understand the conditions for such travel to occur, or, to put it in Gramscian terms, to investigate the conditions of translatability of, say, the right to the city, concentrated-extended urbanisation or the Commune form. If the temporal form of now-time forces us to relate past and present in comparatively varied ways, a formal conception of the urban leaves urban researchers no choice but to specify the character of the differences that converge in particular situations. In other words, it is always a matter of demonstrating how each articulation of centrality and difference is shaped by comparatively distinct traditions of struggle and territorial relations, and the histories of urbanisation, city and non-city these embody. As we will see, these articulations vary in qualitative fashion from Paris to Algiers, Fort-de-France to Toronto. Understood as a level of analysis, the urban also opens up to nuanced (neither diffusionist nor area- or culture-bound) ways of treating urban questions in relationship to macro-political economies and historical geographies of struggle (including the spatial imaginaries generated by these). Given our focus on (neo-)colonial questions, this can only happen if we also turn the tables on Lefebvre, confronting Lefebvrean (or other metropolitan Marxist) traditions of thought and struggle that emerge from within colonised terrains, leading potentially to a 'decolonised right to the city'.[70] In order to do so, I propose to establish a fraught comparative constellation between Paris and Algiers, the Antilles and Canada. In this constellation, we might discover the urban as a modular form that is always co-produced[71] through comparatively specific dynamics rather resulting from linear progression or civilisational uniqueness.

---

68   Lefebvre 1965; Lefebvre 1968a.
69   Perry 1999; Jiang 2014; Bosteels 2013; Lapierre 2008.
70   Grandinetti 2019.
71   On co-production as method, see Mongia 2007.

2   Chapter Summaries

2.1   *Intellectual Dialogues* ....
Two major axes traverse this book. The first one connects a series of intellectual dialogues between Marxist and anti-colonial traditions. Chapter 1 opens
the book by confronting Henri Lefebvre with the colonial realities and anti-
colonial struggles that influenced the Frenchman's work, directly or indirectly.
Originally motivated by reflections on the role of imperialism and multiculturalism in contemporary urbanism,[72] the chapter wants, in a sense, to do with
Lefebvre what Susan Buck-Morss and Matthieu Renault did with G.W.F. Hegel
and V.I. Lenin, respectively. Renault asked how far Lenin had come in 'decolonising the revolution' by translating '1917' to Central Asia and beyond,[73] while
Buck-Morss confronted Hegel's writing on the master and slave dialectic with
his knowledge of the slave revolution in St. Domingue 'to the point where one
cannot think Hegel *without* Haiti'.[74] This chapter traces the 'colonial' in Lefebvre so that we can no longer consider Lefebvre's work without the anti-colonial
struggles (in Morocco, Algeria, Cuba, Vietnam, and Paris) that shaped his work,
notably during the 'long 1968'[75] from the mid-1950s to 1970s. These struggles
transformed Lefebvre's largely metaphorical treatment of colonisation in the
early 1960s to one directly influenced by theories of imperialism in the late
1970s.

    While clearly insufficient on its own for the purposes of anti-colonial social
theory, the evolution of Lefebvre's notion of colonisation is one reason why
it is plausible, at the end of Chapter 1 and then in Chapter 2, to bring Lefebvre into sustained contact with a generation of intellectuals that emerged

---

72   Kipfer and Goonewardena 2004; 2007; Goonewardena and Kipfer 2005; 2006.
73   Renault 2017a, p 17.
74   Buck-Morss 2009, p. 16. Buck-Morss's approach has been scrutinised from various angles.
     It has been accused of being either too fast and certain in its rendering of Hegel (Stephan-
     son 2010) or not dialectical, that is to say not Fanonian and Jamesonian enough in its
     claim to universal history (Scott 2010; Ciccariello-Maher 2014). Despite these limits, the
     merits of Buck-Morss's unfinished project (Scott 2010) are what matter for the purposes
     of this chapter. These merits are to continue building an international intellectual con-
     stellation that must explode the European confines of much Hegel scholarship; and to
     propose an open-ended research agenda attempting to link context (Hegel's knowledge
     of the Haitian Revolution) and content (Hegel's discussion of the master-slave dialectic
     in the *Phenomenology of Spirit*). One might suggest that Buck-Morss's broader and rather
     hurried project for a universal history is only possible by making it subject to a version of
     the left or partisan universalism advanced by Ato Sekyi-Otu.
75   On the 'long' and 'world-wide' character of 1968, see Ali 2005; Amin et al. 1990; Watts 2001;
     Artières and Zancarini-Fournel 2008; Katsifiacas 1987.

from and helped shape the formative years of national and tricontinental anti-colonialism with an unequalled combination of militancy and intellectual depth: Aimé and Suzanne Césaire, Jeanne and Paulette Nardal, Albert Memmi, and Jean-Paul Sartre. Theoretically, this dialogue is rendered plausible by the integral social and political theories and the dialectical humanist orientations that sustain both Lefebvrean and Fanonian traditions, political and intellectual points of divergence notwithstanding. Articulating everyday life with the macro-level of totality and connecting both to a horizon of revolution and liberation, Lefebvre's integral Marxism and Fanon's integral anti-colonialism both escape the divide between political economic and postmodern or postcolonial approaches that has splintered critical theory since the 1980s. As far as Fanon is concerned, my discussion develops the still unparalleled interpretation of Fanon by Ato Sekyi-Otu to focus on the dynamic relationship between time and space in the Martinican's dialectical conception of human liberation, his partisan universalism.[76] It is from this particular anti-colonial vantage point that one can see how Fanon is of great help in redirecting Lefebvrean insights into urbanisation and the production of space.

In the following chapters, Fanon and Lefebvre are put in sustained touch with an additional array of anti-colonial traditions, Marxist-influenced or otherwise.

Chapters 3 and 4 confront both Fanon and Lefebvre with theoretical arguments and colonial realities that exceed the situations they tackled in their lifetimes. Chapter 3 offers an analysis of *Texaco*, the literary text by Patrick Chamoiseau that provides rich insights into the historical transformation of socio-spatial relations and spatial imaginaries of resistance in Martinique. *Texaco* is our window to the creole literary, linguistic and philosophical tradition in the French-dominated Antilles, which is represented by Chamoiseau, Raphaël Confiant and Jean Bernabé and was sharply scrutinised by Maryse Condé. These authors recast Edouard Glissant's conception of *antillanité* to develop an aesthetic project from what they saw as the linguistic, social and cultural particularities of the Caribbean: creole. In so doing, they levelled varied challenges at Césaire's peculiar articulation of communism and *négritude* as well as Fanon's partisan universalist and internationalist take on liberation. Among the conditions of existence of the creole movement were the movements that contested Martinique's and Guadeloupe's status as French administrative districts (*départements*) from the late 1950s to the 1970s. These movements highlighted the contradictions in Césaire's own project to redefine

---

76   Sekyi-Otu 1996.

decolonisation as a struggle for equality in and against the French state, contra-dictions that also explain the often limited and subterranean influence Fanon has had in the French Antilles.

In Chapter 4, we move to another intellectual and political current struggling with persistent colonial realities: the movement for an Indigenous resurgence against settler colonialism in Canada represented by such thinkers as Leanne Simpson and Audra Simpson as well as Glen Coulthard. These thinkers repres-ent a new wave of Indigenous radicals who find themselves in deep conversa-tion with Indigenous traditions of struggle as well as a range of non-Indigenous anti-colonial, feminist and Marxist currents. Coulthard, for example, recon-nects with the Indigenous, socialist and Third World traditions articulated in the red power generation (represented by Lee Maracle and Howard Adams) and the liberation struggles of the 1970s in his Dene nation. Is so doing, he revives Indigenous communist lineages that have emerged in various parts of the Americas since the 1920s. Appropriating both Marxian debates about originary accumulation and Fanonian critiques of recognition, Coulthard elab-orates on the comparative specificities of the colonial relation in the massively majoritarian settler-colonial context of North America. For Coulthard (as well as Simpson and Simpson), these specificities require that the problematic of tradition be reworked through Indigenous perspectives. The results of such intellectual work are relational conceptions of land, time, and territory that challenge colonial-capitalist abstract space in ways that are both relevant for and distinct from Lefebvre and Fanon.

Chapter 5 returns to the metropolitan heartland of France. There we turn our attention to political anti-racist currents. Since the 1980s, these currents have indirectly recast anti-colonial political traditions by taking the baton from their parents, many of whom left (former) colonies for the *hexagone* during the postwar period. While often born in France, the new generations continued to have a fraught relationship to the parties and trade unions of the French left. In fact, they faced what Sadri Khiari has called the colonial counter-revolution,[77] the manifold reactions of French ruling circles against the anti-colonial aspir-ations and migration patterns of the 1950s and 1960s. Generated by waves of movements against racism and police violence, anti-colonial militants and intellectuals have shaped various strands of political anti-racism, which, in a refusal to follow strictly moral anti-racist recipes, developed typically left-leaning orientations: analyses of how colonial histories have been recomposed in French politics as a whole and counter-strategies straddling organisational

---

77   Khiari 2008.

self-determination with alliance formation. Increasingly identified with the 'banlieue', which itself stands in a complex relationship of (dis)continuity with colonial history, political anti-racism offers challenges to Lefebvre's notion of the right to the city (which references 1871 and 1968) and to Fanon's spatio-temporal dialectic (which embodies the stark realities of anti-colonial war).

The goal of these dialogues is not to absorb anti-colonial and Black traditions into metropolitan Marxism but to modify and fortify both traditions in the process. On the Marxist side, the point is to unearth resources to develop an open-ended, and non-Eurocentric conception of Marxism. Such a deprovincialised (Harootunian) or plural, not Western conception of Marxism (Wolfgang Fritz Haug) is anchored in traditions that cross the three worlds that structured the world order in the long twentieth century.[78] No longer centred primarily in Europe, it is in ongoing conversation with anti-colonial traditions within or beyond the universe of Marxism and historical materialism. (One notable reference point for both Harootunian and Haug are the lineages coming together in José Carlos Mariátegui's work.) In turn, the point of confronting Marxist considerations with anti-colonial currents is not to reify (the) colonial question(s) as the always overarching question, as has been the case often during the post- and decolonial turn in social theory. It is to understand (neo-)colonial questions and anti-colonial projects in their nuances and specificities. The point of a dialogue between multiple Marxist and anti-colonial currents is precisely to anchor such encounters in comparatively and historically varied circumstances, in places ranging from North Africa and Europe to the Caribbean and North America, where (neo-)colonial relations have been organised in distinct and historically changing fashion.

Cutting across these Marxist and anti-colonial exchanges are feminist engagements. These do not constitute the core of this book but provide ammunition for future in-depth work. While the chapter on Lefebvre links to Marxist-feminist critiques of everyday life (by Frigga Haug, for example), the chapter on Fanon insists on the importance of feminism in postwar anti-colonial traditions, and feminist arguments (by Drucilla Cornell, Madhu Dubey, and Denean Sharpley-Whiting) about gender relations in Fanon's understanding of national liberation. In subsequent chapters, this transversal feminist thread is woven further into the book's central concerns. In Chapter 3, the opening discussion about the peculiarities of social reproduction in a context of plantation slavery is picked up by Maryse Condé's class-conscious feminist critique of the creole authors. Then a central focus will be on the figure of Marie-Sophie

---

78   W.F. Haug 1987, pp. 7–8, 197–259.

Laborieux (in Chamoiseau's *Texaco*), which points to the gendered character of informal urbanism in post-emancipation social formations. The subsequent chapter highlights the fundamental place of gender relations in the formation of White settler colonialism and the formative character of feminist voices (those of Lee Maracle, Audra Simpson, Leanne Simpson) in traditions of Indigenous liberation, then and now. Finally, Chapter 5 deals also with gendered dynamics in urban redevelopment as well as the feminist components of political anti-racism. All in all, it is safe to say that no dialogue between Marxist and anti-colonial intellectual traditions is feasible without sharp feminist insights.

2.2   *... And Urban Investigations*

The second major axis traversing this book focuses on spatial and urban questions. In fact, a main goal of this book is to advance dialogues between Marxist and anti-colonial traditions through debates about theories of space and urbanisation. In the first instance, the book offers a critical re-reading of Marxist and socialist feminist traditions of urban research as informed by critical and dialectical anti-colonial insights about racialisation, colonialism and imperialism. The goal of this re-reading is to transform these metropolitan traditions theoretically while also developing analytical and conceptual resources to advance urban research, and this in part by reconnecting with earlier waves of historical-materialist work on imperial and colonial urbanisation. Chapter 1 opens with a survey of Marxist and socialist feminist urban theories and then proceeds to unpack the development of Henri Lefebvre's concept of 'colonisation'. This concept wants to capture one way in which states shape the production of space by ordering hierarchical social relations spatially. Encapsulating multi-scalar territorial relations of domination, 'colonisation' helps us understand key dynamics of modern urbanisation (including processes of recasting as well as subverting city-countryside relations) and grasp the idea of the right to the city (as a twin claim to spatial and political centrality achieved in part through spatial dynamics of subaltern mobilisation). I argue that Lefebvre's concept needs to be transformed with the help of anti-colonial traditions if it is to shed adequate, and comparatively nuanced light on the (neo-)colonial aspects of the urbanisation and urban politics.

Secondly, the core of the book offers readings of anti-colonial authors that highlight the 'place' of space and urbanisation in their respective works. From Frantz Fanon, Patrick Chamoiseau, Glen Coulthard, Lee Maracle, Audra Simpson, Leanne Simpson, and Sadri Khiari, one gets a strong sense that colonialism and neo-colonialism represent particular ways of producing space. From these authors, one can also generalise that one key feature of modern capitalism, (neo-)colonial relations, developed in part by through comparatively varied, hierarchical, and racialised territorial relations. These not only shape urban space but structure broader historical-geographical patterns, notably the complex relationship between uneven dynamics of urbanisation and comparatively distinct relations between urban and other social spaces. In turn, one gathers from these texts that anti-colonial liberation represents, among other things, a combination of processes and strategies of appropriating space and time, including moments of struggle that resemble the form of the right to the city (understood as a moment of centrality produced by a convergence of struggle of those peripheralised). This is true across scales, from the body, the household and the neighbourhood to the nation and the globe as a whole.

In Chapter 2, I show how in Fanon, spatial and urban questions help us grasp more precisely the peculiarities of the colonial relation, this deeply racialised relationship of super-exploitation, domination and dehumanisation that Lefebvre failed to grasp sufficiently. Following Fanon, the colonial production of space puts into sharp relief the ossified or thingified relationships of exteriority and incompatibility between colonisers and the colonised. Fanon understands this at various levels and in several contexts, from his comments about everyday interactions, gestures, and looks in the French metropole to his analyses of racialised segregation in Algeria as a whole and the gendered relationship between public, semi-private and private space in the colonial city. In turn, Fanon shows that national and tricontinental liberation movements do not assert the primacy of time over space but represent a multi-scalar dialectic through which colonial space is appropriated in the political struggle to forge novel, genuinely postcolonial social relations. Fanon demonstrates as much in his analysis of gender relations and the rift between European and native quarters during the Battle of Algiers, and then in his analysis of the shifting city-country relationships that mediated the spontaneous revolts, social alliances and political strategies of the Algerian war of independence.

In Chapter 3, I discuss urban and spatial questions in creole literature. My window to these questions is the historically shifting relationship between the old colonial town centre of Fort-de-France, Martinique, and the ring of subaltern neighbourhoods surrounding it on three sides. At the heart of Chamoiseau's *Texaco* and Raphaël Confiant's *L'Allée des Soupirs*, this relationship informs these authors' understanding of creole urbanism, the architectural and daily forms of mixing that represent the material and practised aspects of creole understood as subaltern culture and language. While in *L'Allée des Soupirs*, the revolt of 1959 (a right to the city moment generated when inhabitants invaded the town centre to create the first political crisis in departmentalised Martinique) appears to demonstrate the revolutionary potential of creole urbanism, *Texaco* illustrates how urban strategies (concentrated and extended) helped reorganise and solidify the colonial relation after 1946. Next to a fusion of European and Afro-Caribbean ways of producing space, creole urbanism also represents a political compromise (between shantytown dwellers and Aimé Césaire's City Hall). In turn, *Texaco* harbours spatial imaginaries produced by generations of struggle in and against plantation production. All in all, creole urbanism challenges Lefebvrean research on urban revolutions and Fanonian analyses of genuine decolonisation and its spatial mediations. For such analyses to account for the relationships between city, non-city, and urbanisation on old sugar colonies like Martinique, it must be subtly comparative. This is also true today, when, as Chamoiseau suggested, the imaginaries embodied in creole urbanism are being supplanted by the new wave of extended urbanisation that has engulfed Martinique in the last generation.

In Chapter 4, I push the boundaries of urban research in another context that has resisted formal decolonisation: settler colonialism in Canada. It begins not with territorial relations in concentrated urban space but with extended urbanisation: infrastructural networks like pipelines facilitating resource extraction. Contested through equally networked nodes of mobilisation shaped by Indigenous people, pipelines spontaneously speak to Henri Lefebvre's claim (that planetary urbanisation may harbour unexpected political potentials and give rise to new centralities in part because it mediates daily life and the social order) even as it demonstrates the eminent insufficiency of this claim (which needs to be confronted with the deeply inter-national character of conflicts over land and sovereignty between Indigenous nations, capital and the Canadian state). Like creole urbanism, Indigenous struggles against extended urbanisation force us to understand how urbanisation, urban planning, indeed, that very colonial distinction between city and non-city (the reserve, the bush), highlight the contradictions of settler colonial relations. Pipeline conflicts also alert us to the historical depth of Indigenous struggle. As literary and philosophical reflections by intellectuals Lee Maracle, Howard Adams, Maria Campbell, Glen Coulthard, Leanne Simpson and Audra Simpson show, waves of struggle have generated spatial imaginaries and geographically inflected strategic orientations that subvert settler-colonial time-space, including the distinction between city and reserve, in peculiar and clearly relational ways. Needless to say, these orientations also have major implications for more conventional strategies of urban research and action focused on Canada's urban centres, large or small.

Chapter 5 returns to such a classic focus: urban policies in the metropolitan centres of the global North. The chapter offers an analysis of housing redevelopment (*rénovation urbaine*) in the Paris region. Projects to demolish, renovate and redevelop housing estates have been widespread across Euro-

America. Through well-developed Marxist, left-Weberian and feminist lenses, they are rightly seen as results of state-led strategies to deconstruct welfare state programmes, privatise social reproduction, mobilise real estate investment, and gentrify urban landscapes. These explanations remain pertinent in Paris, but they are doubly insufficient. First, they underestimate the political character of place-based policy, which in the French case responded in no small measure to movements against racism and police violence since the 1980s. In this sense, *la rénovation urbaine* is part of a two-century-old history of state intervention to pre-empt subaltern struggles (and right to the city moments from 1871 to 2005 by way of 1968) by reorganising territorial relations between bourgeois and subaltern social spaces. Second, they give short shrift to the fact that the current round of territorial reorganisation has strongly racialised, indeed specifically neo-colonial dimensions. It targets heavily non-White residential districts in part by reinventing policing and gendered housing policies that were developed in the late colonial period. In fact, place-based strategies inform ongoing projects to reorganise state intervention in authoritarian fashion through urban warfare and states of emergency in France and other parts of the world. In the process, they often propose a form of spatial intervention (social mixing) that rejoins a longer history of organising social relations (including plantation slavery) through hierarchised spatial proximity, not spatial distance. While full of contradictions, this form poses an important challenge for all those Marxist and anti-colonial perspectives (including Lefebvre's and Fanon's) for whom an appropriation of segregated space was to be a medium of emancipation, not a way to reorganise political domination territorially. In response, appropriating mixity for purposes of political strategy may help keep alive such emancipatory horizons.

Beyond Metaphor: Henri Lefebvre and 'Colonisation'

This chapter redirects Henri Lefebvre's work by confronting it with colonial and neo-colonial realities. My interest lies not only in stressing the relevance of Lefebvre's work for research on colonisation, imperialism and racism,[1] but also in tracing his actual, uneven engagement with colonial matters. In the first section of this chapter, I locate Lefebvre within a broader discussion of urban Marxism. I emphasise that even though radical geography and Marxist urbanism since the 1970s were influenced by research on colonial, Third World and dependent urbanisation, colonial and imperial matters appear only selectively in what later came to be known as the most influential formulations of urban Marxism in the English language. The second section highlights the particular ways in which this is also true for Lefebvre. After placing Lefebvre into a broader context of French anti-colonialism from the 1920s onwards, I try to explain his belated foray into explicitly colonial and imperial problematics.

---

1 A number of people have done just that, irrespective of Lefebvre's direct engagements with colonial questions. Crystal Bartolovich (2002) stressed the importance of Lefebvre for a Marxist approach to colonial questions that crosses the divide between political economy and critical theory. Judith Whitehead (2010) demonstrated how Lefebvre's conception of abstract space helps us understand colonial and developmentalist strategies of dispossession in Gujarat. For her part, Manu Goswami (2004) mobilised Lefebvre's theory of the production of space and the state to undermine methodological nationalism and show how India has been produced in the dialectical transformations brought about by colonial territorialisation and anti-colonial nationalism. James A. Tyner (2007) and Eugene J. McCann (1999) have deployed Lefebvre's notions of the right to the city and the production of space to understand Black radicalism and public space in the USA. Tina Grandinetti (2019) has done something similar, proposing a decolonised conception of the right to the city in light of Kanaka Maoli aspirations in Honolulu. Fernando Coronil (2000) and Gillian Hart (2002) have emphasised the focus on labour, capital and land in *The Production of Space* to understand (neo-)colonial situations in the global South. Claudia Fonseca Alfaro (2018), Japhy Wilson and Manuel Bayón (2017) have mobilised Lefebvre and the idea of planetary urbanisation in order to understand the colonial and capitalist dynamics that shape the production of space and its magical aspects in the Yucatan maquila zone and the transport corridor crossing the Ecuadorian Amazon. I want to complement these highly valuable contributions with a detailed discussion of, first, the direct links between Lefebvre and anti-colonial traditions and, second, the ways in which Lefebvre himself uses the term colonisation. In this regard, I follow Kristin Ross (1995).

Three moments in Lefebvre's treatment of these receive our special attention: (1) his work on everyday life in the late 1950s and the early 1960s, where the colonial appears as a form of alienation and a metaphor for neo-capitalism; (2) his urban writing from 1968 to 1972, where colonial and imperial questions are more concretely linked to urban struggles, the world-wide urban revolution, and forms of spatial organisation in the imperial core; and (3) his work on the state from the mid- to late 1970s, where 'colonisation' describes a state strategy of producing space. I underscore that phase two was the transformative moment, pushing Lefebvre's treatment of colonial and imperial questions beyond the metaphorical ways that have been scrutinised by Eve Tuck and K. Wayne Yang.[2] In the third section, I conclude that the anti-colonial substance in Lefebvre's urban phase, while insufficient in itself, warrants and requires efforts to establish closer links between Lefebvre and anti-colonial traditions and, ultimately, a strategy to mobilise both to understand (neo-)colonial urban situations today.

1   Urban Marxism and the Uneven Development of Radical Geography

The 'long' and world-wide '1968' was crucial in shaping the part of the spatial turn in social theory represented by anglophone radical geography. Edward Soja draws significantly upon two sets of Marxist and Marxist-influenced sources to consolidate his observations about the spatial turn in critical social theory: (1) 'geographical' and urban Marxism centred in Euro-America (Lefebvre, Harvey, Castells, Poulantzas, Jameson, Berger) and (2) world-systems and dependency theorists of underdevelopment and unequal exchange (Frank, Wallerstein, Amin, Emmanuel).[3] With the help of Ernest Mandel's multi-scalar observations about uneven development, Soja points out that both currents were vital in effecting a spatialisation of Marxism from the late 1960s to the late 1970s. He ultimately buries these double influences under the weight of his own project to merge the spatial with the postmodern turn of social theory. Both of these turns he relates to the kind of 'restructuring' which he and a number of others have analysed in the supposedly paradigmatic urban region of postfordism: Los Angeles. Nonetheless, Soja's narrative (as well as his own intellectual trajectory from development studies to analyst of core urban regions) indicates

---

2   Tuck and Yang 2012.
3   See in particular chapters 2 and 4 in Soja 1989.

that radical geography and the spatial turn refracted two forces at the heart of the 'long 1968': the metropolitan new left and tricontinental anti-imperialism.

Revisiting Soja's landmark text also reminds us that the proliferation of Marxist urban research in the 1970s and 1980s has taken two main directions. Heavily influenced by permutations of dependency and world-systems theory, the first one moved from the study of colonial and Third World urbanism and anti-colonial revolt in the imperial core to research on the New International Division of Labour, associated new migration patterns and the formation of global cities.[4] The 1960s and 1970s witnessed a new round of Marxist debate on imperialism. In contexts shaped by the transformation of non-revolutionary post-independence regimes into pillars of neo-colonialism, much early debate focused on the implication of dependency and world-systems theory for urban research, which at that time was dominated by modernisation theory and its Eurocentric habits of taking the United States and Western Europe as the benchmark by which to analyse 'urbanisation processes in the Third World', as Terry McGee put it in the early 1970s.[5] In this context, world-systems and dependency traditions conceptualised cities in two ways: as sites whose morphologies, socio-economic structures and relationships to the non-urban world related to their place and function in world-wide divisions of labour framed by imperial surplus transfer and political domination; and as hierarchies of cities interlinked by a myriad of networks (of trade, investment, corporate organisation, migration, and transportation).[6]

World-systems and dependency traditions were important (but not exclusive) influences in the research focused on particular types of cities and urbanisation processes. Researchers insisted that key features of Third World cities/urbanisation (especially disparities within and between cities, a lack of capacity to absorb rural-urban migration, the 'informality' of labour, land-use and planning) were due not to a lack of US-style Development but to the peripheralising dynamics of world capitalism[7] and its disarticulating transformations of Southern urban worlds (into segmented economic circuits, to mention the problem conceptualised by Milton Santos).[8] One historical cause

---

4   Davis 2005.
5   McGee 1971.
6   Timberlake 1985.
7   On the distinction between Development and development, see Gillian Hart 2001.
8   Santos 1979. Milton Santos's work also represents a crucial point of reference for Brazilian researchers such as Roberto Luís Monte-Mór, João Tonucci, and Rodrigo Castriota, who have appropriated Henri Lefebvre's work. For more on these connections, see Chapter 4. For the most part, this chapter focuses on Anglophone engagements with Lefebvre, with selective forays in French, Italian and German literatures. Lefebvre has of course been translated and

of this peripheralisation had to do with the legacy of colonisation and the uneven capacity (or willingness) of post-independence regimes to tackle these. Research on colonial cities unearthed basic patterns of urbanisation in colonial Africa, Asia and Latin America while also insisting on the variegated relationships between pre-colonial history and colonial urbanisation.[9] Pushing beyond world-systems theory, some insisted that these relationships be analysed as elements within wider transformations of modes of production.[10]

In the course of the 1970s and 1980s, the complexity of peripheral urbanisation was also the order of the day for contemporary reasons. Debates about the New International Division of Labour forced researchers to conceptualise the diversification of Third World urbanisation.[11] One avenue to do this was to pay greater attention to the role of the state and class formation, notably with respect to the new, transnationally connected industrial urbanisation dynamics reshaping some *Cities of the South*.[12] Another research path was to study linkages between Foreign Direct Investment and gendered class formation in new manufacturing zones in places like Mexico and Eastern Asia, on the one hand, and new migration patterns from these zones to the central places where FDI flows were coordinated, on the other.[13] One result of these new, more loosely world-systemic debates about the transnational links between investment and migration was research on world or global cities such as London, New York, Tokyo, Paris, Hong Kong and Singapore.[14] The most critical strands of global city research were committed not to treating global cities as paradigmatic cases of global urbanisation (let alone to promoting global-city strategies), but rather seeing them as rarities.[15] Why? In order to think about

received in other parts of the world, including Japan, Turkey, Iran, Israel/Palestine, China, and Spanish-speaking Latin America. On Lefebvre and Tosaka Jun in Japan, see the discussion of Harry Harootunian's work in the introduction and Chapter 3. On the Turkish reception history of Lefebvre's *Production of Space*, see the survey by Husik Ghulyan (2019). On Lefebvre in Israel/Palestine, see Oren Yftachel (2009) and Oded Haas (2020). Aidin Torkameh's extensive translations of Lefebvre texts into Farsi await to be complemented with a discussion of Lefebvre's reception history in Iran. For selective insight on Lefebvre's uses in various parts of the world, see also the handbook edited by Michael E. Leary-Ohwin and John P. McCarthy (2020).

9   Ross and Telkamp 1985.
10   Southall 1998.
11   Armstrong and McGee 1985; Walton 1994; Simon 1992; Smith 1996.
12   Seabrook 1996.
13   Sassen 1988, 1991.
14   Knox and Taylor 1995.
15   Compare Robinson's important critique of the imperious taxonomic tendencies in certain strands of global-city research (2006) and Parneiter's reponse (2013), which insists on the virtue of concentrating on the rare qualities of global cities.

the political leverage to be gained from understanding the geographical concentration of global finance capital, the role of these geographies in imperial and global capitalism, and the local-regional conditions under which global city space is co-produced.[16]

For a period, global city research also served as a reminder about the larger and longer historical links between colonial, Third World and imperial urbanisation. Indeed, the life work of scholars like Janet Abu-Lughod and Anthony King was incomprehensible without a precise grasp of previous rounds of world urban history and the imprint these rounds left in many seemingly small things at the scale of architecture (like the history of the bungalow, in King's case).[17] The work of King and Abu-Lughod provided an empirical and theoretically historical-materialist reference point for the subsequent postcolonial turn in urban research, within which materialist, and specifically Marxist and world-systemic concerns were pushed to the margins but did not die.[18] Other research that incorporated global geographies into analyses of Euro-American space was also built upon Marxist lineages that have all too frequently been left behind by contemporary researchers. One such strand built on all the militant analyses in the 1960s and 1970s (from the Black Panthers and the League of Revolutionary Black Workers to British Black, that is anti-imperial, politics), seeking to establish analytical linkages between anti-colonial liberation politics in the Third World and Black politics in the imperial core.[19] A generation later, cultural geographers influenced by the Birmingham School and the work of Stuart Hall also insisted on the centrality of race, empire and nationalism in Euro-America in metropolitan heartlands and its migratory linkages to global peripheries.[20]

The second Marxist-influenced current in the spatial turn concentrated on the historical development, everyday dimensions and politico-economic dynamics of urbanisation in core capitalist contexts. While these two strands have always overlapped, as we have just seen,[21] some surveys of Anglophone Marxist urban research kept them apart. Ira Katznelson's *Marxism and the City*[22] ignores colonial and imperial aspects of urbanisation. His attempt to

---

16   Ross and Trachte 1990; Hitz et al. 1995; Keil 1993; Kipfer 1995.
17   Abu-Lughod and Hay 1977; Abu-Lughod 1980, 1999; King 1990a, 1990b.
18   Kusno 2000; Freund 2007. Work on colonial and neo-colonial urbanism influenced by
      postcolonial theory will make recurrent appearances in later chapters.
19   Rex 1973.
20   Jackson 1989.
21   See also the well-circulated collection edited by Michael Peter Smith and Joe Feagin 1987.
22   Katznelson 1993. Of course, this book extends some of the Engelsian arguments in *City
      Trenches* (1981).

forge a 'spatialised Marxism' moves quickly past Castells, Harvey and Lefebvre back to Engels to concentrate on the importance of urban research for two
classic debates: class formation and the transition from feudalism to capitalism
in Europe. For his part, Andy Merrifield's breezy, compelling *MetroMarxism*[23]
evokes a Marxism that is at once urban and sensuous, in tune with everyday
contradictions and radical practice. This takes it on a journey from Marx, Engels
and Benjamin to Lefebvre, Debord, Castells, Harvey and Berman, which is carefully shielded from the 'anti-urban skeletons' in the Marxist closet. He rightly
mobilises Gramsci (and his nuanced treatment of city and countryside) to take
to task some of the most egregious cases of anti-urban Marxism (Régis Debray's, for example).[24] Unfortunately, this manoeuvre also disconnects urban
Marxism from numerous and varied treatments of the city in anti-colonial
and anti-imperial traditions (as well as those in Gramsci himself, one might
add). Like Katznelson, Merrifield's urban Marxism remains metropolitan in
two senses of the word:[25] pro-big-city and at home in the imperial core of world
order.

Merrifield's and Katznelson's narratives are by no means implausible. None
of the authors they cover has been primarily concerned with the degree to
which the urban experience in the modern world has been shaped by colonial and imperial relations. But both Merrifield and Katznelson nonetheless
seriously underestimate the points of connection to anti-colonial traditions
that do exist in Marxism viewed from a global perspective, and that could be
explored further in the various exponents of MetroMarxism, particularly those
writing since the 1960s. In this spirit, here is a brief review of key Marxist and
socialist feminist exponents of radical urban and geographical theory. Their
work is situated in and concentrated on Euro-America; it also includes various openings to world-wide processes, including questions of colonialism and
imperialism. The point of this review is to set the stage for an in-depth treatment of Henri Lefebvre's work.

Closest to Henri Lefebvre among MetroMarxists, Guy Debord's ruminations about the various manifestations of the spectacle – concentrated, diffused, integrated – are meant to cast a wide comparative net. They capture
most lucidly Fordism, dwell at length on state socialism, but discuss the Third
World only fleetingly.[26] This is also true for the specifically urban reflections in

---

23   Merrifield 2002a. See also Merrifield 2002b.
24   Merrifield 2002a, pp. 2–4.
25   See Williams 1973, and Jameson 1990.
26   Debord 1977, 1990.

Debord's *Society of the Spectacle*,[27] which, one may argue, ran parallel to the
formation of an autonomist approach to questions of architecture, ideology
and the metropolis in Italy.[28] Much like Lefebvre, Debord transported the situationist critique of colonialism and support for postcolonial self-management
in Algeria into an analysis of the 'colonisation of everyday life', thereby using the
colonial as an analogy to understand the commodification and bureaucratic
administration of life in Western Europe and North America. But in Debord,
we also find glimpses of a more structurally differentiated understanding of
spectacular capitalism. *The Decline and Fall of the Spectacle-Commodity Economy*, his piece on the Watts uprising, argues that the 1965 event was a revolt
against the spectacle-commodity insofar as the latter, while universalising, is
founded on hierarchies structured by class and racism. The form of the revolt –
looting – thus expressed the particular relationship ghettoised looters had to
the spectacle. Therein one could detect its universally radical promise[29]

As one can follow from the *Urban Question* to the more supple *City, Class
and Power*,[30] Manuel Castells's Marxist theoretical claim to the urban question redirected structuralist Marxist concerns for urban sociology (and offered
a brief, if misleading, critique of Lefebvre in the process). Castells's work was
overwhelmingly focused on the role of the state and collective action in struc-
turing collective consumption and reproducing labour power in the metropolitan regions of advanced capitalism. It emerged from ambitious empirical
research projects on urban social movements and had a major influence on
English-speaking structuralist urban Marxism in the 1970s; today, it remains
crucial for researchers on urban social movements. When putting his work
on collective consumption in comparative context in the *Urban Question*,
however, Castells also elaborated on dependent urbanisation and the peculiar relationship between over-urbanisation and under-development that one
can ascribe to a combination of colonial legacies and after-colonial imperialism in the Third World.[31] These themes, Castells took up in his post-Marxist

27   Debord 1977, particularly chapters 5–7. See also Debord 1981a, 1981b. For a broader survey
      of these urban dimensions, see also Sadler 1999.
28   Tafuri's pathbreaking work on the history of architecture, which theoretically culminated
      in his *Architecture and Utopia* (1976) played an indirect role in Anglo-American debates
      about the spatial turn, partly via Fredric Jameson's participation in these debates. Tafuri's
      starkly pessimistic take on state-bound urbanism correlates to the 'metropolitan' per-
      spective forged through the lineages of autonomist Marxism (Negri 2018; Aureli 2008,
      2016).
29   Debord 1981c.
30   Castells 1977, 1978.
31   Castells 1977, pp. 39–63.

work on urban movements (*The City and the Grassroots*), where the relationship between Latin American squatter movements, populism and state power serve as a crucial reference. This line in Castells's work also proved to be important for research on the problematic of informality in world-systemic context.[32]

David Harvey's interest in imperialism is as old as his move from liberal to socialist formulations of urban theory, which he outlined in his *Social Justice in the City*.[33] In this book and subsequent work, Harvey made selective use of Lefebvre's *Urban Revolution* to reconsider geography and urban questions through a rereading of Marx's magnum opus: *Capital*. At this level of theory, Harvey treated imperialism and the urban process (investment in the built environment mediated by land rent) as moments in the metamorphosis of capital. In *The Limits to Capital*, Harvey described both as spatial fixes: temporary geographical embodiments of capital shaped by capital's periodic, crisis-driven search for ways to invest surplus capital.[34] Before his more recent analyses of accumulation by dispossession and the new imperialism,[35] his interest in imperialism remained separate from his urban research, however. In the *Urban Experience* and *Paris: Capital of Modernity*, two books that best bring together and capture his work in the 1970s and 1980s, Harvey brilliantly uses analyses of land rent and the built environment as entry points to studying the broader constellations of production and reproduction that define urban regions such as Paris.[36] At that time, these analyses were undertaken with little regard for colonial and imperial histories, the centrality of these for Paris notwithstanding.

A British contemporary of Harvey, Doreen Massey focused her work in the 1970s on the role of *Spatial Divisions of Labour* in the dynamics of (dis)investment and geographies of growth and decline. Running parallel to debates on the New International Division of Labour, her research on uneven industrial development provided powerful arguments against environmentally determinist and supply-side oriented economic explanations of regional decline (and the relationship between North and South in Britain).[37] Part of a generation of feminists close to the left Labour circles that were decisive in experiments

---

32   Castells 1983, pp. 175–212. On the links between Castells and lineages of research on informality, see Portes, Castells and Benton 1989, and Roy 2009b.

33   Harvey 2001a, 1973.

34   Harvey 1982, pp. 413–15, 431–45; Harvey 2001b, pp. 312–44.

35   Harvey 2003a.

36   Harvey 1989; Harvey 2003b.

37   Massey 1984.

like the Greater London Council in 1980s, Massey also provided an important socialist feminist conceptualisation of space, time and place, partly through a critique of Harvey (on gender) and Ernesto Laclau (for dualistic treatments of time and space).[38] One of her most memorable texts proposed 'a *global sense of place*': the idea that places (including global cities like London) must be understood through the manifold, locally and regionally condensed relations that tie them to other parts of the planet.[39]

Neil Smith, an early student of David Harvey, expanded directly from Harvey's Marxist geography and helped greatly in making Harvey's approach the most influential current in Anglo-American Marxist geography.[40] In his conceptualisation of *Uneven Development* as a dialectic of spatial differentiation and spatial equalisation as well as a process of constructing scale and producing nature, imperialism appears as a key driving force.[41] Even though they appear at distinct scales of social reality, as in Harvey, imperialism and the urban are more frequently brought into contact by Smith. Parallel to Richard Walker's development of land-rent theory to analyse supply-side dynamics of suburbanisation in North America,[42] Smith's work on gentrification (condensed in *The New Urban Frontier*) shows that colonial imaginaries (like US-American frontier myths) can play a role in urban strategies.[43] Later, Smith's interest in imperialism focused also on geography as an imperial discipline and the role of geographers like Isaiah Bowman in giving intellectual shape to the transition from the 'geo-political' geographies of European colonial empires to the territorially more complex 'geo-economic' geographies of *American Empire*.[44]

Parallel to Harvey, Marshall Berman explored the problematic of modernity through literary and cultural theory. His romantic urban Marxism emerged from Rousseau and Goethe before finding its home in the streets of nineteenth-century Paris and New York, and the texts of Baudelaire, Benjamin and Jane

---

38   Massey 1994.
39   Massey 1991.
40   Harvey's and Smith's closely related approaches have helped shape, through internal modifications and articulations with other approaches, research on a wide range of topics, including (urban) political ecology (Heynen, Kaika and Swyngedouw 2006; Ekers and Prudham 2017a, 2017b), regulation and state theory (Duncan and Goodwin 1988; Brenner 2004), and geographies of labour and capital (Herod 2004; Buckley 2013; Buckley and Hanieh 2014), and abolition geographies (Gilmore 2007).
41   Smith 1984, pp. 139–41; Smith 1991, 1993.
42   Walker 1981.
43   Smith 1996.
44   Godlewska and Smith 1994; Smith 2003, 2005.

Jacobs. As he says in *All That is Solid Melts into Air*, modernity is not to be confused with modernisation (capitalist development) or claims to Western supremacy.[45] It represents an experience of time (as rupture and discontinuity, loss and uncertainty) that is endemic to the capitalist world and that can produce contradictory responses, ranging from conservative (yet quintessentially modern) rejections of modernity to multiple modernisms: theories of political and artistic revolution as well as rationalist ideologies of progress and Development. If for Berman, modernity is a universal experience, it takes very different forms. He suggests that the conditions of (capitalist) underdevelopment in Tsarist Russia gave rise to a particularly sharp experience ('modernity without modernisation') that also help explain the anti-urban overtones of early Soviet modernism.[46] These observations may be linked to more genuinely global formulations, such as Harry Harootunian's on the 'co-eval' character of modernity in a highly differentiated and drastically unequal world.[47]

Berman's neo-Benjaminian insistence on the global pertinence of modernity as an experience of temporal rupture can be pushed much further than Berman himself did with his observations about hip hop in the Bronx and gender at Times Square.[48] Susan Buck-Morss did so along lines of gender by exploring the figure of the Prostitute in Benjamin's *Arcades Project* ('The Flaneur, the Sandwichman and the Whore').[49] In turn, Paul Gilroy confronted Berman with Du Bois to unearth the ambiguous meaning of modernity in a world of slavery and radical Black modernism (*The Black Atlantic*).[50] More firmly on the terrain of urban research, Elizabeth Wilson's *The Sphynx in the City* redirects Berman's urban Marxism along socialist-feminist lines.[51] Also borrowing from Benjamin and Jacobs, *The Sphynx* is a wide-ranging survey of the gendered, sexualised contradictions of modernity. Explicating these contradictions takes Wilson on an intellectual journey from Victorian London and Haussmann's Paris to turn-of-the-century Vienna, Berlin, Prague, Chicago and New York and mid-century New York City. Much more than Berman, however, Wilson makes it clear that Euro-American metropolitan life has been infused with imperial culture and is co-defined by the world-wide experience of planning colonial and Third World cities such as Delhi, Lusaka and Sao Paulo.

---

45   Berman 1982.
46   Berman 1982, pp. 173–286.
47   Harootunian 2000.
48   Berman 1997, 2006.
49   Buck-Morss 1986.
50   Gilroy 1993.
51   Wilson 1991.

Next to Marshall Berman, Mike Davis is the most well-known US-American urban Marxist. His oeuvre is arguably the most consistent within metropolitan urban Marxism in linking class and race in US-American cities to questions of imperialism and global urbanisation. His works all insist that in imperial America, class formation, urban politics and ecology cannot be understood apart from deep racialised divides and long traditions of anti-immigrant nativism. This is most famously true of his study on the American labour movement (*Prisoners of the American Dream*) and what may be the most ambitious study about urban politics still today: his tome on Los Angeles, *The City of Quartz*.[52] After pathbreaking work on urban ecology (*Ecology of Fear*), Davis turned his attention to the role of colonial famines in the nineteenth century in producing the Third World (*Late Victorian Holocausts*), and laying the foundation for today's *Planet of Slums*.[53] Davis makes it clear that studying our conflict-ravaged, unevenly informalised urban world today is impossible without taking into account the intertwined legacies of colonisation, post-independence nationalism and subsequent rounds of neo-liberal and neo-imperial structural adjustment.

The case of Henri Lefebvre is similar to many of his MetroMarxist fellow travellers. In his work, too, matters of colonisation, imperialism, Eurocentrism and race are present but often secondary. They are not obviously relevant to his overall theoretical approach. Yet they do make more than a passing appearance, just as they do among the aforementioned urban Marxists. Joining others, above all Kristin Ross, we will argue in the following that anti-colonial concerns lent a particular force to Henri Lefebvre's writing, particularly between the late 1950s and 1980. It has been understood for a while – and Merrifield himself has pointed this out with great effect – that the nexus between critique of everyday life, dialectical urbanism, theories of space and state remain the most explosive in Lefebvre's *oeuvre*. Our point is that anti-colonial concerns are formative in this nexus even though Lefebvre did not elaborate them sufficiently, in contrast to his considerable theoretical achievements concerning everyday life, state and the urban. We will also point out, though, that the full implications of the anti-colonial presence in Lefebvre are impossible to realise without removing Eurocentric roadblocks in his work. Only such a removal – which cannot be achieved without the help of other intellectual influences and broader political horizons – will make it possible to actualise what Lefebvre was grappling with from the mid-1960s on: a properly multipolar global intellectual project.

---

52   Davis 1986, 1990.
53   Davis 1998, 2001, 2006.

2   Henri Lefebvre and the Colonial

> It was the moment when I left the Party, the moment of the Algerian War.
> There was a lot going on ... I was almost fired .... I was research director
> at the CNRS ... and I was almost dismissed for having signed manifestos
> for the Algerians and for having offered support – a feeble support, of
> course – to the Algerian cause. It was a moment of intense fermentation.
> But in France, support for the Algerians didn't happen through the Party,
> nor through the official organisations within the Party or through the uni-
> ons; it went on outside the institutions. The Communist Party only sup-
> ported the Algerians grudgingly, in appearance only. In fact, they hardly
> helped them at all, and afterward the Algerians were very angry with the
> Party. An oppositional group within the Party, and also the movement out-
> side of the Party: these were the only ones that supported the Algerians,
> and that played a role in this story ....[54]

When it comes to questions of anti-colonial engagement, Lefebvre is a typical figure in the 'domestic' French left as well as the broader constellation
of European Marxism. In both contexts, anti-colonialism has always been a
minority current. It strongly shaped the overall orientation of only a few Western Marxists.[55] And in France, anti-colonial concerns achieved broader political significance only during exceptional conjunctures.[56] These included the
mid-1920s (when workers and students from the colonies turned Paris into a
pole of counter-colonial agitation and the young *PCF* embarked on the first of
its few anti-colonial campaigns, against French participation in the Rif War in
Morocco), the late 1940s and early 1950s (during the apogee of the anti-colonial
war in Indochina and the strike waves in West Africa), and finally the early
1960s (in the very last phase of Algeria's war of independence). Lefebvre par-
ticipated actively in some of these conjunctures. In the mid-1920s, the Rif War
was for him a significant politicising influence. Interned briefly for supporting a campaign to convince French soldiers to refuse participation in France's
efforts to defeat the Rif, he was drawn into pro-Communist circles and joined
the party in 1928.[57] In the late 1950s, Lefebvre directly worked against the then
dominant Party line and helped publish two critical internal journals before

54   Lefebvre 2002a, p. 270 (the quotation is from an interview conducted with Lefebvre by
      Kristin Ross in 1983).
55   Parry 2002, pp. 125–6.
56   Liauzu 2007, p. 271; Biondi 1992; Goebel 2017.
57   Burkhard 2000, pp. 49–52, 60; Liauzu 2007, p. 166; Biondi 1992, p. 142.

his exit from the party: *L'Etincelle* (1956) and *Voies Nouvelles* (1958). He facilitated meetings between dissident Communists and the Marseille network of
FLN supporters (*porteurs de valises*).[58] He also supported Algerian independence on his new Strasbourg campus and signed the famous Declaration of the
Right to Insubordination in the War of Algeria (the 'Manifesto of the 121') in
1960.[59] Lefebvre's anti-colonial activities paled in comparison to those of others
(Jeanson, Guérin, Curiel, Maspéro, Sartre) and his own sustained involvements
with the Party, before, during, and after the Resistance. But unlike many other
intellectuals in France, he did not abstain from a critique of French colonialism.

Towards the end of his life, Lefebvre acknowledged the importance of imperialism, inter-imperial competition and French colonialism for world history
and revolutionary politics in the first three decades of the twentieth century.[60]
Yet during the interwar period, Lefebvre's early anti-colonial sympathies left
no significant trace, neither in his engagement with Hegel, Marx and Lenin
nor in his early forays into 'everyday life'. In their work on mystification, Lefebvre and Guterman treated fascism and nationalism as European questions and
informed their reflections with insights from industrial working-class life in
France and visits to Nazi Germany. Others in Lefebvre's immediate milieu –
Paul Nizan and André Breton – pointed to that other side of fascism (imperial
violence and colonial expansion), questioned French imperialism (with Breton's role in staging a counter-exhibit against France's international colonial
exhibition of 1931 and Nizan's book *Aden Arabie*),[61] and took a serious interest
in the French Black Atlantic (and some of its products, *Négritude*).[62] Lefebvre
stayed silent. Why? Lefebvre was always uncomfortable with certain aspects of
official Communist intellectual orientation and repeatedly challenged these.
Yet he was also willing, at that time, to compromise when he deemed it necessary.[63] Lefebvre's silence in effect follows that of the Communist Party, which
started downplaying colonial concerns shortly after the Rif War, subordinating
them to, first, its class war against Social Democracy, and, second, its Common
Front strategy against fascism. Such abrupt manoeuvres led the PCF to pos-

---

58   Hamon and Rotman 1979, pp. 108–9, 167–9.
59   'Déclaration' 1960; Hess 1988, p. 156; Ross 1995, p. 162.
60   Lefebvre 2009a, pp. 296–7.
61   Nizan 1931.
62   Breton 1947. On the broader strands of anti-colonialism that came together in the inter-
      war period in France, see Liauzu 2007, pp. 123–74; Goebel 2017; Dewitt 2008; Levasseur
      2008; Girard 2008; Stora 1992, pp. 23–59; Ndiaye 2009; Brennan 2002; Hayes Edwards 2003;
      Stovall 1996, chapters 2–3; Wilder 2003a.
63   Anderson 1995, pp. 194–7.

itions complicit with French 'reform colonialism' and diminished its appeal among anti-colonial militants.[64]

In Lefebvre's work, specifically colonial concerns only appear during the period of the 'long 1968', a period book-ended with his second phase of work on everyday life (in the early 1960s) and his work on the state (in the late 1970s). In the first phase of work on the quotidian, the colonial enters the vocabulary of Lefebvre, who, finally liberated from the 'narrow, stifling nationalism' of the PCF,[65] was free to engage with the political and intellectual formations that mushroomed in the second half of the 1950s, from the Situationists to the *Socialisme ou Barbarie* group, and from the *FLN* to Fidel Castro's July 26 movement. In a 'revolutionary romantic'[66] mood (inspired not the least by Castro[67] and impressed by the intensity of the war of Algeria and its repercussions in the Hexagon), Lefebvre recognises colonisation as a 'new' form of alienation. Otherwise, the meaning of the colonial remains mostly metaphorical, with only the barest of nods to the specificity of colonial social relations. 'Colonisation' is used to capture the domination of everyday life by capital and state in the imperial metropole.

While in the early 1960s references to the colonial problematic remain fleeting, this is no longer so in the late 1970s. In his four-volume work on the state, Lefebvre explicitly conceptualises 'colonisation' as a particular, state-bound form of organising hierarchical territorial relations. He does so with the acknowledged help of classic (Lenin, Luxemburg) and more recent (Amin, Frank) Marxist theorists of imperialism and colonisation. What explains the shift between the early 1960s – the largely metaphorical use of the term 'colonial' – and the late 1970s – the explicit engagement with theories of imperialism and colonisation? In brief, 1968. As we know,[68] France's May 1968 was shaped (albeit very unevenly) by anti-colonial concerns, either as an after-effect of the war in Algeria or as a result of the anti-imperialist (Third-Worldist, Maoist or Trotskyist) currents present within the French new left. Lefebvre recognised these strands in his writings immediately before and after May 1968 (*The Right to the City* [1968], *The Explosion* [1968]) and subsequent urban reflections (*La Pensée Marxiste et la ville* [1972], *Espace et politique* [1972]). There the role of

---

64   Liauzu 2997, pp. 146–63.
65   Lefebvre 1973, p. 9.
66   Lefebvre's 'Le romantisme révolutionnaire' was published originally in 1957 and re-printed in *Au-delà du structuralisme* (Lefebvre 1971a). See also his 'Towards a New Romanticism?' in *Introduction to Modernity* (Lefebvre 1995).
67   Lefebvre 2002b, p. 270.
68   Artières and Zancarini-Fournel 2008; Boubeker and Hajjat 2008; Ross 2002.

immigrant workers in the uprising is linked, in rapid succession, first, to the political economy of 'internal colonisation' and spatial reorganisation of core-periphery relations in postwar France itself, and second, to the global constellation of revolt that Lefebvre interpreted, in the *Urban Revolution* (1970), as key to grasping the 'world-wide', including the planetary, character of urbanisation. The result is an urban reinterpretation of anti-imperialism and revolution. Driven by the dynamics of '1968', the most intense part of Lefebvre's urban writing from 1968 to 1972 transformed his timid reflections in the early 1960s into a concern with significant conceptual currency (as developed in *De L'état* [1976–78] and encapsulated in *The Survival of Capitalism* [1973]).

2.1   'Colonisation' I: Alienation and the Critique of Everyday Life

Henri Lefebvre has extended the idea of uneven development so as to characterise everyday life as a lagging sector, out of joint with the historical but not completely cut off from it. I think that one could go so far as to term this level of everyday life a colonised sector. We know that underdevelopment and colonisation are interrelated on the level of global economy. Everything suggests that the same thing applies at the level of socioeconomic structure, at the level of praxis.[69]

As Guy Debord so energetically put it, everyday life has literally been 'colonised'. It has been brought to an extreme point of alienation, in other words, dissatisfaction, in the name of the latest technology and of 'consumer society'.[70]

In the early 1960s, Debord and Lefebvre, who had been in conversation in Situationist and other networks since about 1957, come to an important point of agreement: the problematic of everyday life in imperial centres can be understood in *analogy* to the geopolitical situation of colonised countries. Lefebvre establishes this analogy through the concept of uneven development. In the second volume of the *Critique*, he writes that

the critique of everyday life generalises this experience of the 'backward' or 'underdeveloped' nations and extends it to the everyday in the highly developed industrial countries. It lays down the principle that the great

---

69   Debord 1981d, p. 70.
70   Lefebvre 2002a, p. 110.

upheaval which calls on the consciousness of those nations engaged in the drama of uneven development to emancipate themselves should reverberate through 'modernity' via an upheaval of everyday life and a general upheaval in the name of everyday life, given that it is a backward sector which is exploited and oppressed by so-called 'modern' society.[71]

By establishing a parallel between the domination of everyday life in imperial metropoles and the situation in colonial territories, Lefebvre argues that uneven development, far from a concept reserved to questions of world order and the uneven political economies of capitalist development, should also be seen as a category useful to develop the critique of everyday life. With 'colonisation', Lefebvre begins to name the processes by which popular life – everyday routines, symbols and imagination – is (incompletely) dominated by state, capital and technocratic knowledge. A link is made between, on the one hand, the relationship between colonial and colonised countries and, on the other the relationships between dominated and dominated sectors in a new metropolitan capitalism which intensified accumulation within and by means of new sectors such as leisure and urbanism.

Lefebvre's and Debord's early use of the term colonisation is not earth-shattering. As most famously exemplified by Jürgen Habermas's well-known take on the 'colonisation of the lifeworld', various critics have used the notion of 'colonisation' as a metaphor. Metaphors are necessary conduits for language to adapt and transform, as we know from Gramsci, for example.[72] Indeed, metaphors can powerfully link phenomena usually thought of as unrelated to each other. Naming a form of domination 'colonial' can politicise it, as various organisers have discovered.[73] But in bridging distinct contexts – and this is a crucial point for us – metaphorical operations also run the risk of glossing over the specificities of these contexts. To use 'colonisation' indiscriminately may undermine one's regard for the realities of historical colonialism and one's capacity to capture the specifically neo-colonial aspects of postcolonial situations. In

---

71   Lefebvre 2002b, p. 316.

72   Lichtner 2010.

73   An important case was the *Mouvement de libération des femmes* (MLF), an autonomous feminist organisation that formed in the wake of 1968 and subsequently shaped the course of feminism in France. Exponents of the MLF sometimes described women as 'colonised people' or 'the Black continent'. These analogies sidestepped colonialism or racism proper even as they absorbed, in metaphorical fashion, the real-existing anti-colonialisms that carried much weight in that political conjuncture (Boggio Ewanjé-Epée and Magliani-Belkacem 2012, pp. 40–2).

the third volume of the *Critique*, Lefebvre himself indicates self-critically that he may have over-stretched the meaning of 'colonisation'.

> [T]he second volume of the *Critique of Everyday Life* contains a thesis that is possibly excessive, that is, hypercritical, but not meaningless. It was developed in co-operation with the oppositional avant-garde. According to this theory, daily life replaces the colonies. Incapable of maintaining the old imperialism, searching for new tools of domination, and having decided to bank on the home market, capitalist leaders treat daily life as they once treated the colonised territories: massive trading posts (supermarkets and shopping centres); absolute predominance of exchange value over use; dual exploitation of the dominated in their capacity as producers and consumers. The book thus sought to show why and how daily life is insidiously programmed by the media, advertising and the press.[74]

Lefebvre's retrospective summary from the 1980s indicates how, in his own analysis of postwar capitalism, the specifically colonial forms of domination and exploitation quickly receded into the background. In fact, Lefebvre suggests that the 'colonial' problematic of the everyday in the metropole begins precisely at the point of geopolitical *de*-colonisation.[75] With this claim of historical rupture, it remains opaque how exactly transformations in metropolitan capitalism relate to (neo-)colonial pasts or presents.

In this context, what are we to make of Lefebvre's own claim, made in 1961, that the reference to colonial matters and uneven development is not just a 'metaphor' or 'a superficial analogy'?[76] Derek Gregory argues that in contrast to Habermas, Lefebvre deploys '"colonisation" more than as a figure of speech'. He articulates it as a form of producing space and was aware of how the language of colonisation is 'freighted' by the 'the implications of occupation, dispossession, and reterritorialisation'.[77] This is true, but only incompletely so in the early 1960s. His shift to empirical urban research, which began in the late 1940s and was in full force only in the 1960s, provided a veritable theoretical labour process through which he formed his major spatial concepts.[78] This research in turn emerged from his various rural sociological investigations,

74   Lefebvre 2008, p. 26.
75   Lefebvre 1995, pp. 195–6.
76   Lefebvre 2002b, p. 316.
77   Gregory 1994, p. 403.
78   Stanek 2011.

which go back to the time of the Resistance and his doctoral research on the Campan valley and continued apace into the postwar period. His analyses of growth pole and company-town planning in Lacq-Mourenx were particularly important for his subsequent theorisation of urbanisation and abstract space, which we will highlight specifically in relationship to Lefebvre's conception of planetary urbanisation (in Chapters 3 and 4).[79] The urban transformation of the Pyrénées region, the very milieu that provided him with rich materials for his early sociological investigations, could have been viewed as a form of semi-colonial implantation.[80] Yet Lefebvre only resorted to such language consistently in the late 1960s, in close historical proximity to May 1968. He did so then to describe how everyday life in the 'bureaucratic society of controlled consumption' is mediated by spatial organisation ('imprisoning', 'fencing in'[81]), urban forms (the bungalow, new towns) and mobilities (the car).[82]

In the Lefebvre of the *early* 1960s, a search for references to 'colonisation' as a specific relationship and experience leads to the question of alienation. For him, the critique of everyday life was always meant to render alienation concrete,[83] helping us show exactly how daily experiences are subjectively experienced points of tension between reality and possibility, routine and imagination, or, as he also says, contradictory articulations of 'maximum alienation' and 'relative disalienation'.[84] It helps to recall that in his formative *Dialectical Materialism* from the late 1930s,[85] Lefebvre argued that alienation remains central not only to all aspects of Marx's work but to any dialectically humanist Marxism that wishes to transcend political economy as positive science. For this purpose, the critique of alienation must be brought down to earth (to 'start

---

79   Lefebvre 1970b pp. 109–28.
80   Wilson (2011) has developed Lefebvre's formative analysis of Lacq-Mourenx to understand the Mexican state's counter-revolutionary urbanism in Chiapas. Another empirical case was the production of standardised spaces for mass tourism along the Mediterranean and Atlantic beaches. Lefebvre called these examples of 'neo-colonisation' in the early 1970s, in the *Production of Space* (1991b, p. 58). Beyond the general historical line of intellectual development traced in this chapter, there is also a very specific story behind Lefebvre's choice of language to describe Fordist (and functionalist) leisure spaces. As Stanek (2014, pp. xi–xxxiii) has pointed out, Lefebvre's take follows years of collaboration with Mario Gaviria, who interpreted the Benidorm project on the Costa Blanca as a case of neo-colonialism (1974). Lefebvre idea of an *Architecture of Enjoyment* is another result of Lefebvre's long-standing relationship with Gaviria (2014).
81   Lefebvre 1971c, pp. 144–5.
82   Lefebvre 1971c, pp. 123, 189.
83   Lefebvre 1970c, p. 106.
84   Lefebvre 2002b, p. 67.
85   Lefebvre 2009b.

from man as actual and active, from the actual process of living') and capture a variety of lived experiences – from the labour process to productivism, individualism and the division of intellectual and manual labour. Eight years later, in 1947, Lefebvre takes up this theme to suggest that this notion of alienation – neither Hegelian objectification of mind nor economic category of exploitation *alone* – is the 'driving force behind the *Critique of Everyday Life*'.[86] An expanded critique of alienation grasps the lived contradictions of postwar capitalism.[87] In his foreword to the fifth edition of *Dialectical Materialism* (1961), he insisted that such an expansion can capture the salient features of this capitalism, enabling us 'to uncover and criticise numerous forms of alienation', including the alienation of 'women', of 'work and the worker', of 'consumer societies', and 'of colonial or ex-colonial countries'.[88]

Lefebvre's remarks indicate how the (largely metaphorical) references to the 'colonisation of everyday life' run parallel to an expanding number of alienations, including the specific one termed colonial. At the very least, this underscores the *social* unevenness in which the domination of everyday life takes place. Already in the first volume of the *Critique*, Lefebvre had pointed out how the domination of everyday life in the new capitalism was a counter-revolutionary way of disorganising the working class. As he underlines in all his *Critiques*, key to understanding this mundane counter-revolution was the situation of women, including middle-class women. While often essentialising, Lefebvre's ruminations do grasp gendered elements of the postwar world, neo-capitalism in Euro-America. With reference to one of his preferred subjects, advertising and the new genre of women's magazines (like *Elle*), Lefebvre sug-

---

86   Lefebvre 1991a, p. 76.
87   For a significant period, Lefebvre's double claims (about the centrality of alienation in Marx and Marxisms which eschew hostile divides between philosophy and political economy, idealism and materialism, Hegel and Marx; and the need to expand the notion of alienation to forms beyond the multiple ones already identified by Marx himself) were controversial: they defied Communist party doctrine for decades and ran against the grain of anti-humanist Marxism. As a result of debates in and beyond Marxism since the 1970s, this has long stopped being the case. As Meszaros (1970, p. 227) argued in particularly forceful if overly architectural terms during the heyday of structuralism, 'the concept of alienation is a vitally important pillar of the Marxian system as a whole, and not merely one brick of it. To drop it, or to translate it one-sidedly, would, therefore, amount to nothing short of the complete demolition of the building itself and the re-erection, perhaps, of its chimney only. That some people have been – or are still – engaged in such operations, trying to build their "scientific" theories on chimney-tops decorated with Marxist terminology, is not in doubt here. The point is that their efforts should not be confused with the Marxian theory itself'.
88   Lefebvre 2009b, pp. 4–5.

gested that the situation of women embodied with particular clarity the ambiguities and contradictions of everyday life more generally. The daydreams for a 'new femininity' promoted by these magazines held out promises: economic independence, sexual liberty and fulfilling love. Yet, these promises were false insofar as they came along with an acute reprivatisation of life, 'at home' and in new realms of 'leisure'.[89] As a result, 'everydayness weighs particularly heavily on women',[90] guarded as it was by the enclosures of the bungalow and other such 'family units'.[91]

Lefebvre's critique of the bourgeois family highlights that the homogenisation and standardisation achieved by neo-capitalism proceeded unevenly, for example through the contradictions of consumerist and spatially reorganised domesticity. Despite its limits, this critique constitutes a point of connection to feminist urban and geographical work as well as Marxist feminist research on everyday life.[92] It also sheds light on the uneven development of everyday

---

89   Lefebvre 2002b, pp. 11–15, 80–7, 210–12, 222–3; Lefebvre 1971, p. 86; Lefebvre 2003b, pp. 100–6.
90   Lefebvre 1971, pp. 76–7; Lefebvre 1971a, pp. 103–4; Lefebvre 1970c, pp. 103–4.
91   Lefebvre 1991a, pp. 34–5, 99, 262; Lefebvre 1991b, pp. 49–50.
92   Mary McLeod, Kristin Ross and Doreen Massey have mobilised Lefebvre for feminist (urban and geographical) research on gender and sexuality (McLeod 1997, pp. 18–19; Ross 1995, pp. 79–81, 89; Massey 1994; see also Hubbard and Sanders 2003; Friedman and van Ingen 2011). A crucial author connecting Marxist feminist research on everyday life and Henri Lefebvre has been Frigga Haug. Considering Lefebvre as a counterpoint to Habermas's notion of the life-world (which flattens the lived ambiguities and tensions of everyday life), Haug placed Lefebvre as well as Marx and Gramsci amidst the lineages that inform her research project on everyday life (*Alltagsforschung*) (1994, 2003). Unlike Lefebvre, but like Dorothy Smith (1989) and Himani Bannerji (1995), Haug starts with (and returns to) the standpoint of women's experiences to challenge the false universalism of male-dominated approaches and unpack relations of domination and exploitation in the social formation as a whole. Like Lefebvre, Haug wants to articulate, not separate, the subjectively lived micro worlds of daily life from the 'larger' institutions of the social order. Analogous to Lefevre's notion of everyday life as an (often fleeting) meeting point of possibility and routinised reality, she considers everyday life in its contradictions, demonstrating, for example, the ways in which women's memories and daydreams often combine aspirations for a changed world with dominant conceptions and sensibilities (Haug 1992, 1987). More recently, Simona de Simoni has also elaborated on links between Lefebvre and feminist critiques of everyday life, thereby recasting, enlarging and supplanting Lefebvrean horizons through the revolutionary problematic of social reproduction theorised by Silvia Federici, Leopoldina Fortunati, Selma James and Mariarosa Dalla Costa (2014). Given the sources she mobilises, Simoni's intervention points to the possibility of exploring resonances between the critique of everyday life and queer communist lineages from Daniel Guérin, Mario Mieli, Rosemary Hennessy, Peter Drucker, and Kevin Floyd up to the most recent queer Marxist contributions (for example Rebucini 2017; Sears 2017; Lewis

life which Lefebvre occasionally calls 'colonisation'. But the social specificities of this uneven development are, at this point, not discussed in terms that
are expressive of colonial social relations. While *colonisation* as conventionally
understood *is* mentioned in this context as a particular form of alienation, *this*
form is of little to no consequence for how Lefebvre proceeds with his analysis of everyday life, as promising as it is otherwise. Only in the most fleeting
passages does Lefebvre refer to the concrete relationships between the French
quotidian and the French empire. In 1957, in the foreword to the second edition
of *The Critique* volume I, he acknowledges how the dreamscape of the suburban
bungalow excluded 'the Algerian workers at Renault, and many others'.[93] It was
only a decade later that Lefebvre would move to expand on such remarks and
prepare the ground for a fuller discussion of the relationship between 'colonisation' and spatial organisation. Before we get to that point, let us fast forward
to the late 1970s, when Lefebvre provides a more formal conceptualisation of
'colonisation'.

2.2   *'Colonisation' II: State, Imperialism and Territorial Organisation*

> Having become political, social space is on the one hand centralised
> and fixed in a political centrality, and on the other hand specialised and
> parcelled out. The state determines and congeals the decision-making
> centres. At the same time, space is distributed into peripheries which
> are hierarchised in relation to the centres; it is atomised. Colonisation,
> which like industrial production and consumption was formerly local-
> ised, is made general. Around the centres there are nothing but subjected,
> exploited and dependent spaces: neo-colonial spaces.[94]

De l'état was Lefebvre's project to 'spatialise political theory', to counter the
mystification of the state-like (*l'étatique*).[95] In English, Lefebvre's writing on
the state has received little systematic attention until recently, with the publication of a series of annotated excerpts and related texts.[96] The four-volume
work is still mostly known for the formative discussion on scale and state in

---

2016, Adamczak 2017). Another theoretically plausible way of pushing Lefebvre's critique
  of everyday life beyond heteronormativity has been suggested by Eden Kinkaid, who has
  linked the phenomenological aspects of Lefebvre's work to queer phenomenology, including Sara Ahmed's crucial contributions (2019).

93   Lefebvre 1991a, p. 43.
94   Lefebvre 1976a, p. 85.
95   Lefebvre 1978, p. 165.
96   Lefebvre 2003c; Lefebvre 2009c.

volume four, thanks to Neil Brenner's pioneering work on this subject and the question of *autogestion*.[97] In German, Christian Schmid and Hajo Schmidt have emphasised the importance of volumes 3 and 4 for Lefebvre's understanding of social relations as exchange[98] and his critique of base-superstructure models.[99] While Schmid incorporates *De l'état* into his systematic reconstruction of Lefebvre's theory of the production of space, Schmidt mobilises Lefebvre's state-theoretical writings (including his argument about the intrinsic connection between warfare and the violence of equivalence embedded in commodity and state forms) for a critique of militarism, mystification and fascism.

Lefebvre's understanding of state-space can be of great analytical value for an understanding of colonisation and anti-colonial nationalism, as Manu Goswami has demonstrated in detail.[100] I argue that one can also take *De l'état* directly into anti-colonial and anti-imperial directions. For what one finds in these volumes is Lefebvre's explicit engagement with Marxist theories of state and imperialism (volumes 2 and 3), which culminate in a chapter on 'colonisations and colonisers' (volume 4). In his review of Marxist thought, Lefebvre is drawn to Rosa Luxemburg and Antonio Gramsci more than Lenin, Trotsky, Stalin and Mao. In the specific field of theories of imperialism, he treats Luxemburg's work as the key conceptual 'nodal point' of twentieth-century Marxism.[101] Accordingly, Lefebvre insists that rather than a specific stage of capitalism (as Lenin suggested), imperialism develops together with capital-

---

97 Brenner 2001; Brenner 2004; Brenner and Elden 2009.
98 At first sight, it appears that Lefebvre's notion of social relations as material exchange makes him a candidate for inclusion into the (tendentially Eurocentric) exchange-centric views on capitalist development criticised forcefully by some (Wood 2003). But the thrust of Lefebvre's critique of capital and state (in *De l'état*) assumes not a timeless form of exchange modelled on modern capitalism but insists on the historically contingent and constitutive role of the state and political violence in bringing about a generalisation of relations of equivalence (the politically enshrined and codified commodity form) and thus a qualitative shift of the commodification process under industrial capitalism: labour markets and generalised clock time (Lefebvre 1976b, p. xlviv; Lefebvre 1977, pp. 86–100). Lefebvre's insistence on the constitutive role of the not-just-national state is rooted in a critique of economistic conceptions of original accumulation and leads to a critique of the economism found in theories of dependency and unequal exchange (Lefebvre 1977, p. 127; see also Brewer 1980; Cooper 2005). In turn, Lefebvre's notion of 'colonisation' does not make the common mistake of reducing the territorial to nation-state politics, as Wood and many old and current theorists of imperialism and world system do. Finally, it escapes the dualist character of the debates (between Ernesto Laclau, Andre Gunder Frank and Immanuel Wallerstein, for example) about class and space in the 1970s.
99 Schmidt 1990; Schmid 2005.
100 Goswami 2004.
101 Lefebvre 1976c, p. 422.

ism and in this, perfects methods of plunder already developed in colonial empires.[102] Coterminous with the formation of capitalism, imperialism thus forms an integral part of original accumulation and points to a more permanent role of systemic political violence in economic processes than Marx and Engels allowed for.[103] Even though she, too, underestimates the degree to which original accumulation is a recurrent rather than terminal aspect of accumulation,[104] Luxemburg reminds us that capital accumulation depends on the destruction of pre-capitalist formations and 'an inverted world' of 'misery', 'permanent insecurity' and 'unbearable labour'. She gives us one of the first Marxist analyses of the world-wide scale[105] and forces us to heed the spatially and socially uneven nature of exploitation.[106]

At this point, Lefebvre takes us beyond Luxemburg, suggesting that her account neglects key aspects of original accumulation. He argues that the decomposition and transformation of historic cities plays a role in primary accumulation as well, as do peripheries within imperial countries themselves[107] and criticises Luxemburg for missing the multi-faceted aspects of the production of space and its importance for capital accumulation:

> Rosa Luxemburg's thesis about accumulation can only be confirmed if it is modified, taking into account space and its conquest by capitalism: agriculture, historic cities, leisure industry (which occupy sterile spaces: beaches, seasides, mountains etc.). Capitalism takes over space as a whole. Without appropriating its use, it dominates space and modifies it for exchange; it produces its proper space of domination, in the form of centres of decision-making, wealth, knowledge (*savoir*) and information.[108]

In her crucial emphasis on peripheries understood in the non-capitalist sense, Luxemburg thus neglects the 'politico-economic constitution of *centres* (capital concentration, decision-making power, the formation of giant cities etc.) and the associated role of the state' in the formation and expansion of capital

---

102 Lefebvre 1978, pp. 113–14.
103 Lefebvre 1977, pp. 87–8.
104 Lefebvre 1977, p. 122. On this point, Lefebvre is on the same wavelength as Harvey and his work on accumulation by dispossession (Harvey 2003a).
105 Lefebvre 1976c, p. 261.
106 Lefebvre 1977, p. 114.
107 Lefebvre 1976c, p. 310.
108 Lefebvre 1976c, p. 120.

and capitalism.[109] In particular, she fails to account for the way in which the shattering and transformation of pre-industrial cities facilitate the realisation of surplus value.[110] The opposition between centre and periphery can thus be found not only in the formally colonised countries but 'extends to the heart of metropoles'.[111] 'Internal colonisation' must thus be incorporated in any analysis of colonisation.

Based on this engagement with classical and neo-Marxist debates on state and imperialism, Lefebvre furnishes a more formal definition of 'colonisation'. This can be seen most clearly in the chapter entitled *Colonisations and Colonisateurs* in the fourth volume of *De l'état*, where he suggests that 'colonisation' refers to the political organisation of territorial relations:

> Colonisation exists as soon as political power (of a feudal lord, a conqueror, but also a military authority or 'monied power') ties a territory, and thus a productive activity or function, to a weak social group by organising domination as well as production. Utility (productive use) is a mere indicator of the subjection of an 'inferior' group to a 'superior' one, and, consequently, of dominated space to dominant space, which is generally centralised in a fortified point (city, castle, fortress, military camp ...). Wherever a dominated space is generated and mastered by a dominant space – where there is periphery and centre – there is colonisation.[112]

Rather than a delimited historical era of European territorial expansion followed by non-territorial imperialism, 'colonisation' in Lefebvre thus refers to the role of the state in organising relationships of centre and periphery. This, Lefebvre holds, is vital not only for the purpose of reproducing relations of production.[113] At the heart of 'colonisation' is also the reproduction of *relations of domination* with all the humiliating and degrading aspects that sometimes escape economistic analyses of imperialism.[114] 'Colonisation' is *one* part of the

---

109   Lefebvre 1976c, p. 327.
110   Lefebvre 1976c, p. 310.
111   Lefebvre 1977, pp. 18–19. This is also the point at which Luxemburg's notion of the state and politics reaches its limits. While her understanding of original accumulation rightfully insists that 'political force is inherent in social and economic relations' (Lefebvre 1976b, p. xxx), her neglect of centre and periphery relations within metropolitan social space partly explains why she 'does not entirely escape Gramsci's accusation of economism and spontaneism' (Lefebvre 1976b, p. 327).
112   Lefebvre 1978, pp. 173–4.
113   This is the main theme in *Survival of Capitalism* (1976).
114   Lefebvre 1978, pp. 237–8.

role of the state in the reproduction of relations of production and domination:[115] the coordination of 'pulverised' abstract space of capital[116] and the thwarting of opposition with hierarchical separations of social space.[117]

Lefebvre's notion of 'colonisation' therefore alerts us to a key aspect of how the state produces abstract forms of space: homogenous, fragmented, and hierarchical.[118] Of particular interest is how in Lefebvre, the notion of 'colonisation' demonstrates how the state reaches far beyond its institutionally fortified and condensed core to permeate everyday life. Mediated by the urban level (level M, as we will see in the next section), 'colonial' state strategies, while operating at the level of the social order as a whole (level G), must be understood in their (contingent) capacity to organise everyday life (level P).[119] Situated in this way, Lenin's analyses of state, finance capital and imperialism 'somewhat occludes the concept colonisation' because they remain restricted to level G. But 'colonisation' is not only more diverse and widespread than the 'specific modalities of capitalist expansion at the beginning of the 20th century'. It cannot be reduced to a 'consequence of finance capital'.[120] An analysis of 'colonisation' includes but takes us beneath 'economic facts' (such as capital exports, as in Lenin; or external market expansion, as in Luxemburg).[121] Mediated by urbanisation, Lefebvre's concept of 'colonisation' allows us to link macro-political economies of imperialism not merely to relations between nation-states but also to the experiences of everyday life.

If it reaches beyond level G, 'colonisation' also operates at multiple scales (inter-national, inter-regional, intra-regional). 'Colonial' strategies are by no means confined to the *nation* state. This, Lefebvre illustrates with a brief sketch of historical forms of 'colonisation' from the era of commercial capitalism to mid-twentieth-century 'neo-capitalism'. In the period of post-liberal industrial capitalism, for example, colonial exploitation intensifies under the pressures of inter-imperialist competition for territorial control.[122] In this general context, Lefebvre identifies an emerging 'suburban style' of homogenising and peripheralising workers and 'native' peoples in colonial cities as

115   Lefebvre 1978, pp. 380–2.
116   Lefebvre 1978, p. 310.
117   Lefebvre 1978, pp. 308–9.
118   Lefebvre 1980, pp. 151–6.
119   Lefebvre 2003f., pp. 77–102.
120   Lefebvre 1978, pp. 170–1.
121   Ibid.
122   These historical dynamics are explored further in Chapters 2 and 5 with reference to the French empire.

well as Haussmann's Paris.[123] In twentieth-century neo-capitalism and neo-imperialism, formal decolonisation goes hand in hand with a 'world-wide extension of the colonial phenomenon'.[124] This world-wide generalisation of 'colonisation' includes not only neo-imperial relations of world order. It also extends to 'internal colonisation' of peripheral regions in metropolitan countries,[125] for example, the relationship between the *Ile de France* and declining regions like the *Pyrenées*, *Bretagne* and *Pays Basque*. Most importantly, 'colonisation' in neo-capitalism includes a transformation of cities according to the vulgar modernist 'model of isolated units'. This model orders space into a hierarchical 'collection of ghettos',[126] facilitates the dispersal of workers[127] and, especially in the metropolitan France of state-led Fordist expansion, furthers the gendered 'colonisation' of everyday life, with men acting as 'foremen' for the 'big phallocrats' of state and industry.[128]

Being not only a multi-level, but also a multi-scalar concept, 'colonisation' becomes one window through which Lefebvre grasps 'the world-wide'. (The other contemporaneous concept through which Lefebvre approaches the latter is course 'the urban revolution', which mediates 'colonial' state strategies.)[129] With this world-wide conception of 'colonisation', Lefebvre establishes a connection between various socio-spatial 'peripheries' – underdeveloped countries, displaced peasants, slum dwellers, immigrant workers, inhabitants of suburbs, women, youth, homosexuals, drug addicts – that nourish revolt.[130] It allows us to connect 'far' and 'near' peripheries that are subject to forms of territorial control in (ex-)colonies and metropolitan centres. It offers a way of tying geo-political aspects of imperialism and colonisation to the relations of centre and periphery within metropolitan regions themselves.[131] This becomes clearest when considering the *crisis* of this postwar 'colonial' model:

> Crisis ... or, rather, the critical state (*l'état critique*) shook up modern colonialism and its hierarchy. The movements of people rendered dependent (humiliated, dominated, exploited, with the primary emphasis on 'humiliation', which is underestimated by economism) loosened *relations of*

123 Lefebvre 1978, p. 178.
124 Ibid.
125 Lefebvre 1978, p. 180.
126 Lefebvre 1978, pp. 308–9.
127 Lefebvre 1978, pp. 174–5, 183.
128 Lefebvre 1978, pp. 84, 186.
129 Lefebvre 2003f.
130 Lefebvre 1976a, pp. 115–16.
131 Lefebvre 2003f., p. 113.

domination. Their effectiveness has extended from peripheries to centres. It would be imprecise to limit their impact to countries in revolt. Should we forget that the last phase of war in dependent countries in Asia and Africa found its extension in the contestations and protests of youth, women, intellectuals, the working class, the everyday, suburbs, in short, all *peripheries*, even those strangely close to the centres?[132]

The neo-capitalist version of 'colonisation' crumbled under the pressure of resistance in both 'far' and 'near' peripheries, ex-colonies and Parisian suburbs. But this 'world-wide front' – of 'women, youth, students, foreign workers, oppressed nations and regions, the more or less engaged working class' – against the 'planetary hegemony of imperial power' never consolidated. It never managed to do more than question 'relationships of subordination-dependency-exploitation' in their 'world-wide hierarchy'.[133]

In these last remarks, Lefebvre speaks of the failure of '1968' to break and permanently undermine the power of imperialism and neo-colonialism. This gives us a good indication of the origins of Lefebvre's more general insight into the character of 'colonisation' in *De l'état*. If in *'Colonisations and Colonisateurs'*, 'colonisation' appears in a more explicitly anti-colonial and anti-imperialist fashion than was the case in his critique of everyday life in the early 1960s, this is in large part because of his observations of the nature of revolt and revolution in the late 1960s. Lefebvre's understanding of 'colonisation' as a multi-scalar political form of producing space – hierarchical territorial relations of core and periphery – emerged from his analysis of the spatial dynamics of May 1968 and how these dynamics related to other points of mobilisation, from Algeria to Latin America and the ghettos of the United States. Far from a mere result of one-sidedly abstract conceptualisation, Lefebvre's state-theoretical understanding of 'colonisation' takes its cues from the social struggles that were either on the wane or defeated by the time he wrote *De l'état*. So let us return to the late 1960s and the urban question.

---

132   Lefebvre 1978, pp. 237–8.
133   Lefebvre 1978, p. 247.

2.3   *From 'Colonisation' I to 'Colonisation' II: The Right to the City and the Urban Revolution*

The figureheads of imperialism have changed, but not imperialism. The most intelligent leaders of the capitalist countries, winners or losers of the Second World War, have succeeded in extricating themselves from the colonialist impasse. They also managed to bank on the internal market, which leads to 'consumer society'.[134] Paradoxically, under neocapitalism, exploitation has taken the form of internal colonisation. People are waking up to these developments. Organised capitalism now has its colonies in the metropoles and it deploys the colonial mode of control when it banks on the internal market. The double exploitation of the producer (as such and as consumer) transfers the colonial experience into the midst of formerly colonising peoples. These global repercussions for the national take varied forms. Metropolitan populations are regrouped into ghettos (the suburbs, foreigners, factories, the students) and new towns have certain features that remind us of colonial cities. Complex differences thus appear within general oppression, revalorising democracy, speech, the exchange of ideas and the discussion of projects. These are the only ways of breaking the isolation of the ghettos.[135]

In 1966, Lefebvre published some reflections on generalised self-management. He suggests that *autogestion* tends to emerge from the weak points within the unevenly developing dynamics of world order. Next to the *Commune* and the *Soviet* revolution, Lefebvre uses the case of Algeria between independence in 1962 and Boumedienne's coup in 1965 to buttress his case. There, *autogestion* was being set up 'in the domains abandoned by the colonists', throwing 'into question society as a whole and the apparatuses that were inherited from the colonial era, or that were established at the time of independence'.[136] Running parallel to the Situationists' more programmatic comments on the Boumedienne coup,[137] this harsh rupture in the 'red' years of post-independence Algeria,[138] Lefebvre's are rare observations about politics in the former colonial world. In fact, as the opening quote from *The Explosion* indic-

---

134   Lefebvre 1968a, p. 45.
135   Lefebvre 1968a, p. 103.
136   Lefebvre 2003d, p. 145.
137   Situationist International 1981a, 1981b.
138   On the role of 'red' collaborators with post-independence Algeria in this context, see Simon 2009.

ates, much of his emerging insights into the direct links between 'far' and 'near' colonies stem from his observations of how in Paris, the dynamics of May 1968 were driven by the students, workers, and immigrants, who took action in their segregated 'ghettos' – suburban dormitories, factories and shantytowns – before converging on the Left Bank and the Latin Quarter.[139] It is *this* dialectic of periphery (popular suburb) and centre (central Paris) that led Lefebvre to suggest, in the same year, that demands for the right to the city/difference emerge out the 'refusal to allow oneself to be removed from urban reality by a discriminatory and segregative organisation'.[140]

Lefebvre's critique of alienation and everyday life from earlier in the 1960s is now activated, as it were, by concrete urban struggles. Upon his participant observations about 1968, Lefebvre takes us beyond a metaphorical treatment of 'colonisation'. In rapid succession, Lefebvre aligns a series of arguments that concretise his understanding about the relationships between colonisation 'proper' and the neo-'colonial' reorganisation of the metropole. Encapsulated in the two works most directly informed by May 1968, *The Explosion* (1968) and the *The Right to the City* (1968), these arguments are elaborated more fully in *The Urban Revolution* (1970), *La pensée Marxiste et la ville* (1972) and the articles collected in *Espace et Politique* (1970–73). It is in these tomes that Lefebvre decides to discuss 'colonisation' with the theorists of imperialism and colonisation, who also inform *De l'état*.

In the first instance, Lefebvre links metropolitan capitalism to the colonial world with shifting accumulation strategies and migration. As he summarises succinctly in his review of Marxist engagements with the city, *La pensée Marxiste et la ville*, urbanisation is key to the reproduction of capital not only in the formation of surplus value (as productive force) and the distribution of it (through land rent). It is also crucial for the realisation of surplus value (as part of the *internal* market). This is of particular importance in the shift to intensive accumulation during Fordism, when a new capitalism needs and creates new consumers and when a growing proportion of workers are recruited from past or present colonies. With explicit reference to Lenin, Luxemburg and Samir Amin's *Accumulation on a World Scale*, Lefebvre suggests that

> social space itself is produced at the same time as it is under surveillance and control, in the extension of the big cities and the planning of territory. If the bourgeoisie of a particular industrial country loses its

---

139   Lefebvre 1968a, p. 103; Lefebvre 1996, p. 144.
140   Lefebvre 1996, p. 195.

external markets, it transports colonialism into the country. In relationship to the centres (of economic production and of political decision-
making), the peripheries give rise to phenomena of neo-colonialism,
of neo-imperialism. Among the social strata which are juxtaposed in
urban space, there are few peasants but many populations which are both
dispersed and dominated by the centres. The modern city (metropolis,
megalopolis) is seat, instrument and centre of action of neo-colonialism
and neo-imperialism all at the same time.[141]

In this formulation, 'internal colonisation'[142] refers to more than ways of controlling everyday life for mass consumption. It is spurred on by the mortal crisis
of the colonial economic system. And it thrives on the processes of dispersal,
migration and settlement, which reconnect various peripheries – former colonies, relegated regions – to metropolitan (imperial- and large-urban) centres. It
is in this sense that cities must be placed at the heart of any analysis of neo-
colonialism.

What is also clear from the above quote is how neo-colonial arrangements
are organised spatially. 'Internal colonisation' is refracted through dynamics of
uneven development. As Lefebvre argued in 1970, 'the introduction of colonialism into the metropole' entails

> a semi-colonisation of the underdeveloped regions and zones by the
> decision-making centres, especially the Parisian centre. There are no
> longer colonies in the old sense of the word, but there is already a metro-
> politan semi-colonisation that subjects rural populations, large numbers
> of foreign workers, and also many French workers and intellectuals, to a
> concentrated exploitation through the methods of maintaining the ele-
> ments of a state of spatial segregation.[143]

The spatial inequalities of 'semi-colonisation' in France can be observed in
inter-regional relations between the Paris area and other 'overdeveloped' regions, on the one hand, and peripheral regions such as the *Bretagne*, on the
other.[144] Of particular salience in these processes of peripheralisation is urbanisation: the creation of mono-functional industry towns in peripheral regions

---

141   Lefebvre 1972a, pp. 130–1.
142   Lefebvre 1972a, p. 130.
143   Lefebvre 2003e, p. 181.
144   Lefebvre 1972c, pp. 257–8.

(such as Lacq-Mourenx) and suburban segregation in large urban regions. The degree to which the reorganisation of everyday life in postwar France is both a response to geopolitical decolonisation and an aspect of neo-colonial arrangements thus becomes clearest within the unevenly expanding field of the urban itself.[145]

Lefebvre is often vague about the socially concrete ways in which the 'manipulation of space' helps disorganise the working class by re-organising core-periphery relationships.[146] But at a descriptive level at least, he mentions repeatedly that peripheralisation does not mean the same thing for every worker. We have already learned (at least in rudimentary form) that this is true for women. In the late 1960s, Lefebvre makes increasing references to immigrant workers as well. In a talk about 'the bourgeoisie and space' in Chile in 1972, he insists that in France, the housing question is

> far from being completely resolved, in capitalism, as Engels once said in a famous book. This is particularly the case for foreign workers. Many hovels and slums still exist, either in the centre of old cities or in the suburbs. Nevertheless, an important part of the working class is relatively well housed ... (in bungalows [*pavillons*] and large estates [*grands ensembles*]).[147]

At the time when Lefebvre wrote these lines, many immigrant workers (particularly those from North Africa and the Iberian peninsula) were still living in sub-standard housing (single rooms in cheap hotels and transitional housing estates called *cités de transit*). The largest burden of residential segregation was shouldered by those in the most precarious segments of the labour market. In this most concrete form, semi-colonisation produced demarcations *within* the peripheralised working class.[148]

In a rare observation about the status of immigrant workers, Lefebvre notes a particular kind of contradiction that is brought to bear on '1968':

> The most notable characteristic of France is a big contradiction between the democratic revolution, the great French revolution (with its consequences: the Rights of Man), on the one hand, and, on the other, imperialism, the clever and very tough bourgeois dominant class, the super-

---

145   Ross 1995.
146   Lefebvre 1972d, pp. 276–8.
147   Lefebvre 1972c, pp. 258–9.
148   Ibid.

exploitation of foreign workers (which number three and a half mil-
lion in France). The combination of these contradictions was revealed in
1968.[149]

In a context shaped by a tension between the French revolutionary tradition, neo-imperialism, and the realities of semi-colonisation, demands for the
right to the city must mean more than a generic critique of commodification: the process through which exchange value occupies the street with
images and objects, publicity and spectacle.[150] Directed against the super-
exploitation and spatial segregation through which commodification is experienced by some workers, demands for the right to the city must be channelled
through demands for the right to difference:[151] the quest for a different world
expressed as the liberation from the alienated, minimal differences of the
here and now. To do justice to the *complex* differences that arise within 'general oppression' means also to 'break the isolation of the ghettos'[152] that, in
1968, formed the minimally different starting points for the spatial dialectic of
revolt.

The upshot of Lefebvre's discussion of the 'colonial' aspects of '1968' are not
restricted to metropolitan France. In the *Urban Revolution*, he discusses the
revolts in the African-American ghettos and the rise of urban guerrilla movements in Latin American *barrios* to buttress his arguments that revolt and
revolution are taking place in a rapidly progressing, if very uneven and disrupt-
ive field of urbanisation. While agrarian reform and peasant rebellion informed
a significant part of the successful revolutions in 1789, 1917, 1949, even 1959,
the anti-urban imaginaries that emerged from some of these revolutions are
increasingly anachronistic. As he asks with reference to the Maoist conception
of revolutionary strategy,

> Can such a [Maoist] strategy assume, however, that the countryside will
> encircle the city, that peasant guerrillas will lead the assault on urban
> centres? Today, such a vision or conception of the class struggle on a
> global scale appears old-fashioned. The revolutionary capacity of the
> peasantry is not on the rise; it is being reabsorbed, although not consist-
> ently. On the contrary, a kind of overall colonisation of space by 'decision-
> making centres' seems to be taking shape. Centres of wealth and inform-

---

149   Lefebvre 1972c, p. 257.
150   Lefebvre 2003f., p. 21.
151   Lefebvre 1972c, p. 259.
152   Lefebvre 1968a, p. 103.

ation, of knowledge and power are beginning to create feudal dependencies. In this case, the boundary line does not divide city and country but cuts across the urban phenomenon, between a dominated periphery and a dominating centre.[153]

Here Lefebvre reacts to the globally rescaled version of Maoist strategy. Articulated by Lin Pao in 1965, this strategy transposes the notion of a peasant-centred strategy to encircle cities *in toto*, by establishing a global opposition between the 'rural areas of the world' (Asia, Africa, and Latin America) and 'the cities of the world' (North America and Western Europe).[154] At the same time, Lefebvre takes issue with Che Guevara. In Latin America, he suggests, rapid urbanisation and another round of agricultural destructuring have undercut the socio-spatial bases for the kind of *foco* strategies pursued by Guevara. The ensuing mass migration to 'the outskirts of the already overcrowded cities' has created the conditions for 'urban guerrilla activity' 'in the favelas and shantytowns, which have become outlets for struggle, intermediaries between the dispossessed peasants and industrial labour'.[155] Read together with Lefebvre's points about May 1968, these observations push beyond Frantz Fanon's insistence on the role of the peasantry and the lumpenproletariat in liberation struggles, as we will see in Chapter 3. They underscore that the revolting peripheries, 'far' and 'near', have become linked by world-wide urban transformations, too. The urban revolution now mediates the terrain for colonial problematics. As a consequence, the revolution requires urban strategies.

2.4 Beyond Homological Arguments: Globalising Lefebvre

From the early 1960s to the late 1970s, Lefebvre's understanding of 'colonisation' undergoes significant specification. While in the second volume of *The Critique of Everyday Life* Lefebvre refers to 'colonisation' as a metaphor to grasp the general domination of everyday life under neo-capitalism, in *De l'état*, 15 years later, 'colonisation' appears in a more explicit anti-colonial register, as a particular, state-bound strategy of producing abstract space: territorial relations between dominant and dominated social spaces. It was the most intense part of Lefebvre's urban turn, from 1968 to 1972, that helps us understand how the critique of everyday life can translate colonial problematics into the study of imperial centres themselves. Lefebvre's observations of urban struggles from Paris to

---

153   Lefebvre 2003f., p. 113.
154   As Stuart Schrader (2018) has pointed out, the source of this rescaling of Maoism is Lin Pao's *Long Live the Victory of the People's War*.
155   Lefebvre 2003f., p. 146.

Chicago, and from North Africa to Latin America, alerted him to some of the specific connections that link socio-spatial peripheries in imperial centres with those in former colonies: accumulation strategies, dynamics of displacement, forms of spatial organisation.

'Colonisation' can thus be taken to be a more concretely elaborated aspect of Lefebvre's understanding of the urban revolution as a mediation of totality in the modern world. On the one hand, the explosion of historically circumscribed city forms under conditions of world-wide urbanisation engulfs core-periphery relationships in a notably uneven and hierarchical urban field. On the other hand, the couplet 'the right to the city'/'the right to difference' appears as a set of 'decolonising' claims that, in the postwar period, emerge out of fragmented and homogenised peripheries such as the Algerian shantytown or the Parisian banlieue. In this context, Lefebvre suggests (in telling comments about nationalism and Eurocentrism) that a successful challenge to 'colonisation' must develop the capacity to 'modify particularities' (of homogenised-segregated groups) and 'transform' them into non-reified, dynamic and situated 'differences'.[156]

As a struggle concept, 'colonisation' – which, much like urbanisation, Lefebvre saw as a transnational, multi-scalar phenomena – played a significant role in Lefebvre's discovery of the global. As he says in an interview on *autogestion* in 1976 and again in *Le Retour de la dialectique* ten years later, the world-wide revolt and proto-revolution that was '1968' was critical in how it became possible, from 1960 to 1975, to grasp the 'world-wide as a problem'.[157] He suggested that the contingent possibility of knowing and experiencing the world as a whole was clarified to him not the least by the world-wide constellation of multiple, unevenly developed points of opposition and uprising.[158] An awareness of this constellation led Lefebvre to caution against the notion that the globalisation of knowledge proceeded as a singular quest for intellectual unification. As he argues in the last volume of *De l'état*, the notion of *'mondialité* denies the existence of one, unique centre and affirms the *differential* multiplicity of centres, as well as their relative (moving, precarious, uncertain) character'.[159] Connecting knowledge and the world is thus not about claiming the world as a whole only from one, fixed centre. Such unilateral claims to the world-wide, Lefebvre considered potentially complicit with strategies of globalising the state and enveloping the world in a web of rationalist, state-bound know-

---

156   Lefebvre 1978, p. 207; Lefebvre 1970h, pp. 182–3.
157   Lefebvre 2009a, p. 301. See also Brenner and Elden 2009, p. 8.
158   Lefebvre 1976d, p. 125.
159   Lefebvre 1978, p. 330.

ledge (*savoir*).[160] Globalising knowledge is about connecting multiple centres of knowledge creation from a range of possible vantage points. What emerges from this is an incomplete historical intellectual praxis with multiple centres of gravity, each of which is caught in a dialectic of universality and particularity akin to the dynamics of revolt in the long 1968.

Given these extrapolations (from anti-colonial social struggles to the philosophical problem of the world-wide), one is struck by how little discernible effect Lefebvre's engagement with colonial problematics otherwise has on the most theoretical of his works. Consistent with his observations about the need to situate a critique of alienation in the midst of lived reality, all of Lefebvre's major philosophical works, from *Dialectical Materialism* (1939) to *Métaphilosophie* (1965), *Hegel, Marx and Nietzsche* (1975) and *Le retour de la dialectique* (1986) aim at a dialectical transformation of philosophy. Yet the increasingly world-wide character of everyday life Lefebvre noticed has virtually no effect on this intellectual transformation, which continues to take place in a rather conventionally conceived forcefield of European philosophy. Within this context, the dominant critiques of Eurocentrism he mobilises only aim at abstract targets (logocentrism in the 'West', the 'Occident' or 'Judeo-Christianity') and stem, paradoxically, from writers otherwise patently committed to explicit European supremacy:[161] Nietzsche and Heidegger. Not surprisingly, when Lefebvre mobilises these critiques of the West, as he does in the *Production of Space*, they leave intact his own Eurocentric history of space.[162]

Lefebvre himself thus failed to fulfil the promises of his own reflections about the meta-theoretical implications of social struggle in a neo-colonial urban world. His search for a more genuinely world-wide form of knowledge was frustrated by the limits of his own engagements. This has consequences also at a more analytical level. Lefebvre's conceptualisation of 'colonisation' as

---

160 Lefebvre 1978, pp. 331–9.

161 As Robert Bernasconi (1997, p. 213) has argued more generally, even critics of Eurocentric philosophy have a tendency to return to the very 'paradoxically parochial' conceptions of the history of 'Western philosophy' that inform such intellectual Eurocentrism.

162 Our concern with Lefebvre's histories of city and space is not that they are rooted in European experiences or that the concepts they yielded are impossible to disentangle from these experiences (they can be). The problem is that they make it difficult to understand how world-wide relations (including the links between colonial and imperial cities) have over-determined or mediated urbanisation and the formation of abstract space in the modern world (including Europe). As Goswami's (2004) work on the production of India indicates, Lefebvre's theory of the production of space is useful to understand the production of colonial space only once it is re-articulated and re-contextualised accordingly.

territorial relation of domination, although much less generic than his critique of everyday life, does not adequately specify the distinction between *different varieties* of 'colonisation' and their *particular* forms of determination. While Lefebvre repeatedly mentions the degree to which 'colonisation' means different things for students, workers, women, immigrant workers, he does so descriptively, without theorising fully why this might be the case. As a result, even the Lefebvre of the 1970s has still not fully met his earlier claim that importing colonial problematics into a critique of everyday life goes beyond superficial analogies.[163] As Jost Müller has argued with respect to the relevance of Lefebvre's critique of alienation and everyday life for an analysis of everyday racism,[164] connecting the experience of colonial spatial strategy to analyses of neo-capitalism, racialised ghettoisation or slum settlements in a neo-colonial world runs the risk of substituting a theoretically nuanced analysis with argumentation by homology.

The limitations of Lefebvre's foray into colonial problematics are rooted in his unwillingness to fully explore the specificity of colonisation as a particular form of alienation. Lefebvre muses here and there about the role of super-exploitation, surplus transfer and racially inflected civilising missions in shaping the alienations peculiar to colonisation[165] and, more specifically, the nature of racism as a form of mystification: a blind way of generalising, extrapolating, systematising particularities such as physical traits or ethnic forms.[166] Noting the time when these fleeting remarks were published (in 1966, 1968, and 1981), one cannot help but notice how cryptic they are compared to the kind of analyses Lefebvre then had at his disposal. Not only did the famous accounts of colonisation as thingification (Césaire 1950), a violent system of super-exploitation (Sartre 1949; Sartre 1960), exploitation and humiliation (Memmi 1957) and racialised and gendered spatial organisation (Fanon 1959; Fanon 1961) fail to make an explicit dent in Lefebvre's work; even analyses like Balandier's (1951) 'the colonial situation',[167] which emerged from within the very post-Communist intellectual milieus Lefebvre frequented in the late 1950s,[168] are absent in his work. But it is precisely these *sustained* counter-colonial sources, which in other respects shared with Lefebvre a broadly con-

---

163   See footnote 58.
164   Müller 2001, pp. 9–11.
165   Lefebvre 1970h, pp. 182–3.
166   Lefebvre 1972b, p. 75; Lefebvre 2008, pp. 111–12.
167   Balandier 1951.
168   Balandier and Lefebvre were both leading figures and contributors to two journals (*Arguments* and *Cahiers internationnaux de sociologie*) that functioned as meeting points for disaffected party Communists in the late 1950s. See Trebitsch 2002, pp. xvi–xxi.

ceived new humanist theoretical orientation, that must be brought to bear on Lefebvre himself. As we learn from Kristin Ross's brilliant attempt to link the internally related logics of the Algerian War and suburban planning in Paris,[169] only with the help of intellectuals like Fanon is it possible to avoid glossing over the specificities of distinct forms of 'colonisation' ('near' or 'far') and actualise the promising elements in Lefebvre's notion of 'colonisation'. This will be the subject of the next chapter.

3   Conclusion

> Has the intellectual tool that is the notion of the colonial situation, and the theorisation that preceded it, become obsolete with the end of the forms of colonisation that emerged from the imperialisms of the 19th century? We must begin with the observation that the 'post-colonial' erases the 'colonial' only in its most apparent forms. It leaves a vast terrain of influence, of indirect domination, by making use of the ties which were created in colonial times but whose partners and forms have changed: economic, political, religious, cultural ties, which, through shared interests, link the dominant minorities of the old metropole with the dominant minorities ushered in with independence .... Colonial relations are also maintained when they direct immigrants from the old colonies to the former colonial countries. Once only 'outside', in the colonies, the social and cultural pluralism that was produced by conquest and settlement now extends into the metropoles, the former imperial countries. This pluralism internalises in different forms what remains of the colonial relation. It is as if this relation still occupied people's consciousness even as it expresses itself in different languages and cultural dynamics.[170]

In 1961, Lefebvre stressed the almost complete failure of Marxist political theory to come to proper terms with colonisation and the Third World.[171] Looking back at the progression of his work (and that of many others) since then, one is tempted to be less pessimistic. A generation before Balandier's comment about the currency of the colonial in (neo-)colonial times, Lefebvre's concept of 'colonisation' infused our sense of global urbanisation explicitly with problematics of colonisation and imperialism. Articulated formally in his writing on

---

169   Ross 1995.
170   Balandier 2002, p. 4.
171   Lefebvre 1971b, p. 129.

the state in the late 1970s but noted with accentuated frequency in his observations about the various struggles which converged in '1968', Lefebvre's concept describes state-bound territorial relationships of domination. It develops his critique of everyday life and specifies aspects of his dialectical notion of the urban as (spatial) form, (social) level and mediation (of totality). Originally a struggle concept (like his notion of difference), Lefebvre's 'colonisation' redirects Marxist theories of state and imperialism (particularly those of Lenin and Luxemburg) into urban directions. It also alerts us to the strategic role socio-spatial peripheries play in revolution. A key aspect of how state intervention helps produce space, 'colonisation' articulates world order and reaches into the contradictions of everyday life. It can be analysed at various spatial scales, as a territorial relation among neighbourhoods, regions, and nations. In any historical period, spatial forms can be compared directly across scalar divides, thus making it possible to link 'colonisation' in former colonies to segregated areas in metropolitan countries. Since socio-spatial peripheries are increasingly linked through a transnational urban field, their comparison takes on a distinctly relational character. This is now increasingly well recognised in research on planetary urbanisation, as we will see in Chapters 3 and 4.

To realise its full potential, however, Lefebvre's concept of 'colonisation' needs to be liberated from the limits of his overall work. To rigorously account for the socio-spatial specificities of 'colonial' spatial forms, it needs to be redirected with counter-colonial influences proper. In the next chapter, I propose to do this with the help of the particular form of counter-colonialism embodied by Aimé and Suzanne Césaire, Albert Memmi, Jean-Paul Sartre and, above all, Frantz Fanon. In the spirit of articulating points of contact between European Marxism and colonial liberation theory,[172] one can also broaden our field of investigation, bringing Lefebvre into more sustained contact with other counter-colonial currents, including his own occasional interlocutors Lenin, Mao and Samir Amin. As I will point out in Chapters 3 and 4, one avenue to pursue this line of investigation could be the considerations of land, city and countryside so central to anti-colonial and Southern Marxisms.[173] Much of Lefebvre's work on land rent, agricultural class relations in Tuscany, the festival in Southern France and Rabelais[174] underscored that, for him, the rural and the urban do not relate to each other as markers of ideal types (tradition or modernity), nor did they succeed each other in the linear fashion of modernisation theory or other Euro-centric diffusionisms. Lefebvre's investigations were

---

172   Parry 2002, p. 126.

173   Coronil 2000; Hart 2006.

174   Lefebvre 1970d, 1970 g; Lefebvre 1955.

directed against transhistorical conceptions of rurality and emphasised the historically and geographically varied ways in which social relations and cultural
forms undergo structural change in long transitions to capitalism. Combining
rupture with continuity, this change is not a linear shift from rural tradition to
urban modernity. Rather, the urban revolution unevenly transposes city and
countryside into an urban field of central and peripheral social spaces. Today,
Lefebvre's insights could be put to good use to study comparatively the specific
ways in which dynamic city-countryside relations sustain world-wide urbanisation, thus heeding calls for a more genuinely global geography of urban
theory.[175]

Lefebvre's non-diffusionist understanding of urbanisation as a world-wide
but uneven and incomplete process is more important than ever to understand
the geographies of our capitalist world, where imperialism is no longer primarily organised in formal colonial terms. It represents a remarkably prescient
statement about the 'urbanisation of empire' today.[176] Once transformed with
Fanon, Lefebvre's notion of 'colonisation' helps shed light on how imperial capitalism is mediated by struggles over the spatial organisation of political domination. This is true with respect to a variety of often racialised spatial strategies –
military urbicide, slum clearance, and, the subject of Chapter 5, public housing redevelopment.[177] These strategies attempt to pre-empt or counter forms
of anti-systemic politics by destroying, dispersing, fragmenting or obfuscating
subaltern social spaces. Within current debates about the geography of imperialism, the advantages of the notion of 'colonisation' derived from Lefebvre and
Fanon are at least three-fold. By looking at territorial organisation as a multi-
scalar affair, it avoids treating 'Empire' as deterritorialised 'smooth space'[178]
without reaffirming territory as a marker of a fixed scalar ontology centred
on nation-state-space. With 'colonisation', Lefebvre and Fanon take us 'under-
neath' the macro-political economies of imperialism.[179] They offer us tools for
understanding territorial forms of domination that cut across the 'geo-political'
and 'geo-economic' aspects of Empire (to speak with Neil Smith)[180] or the 'territorial' and 'capitalist' logics of power in the new imperialism (in David Harvey's terms).[181] Finally, by focusing on territory as a mediation of socio-political

---

175   Roy 2009.
176   Davis 2004; Mendieta 2008.
177   Kipfer and Goonewardena 2007.
178   Hardt and Negri 2000; for critiques of deterritorialisation in *Empire*, see Sparke 2001 and
      Hart 2006.
179   Harvey 2003a; Smith 2005.
180   Smith 2003, pp. 24–5.
181   Harvey 2003a, pp. 101–15.

relations, the notion of 'colonisation' provides a useful counterpoint to neo-Foucauldianism, where neo-colonial and imperial geographies appear primarily as effects of discursive practices and geographical imaginaries[182] rather than as relational and integral products of struggle over the appropriation of social space.

182   Gregory 2004.

CHAPTER 2

Times and Spaces of Liberation: Frantz Fanon on (De)Colonisation

This chapter presents Frantz Fanon as a dialectical thinker who developed an eminently dynamic conception of the times and spaces of anti-colonial liberation. In the following, I begin by reviewing key strands of debate in English-speaking Fanon scholarship and what these debates tell us about the 'spatial' Fanon. Taking into account the recent publication of previously unavailable Fanon texts, I concentrate on the supersession of postmodern interpretations and the formation of a heterodox state of the art in Fanon scholarship that emphasises the Martinican's consistent quest for a new, dialectical humanism. In the second section, I place Fanon in broader intellectual context, situating his work within the francophone current of counter-colonialism that emerged in the 1930s and flourished in the postwar period. In the third section, I offer an integral reading of Fanon that demonstrates, among other things, one of his key contributions to counter-colonial theory: his spatio-temporal conception of colonialism and anti-colonial struggle. In the last section, I reconnect Fanon to Henri Lefebvre. I show how Fanon's work can transform Lefebvre's notion of 'colonial' territorial relation and offer suggestions about how to develop Fanon's work further, particularly as far as research on urbanisation and the state is concerned. The concluding paragraphs open up to subsequent chapters by confronting Fanon with strategic political debates in mainland France, Indigenous Canada, and Martinique.

1 Debating Fanon

For a while, from the late 1980s to the early 2000s, postmodern theories of post-colonial conditions greatly influenced English-speaking Fanon scholarship. They did so in part by inverting earlier, revolutionary and anti-imperialist interpretations of the Martinican, as Saïd Bouamama recently reminded us.[1] The question of 'space' in Fanon's work has been a crucial, if paradoxical problem for postcolonial interpretations. Theorists like Edward Said and Homi Bhabha

---

1 Bouamama 2014, p. 10.

applauded the stark spatial formulations in some of Fanon's works insofar as they seem to signal a welcome move away from 'historicism' and dialectical thought.[2] In this respect, Bhabha went much further than Said (who ultimately rejected the label 'postcolonial') when he mobilised Fanon for his notion of 'third space': the empty space of non-representability that opens up between signifiers (identity and difference, self and other) in performative play.[3] Fanon thus became part of a deconstructive third space, this 'spatial relation between signifiers'[4] that allowed Bhabha to hybridise the fixities of Black and White. It was *this* spatial Fanon, Bhabha's, which has been the most influential in postcolonial geographical attempts to merge the spatial with the cultural and linguistic turns in social theory. For Ed Soja and Barbara Hooper in particular, Fanon was an early thinker of 'the spatialisation of cultural politics' and can be understood, *pace* Bhabha, as an embryonic thinker of 'third space', that space of 'hybridity' where 'everything comes together' in an 'all-inclusive simultaneity'.[5]

Mobilising the spatial Fanon for deconstructive or discourse-theoretical purposes requires that Fanon's work be divested of its constitutive, Hegelian-Marxist and phenomenological influences and its radical humanist proclivities. On this count, Fanon's spatial formulations must appear dangerous because they point to the ostensibly essentialist and binary character of his writing. Bhabha's deconstructive and hybridising moves reinscribe, even eternalise, Fanon's spatial binaries, but only as elements in an indeterminable play of signifiers.[6] The 'spatial' aspects of Fanon's work are thus highlighted in an anti-dialectical and anti-humanist register that runs counter to Fanon himself. Bhabha's more recent selective reassessment of the spatial Fanon still disarticulates time and space in Fanon's understanding of decolonisation and thus fails to grasp the dialectical movement that operates in his work.[7] This failure points to a deeper deterritorialising streak in the epistemological radicalism of Bhabha (and Gayatri Spivak), which, despite the 'apparent suspicion of post-modern in-difference to placelessness', 'can only be read as making a still more emphatic claim to a paradoxical place of *placelessness* itself'. There, 'any carefully delineated border of periphery and metropole, colony and empire become blurred, de-territorialised, and unbounded'.[8] This *a priori* commitment to blur-

2   Said 1999, p 208; Bhabha 1999, p. 184.
3   Bhabha 1994, pp. 36–7, 50.
4   Bhabha 1994, p. 36.
5   Soja 1996, pp. 96, 139, 12–14, 56–7; also Pile 2000.
6   Bhabha 1994, pp. 241–2, 247; 1999, p. 191.
7   Bhabha 2004; Haddour 2006, p. xx.
8   Hallward 2001, p. 22, p. 34.

ring boundaries can downplay 'the historical polarisation of the experience of colonisation and slavery, as well as the ongoing effects of its legacy in the present global divide'.[9] Most clearly, it runs up to the major concern of this chapter, which is to delineate Fanon's *counter*-colonial project to *transforming* colonialism with a dynamic understanding of time and space, history and geography.[10,11]

Deconstructive radicalism, which forms a part of what has been called 'French theory' in the English-speaking academy[12] has lost its hegemonic position in Anglophone Fanon scholarship as well as in postcolonial discourse. At the same time as it has become common to distinguish between research on after-colonial situations and the specificities of deconstructive postcolonialism (which only represent one set of approaches to this field),[13] English-speaking Fanon scholarship has been profoundly reoriented by new waves of interpretations since the 1990s. Perhaps best exemplified by the richest among

---

9   Majumdar 2007, p. 253.

10   Hallward and Majumdar effectively pinpoint the most radical aspects of deconstructive postcolonial theory: their uncompromising epistemological critique of representation. This epistemological radicalism has twin effects. The very deconstructive moves that undermine any sense of stability in (neo-)colonial relations (territorial or otherwise) also must reinstate the binaries they mean to disturb. As Spivak has pointed out herself, the project of deconstructing Western metaphysics depends on a 'methodological presupposition': the 'necessary theoretical fiction' of this very history of metaphysics (1990, p. 136; 1998, p. lxvv). This unifying procedure represents the counterpoint to deconstruction, and a basis for strategic essentialism. In Bhabha's project of disturbing the signifying binaries of the colonial world, these very binaries – and the discursive marker of race – become eternalised. They remain 'necessary' – epistemologically prescribed – parts in the interplay of identity and difference, self and other (1994, pp. 241–2, 247; 1999, p. 191). And in Dipesh Chakrabarty, who is admittedly less committed to deconstructive radicalism than Spivak and Bhabha, the project of questioning Orientalist binaries in Indian historiography is built upon a stark set of a priori dualisms (West and non-West, 'History I' and 'History II', the modern and the subaltern, Marx and Heidegger). As we have noted already in the introduction, his eminently important project to provincialise 'Europe' (and question its claim to the privilege of being ignorant about the rest of the world) thus comes close to achieving the opposite. It threatens to recreate a superhuman figure of 'Europe' (which is claimed to be in possession of such goodies as reason, progress, democracy and secularism) while identifying the 'other' (India, the non-West) with the now revalorised opposite qualities: gods and spirits (Chakrabarty 2000; for critiques, see Cooper 2005, pp. 31, 133, 136, 140; Lazarus 2002, pp. 59–60; Harootunian 2000, pp. 50–1, Harootunian 2015, pp. 225–33; Matin 2011, Kaiwar 2013, pp. 152–80, Bannerji 2011).

11   On the specifically Algerian reference points in Derrida's own strategies to 'blur' distinctions between coloniser and colonised, see Huffer 2006.

12   Cusset 2005.

13   See Lazarus 2004 and McLeod 2007.

these interpretations, Ato Sekyi-Otu's *Dialectic of Experience*, these waves have highlighted with great precision a number of crucial and formative features in Fanon's work.[14] They have not only rescued a lost 'radical' Fanon, whose work is very much compatible with certain Hegelian, Marxist, phenomenological and modernist Black radical currents. Avoiding any suggestion that Fanon's work was cut in two by some sort of epistemological break brought about by shifts in Fanon's biography,[15] they have also insisted on the continuities between Fanon's early phenomenological analyses of everyday racism, his psychiatric work and his more explicitly political and historical-materialist writing on national liberation. Fanon's shift to explicitly political writing notwithstanding, his work was a life-long search for human-subjective potentials and capacities against the seemingly iron-clad, 'ontological', divides of the colonial world and its dehumanising racialised fixities. These persistent new humanist concerns allow us to understand why and how Fanon recast dialectical thought and 'stretched' (extended and modified) the Marxisms available to him.[16] They also help us understand the ways in which the Fanon of the late 1950 and early 1960s placed the art of politics at the heart of his internationalist, tricontinental project of liberation.[17]

---

14 Ato Sekyi-Otu 1996, also 2018; Lewis Gordon 1995, 2015; Gordon, Sharpley-Whiting, and White 1996; Gibson 1999; Bernasconi with Cook 2003; Macey 2000; Gibson 2003a; Ahmed 2007; Rabaka 2010; Gibson 2011; Jane Gordon 2014; Hudis 2015; Zeilig 2016; Cicciarello-Maher 2017; Gibson and Beneduce 2017.

15 This view was frequently implicit in decisions to foreground either *Black Skin, White Masks* or the *Damned of the Earth* at the expense of the other, with post-readings typically focusing on the first and revolutionary political readings (Black, Third Worldist or Marxist) zeroing in on the second. In a certain sense, this divide is also reproduced indirectly by those who read Fanon's political writings from the middle of the 1950s in biographic and psychologising terms, in part by extrapolating from a reading of *Black Skin, White Masks*. Albert Memmi (1971) and Françoise Vergès (1997) both suggested that Fanon's Algerian involvement was a case of impossible and gendered subjective identification with Algeria, and a concomitant rejection of his own mixed-race Martinican self. The sociological parallel to this view is that of Cedric Robinson, who argued, in this case approvingly, that Fanon's decision to join the Algerian struggle was crucial in shedding the petty-bourgeois and *évolué* sensibilities that Robinson said informed *Black Skin, White Masks* (1993). Robinson did overlook, however, Fanon's own incipient and self-critical class analysis of colonial alienation in that text (see Blérald 1984, p. 142).

16 For the latest contributions that argue that Fanon made major contributions to historical materialism even though he himself was not a card-carrying Marxist, see Hudis (2015) and Zeilig (2016).

17 Sekyi-Otu 1996, Jane Gordon Turner 2014. In the last five years of his life, politics (understood not as derivative of cultural or economic forces but as the art of dialectical, partisan universalisation) becomes a partly autonomous agent not only in the creation of new nations but in the process of human-subjective transformation he had longed for

This post-postcolonial state of the art in Fanon scholarship has held up very well to closer scrutiny informed by volume of additional works by Fanon published in 2015 (*Ecrits sur l'aliénation et la liberté*) and translated into English as *Alienation and Freedom* in 2018.[18] This volume includes a range of as yet unavailable Fanon texts: three plays written in politically coded existentialist registers, psychiatric writings (his doctoral thesis, notes, letters, academic articles and hospital journal entries from his work in St. Alban, Blida and Tunis), additional political texts (including anonymous articles in *El Moudjahid* he may have (co-)authored), his correspondence with Ali Shariati, François Maspéro, and Giovanni Pirelli, and an annotated list of books in his library, which is stored in Algiers. As the editors Jean Khalfa and Robert Young point out, corroborating in effect *Fanon's Dialectic of Experience* as well as a range of Marxist, Black radical and existential-phenomenological readings, the collection makes it impossible to separate Fanon's philosophical, historical and political interests from his continuous concern with the human, including his psychiatric practice that became a sustained entry point to analysing the contradictions of everyday life in colonial-imperial contexts and racialised situations. As they point out, the link between the two aspects of Fanon's work is provided by the 'the spatial and social relations involved in shaping consciousness' and his newly humanist concern with the imperative to 'think and construct liberty as disalienation'.[19]

In this volume, one does indeed learn, once again, that Fanon knew more than anybody that the project of 'humanising man', which involves transforming the character of humanity by means of 'relations ripe with generosity', was not a liberal-humanist one, as he lectured in Tunis in 1959 and 1960.[20] Such a humanisation cannot happen by extrapolating from colonial and bourgeois worlds. It demands nothing less than social and political revolution to facilitate a deep, protracted challenge to all aspects of the colonial world, including the racist naturalisms he encountered in colonial psychiatry itself. With respect to political revolution, Fanon underlined, again in *El Moudjahid* in 1957, that national liberation was a 'struggle with a two-sided character'.[21] It entailed free-

---

all his life. In this emphasis on political agency, Fanon has much in common with other anti-colonial revolutionaries. One obvious among these, a range of nuanced differences notwithstanding, is Amilcar Cabral and his understanding of the role of political struggle in mediating the relationship between living culture and economic forces (1973). See also Idahosa 2004.

18   Fanon 2015, 2018.
19   Khalfa and Young 2015, pp. 8, 11.
20   Fanon 2015, p. 446.
21   Fanon 2015, p. 478.

ing promising historical aspects of colonised societies from colonial shackles while transforming other aspects of these same societies in open-ended processes of building something new: 'a nation to come', as he said in his letter to Ali Shariati the following year.[22] This project of building a new world through struggle has liberatory implications even for those in the imperial heartland. As he makes clear in his comments about the future of democracy, victory against the spectre of fascism in the France of the late 1950s depended on the prospects of Algerian independence, period.[23]

Those who had already interpreted Fanon in an anti-humanist register recognise the evidence to the contrary presented in this new edition of Fanon texts. One of these is Achille Mbembe. For various reasons, including Foucauldian and Afrofuturist ones, Mbembe's commentary on *Ecrits sur l'aliénation et la liberté* remains sceptical about Fanon's project of personal and political transformation.[24] But he entertains positions that are closer to Fanon's own. Among the latter is Sylvia Wynter's, the eminent feminist writer based in the English-speaking Caribbean, who has become increasingly central to a range of fields since the turn of the millennium.[25] Wynter has mobilised multiple sources, Fanon included, for the purpose of 're-enchanting humanism'. Like Fanon, she is well aware that such a re-enchantment is fraught with obstacles. For her, it must be a 'new' humanism: 'embattled', 'dissonant', 'non-identitarian', 'comprehensive', and 'planetary'.[26] This humanism cannot be a property of Europe; it must be wrested away from the 'ethno-classes' that have imprisoned (and falsified) humanism within the confines of bourgeois-colonial particularisms,[27] thus drowning out the possibilities of the human with typically naturalising, economistic, and gendered claims to Man. According to Wynter, the conditions of intelligibility of the contradiction between the human and Man can be found in the works by Frantz Fanon and Aimé Césaire and what made them possible: the liberation struggles that peaked in the 1960s and 70s.[28]

22   Fanon 2015, p. 543. Further on the relationship between Ali Shariati and Fanon, see Sara Shariati (2016).

23   Fanon 2015, p. 501.

24   Mbembe 2016.

25   Bogues 2006; McKittrick 2015.

26   Wynter 2000, pp. 121, 158. For more on the Fanon-Wynter connection, see Thomas 2018b and Gordon 2006.

27   Wynter 2000, pp. 195–7.

28   Wynter 2003; Wynter and McKittrick 2015. While McKittrick has offered to rearticulate Wynter's insight into spatial directions, Rinaldo Walcott has suggested that her search for new forms of human life can be fruitfully urbanised (2016, pp. 35–66).

Fanon's psychiatric writings contained in the new volume offers a wealth of insight into his new humanism. In 2000, Alice Cherki had already helped us improve our understanding of Fanon's life, notably as far as his psychiatric work and the problematic of violence is concerned.[29] In their monograph, Nigel Gibson and Roberto Beneduce provide additional context to the psychiatric dimensions of Fanon's *Oeuvres II*. Corroborating Cherki, Khalfa and Young, they highlight that psychiatric work constitutes a crucial thread of continuity to Fanon's life work.[30] Not unlike Henri Lefebvre's detailed analyses of architecture and planning projects (through which he ended up generating theories of space and urbanisation), Fanon's reflections on psychiatry function as a sort of labour process through which he solidified key concerns and concepts. His double psychiatric project (his critique of colonial and bourgeois psychiatry and his efforts to (re)build human-subjective capacities with his patients through various forms of socio-medical experimentation) helped concretise his understanding of uneven racialisation in France and the colonies. It also helped forge his conceptions of thingification,[31] (dis)alienation and (de)humanisation, including 'absolute depersonalisation'.[32] In fact, as Gibson and Beneduce suggested, Fanon's view of colonial social space (which was not merely metaphorical) was sharpened by his intimate knowledge of how space was produced in the colonial mental hospital, through the segregating physical arrangements and staff-patient relationships in the microcosm of Blida-Joinville.[33]

If Fanon's *Ecrits sur l'aliénation et la liberté* corroborate the main claim made in this chapter (about the dynamic spatial and historical character of Fanon's work), we also get from this work further clarity about the multiple temporalities of Fanon's politicism. For him, the primacy of politics did not mean that anti-colonial revolution could resolve everything at once. He was clear that ongoing 'healing work' would remain a key task in the construction of a genuinely postcolonial world.[34] But Fanon's new humanist concerns and political commitments keep overwhelming his psychiatric work, pushing Fanon beyond the boundaries of psychiatry as real-existing institutional practice. All in all, Fanon scholarship since the 1990s has thus clarified the range of plausible Fanon interpretations, a range that has pushed to the margins the postmodern-

---

29   Cherki 2006.
30   Gibson and Beneduce 2017.
31   Gibson and Benefuce 2017, pp. 127, 232.
32   Gibson and Beneduce 2017, pp. 113, 249.
33   Gibson and Beneduce 2017, p. 143.
34   Gibson and Beneduce 2017, pp. 5, 234.

postcolonial readings that infused Fanon scholarship in the 1990s with strong anti-humanist sensibilities if not a veritable 'essentialist anti-essentialism'.[35] The author of this expression, Lewis Gordon has extended his long-standing existentialist-phenomenological take on Fanon[36] to underline Fanon's work has helped the shaped all three overarching concerns of Africana philosophy with the human, with liberation and freedom, and with reason and rationality.[37] To put this insight into the complementary ways of Reiland Rabaka, one can say that Fanon's variegated insights can be developed in various theoretical and political directions (anti-racist, anti-colonial, Marxist, feminist) provided that one does not lose sight of Fanon's consistent and eminently transdisciplinary commitment to a revolutionary form of humanism.[38]

Building on these heterodox insights, I will proceed to treat the spatial Fanon not as a precursor to postmodern postcolonial theories and their spatial metaphors but as a crucial contribution to what one could call, jokingly, a different kind of French theory: the counter-colonial generation represented also by Aimé and Suzanne Césaire, Jeanne and Paulette Nardal, Albert Memmi, and Jean-Paul Sartre. Read in this context, Fanon's 'geography' is not anti-dialectical but infused profoundly with temporal concerns. The spatial aspects of his work are not in contradiction with his concerns about temporal transformation. To the contrary, his treatment of everyday racism (as alienating spatial relation), colonisation (as spatial organisation), and decolonisation (as a way of appropriating spatial relations at multiple scales from body to world order via the spatial relations permeating the colonial city and the emerging postcolonial nation) is thoroughly historical and geographical all at the same time. As Katherine McKittrick has pointed out, Fanon understood 'human liberation ... in tandem with a radical remaking of human geographies'.[39] In the context of this book, the ultimate point of discussing 'space' in Fanon's work is to arrive at a richer conception of colonial territorial relation than the one we could derive from the work of Henri Lefebvre. To put it differently: if Chapter 1 searched for the traces of the colonial in Lefebvre's work, this chapter will excavate the territorial and spatio-temporal aspects of colonial social relations in Frantz Fanon's contributions.

---

35   Lewis Gordon 2012.
36   Lewis Gordon 1995, 2015.
37   Lewis Gordon 2000, 2008, 2013.
38   Rabaka 2010, pp. 12, 37.
39   McKittrick 2006, p. 24.

2   Counter-Colonialism and Colonial Relations

Fanon's work was part of a broader socio-political and intellectual wave. Together with the Césaires, Memmi, and Sartre, Fanon belonged to a constellation of intellectuals, who, between World War II and the 1960s, generated
highly influential analyses of colonisation. Some of these built upon intellectual developments in the interwar period that were built on migrant networks
and political practice condensed and refracted in urban space.[40] From the
1920s on a growing presence of soldiers, workers, artists, and students of colour
turned Paris (and Marseille) into a thriving intellectual and artistic diaspora as
well as a hub for Communists, Algerian and Indochinese nationalists and pan-
Africanists. Critiques of European colonialism were advanced through a dizzying array of political organisations like *L'Union Anti-coloniale, l'Etoile Nord-
Africaine, L'Union culturelle des Vietnamiens, La Fédération des travailleurs vietnamiens en France, La Ligue universelle de défense de la race nègre*, and *le Comité
de défense de la race nègre*. They were articulated through heated debates in
journals such as *Paria, El Ouma, Viêt Nam Hôn, Lao Nông, La voix des nègres,
Le cri du nègre, Revue du Monde Noir, Légitime Défense, La Dépêche Africaine*,
and *Tropiques*. These debates dealt with, for example, the relationship between
Communism, nationalism and Pan-Africanism, the links between European
avant-gardes and non-European cultural forms, the role of Islam in colonialism
and anti-colonialism, and the tension between petty bourgeois and proletarian
perspectives.[41]

     Of particular importance for our purposes were Jeanne and Paulette Nardal
and Aimé and Suzanne Césaire, who helped forge Black Atlantic networks
and advanced internationalist, comparatively nuanced, and gender-sensitive
notions of Blackness (*négritude*).[42] In this, they were influenced by, reacted to
or worked with intellectuals such as René Maran, Lamine and Léopold Senghor, Claude McKay, Una Marsdon, Nancy Cunard, C.L.R. James, W.E.B. Du Bois,
Claudia Jones, Nicolas Guillen and Alejandro Carpentier. In their influential critique of French racism and Caribbean cultural assimilationism, the four intellectuals refracted the meaning of surrealist cultural practice and Communist
politics. While not all yet on the path towards national liberation – demands
for equality and emancipation *within* the Empire were still influential then –

---

40   Goebel 2017.
41   See Liauzu 2007, pp. 123–74; Dewitt 2008; Levasseur 2008; Girard 2008; Stora 1992, pp. 23–
      60; Ndiaye 2009; Brennan 2002; Hayes 2003; Stovall 1996; Wilder 2003a; Goebel 2017.
42   See in particular Khalfa 2009, Sharpley-Whiting 2002; Bouvier 2010, pp. 57–111; Maximin
      2009, pp. 7–23; Ndiaye 2009, Tomic 1979.

their nuanced anti-assimilationist stance helped prepare the ground for post-war radicalisation.

The impasse of the popular front and its reform colonialism, the rise of fascism and World War II demonstrated both the vincibility and hypocrisy of colonial powers. In this context, counter-colonial writing reached a new intensity as empires crumbled and wars of decolonisation became the defining feature of a new world order. In the French case, the massacres committed by French colonial authorities across the empire at the end of the war, the subsequent wars in Indochina and Algeria, and the protracted strike waves in West Africa were of primary importance in shaping the intellectual atmosphere in the diasporas and anti-colonial circles of the hexagon.[43] There, struggles in the colonies resonated with a new wave of colonial migrants (soldiers, intellectuals, students, and workers) as well as small numbers of sympathisers, both of whom helped sustain anti-colonial organisations (most prominently of course the *PPA-MTLD*, the *MNA*, and *the FLN*), underground solidarity networks and anti-colonial intellectual nodes (notably those organised by François Jeanson, Henri Curiel, François Maspéro and Marcel Manville).[44] Intellectual debates crystallised in journals (*Présence Africaine, Les Temps Modernes, l'Esprit, Partisans, Jeune Résistance, Vérité Pour,* and *Révolution Africaine*), publishing houses (*Présence Africaine, Maspéro*) and high-profile congresses (notably the Congress of Black Writers and Artists held in 1956 and 1959).[45] With their interventions, Césaire, Sartre, Memmi, and Fanon helped shape the direction of many of these debates.[46] Together with a few other, allied intellectuals such as Richard Wright and James Baldwin, they influenced a new generation of anti-racist and national liberation activists (including those committed to a tricontinental perspective).[47] In so doing, they also inspired allied dissident Marxists and segments of the fledgling new left in the metropole.

Césaire, Sartre, Memmi, and Fanon represent perhaps the most cogent concentration of a counter-colonialism that fused open-ended Marxisms with existential-phenomenological and modernist Black currents. Their work demonstrates clearly how postwar anti-colonialism remained suffused with 'Marx-

---

43 On this conjuncture, see Liauzu 2007, chapter 6; Liauzu 2004; Stora 1992.

44 Hamon and Rotman 1979; Gallissot 2009; Macey 2000, pp. 19–20.

45 On the various currents coming together in *Présence Africaine*, see the recent special issue of Gradhiva 2009, particularly Howlett and Fonkoua 2009. For Manville's account of Fanon's particular significance in this context, see the conference proceedings of the 1984 conference on Fanon organised by Manville's *Cercle Frantz Fanon* (Dacy 1986).

46 On Fanon and Césaire in particular, see the richly documented accounts by Bouvier 2009, Macey 2000.

47 Bouamama 2016; Gallissot 2005; Ben Barka 2007; Prashad 2007, pp. 105–15.

ist premises and vocabulary'[48] even as these premises were undergoing rapid modification, ushering in attempts to revise Marxism and 're-define the "universal" in a way that did not privilege Europe'.[49] In the face of national liberation struggles and attendant variants of anti-colonial cultural practice, Marxism could not be confined to the rigidities of pro-Soviet Party communism (particularly those of the *PCF* and its colonial outlier organisations in Algeria and Martinique). It needed to be revised to account for the specificities of colonisation, including the subjective and personal dimensions of the colonial experience.[50] For our authors, versions of Marxism remained central, but, as Fanon put it, needed to be 'slightly stretched every time we have to do with the colonial problem'.[51] Of course, Marxist elements were articulated with other influences differently in our authors. Their respective works did thus not add up to a seamlessly integrated approach. But despite a number of well-known points of disagreement, some of which we will revisit in Chapter 3 on Martinique, they did yield common and consistent insights.[52] Here are a few.

---

48   Wallerstein 2009, p. 6.
49   Kelley 1999.
50   'Motion d'un groupe de Marxistes' 1959, p. 419.
51   Fanon 1963, p. 40; 1970, p. 9.
52   According to Robert Bernasconi (2002), Fanon's theoretical relationship to Césaire and Sartre is characterised by a complex combination of serious but immanent critiques. This is perhaps the best to way to understand the well-known disagreements that exist among the authors we bring together in this section. (1) Aimé Césaire's dismissal of Paulette and Jeanne Nardal's salon underscores the struggle required by women to assert their role and the importance of gender in the history of *Négritude* and transatlantic Black internationalism (Sharpley-Whiting 2002, pp. 12–21; Hayes 2003, pp. 119–29, 147–52). (2) Fanon's critiques of Sartre's introduction to Senghor's *Black Orpheus* as well as Sartre's *Réflexions sur la question juive* testify to the centrality of Sartrean themes in this anti-colonial intellectual lineage and the importance of linking anti-Semitism and colonial racism even as they underline the dangers of premature attempts to marshal anti-racist response to universal dialectical movement (in Sartre) and the pitfalls of minimising the corporeal dimensions of anti-Semitism (in Fanon) (Fanon 1967, pp. 132–40, 115–16, 160–3, 180–4; 1952, pp. 93–4, 106–14, 130–3, 144–50; Bernasconi 2002; Cheyette 2006). (3) Memmi's critique of Fanon's 'impossible' geopolitical affinities underscores the fundamental limits of such psycho-biographical, even racialised reductions of thought, analysis and political involvement (Memmi 1971; Macey 2000, pp. 423–6; Lewis Gordon 2015, p. 5). Note, however, that Memmi made this critique at a time when he had already moved away from our reference point in this text, his double portrait of the coloniser and the colonised (1985). (4) Fanon's nuanced engagement with *Négritude* (which differentiates between Césaire, Senghor and Alioune Diop and distinguishes between different aspects of Césaire's own understanding of the matter) underscores how much Fanon shared Suzanne and Aimé Césaire's critique of cultural assimilationism in the French Caribbean and appreciated claims to Blackness in the context of racist inferiorisation and falsely univer-

- Colonisation is a particular relation of domination which is linked to systems of economic super-exploitation and cemented by the direct or indirect exercise of territorial rule of colonial subjects by usually European colonial rulers, settlers and their allies: administrators, merchants, religious leaders and professionals taken from local or intermediary populations. This and the following qualifications notwithstanding, 'the language of pure force' is ever-present in colonial relations of domination.[53] To put it differently, with Fanon, 'from the perspective of the colonialist, there must exist a minimum of terror on occupied soil'.[54] As we learn from Fanon himself, however, the violent character of colonialism does not mean that considerations of hegemony are foreign to the exercise of colonial rule.
- Colonial relations of domination are multi-dimensional and can be analysed at multiple levels. While organised through political economies of colonial rule and exploitation, they are linked to daily rounds of humiliation that shape the subjectivities of coloniser and colonised. 'Colonial privilege is not solely economic'.[55] The colonial relation of domination forms part of a politico-economic 'system' but this system must also be understood in its everyday manifestations,[56] as a 'lived experience' to put it in the phenomenological terms so important at the time.[57] One can thus see the

---

sal civilising missions. In turn, it also highlights Fanon's consistent plea to consider dehumanisation as a future-oriented, political, and internationalist claim to human possibility instead of an inversion of the White and colonial gaze by means of historical, cultural or racial claims to being, pre-colonial or otherwise (Fanon 1967, pp. 225–32; 1952, pp. 182–8; Fanon 1988, pp. 21–7; 2006, pp. 26–36; Fanon 1963, pp. 214, 234, 245–6; 1970, pp. 162–5, 172–7; Bernasconi 2002; Khalfa 2009, pp. 62–3; Irele 2011, pp. 117, 138, 141; Bouvier 2010, p. 93; Gordon 2015, pp. 52–9). (5) On a more directly political level, Fanon shifted from supporting Césaire's move into Communist party politics in 1945 to criticising Césaire's decision to pursue *départementalisation* (in the Fourth and Fifth Republics) as a project to pursue social emancipation in Martinique within a French imperial framework. He was equally dismayed by Césaire's position on the Algerian question: Césaire's support for special emergency powers in 1956 and his yes vote in the 1958 referendum that cleared the way for President De Gaulle's Fifth Republic. These two cases point to the growing gap between Fanon's and Césaire's respective political engagements, Césaire's repeated but always partial auto-critiques of *départementalisation* notwithstanding (Fanon 1988, pp. 167–9; 2006, pp. 186–8; Aimé Césaire 1956b, pp. 9–17; Manville 1988; Bouvier 2010, pp. 86, 169; Fallope 1986, pp. 303–8; Wilder 2015, pp. 170–81; Pierre-Charles 2011, pp. 168–9).

53   Fanon 1963, p 38; 1970, p. 6.
54   Fanon 2015, p. 510. Trans. Kipfer.
55   See Memmi's Preface to the 1966 edition, Memmi 1985, p. 16.
56   Sartre 2001a, p. 51.
57   Lewis Gordon 1996, p. 77.

colonial social relation as an 'ensemble of lived situations'[58] through which the broader infrastructure of colonisation is experienced, enacted and contested.[59]

- The multi-dimensional reality of colonisation is profoundly mediated by racism and racialisation. To speak with Fanon, racism is not everything but it is one 'element of a vaster whole', the 'most visible, the most day-to-day' element of the 'systematised oppression of a people' that is colonialism.[60] 'Emotional, affective, sometimes intellectual explanation of [colonial] inferiorisation',[61] racism is not only doctrine but also lived reality embodied in daily gesture, speech and emotive response.[62] As such racism is a crucial element in the organisation of economic plunder and the justification of violent systems of super-exploitation. It helps insulate colonial powers from claims to equality and citizenship and translates the class relations of exploitation into people-to-people relations.[63] Whether biological or cultural, 'crude' or more 'nuanced', colonial racism achieves this translation by opening an unbridgeable – pseudo-biological, cultural, 'civilisational' – gulf between the colonisers and the colonised.[64] As Sartre put it without mincing words: 'if the bourgeois was a man, while the worker, his compatriot, was merely sub-human, how could an Algerian, a distant enemy, be anything but a dog'?[65]
- As a racialised form of domination, the colonial relation heralds a particular type of alienation. This form of alienation is subjective and experiential as well as socio-economic and makes it impossible for the colonised to be recognised as (fully) human beings.[66] The divide is rendered possible by the depth of modern racism and the brutality of colonial violence establishes a relationship of exteriority between coloniser and colonised, which seems to prevent any form of dialectical transformation.[67] Césaire describes the alienating stasis of colonial life as thingification (*chosification*). Built on violence, brutality and exploitation, colonial thingification is fundamentally dehumanising: it empties colonised societies of their culture, confis-

---

58   Memmi 1985, p. 43.
59   See also Balandier 1951.
60   Fanon 1988, pp. 32, 33; 2006, pp. 39, 41.
61   Fanon 1988, p. 40; 2006, p. 48.
62   Memmi 1985, pp. 89–90.
63   Memmi 1985, pp. 60.
64   Césaire 1955, p. 10.
65   Sartre 2004, p. 718.
66   Fanon 1967, pp. 11, 111–14; 1952, pp. 8, 90–4.
67   Sartre 2004, p. 728.

cates their land, rids them of their historical possibilities.[68] Colonial thingification simultaneously fragments the colonised into sub-human instru-
ments and homogenises their existence by denying their historicity, their
capacity for self-government, their humanity. Life under thingified colonial
rule becomes 'mummified': 'fixated', 'straightjacketed' and 'sclerotic'.[69] The
potentialities of human existence are systematically denied and aborted.[70]

- The dehumanising character of the colonial relation comes back to haunt
imperial metropoles. It deforms not only colonial subjects but the coloniser as well. As Césaire puts it, 'colonisation ... dehumanises even the most
civilised man; ... colonial conquest, founded and justified as it is with the
contempt of the colonised, inevitably modifies those who embark on it'.[71]
The application of colonial technique and racist brutality unleashes a 'law
of progressive dehumanisation' – violence, corruption, barbarism – onto the
colonisers. It can 'return as practical violence to be used immediately in the
metropolitan power against the exploited masses'.[72] As all our exponents of
counter-colonialism knew well, whether as subjects or refugees from Vichy
France, victims of anti-Semitism, soldiers in the Free French army, or wit-
nesses of the OAS's putschism, the relationship between colonialism and
European fascism is intimate. 'Every colonial nation carries within itself the
seeds of fascist temptation'.[73] In turn, that means that the struggle for democracy in metropolitan heartlands (France) depends on 'peace and independence' in the colonies (Algeria).[74]

- The colonial relation is deeply gendered. Colonial rule imposes a double
burden on colonised women. Claims by some colonisers about the role of
colonisation in 'emancipating' women notwithstanding, colonial rule established or attempted to further entrench patriarchal divisions of labour. As
we will see, Fanon and writer Assia Djebar observed this form of colonial
patriarchy with particular acuity in the North African context. Colonial culture is also highly sexualised. Long before Fanon, the Nardal sisters and
Suzanne Césaire, who were instrumental in organising the Black Atlantic
diasporic circles of the 1930s and 1940s, drew our attention to how the control of women's sexuality is instrumental to colonial rule even as the fear

---

68   Césaire 1955, pp. 19–20.
69   Memmi 1985, p. 116.
70   As a result, to insist that 'the Black is a Man' is not at all as banal as it may seem (Balandier
      1947).
71   Césaire 1955, p. 18.
72   Sartre 2004, p. 719.
73   Memmi 1985, p. 83; also Césaire 1955, pp. 16, 47, and Sartre 2001b.
74   Fanon 2015, p. 501.

of the colonised men's sexuality informs the paranoia of the coloniser.[75] Jeanne Nardal in particular captured the peculiarly exoticising proclivities of French colonial culture in its interwar manifestations:[76] colonial *doudou* literature, the cult of Josephine Baker, and the grandiose colonial exhibition of 1931. The exoticising proclivities of French colonial culture provided serious challenges for internationalist and counter-colonial cultural practices.[77]

– Colonial relations are historically and comparatively variable. They cannot be humanised by reform, however. Colonisation does not rhyme with idyll.[78] Contrary to the socialist 'reform colonialists' (of the Popular Front or the 4th Republic in France), and the demands for emancipation within the empire (which were very common among North African nationalist and transatlantic Black networks between the wars), Sartre reiterated the views of many when he argued, in the late 1940s, that 'it is not true that there are some good *colons*, and others who are wicked. There are *colons* and that is it'.[79] Despite their seeming mutual externality, coloniser and colonised are locked in an inextricable relationship of mutual dependency.[80] Overcoming this relationship is impossible without breaking with the colonial empires. As Aimé Césaire put it, in significant tension with his own role in the departmentalisation of Martinique and his positions on Algeria, 'true decolonisation will be revolutionary, or not at all'.[81]

– The very intransigence of the colonial relation makes it brittle. Colonisation comes with deep contradictions. Despite attempts to legitimise colonial rule with 'pseudo-justifications',[82] despite the 'mystifying' quality of colonial rule,[83] despite the presence of a minority of Indigenous allies or intermediary groups between coloniser and colonised, the colonial relation is unstable, thus limiting the scope of hegemonic organisation.[84] The imperatives of super-exploitation and primary accumulation seem to make it impossible to grant substantial reforms. And the very depth of racialised separation and homogenisation – thingification, mummification – sought

---

75   Sharpley-Whiting 2003, pp. 115–28.
76   Jeanne Nardal 2002a [1928]. p. 108.
77   Suzanne Césaire, cited in Sharpley-Whiting 2003, p. 123; Hayes 2003, pp. 119–86; Jeanne Nardal 2002b, pp. 105–7; Paulette Nardal 2002, pp. 119–24.
78   Césaire 1956a, p. 196.
79   Sartre 2001a, p. 36.
80   Memmi 1985, pp. 107–8; also Sartre 2001a, p. 48.
81   Césaire 1959, p. 119. See also footnote 51.
82   Balandier 1951, p. 26.
83   Memmi 1985, pp. 36–7.
84   Memmi 1985, p. 136.

by colonial rule represents an insurmountable obstacle to assimilate colonial subjects into colonial culture, the claims of universalising civilisers notwithstanding. The cases of Indochina and Algeria showed, among other things, how the brute force of colonial domination was a factor in unifying revolutionary anti-colonialism despite the homogenising and fragmenting features of colonialism.[85] The less bloody strike waves in French-dominated West Africa after the end of the *Code d'indigénat* in 1946 showed that the empire could not contain demands for equal rights.[86]

– If colonial reform is an oxymoron, and if cultural assimilation, a retreat to (statically conceived notions) of tradition, and, worse, the fantasy of racial purity are dead ends,[87] in the eyes of our authors, this leaves for some, and Sartre, Fanon, and Aimé Césaire in particular, the perspective of counter-colonial liberation as a double, political and social revolution. Genuine independence requires liberating colonised populations from the manifold economic, social and cultural dimensions of colonial rule. *Ideally*, and deep obstacles notwithstanding, this should include a 'proletarian revolution',[88] and a 'dialectical strengthening' between anti-colonial movements and metropolitan class struggle.[89] Even if this broader political dynamic is foreclosed, political revolution, base-democratic self-government and a structural social transformation of colonial political economies remain indispensable for this tradition of counter-colonial and national liberation politics.

– What is the ultimate horizon of counter-colonial revolt and revolution? Nothing less than a new humanism, a transformation of the human in the face of colonial dehumanisation. Contrary to the falsely universal European-colonial humanism, this quest for a 'true humanism' has genuinely universal potential.[90] It concerns humanity as a whole, including Europe.[91] It aims to achieve a double dis-alienation of colonised and coloniser. 'If the European must annihilate the coloniser within himself, the colonised must overcome the colonised'.[92] A new humanist perspective proposes that the full possibilities of human life can only be envisaged through the trials of a deep, existential transformation of the subjectivities of the colonised and the colonised

---

85   Fanon 1965, p. 120; 2011, p. 105.
86   Cooper 2005, pp. 204–30.
87   See Suzanne Césaire's still uniquely succinct comment on these pitfalls, 2009, pp. 67–75.
88   Césaire 1955, p. 59.
89   Fanon 1988, p. 144; 2006, p. 162.
90   Césaire 1955, p. 54.
91   Fanon 1988, p. 144; 2006, p. 162; Fanon 1963, p. 316; 1970, pp. 232–3.
92   Memmi 1985, p. 161. See also Césaire 2005, p. 63; Bernasconi 1996, p. 113.

as they were constructed under colonial rule. This transformational humanism goes far beyond the tactics of colonial mimicry, parody, and boundary
shifting proposed by Bhabha[93] and deconstructive postcolonial theory.[94]
This situated appeal to 'human fraternity', as François Maspéro called it with
reference to Fanon,[95] entails, on the one hand, a critical and selective *appropriation* of European history, language and technology on the terms of colonised,[96] and, on the other, an inscription of anti-colonial revolution into
universal history, as Césaire put it with reference to the Haitian Revolution.[97]
As we will see, for Fanon, human liberation must also mean the end of patriarchy.

3   Fanon: The Times and Spaces of (De)Colonisation

There is nothing ontological about segregation.
FRANTZ FANON[98]

∴

Within the context of these broader anti-colonial arguments, Frantz Fanon
distinguished himself with a critical modernist scepticism about culturalist
anti-colonialism that went beyond that of Suzanne and Aimé Césaire. He also
revealed a capacity to link the everyday experience of racism and colonial life to
the political and historical dynamics of (de-)colonisation superior to Memmi's
and Sartre's. Most important for our purposes is the particular degree to which
Fanon dealt with the spatial dimensions of (de-)colonisation. *Contra* Bhabha
and Said, the 'spatial' Fanon stands neither in opposition to the 'historical'
Fanon nor in contrast to the 'dialectical' Fanon. Fanon's starkly spatial passages, both in *Black Skin, White Masks* and the *Damned of the Earth*, certainly
'disturb' Hegel's slave-master dialectic. They do so because they speak to the
seemingly unsurmountable, ontological gulf between master and slave that is
opened by *racial* slavery and its project to condemn slaves to a veritable 'zone

93   Majumdar 2007, p. 77.
94   Haddour 2001, p. 17.
95   Maspéro 1962, p. 133.
96   Césaire 2005, p. 69; Fanon 1965, pp. 62–3, 89; 2011, pp. 44–5, 73–4.
97   Césaire 1961a, p. 310.
98   Fanon 1967, p. 186; 1952, p. 150.

of non-being'.[99] And yet the spatial formulations Fanon deploys to underline the particular stasis of the colonial world do not permanently displace Fanon's very much dialectical, and constantly questioning 'thought in movement',[100] nor do they undermine the ever-present, if occasionally repressed 'discourse of temporality' which suffuses his work.[101] To speak with Sekyi-Otu: the Martinican's spatial formulations are best understood as 'dramatic speech acts in the moving body of a dramatic narrative' which is his life work, and, most strikingly, his *Damned of the Earth*.[102] This narrative yields a 'partisan-universalism', a perspective placed in determined, contradictory situations and oriented by 'revolutionary humanist visions' and an 'irrepressible openness to the universal'.[103]

Fanon's spatial representation of colonisation captures the peculiarly ossified character of colonial relations and seemingly permanent ontological divides these relations inscribe in the social landscape. But to take his spatial formulations as an indication of a phenomenology of violence generated by the anti-Black terror of slavery and colonialism *only* risks equating the spatial Fanon with a non-dialectical ontology of human existence and power.[104] Fanon's conception of human-social realities and possibilities resists turning an uncompromising critique of racist dehumanisation into a strategy of ontologising (making eternal) racial divides.[105] His conception of White and Black does not cease to be relational, reaching beyond itself.[106] What is more, Fanon powerfully underscores the contradictions (including the contradictions revealed by very brutality of colonial rule), which make the transform-

---

99   On the zone of non-being, see Fanon (1967, p. 8; 1952, p. 6) and Lewis Gordon (2005, 2015, pp. 19–74). On the challenges Fanon brings to the Hegelian and Marxian dialectic, see Sekyi-Otu 1996; Bernasconi 1996; Turner 1996, pp. 134–55, 1999, 2001; Gibson 1999; Gidwani 2008; Ciccariello-Maher 2017; and Hudis 2017, pp. 869–71.

100 Cherki 2002, p. 15.

101 Sekyi-Otu 1996, p. 76.

102 Sekyi-Otu 1996, p. 236.

103 Sekyi-Otu 1996, pp. 3, 16.

104 Despite its multifaceted insights, Mbembe's earlier treatment of Fanon is heavy in its emphasis on power and violence as desire and pleasure, thus coming close to ontologising colonial rule. In this, Mbembe draws heavily on Nietzsche, Freud, Bataille, Schmitt and Foucault. See Mbembe 2001, pp. 103, 174–5, 181–2, 212; 2003, pp. 8–9; 2007, pp. 30–54. For a critique of *Postcolony*, see Lewis Gordon 2008, pp. 237–42.

105 Fanon's work is thus not to be confused with what today is the most influential source for such ontologising and dehistoricising/despatialising strategies: Afro-pessimism and its conception of (anti-)Blackness as absolutely exceptional (Sexton 2016). For detailed engagements and critiques, see Thomas 2018a; Olaloku-Teriba 2018; Ajari 2019; Okoth 2020.

106 Lewis Gordon 2015, p. 127.

ation of the colonial relation possible. He not only suggested that colonialism and racism must be understood in spatial as well as historical terms; he also indicated that the transformation of (weakly hegemonic) colonial space must be understood as a historico-geographical process and a strategy of appropriating and transforming both space and time.[107] Space and geography in Fanon's work thus exist in an integral relationship with time and historical change; they are part of an overarching project of liberation. While both inevitable and understandable under structurally violent conditions, violence is not necessarily a liberatory part of the anti-colonial struggle. As Aimé Césaire said, 'Fanon's violence is, without paradox, that of the non-violent' aiming to 'rehabilitate the human'.[108] Violent though it might be, the goal of genuine decolonisation should be to relegate violence to the dustbin of history.[109]

3.1   *The Colonial as Spatial Relation*

Fanon's phenomenology of everyday racism in *Black Skin, White Masks* is infused with spatial terminology. Fanon describes racialisation as a form of being immobilised, of being 'walled in',[110] a description which was echoed shortly afterwards by James Baldwin's view that, weighed down by White people and White power, Blackness can 'fix bleak boundaries' to someone's life.[111] Through racialisation, Fanon said, 'the White man is *sealed* in his Whiteness and the Black man in his Blackness'.[112] These expressions are not only metaphoric. Fanon alludes to how the experience of Blackness in the metropole is shaped by body language, gestures, looks and physical distance, all of which establish a spatial relation of separation between Black and White as they meet on a street corner or in a queue. Thus,

> I am the slave not of the 'idea' that others have of me but of my appearance. I move slowly in the world, accustomed now to seek no longer for upheaval. I progress by crawling. And already I am being dissected under white eyes, the only real eyes. I am *fixed*. Having adjusted their micro-

---

107   Weate 2001, p. 178.
108   Césaire 1961b, p. 110.
109   See Cherki 2004, pp. 170–84; Gopal 2013.
110   Fanon 1967, p. 117; 1952, p. 94.
111   Baldwin 1984, p. 87. One can say that Fanon's contribution is a tricontinental, political and revolutionary analogue to James Baldwin's self-described maverick literary work. To put it in Baldwin's terms, both writers shared a commitment to 'make the question of colour obsolete' (Baldwin 2014 [1984], p. 53). For Baldwin, this commitment was based on the assessment that the most dangerous thing one can do as a Black person is to 'refuse to accept the White world's definition' (1993 [1963], p. 69).
112   Fanon 1967, p. 9, emphasis added; 1952, p. 7.

tomes, they objectively cut away slices of my reality. I am laid bare. I feel,
I see in those white faces that it is not a new man who has come in, but a
new kind of man, a new genus. Why, it's a Negro!

I slip into corners, and my long antennae pick up the catch-phrases strewn
over the surface of things .... I slip into corners, I strive for anonymity, for
invisibility. Look, I will accept the lot, as long as no one notices me![113]

Reducing human beings to their physical appearance – and the weight of histories of racism tied up in bodily image – is achieved by putting Black bodies in
place. This form of thingification makes it impossible to escape bodily confinement and denies the possibility of freedom, that is to say a reciprocal spatial
relation between body and the world.[114] Given the extent to which everyday
racism imposes peculiar spatial limits on colonised subjects, it is no wonder
that dreams for humanity can take the form of 'leaping-out' of the socio-spatial
constraints of race or at least of 'slipping into corners', of minimising the degree
of visibility in racially charged public space. Although the violently homogenising and standardising aspects of racism render anonymous and make invisible by making individuality impossible, being an invisible Black *flâneur* in
1950s Lyon is also out of the question.[115] The relentlessly visibilising side of
everyday racialisation makes the 'relief of anonymity'[116] or the 'melting pot' of
the modern city[117] difficult to experience for those who are racialised as non-
White (and thus rendered anonymous, indistinct in other ways). Racism is a
form of spatial separation insofar as it relegates people to their racialised bodies even when they can avoid or move across the divides of spatial segregation.

The degree to which racism is implicated in spatial organisation becomes
even more evident in Fanon's historical-geographical analyses of life in the

---

113   Fanon 1967, p. 116; 1952, p. 93.
114   Gibson 2003, p. 133. For Fanon's reading of Richard Wright and his consequent adapta-
       tion of Sartre's critique of anti-Semitism and Merleau-Ponty's notion of lived experience
       as well as Fanon's double substitution of the latter's *schéma corporel* with the *schéma
       historico-racial* and *the schéma épidermique-racial* in his 'Lived experience of the Black',
       see Weate 2001; Gibson 2003b; Turner 2003; and Ahmed 2007, pp. 152–5.
115   Kristin Ross makes a point similar to Fanon's when she contrasts the image of the flân-
       eur in postwar French film with the experience of *FLN* organisers in 1950s Paris, who were
       'driven to walking the streets at night despite the curfew because they have nowhere else
       to be together, and limited to only a very few areas deemed "safe" and experienced Paris as
       an enormous ambush through which we moved with ludicrous precautions' (1995, p. 176).
       See also James Baldwin's observations about the status of Black African students in the
       Paris of the 1950s (1984, pp. 117–23).
116   Kahn 1987.
117   Berman 1982.

colonies. There, racism is best understood as a crucial element of the territorially organised colonial social order.[118] Fanon encountered the stark realities of segregation in the colonial city. This was true less in Fort-de-France and more in Algiers and Blida, first as an employee of the French authorities in Blida's psychiatric clinic, then as a member of the FLN.[119] Fanon's analyses suggest that the brittle but real hegemony of colonialism is predicated on processes of spatial separation that exist as segregation in colonial cities and forms of demarcating city and countryside through colonial administration. In the *Damned of the Earth*, Fanon describes this spatial relation as a form of compartmentalisation:

> The colonial world is a world divided into compartments. It is probably unnecessary to recall the existence of native quarters and European quarters, of schools for natives and schools for Europeans; in the same way we need to recall apartheid in South Africa. Yet, if we examine closely this system of compartments, we will at least be able to reveal the lines of force it implies. This approach to the colonial world, its ordering and its geographical layout will allow us to mark out the lines on which a decolonised society will be recognised. The colonial world is a world cut in two. The dividing line, the frontiers are shown by barracks and police stations. In the colonies it is the policeman and the soldier who are the official, instituted go-betweens, the spokesmen of the settler and his rule of oppression.[120]

Colonial administration has far-reaching consequences. As expressions of social inequality and seemingly ontological forms of exclusion, colonial spatial segregation heralds an irreconcilable conflict between coloniser and colonised. As he points out, relations between the European and the 'native' zones are 'not complementary'; they are 'opposed', 'not in the service of a higher unity' but 'following the principle of reciprocal exclusivity'. 'No conciliation is possible' between the sturdy, properly serviced, well-fed, and easy-going but defensive 'settlers' town', on the one hand, and the ramshackle, overcrowded, hungry, and envious 'native town', 'medina' or 'reservation', on the other.[121]

With his spatial formulations, Fanon paints a picture of Manichean dualism that *appears* to forbid dialectical transformations and hegemonic projects alike. The socio-spatial organisation of colonialism remains stark. It helps

---

118   Fanon 1988, p. 33; 2006, pp. 39, 41.
119   Macey 2000, pp. 213, 260–1, 271.
120   Fanon 1963, pp. 37–8; 1970, p. 7.
121   Fanon 1963, p. 39; 1970, p. 8.

ensure that 'economic reality, inequality, and the immense difference of ways of life never come to mask the human realities'.[122] It expresses the transformation of class-based relations of exploitation by caste-like divisions along lines of race. Indeed, in the colonial world, spatial relations are characterised by a peculiar form of stasis; they bring forth a 'world of statues: the statue of the general who carried out the conquest, the statue of the engineer who built the bridge; a world which is sure of itself, which crushes with its stones the backs flayed by whips: this is the colonial world'.[123] As he says in 'Algeria Unveiled', in the colonial city, spatial organisation appears to be imposed entirely from the outside:

> The European city is not the prolongation of the native city. The colonizers have not settled in the midst of the natives. They have surrounded the native city; they have laid siege to it. Every exit from the Kasbah of Algiers opens on enemy territory. And so it is in Constantine, in Oran, in Blida, in Bone. The native cities are deliberately caught in the conqueror's vise. To get an idea of the rigor with which the immobilising of the native city, or the autochthonous population, is organized, one must have in one's hand the plans according to which a colonial city has been laid out, and compare them with the comments of the general staff of the occupation forces.[124]

In colonial society, spatial organisation is seemingly without contradiction and fluidity. It appears to express a strictly one-sided form of rule 'where the first thing the native learns is to stay in his place',[125] or, as C.L.R. James put it with reference to Saint-Domingue/Haiti, the system makes sure that 'everyone is in their place'.[126]

A closer look at everyday life in the colonial city reveals, however, that colonial space does not reflect an immutable, historically eternal character of racial distinction. 'There is nothing ontological about segregation', Fanon had already said in his *Black Skin, White Masks*.[127] Like human history broadly speaking, real-life racial segregation is full of complexities and tensions, which makes change possible. In addition, spatial segregation is not restricted to the extern-

---

122   Fanon 1963, p. 40; 1970, p. 9.
123   Fanon 1963, pp. 51–2; 1970, p. 18.
124   Fanon 1965, pp. 51–2; 2011, pp. 33–4.
125   Fanon 1963, p. 52; 1970, p. 18.
126   James 1989, p. 45.
127   Fanon 1967 p. 186; 1952, p. 150.

ally imposed and brutally coercive forms of social space *conceived* by the colonial administrators. Colonial spatial relations, as violent as they are, produce forms of homogeneity that are embedded in daily spatial practices and infused in the bodily and affective representational spaces of the colonised even as they are separated from the coloniser. For Fanon 'colonisation standardises relations, for it dichotomises the colonial society in a marked way'.[128] It does so through violence, of course, but also through the 'emotional, affective' aspects of cultural racism[129] and the 'unreflected imposition of a [colonial] culture'.[130] This peculiar colonial production of homogenisation/separation (what Sartre would have called seriality and what Lefebvre called abstract space and linear time) is both spatial (demarcating) and temporal (linear-repetitive).[131] 'Not wholly coercive or repressive',[132] colonial time/space has a profound impact on the imaginary worlds and bodily experiences of the colonised. It 'normalises the pathological' in colonial situations[133] to the point of tempting the colonised to 'racialize their claims'[134] and revert to unmediated forms of 'action and aggression', or alternatively, dream of escaping confinement by 'jumping, swimming, running, climbing'.[135] As Fanon indicated in his observations about certain versions of *Négritude* and 'the pitfalls of national consciousness', such immediate reactions to colonial time/space are difficult to avoid but can lead to an impasse in the quest for a future beyond race and true national liberation.[136]

3.2   *Patriarchy and the Contradictions of the Colonial Order*
The incorporation of colonial rule in everyday spatial relations becomes obvious also when one analyses the ways in which colonial spatial organisation is gendered. As he argued famously in 'Algeria Unveiled',

> Apart from the charwomen employed in the conquerors' homes, those whom the coloniser indiscriminately calls the 'Fatmas', the Algerian women, especially the young Algerian women, rarely venture into the European city. Their movements are almost entirely limited to the Arab city.

---

128   Fanon 1965, p. 126; 2011, p. 114.
129   Fanon 1988, p. 40; 2006, p. 48.
130   Fanon 1967, p. 191; 1952, p. 154.
131   Weate 2001, p. 178.
132   Sekyi-Otu 1996, p. 85.
133   Lewis Gordon, cited in Persaud 1997, p. 174.
134   Fanon 1963, p. 214; 1970, p. 147.
135   Fanon 1963, pp. 51–2; 1970, p. 18.
136   Kruks 1996, p. 130.

And even in the Arab city their movements are reduced to the minimum. The rare occasions on which the Algerian woman abandons the city are almost always in connection with some event, either of an exceptional nature, or more often, traditional family visits for religious feasts, or a pilgrimage. In such cases, the European city is crossed in a car, usually early in the morning. The Algerian woman ... must overcome a multiplicity of inner resistances, of subjectively organised fears, of emotions. She must at the same time confront the essentially hostile world of the occupier and the mobilized, vigilant, and the efficient police forces ....[137]

Under colonisation, Algerian women were subjected to spatial confinement in two ways. The homogenisation of the colonised produced by French colonial apartheid reinforced the legacy of domesticity and gender division in embedded in architecture and interior design dating back to Ottoman rule or the Arab dynasties.[138] While women carried much of the weight colonialism imposed upon the colonised, 'colonial bondage served as a kind of an epic simile for the portrait of women's subjugation'.[139]

The double confinement of Algerian women – novelist Assia Djebar calls it imprisonment[140] – are products of both colonial spatial organisation and defensive reaction on the part of the colonised. Colonial abstract space is profoundly patriarchal, but this patriarchal organisation of space in the colonial city is quite different from that in postwar France because it cannot be understood without reference to the strategies of colonial control. For the Orientalist coloniser, for whom the Arab or Islamic city is symbolised by the colonised woman and the Algerian house,[141] full colonisation can only be achieved by 'liberating' women from the stranglehold of seclusion. Controlling Algeria thus means 'unveiling' its women both in a literal sense and figuratively, through planning and architectural strategies that 'open up' Algerian domestic spaces (courtyards, rooftops) in modernist housing blocks that are more open to

---

137   Fanon 1965, p. 52; 2011, p. 34.
138   Çelik 1996, pp. 129–30.
139   Sekyi-Otu 1996, p. 228.
140   In novels such as *L'Amour – la Fantasia* (1985) and *La Femme sans Sépulture* (2002), Djebar, herself a participant in the liberation struggle and contributor to *El Moudjahid*, describes the relationship between colonisation and spatialised patriarchy and, in turn, the variegated and rich role of women in the independence movement, as victims of French reprisals, active, if all too often publicly 'invisible', supporters, and heroic figures of the resistance in the field.
141   Çelik 1996, pp. 130–1; Çelik 1997, pp. 21–7.

external access.[142] In a colonial context such a strategy of unveiling has effects on women's daily spatial practices and affective experiences of public space that are not liberatory:

> These patterns [of strengthening the traditional patterns of behaviour], which were essentially positive in the strategy of resistance to the corrosive action of the colonizer, naturally had negative effects. The woman, especially the city woman, suffered a loss of ease and of assurance. Having been accustomed to confinement, her body did not have the normal mobility before a limitless horizon of avenues of unfolded sidewalks, of houses, of people dodged or bumped into. This relatively cloistered life, with its known, categorised, regulated comings and goings, made any immediate revolution seem a dubious proposition.[143]

The combination of colonial confinement and reaction on the part of the colonised has profound effects on the bodily experience of colonised women.

While obviously counter-revolutionary, the gendered organisation of colonial space also bears profound contradictions, which emerge in various points of the colonised social formation. The commodification of agriculture in Algeria not only allowed land transfer to settlers and colonial authorities but also produced displacement, proletarianisation, rural-urban migration and sprawling shantytowns (*bidonvilles*) that undermined the caste-like divisions of colonial urban society and sustained the growth of independence movements.[144] Similarly, gendered strategies of 'unveiling' Algeria had unintended effects. The 'veil' and the 'native' house become elevated to symbols of passive resistance – and some modernist developments meant to appease and control Algerian aspirations became hotbeds of anti-colonial mobilisation in the 1950s.[145] In contrast to Paris – the Capital of the nineteenth century and imperial metropole – colonial city life is thus antithetical to the kind of gendered commodification Walter Benjamin describes in his passages on fashion in his *Arcades Project*,[146] a commodification that produced hand-wringing because it posed a constant threat to the rigidity of early modern – Victorian, Haussmannian, and Wilhelminian – patriarchy and its project to consolidate the separation of

---

142 Çelik 1996, pp. 130–1; Çelik 1997, chapter 5; Deluz-Labruyère 2004, pp. 183–98.
143 Fanon 1965, p. 49; 2011, p. 31.
144 Stora 2004, pp. 95–7.
145 Çelik 1996, pp. 132, 138.
146 Benjamin 1982.

public and private space.[147] In Algiers, the very colonial forms of political and spatial separation posed the opposite threat by making it difficult for the colonisers to assimilate Algeria by 'unveiling' its women and sexualising space by treating women as merchandise:

> This woman who sees without being seen frustrates the colonizer. There is no reciprocity. She does not yield herself, does not give herself, does not offer herself. The Algerian has an attitude toward the Algerian woman which is on the whole clear. He does not see her .... In the case of the Algerian, therefore, there is not in the street or on a road, that behavior characterizing a sexual encounter that is described in terms of a glance, of the physical bearing, the muscular tension, the signs of disturbance to which the phenomenology of encounters has accustomed us. The European faced with an Algerian woman wants to see. He reacts in an aggressive way before this limitation of his perception.[148]

This lack of gendered commodification, while a product of 'successful' colonial and patriarchal confinement, also represents an Achilles heel for the colonial order. It signals the real but limited hegemonic nature of the peculiar strategy and process of *separation* that define the territorially mediated colonial social relation.

3.3   Decolonisation: From Reappropriating Urban Space ...

Fanon describes not only colonial administration and its contradictions but also anti-colonial struggles in spatial terms. In what are among the most brilliant passages in Fanon's overall work, in 'Algeria Unveiled' and 'The Algerian Family', Fanon describes the war of movement of national liberation as *a claim to the city* and a practice of *reappropriating – and thus transforming* – colonial space. Clearly reflecting on the experience of the Battle of Algiers, Fanon starts his observation with comments on the role of women in urban uprising.[149] At that time, the Soummam declaration of 1956 had defined anti-colonialism as an endogenous, mass-based, democratic, politically defined social liberation movement that includes women as active resistance fighters.[150] In Algiers, this

---

147   Wilson 1991.

148   Fanon 1965, p. 44; 2011, p. 26.

149   As Khaoula Taleb Ibrahimi reports, the majority of women involved in the war were not to be found in urban guerrilla action but in civil resistance and the *maquis* outside the major cities and towns (2004, pp. 199–203).

150   Front de Libération Nationale 2004; Abane 2011; Turner 1999, pp. 371, 377–86; Macey 2000, pp. 276–8.

could mean that women crossed the increasingly tight controls between the European city and the Casbah (the historic city centre inhabited predominantly by the colonised) to fulfil supply, reconnaissance, or bombing missions. It sometimes required leaving the veil at home in order to pass the controls more easily and appear as a European woman. Women became more visible agents of liberation.

> Initially subjective, the breaches made in colonialism are the result of a victory of the colonized over their old fear and over the atmosphere of despair distilled day after day by a colonialism that has incrusted itself with the *prospect of enduring forever*. The young Algerian woman, whenever she is called upon, establishes a link, Algiers is no longer the Arab city, but the autonomous area of Algiers, the nervous system of the enemy apparatus. Oran, Constantine, develop their dimensions. In launching the struggle, the Algerian is loosening the vise that was tightening around the native cities. From one area of Algiers to another, from the Ruisseau to Hussein-Dey, from El-Biar to the rue Michelet, the Revolution creates new links. More and more, it is the Algerian women, the Algerian girl, who will be assuming these tasks.[151]

Further loosening the divide between domestic, semi-public and public space and leaving the segregated 'Arab' city denigrated and glamorised by colonial planners,[152] the actions of revolutionary women prefigured a truly liberated postcolonial society by transgressing boundaries and re-appropriating space.

Temporarily reappropriating urban streetscapes meant not only confronting the European city and the spatial restrictions on the 'native' city, however. It also meant overcoming the 'considerable number of taboos'[153] presented by the peculiarly gendered forms of bodily confinement in the colonial city. The freedom acquired by walking not along the walls but 'in the middle of the sidewalk,

---

151   Fanon 1965, pp. 52–3, 2011, p. 35.
152   Replicating the 'arabophile' leanings of Napoleon III (Stora 2004, pp. 18–19), the Orientalist idolatry of the Casbah and the Algerian house as the gendered embodiment of 'Arab' or 'Islamic' culture was strongly present in French planning and architecture circles, including Le Corbusier. From the 1930s on, it also informed policies of preserving the architectural (but not social) integrity of spaces like the Casbah (Çelik 1999, pp. 38–43). This early strategy of 'accommodating diversity' within the confines of the colonial order can be taken as spatial dimension of the 'humane' racism criticised by Fanon at the First Congress of Negro Writers and Artists in 1956; it represents a colonial precedent of current culturalist racisms.
153   Fanon 1965, pp. 51–2, 2011, p. 34.

which in all countries in the world belongs rightfully to those who command',[154] presupposes a transformation of the relationship between body and the world.

> The absence of the veil distorts the Algerian women's corporeal pattern. She quickly has to invent new dimensions for her body, new means of muscular control. She has to create for herself an attitude of unveiled-women-outside. She must overcome all timidity, all awkwardness (for she must pass for a European), and at the same time be careful not to overdo it, not to attract notice to herself. The Algerian woman who walks stark naked into the European city relearns her body, re-establishes it in a totally revolutionary fashion. The new dialectic of the body and the world is primary in the case of one revolutionary woman.[155]

The revolutionary dialectic of body and world requires transforming urban space in all its dimensions, for urban space articulates everyday life with the entire social order. Doing justice to the Fanon of 'Algeria Unveiled' and the *Damned of the Earth*, these gendered muscular and psycho-somatic transformations brought about by spatially mediated political struggle were again in full view during the 1960 uprisings, which mobilised large numbers of women and young people.[156]

It is important to note that Fanon expected women's revolutionary role not 'just' to further national liberation. He supposed that the publicly visible role of revolutionary women would provide an example for colonised women more generally, undermine patriarchy and lay the foundation for new gender relations in post-revolutionary Algeria. Indeed, he observed in the 'Algerian Family' that the public role of FLN women was creating situations where 'the men's words [in the Algerian family] were no longer law, the women were no longer silent, ... the woman ceased to be a complement for man, [and] *she literally forged a new place for herself by her sheer strength*'.[157] Fanon thought that the process of individualisation that (necessarily) failed in France's quest to 'unveil' Algeria would work to break up patriarchal homogeneity in postcolonial society. Fanon effectively describes the possibility of blurring the gendered division between public and private space *without* the patriarchal mediation of sexualised commodification so common in the advanced capitalist world. The veil, once stripped of its traditional or religious aura, could come off on terms

---

154   Fanon 1965, p. 59; 2011, p. 40. See also Ibrahimi 2004, pp. 212–15.
155   Fanon 1965, p. 59; 2011, p. 41.
156   Rigouste 2020a, pp. 325–40, 289–316.
157   Fanon 1965, p. 109, 2011, p. 95.

defined by the colonised, not the coloniser. Its further use, which was sometimes necessary after the French caught on to the FLN's initial strategy and
women used the veil to conceal weapons, would be instrumental, without the
weight of unexamined common sense.

Given how the FLN was transfigured into the core of a post-independence
regime with remarkably enduring military and security apparatuses, which
Fanon himself warned against, Fanon's expectations about the role of women
revolutionaries were clearly too optimistic.[158] But far from equating decolonisation with 'male liberation',[159] Fanon saw the transformation of patriarchy
as a key aspect (and ultimate goal) of true independence, where 'women will
have exactly the same place as men, not in the clauses of the constitution but
in the life of every day: in the factory, at school, and in the parliament'.[160] Even
though women's political agency receded again into the background in the sections of the *Damned of the Earth* that follow these words,[161] these remarks have
sustained an interpretative lineage that has liberated Fanon from masculinist
aspects of his work to buttress anti-colonial feminisms[162] and, in the process,
recast anti-colonial struggle as an 'erotics of liberation' aimed also at a decolonisation of sexuality.[163] As Drucilla Cornell put it, with specific reference to
'Algeria Unveiled': While 'Fanon was not a feminist, his understanding of culture and revolutionary struggle, the prominent place he gives to the creation of
new forms of being a woman as these arise from that struggle, keep his work
at the heart of anti-imperialist feminism, a feminism that does not succumb to
Western projections of "Third World" women as passive victims or fetishistic
objects'.[164]

---

158   Ibrahimi 2004; Zouligha 1999, pp. 354–66.
159   hooks 2000 p. 41.
160   Fanon 1963, p. 202; 1970, p. 136.
161   McClintock 1995, p. 367.
162   See Dubey 1998; Sharpley-Whiting 1996, 1999; Sekyi-Otu 1996; Lewis Gordon 2015, 29–44,
       59–69.
163   This is Matthieu Renault's conclusion from his work on the relationship between Simone
       de Beauvoir, Richard Wright, and Frantz Fanon, and these authors' respective sugges-
       tions about how to redirect and recast Hegel's dialectic (2011a; 2011b, pp. 145–7; 2014). On
       equally nuanced observations about the distinct but related questions of heterosexuality
       and homophobia in Fanon's *Black Skin, White Masks*, see Rinaldo Walcott (2006, pp. 121–2)
       and Lewis Gordon (2005, p. 23).
164   Cornell 2001, p. 34.

3.4   ... *To Pursuing National Liberation as a Multi-Scalar Project*

In colonial Algeria, gendered strategies of reappropriating urban space were moments within a national struggle. These geographies of national liberation had to rest on socio-spatial alliances and the spontaneity of urban or rural uprisings had to be complemented by patient intellectual leadership and an effective party organisation rooted in both city and countryside.[165] Fanon wrote years after the (temporary) defeat of the Battle of Algiers. Then, the relationship between the FLN leadership in Tunis and the base organisers in Algeria was increasingly distant. The military wing of the struggle concentrated in the army of the exterior (which furnished the core cadres of the post-independence regime) was tightening its grip over the party even as new mass mobilisations developed in Algeria, notably the 1960 mass uprising Fanon also had in his mind as he feverishly wrote the *Damned of the Earth*. In this contradictory context, two pitfalls must be avoided in the construction of these alliances, according to Fanon. First, the wide-spread urban bias of nationalist parties must be avoided, for it is among the 'workers, primary schoolteachers, artisans and small shopkeepers' in urban centres that one is most likely to find people who profit – in small measure – 'from the colonial setup'.[166] Otherwise, the nationalist parties tend to disregard the peasants, who 'have nothing to lose and everything to gain'[167] and organise them in a top-down fashion, by 'parachuting' inexperienced organisers into the villages.[168] Alliances must be built with militant organisers that organise close ties with the villages 'instead of playing hide-and-seek with the police in urban centres'.[169]

With his emphasis on the primacy of the peasants in national liberation, Fanon arguably played a role in constituting the 'rural' self-image of the FLN (a party with definite urban roots) after the defeat of the urban guerrilla movements in 1957.[170] But Fanon did not abandon his earlier insistence on the urban

---

165   Gibson 1999, pp. 408–45; Sekyi-Otu 1996; Turner 1999.
166   Fanon 1963, p. 60; 1970, p. 24.
167   Fanon 1963, p. 61; 1970, p. 25.
168   Fanon 1963, p. 113; 1970, p. 67.
169   Fanon 1963, p. 126; 1970, p. 77.
170   See Mohammed Harbi's insider account and Belaïd Abane's more recent analysis of the relationship between Fanon's writings and the shifting relations of force within the FLN after the defeat of the Battle of Algiers, the assassination of Fanon's erstwhile ally, Abbane Ramdane, the increasingly explicit control of the FLN by the commanders of the ALN, and the consequent reversal of the Soummam declaration, of which Ramdane was a key architect, and which had stressed the primacy of the political over the military struggle as well as the secular and democratic aspects of liberation in a postcolonial society (Harbi 1980, pp. 248, 251–3, 290; 2008, pp. 11–15; Abane 2011, pp. 27–44).

dimensions of revolution. He could not do so in part because the 1960 uprisings (which provided a crucial counterweight to French counterinsurgency
strategies as well as the putschist forces of the OAS) also swept through Algeria's
cities, returning to the sites of struggle in 1956 and 1957 to help prepare the
ground for independence.[171] According to Fanon, then, the second pitfall that
thus must be avoided is categorical anti-urbanism. Just as the unmediated
spontaneity of revolt tends to give rise to 'the most everyday, practical real-
ism'[172] in order to move from nationalism and racial hatred to hegemonic 'social
and economic awareness',[173] he suggests that national liberation movements
cannot bypass colonial urban centres.

> The leaders of the rising, however, realise that some day or another the
> rebellion must come to include the towns. This awareness is not fortuit-
> ous; it is the crowning point of the dialectic which reigns over the develop-
> ment of an armed struggle for national liberation. Although the country
> districts represent inexhaustible reserves of popular energy, and groups
> of armed men ensure that insecurity is rife there, colonialism does not
> doubt the strength of its system. It does not feel that it is endangered fun-
> damentally. The rebel leaders therefore decide to bring the war into the
> enemy's camp, that is to say into his grandiose, peaceful cities.[174]

In the cities, Fanon centred his hopes on the lumpenproletariat, 'the people of
the shanty towns', where 'the rebellion will find its urban spearhead'[175] and,
from there, recapture the more established proletarian and petty-bourgeois
segments of urban life. Fanon's comments about the lumpenproletariat must
be understood from within a social formation where full proletarianisation was
limited and urbanisation was a function of agricultural restructuring and military population relocation rather than mass industrialisation.[176] Furthermore,
Fanon's cautionary remarks about unmediated spontaneity, which apply not
only to the peasantry but also the lumpenproletariat, do not lend themselves to
anti-urban revolutionary strategies (such as Régis Debray's *foco* theory), nor do
they sanction the millenarianism that may follow such conceptions of revolution.

---

171   Rigouste 2020a, 2020b.
172   Fanon 1963, p. 134; 1970, p. 83.
173   Fanon 1963, p. 144; 1970, p. 91.
174   Fanon 1963, p. 128; 1970, p. 79.
175   Fanon 1963, p. 129; 1970, p. 80.
176   Sekyi-Otu 1996, pp. 120, 124–5; Stora 2004, p. 96.

Only an organisation of national liberation that spans the colonially administered divide of city and countryside can hope to overcome the social divides of the colonial city.[177] Indeed, without such a broad socio-spatial alliance, Fanon, who bases his comments in part on observations he made in Accra as a representative of the Algerian exile government, fears that postcolonial regimes are likely to degenerate into neo-colonial caricatures governed by overblown administrative centres and anti-democratic centralism:

> Only too frequently the political bureau, unfortunately, consists of all the party and its members who reside in the capital. In an underdeveloped country, the leading members of the party ought to avoid the capital as if it had the plague. They ought, with some few exceptions, to live in the country districts. The centralization of all activity in the city ought to be avoided. No excuse of administrative discipline should be taken as legitimizing that excrescence of a capital which is already overpopulated and overdeveloped with regard to nine-tenths of the country. The party should be decentralized in the extreme.[178]

Without socio-spatial balance and deep democratisation, the pitfalls of 'national consciousness' and the structural weaknesses of the native bourgeoisie will find its equivalent in a neo-colonial mimicry of bourgeois urbanism:

> Since the bourgeoisie has not the economic means to ensure its domination and to throw a few crumbs to the rest of the country; since, moreover, it is preoccupied with filling its pockets as rapidly as possible but also as prosaically as possible, the country sinks all the more deeply into stagnation. And in order to hide this stagnation and to mark this regression, to reassure itself and to give itself something better to do than to erect grandiose buildings in the capital and to lay out money on what are called prestige expenses.[179]

Truly liberating strategies for democratic, socialist self-determination must thus rest on socio-spatial alliances that do not replicate colonial spatial arrangements, including the very divide between city and countryside as it is (re)organised by colonial rule. The alternative is a passive revolution centred in the former European quarters of the colonial city. What Fanon anticipates here

---

177   Turner 1996, p. 135.
178   Fanon 1963, p. 185; 1970, p. 123.
179   Fanon 1963, p. 165; 1970, p. 108.

is the neo-colonial urban modernism that expresses the socio-spatial seclusion of the comprador bourgeoisie from the arid hinterlands and was immortalised in Ousmane Sembène films set in Dakar, notably *XALA* and *FAAT KINE*.

Built upon a transformation of city and countryside, national independence is not an end in itself. It is a stepping-stone towards an internationalism which opens up horizons of human liberation. Given his non-ethnic, anti-traditionalist, socialist and proto-feminist conception of national liberation, Fanon sees independence as an opportunity to build something new, an 'indispensable condition' to master 'all the material means which make possible the radical transformation of society'.[180] Built on the kind of socio-spatial arrangements Fanon sketched in broad strokes, this 'domestic' transformation of material conditions provides the precondition for a new internationalism: 'It is at the heart of national consciousness that international consciousness lives and grows'.[181] Not to be confused with nationalism, 'national consciousness ... is the only thing that will give us an international dimension'.[182] For Fanon, this new internationalism extends from African and tricontinental strategies of anti-colonial solidarity to a new, internationalist humanism:

> We believe that the conscious and organized undertaking by a colonized people to re-establish the sovereignty of that nation constitutes the most complete and obvious cultural manifestation that exists. ... The struggle for freedom does not give back to the national culture its former value and shapes; this struggle which aims at a fundamentally different set of relations between men cannot leave intact either the form or the content of the people's culture. After the conflict there is not only the disappearance of colonialism but also the disappearance of the colonized man. This new humanity cannot do otherwise than define a new humanism both for itself and for others. It is prefigured in the objectives and methods of the conflict.[183]

The articulation of national consciousness and internationalism represent a scalar interface for a profound transformation of social relations. Only through the trials of genuine decolonisation (full political independence and a deep, micrological transformation of everyday life) is it possible to avoid the twin pitfalls encapsulated by Europe's false colonial humanism and the compra-

---

180   Fanon 1963, p. 310; 1970, p. 228.
181   Fanon 1963, pp. 247–8; 1970, p. 175.
182   Fanon 1963, p. 247; 1970, p. 174.
183   Fanon 1963, pp. 245–6; 1970, p. 173.

dor bourgeoisie's narrow nationalism. Seen in this light, Fanon's 'partisan-universal' politics of opening up 'immediate knowledge' to a 'progressive en-lightening of consciousness'[184] rests on a three-fold, multi-scalar transforma-tion of colonial space: the gendered colonial city; national geographies of colo-nial administration; and unequal international relations.

4   Conclusion

> Yes, revolution demands the seizing of state power; yes, revolu-tion demands the constituting of a new government; yes, revolution demands complete control of the economy by the people. But it also demands that we be different in every aspect of our daily lives.
>
> DRUCILLA CORNELL on Fanon[185]

∴

Fanon's analyses provide profound insights into the spatial dimension of (de)colonisation. These analyses are essential for a conception of 'colonisa-tion' as territorial organisation that avoids Lefebvre's blind spots. But is this linkage between Fanon and Lefebvre plausible? We have already seen that what was central to Fanon – racism, imperialism and colonisation – was either marginal or secondary in Lefebvre's overall work. While Lefebvre's overarch-ing historical and philosophical concerns were centred on Europe, Fanon's radical Black and anti-imperialist preoccupations were focused predomin-antly on the colonial realities in various part of the French empire. Simil-arly, Fanon, whose work was even less traditionally academic than Lefebvre's, did not share the latter's growing interest in explicit theorisations of the pro-duction of space. Drawing connections between Fanon and Lefebvre is not impossible, however. This is true once we consider the similarities between Lefebvre and Fanon's intellectual universes and examine the conceptual bene-fits of tying Fanon's spatial remarks on (de)colonisation to Lefebvre's the-ories of everyday life, urbanisation, the production of space, and 'colonisa-tion'.

---

184   Sekyi-Otu 1996, pp. 26, 104.
185   Cornell 2015, p. 147.

A Lefebvre-Fanon lineage makes eminent sense for at least six reasons. First, Lefebvre's and Fanon's respective engagements with Marx, Hegel, surrealism, existentialism and phenomenology emerged from intellectual networks that overlapped in key figures like Sartre, Merleau-Ponty, Balandier, Jeanson, and Maspéro. Second, both Fanon and Lefebvre developed a critical modernist (and critical historicist)[186] philosophical perspective that mobilises heterodox Marxist insights for a dialectical form of humanism. While situated and inflected differently, their respective takes on difference, modernity and alienation were similarly oriented towards the liberation of human potentialities and a transformation of subjectivities. Such an orientation is at odds with the structuralist or deconstructive linguistic turns of the 1960s, 1970s, and 1980s.[187] Third, both Fanon's and Lefebvre's respective concerns with alienation revolve around analysing concrete daily situations. Not an anti-dialectical refusal of Europe but a dialectical quest for liberation ('maximal difference' in Lefebvre's terminology), Fanon's critique of everyday racism resonates with Lefebvre's critique of everyday life, which itself translates Marx's original work on alienation. Fourth, as Drucilla Cornell's comment at the beginning of this section indicates, Fanon, like Lefebvre, considered revolutionary change as a multi-temporal confluence of social transformation, political strategy, and molecular transformations of everyday human relations. Fifth, Fanon's and Lefebvre's new humanist perspectives were ultimately contrary to Third International Party Communism, which was unwilling to give anti-colonialism its proper political due and for which a concern with alienation was a potentially subversive sign of intellectual immaturity.[188] Sixth, Fanon, like Lefebvre, treats space a crucial mediation in the organisation and transformation of the social order.

4.1   *Transfiguring Lefebvre ...*
In what ways, then, does Fanon help deepen and reconfigure Lefebvre? In the last chapter, we have seen that Lefebvre's notion of 'colonisation' as state-bound territorial relation between dominated and dominant social spaces remains underdeveloped even in its most articulated form of the late 1970s. This, we have argued, is in large part because Lefebvre only alludes to the colonial as a particular form of alienation. It is from Fanon (and the wider counter-colonial networks to which he belonged) that we learn about colonial social relations. Shaped by the modality of racism, colonial relations are

---

186   Sekyi-Otu 2011.
187   Ross 1995, pp. 157–65, 176–96.
188   Macey 2000, pp. 205, 243, 258, 342–5.

characterised by a combination of super-exploitation and everyday humiliation that reduces the colonised to sub-human and non-historical status. Peculiarly standardised (Fanon), thingified (Césaire), and mummified (Memmi),
colonial relations seem to defy the forces of historical transformation. One of
Fanon's most important contributions is to show how the form of standardisation peculiar to the colonial relation can only really be understood in its
complexities and contradictions when taking into account its spatial organisation.

Fanon's analysis of the spatio-temporal character of colonisation sharpens
our understanding of colonial abstract space. To analyse the three – homogenous, fragmented, and hierarchical – dimensions of abstract space in a colonial
context, one must take into account the particularly uncompromising brutality of state violence and the formally racialised character of the commodity
form that obtain under these conditions. Hierarchised by state-sanctioned violence and caste-like racial categorisations, colonial space is characterised by
a profoundly gendered duality of homogenisation and serialisation (of coloniser and colonised) and separation and confinement (of these same subjects, who are segregated in both public and private space). In colonial contexts, abstract space is ridden with particular contradictions as well. Colonial
social relations are not purely coercive – they can become part of lived space
through routinised spatial practices and imaginations. But their hegemonic
integrity is limited by the super-exploitative and ruthless character of colonial economies of dispossession (which make colonial reforms largely illusory)
and by their socio-spatial Manicheism (which establish fundamental limits
to assimilationist and civilising missions). Fanon analysed these contradictions astutely with reference to the twin pressures of unveiling/assimilation
and segregation/separation imposed on patriarchal households in the Algerian
Maghreb.

Translated into after- or neo-colonial contexts, Fanon's work asks us to treat
'colonisation' as a form of hierarchical territorial organisation, which, first,
refracts specific elements of colonial social relation, and second, is shaped by
modalities of racism and racialisation that have a determined link to colonial past and presents. Once translated in this manner, Fanon corroborates
Lefebvre's suggestion that 'colonisation' can be analysed at multiple, world-
wide, national and local-regional/metropolitan scales. For him, colonial territorialisation and counter-colonial spatio-temporal appropriation are not only
national questions. In fact, Fanon's discussion of spatial separation in colonial
cities also helps enrich Lefebvre's tendency to capture 'colonisation' as an urban
question. As we recall, Lefebvre proposed to periodise 'colonisation' into: (1) a
global Haussmannian phase of organising urban space in the post-liberal era

of capitalism and inter-imperialist competition in the late nineteenth century; and (2) the era of functional segregation (the 'model of isolated units') which during Fordism and the last phase of colonial rule in Africa and Asia. Fanon encountered particular articulation of these periods as he wrote about the anti-colonial revolution in Algeria (as well as Tunisia and West Africa).

Fanon paid little attention to the historical specificities of colonial urban-isation.[189] He was concerned with the overall dynamics of liberation, not with Algiers' urban history or the particular ways in which French colonial urb-anism reinforced or modified forms of socio-spatial separation dating back to the times of the Arab dynasties and the Ottoman Empire.[190] But as Alice Cherki points out, his comments about spatial organisation give us clues about Algiers, which in the 1950s was already a multi-layered colonial city where 'partition was a non-negotiable fact': 'implacable, unspeakable and beyond for-mulation' and 'physically inscribed in the urban topography'.[191] By the time Fanon reached Blida and Algiers in 1953, the European quarters dating from the 'Haussmannian' era (the new blocks built on the lower part of the Casbah and along the waterfront, the central administrative districts and the bourgeois residential areas south of the Casbah, and the working class areas *Bab-el-Oued* and *Belcourt*) had already come of age but remained socially demarcated from what remained of the Casbah. These Haussmannian legacies were being over-laid with the functionalist urban and regional plans that were developed and (in some cases) implemented since the 1930s, and the informal urbanisation patterns that produced Algerian-dominated peripheral social spaces. Shortly after Fanon was forced to leave Algeria, the Constantine plan of 1958 added a number of large-scale public housing complexes to those built between the World Wars. Like the previous round of colonial city planning, this functional-ist round redeveloped some shantytowns (*Mahieddine, Climat de France*) but could not contain informal urbanisation. Despite its complexities and con-tradictions, and De Gaulle's counter-revolutionary project to sustain colonial

---

189   In a sense, it would be absurd to suggest he should have given urbanisation its due given the role he played as a psychiatrist and political militant in the 1950s. In addition, the bulk of the critical research on the topic had not arrived on the scene yet (although some work on colonial urbanism was available then, including in Algeria). See the discussions about colonial urbanisation Chapters 2 and 4. The key references are, again, Abu-Lughod 1980; Ross and Telkamp 1985; King 1990a; Goerg and Huetz 2003; Wright 1991; Rabinow 1989; Hugill 2017.

190   On some of these Algerian complexities and antecedents, see Çelik 1997; Deluz-Labruyère 2004; Stora 1994, pp. 7–11, 50–3; Almi 2002; Hakimi 2005, pp. 59–82; Miège 1985, pp. 156–70; Picard 1996, pp. 135–66; Hadjri and Osmani 2004, pp. 29–58; Henni 2016, 2017.

191   Cherki 2006, pp. 40–1.

rule by 'blurring' colonial compartmentalisation with the late colonial *Plan de Constantine*,[192] segregation remained entrenched. 'Algerians rarely ventured outside the areas in which they were concentrated' while 'the quasi-totality of Europeans, both the young and not so young, never set foot in the Casbah and never "saw" the slums'.[193]

What we know now is that spatial planning in Algeria was not a simple adaptation of French and Parisian models to colonial conditions. In both historical periods, Algiers (and Algeria) also functioned as a point of experimentation, which in turn influenced Haussmann's much better-known Parisian strategies in the 1850s and 1860s and informed the large-scale suburban and region-wide planning projects for the Paris of the 1950s and 1960s. For the second period in question, Kristin Ross argued that the peculiar production of abstract in colonial Algeria is internally related to the production of abstract space in postwar France. This was true not only because Algeria was then considered part of France itself, but also because 'administrative techniques developed in the colonies were brought home and put to use side by side with new technological innovations such as advertising' to re-plan French cities and reorient domestic life in France.[194] Before, during, and after the *Plan Constantine* and its plan to 'pacify' Algeria, colonial cadres were re-assigned to administer the rapid urbanisation of Paris urban region and organise the lives of migrant workers from colonies there, as we will see in Chapter 5. Even before the latest round of gentrification and urban renewal since the late 1970s, the construction of 'neo-bourgeois' space meant a neo-Haussmannian exercise of 'cleaning out' 'rotten' areas like *Les Halles* and the remaining 'unsanitary' working-class and immigrant areas in central Paris (*les îlots insalubres*) while relegating immigrants and workers (particularly those from North and West Africa) to the *bidonvilles*, *cités de transit* and *grands ensembles* at the edges of

---

192 Henni 2017, p. 117.

193 Cherki 2006, pp. 41–2. In Algiers, the dichotomy between the European city and the Casbah – the main terrain for the Battle of Algiers and a key divide also in Fanon's work – was complicated by the presence of a minority of colonial subjects in the European quarters, social differentiation among Algerians and Europeans (along lines of class and nationality), the presence of a strong Kabyle resident population, and the tension between competing urbanist imperatives: real estate speculation, military planning, production and distribution. In a few areas, associations between French and Algerians did exist and provided the openings that allowed Fanon himself to link up with the emerging liberation struggle (Cherki 2006, pp. 42). In general, however, Cherki's description is corroborated by Jean Pelletier's classic social-scientific statement about social separation and spatial segregation in the late colonial period (2015 [1959]).

194 Ross 1995, pp. 7–8.

Paris.[195] In these cases, a contextualised Fanon helps us understand why Algeria represented the 'double' of postwar French urban politics.[196] With its focus on public housing redevelopment, Chapter 5 will return to the story of French neo-colonial urbanism.

4.2   ... Urbanising Fanon ...

Only with Fanon's help does Lefebvre's notion of 'colonisation' move closer to its analytical and political promise. But the confrontation of Lefebvre and Fanon does not only make it possible to absorb the former into the counter-colonial universe of the latter (which helps us make a qualitative step towards the kind of multi-polar global knowledge Lefebvre advocated). Bringing to-gether Fanon and Lefebvre also yields a modified Fanon. As we have seen, Fanon defies simplistic anti-urbanism. He insisted on linking social forces in city and countryside in a project of true decolonisation. His faith in the peas-antry was not blind but cognisant of the dangers of millenarianism and ethno-nationalist (sub-)nationalism. Yet Fanon's analysis continued to be wedded to the distinction between city and countryside.[197] At the end of Fanon's life, Lefe-bvre's 'urban revolution' started to question this very distinction as the basis for revolutionary theory. Lefebvre did so in terms of some of the same empirical references and political assumptions Fanon made. At some distance from clas-sical Marxism, the 'new left' Lefebvre shared with Fanon the idea that revolu-tionary change comes from the socio-spatial peripheries within an unevenly developing world order. Fanon tended to treat one such peripheralised force – the lumpenproletariat in the shantytowns – as an extension of the peasantry[198] even though he called it the 'urban spearhead' of the revolution.[199] In con-trast, Lefebvre saw the growth of shantytowns and the rise of urban guerrilla movements as examples of a world-wide urban explosion that would under-mine the usefulness of anti-urban revolutionary theories (represented most sharply not by Fanon but by Régis Debray). One can say that Lefebvre's work in effect echoed a growing recognition that to neglect urban questions can add to the social isolation a number of revolutionary movements experienced in the 1960s.[200]

---

195   Ross 1995, pp. 145–56. For the latest on these Algerian-French lineages in the urban design, regional planning and the production of standardised mass housing, which we will revisit in Chapter 5, see Henni 2017, pp. 79–290.

196   Ross 1995, p. 110.

197   Persaud 1997, pp. 177–8.

198   Fanon 1963, p. 111; 1970, p. 66.

199   Fanon 1963, p. 129, emphasis added; 1970, p. 80.

200   Bouamama 2016, p. 150.

The Algerian case itself pokes some holes in Fanon's insufficiently differentiated view about city and countryside, proletariat and peasantry.[201] As we have seen, Fanon made his case about the revolutionary role of the peasantry partly for conjunctural reasons after the temporary defeat of urban guerrilla struggle, the exile to Tunis, and the 'rural' shift in the FLN's self-representation (which was partly contested on the ground by the 1960 uprisings). However, already at the beginning of the war, in 1954, more than a century of war, land dispossession and commodification, population relocation, proletarianisation and urbanisation had deeply destructured Algeria's agricultural populations. During the war of independence, these long-term developments were accentuated by the brutal and massive population relocation projects the French undertook to undercut the socio-spatial basis for the *Armée de Libération Nationale*. With their mobilising capacities compromised, the links between agricultural populations and the *FLN/ALN* remained highly uneven and often inorganic.[202] Partly 'depeasantised', Algeria's agricultural populations could no longer be described adequately under the twin rubrics of 'rurality' or 'peasantry'. Indeed, the migrant circuits linking agricultural districts with the informal settlements in and around Algeria's towns and urban regions as well as the diaspora in France signalled an unsettling and transformation, not an extension of rural life.[203] Recent Fanon-inspired research on South Africa has shown clearly, that today, too, socio-spatial strategies of land dispossession and opposition testify both to the relevance of Fanon's analysis of colonial spatial relations in a post-colonial context, and, in turn, the inadequacy of the city-countryside distinc-

---

201 On Fanon's general limitations on this front, see De Andrade 1984; Blérald 1984; Pierre-Charles 2011; Zeilig 2016, pp. 62, 120–1, 187, 203, 207, 243. We will return to these limitations in the following chapter devoted to Martinique.

202 Harbi 2008, pp. 13–14.

203 Harbi 1980, pp. 251, 332–3; Stora 2004, pp. 22–4, 40–6. A classic reference on agrarian destructuring in colonial Algeria is still Bourdieu and Sayad (1964). One can say this even though Bourdieu's neo-Weberianism limited their analyses in various ways and ran counter to both Marxist and Fanonian alternatives (Gallissot 2016 [1969]; Martín-Criado 2008). The cutting-edge research on one of Bourdieu and Sayad's key points of interest, namely military strategies of population displacement and resettlement in French Algeria, is that of Samia Henni. She places her investigation of the *camps de regroupement* in the late 1950s in longer context (from the period of conquest to the Vichy era). However, she frames her work as a contribution not to rural sociology but to the history of architecture and the role of spatial intervention in colonial military doctrines and pacification strategies (2016; 2017, pp. 20–96, 179–204). Of course, a full appreciation of these counterinsurgency strategies needs to take into account their contradictions and limitations, some of which were deepened if not brought about by anti-colonial mass mobilisation (Rigouste 2020a, 2020b).

tion Fanon still held on to.[204] In short, it is hardly sufficient to suggest today in general, undifferentiated terms that shantytown dwellers represent an extension of the peasantry and the countryside. We will pursue this point in Chapters 3 and 4 when we revisit Fanon's Martinique and engage debates on planetary urbanisation.

4.3   ... Revisiting the State ...

With Lefebvre, Fanon's insights about the spatial mediations of the colonial social relation reappear today within an unevenly and incompletely urbanised field. As both our authors agree, the state plays a crucial role in organising the colonial (and a few other) dimensions of this urban field. Fanon deals with the role of the state at a descriptive level; for him state agents (policemen, soldiers, administrators, planners) are the most visible actors demarcating the colonisers from the 'natives'. Lefebvre's notion of 'colonisation' emerges from his observations about social struggle in the world-wide urban field but becomes inseparable from his engagement with state theory, an engagement aimed at foregrounding the spatial dimensions of state apparatuses and the social relations they refract.

As Manu Goswami has pointed out (with Lefebvre), a full understanding of the production of space under colonial conditions requires a more sustained theoretical treatment of the state.[205] Even though she does not engage with Lefebvre's own treatment of 'colonisation' and largely refrains from delving into urban questions, she has shown, in the case of India, how the colonial state, with its built environments, public works, land tenure regimes, and accounting practices, was integral to the formation of a colonial political economy by producing abstract space and linear time. Simultaneously homogenising, hierarchical and differentiating/fragmenting, colonial state space was riddled with contradictions it was ultimately powerless to contain. What we also learn from Goswami is that an analysis of (post-)colonial state space levels a challenge to 'methodological nationalism' as profound as Lefebvre's hypothesis about the complete urbanisation of the world. For the formation and transformation of the (post-)colonial state cannot be understood by presupposing an already existing national context. It is a *product* of multi-scalar processes and strategies, notably world-wide (imperial and inter-imperial) dynamics of restructuring and emerging nationalist and anti-colonial resistance.[206] Contemporaneous to modern state-formation in the metropole, the (post-)colonial state is thus best

204   Hart 2002; Gibson 2011b, pp. 144–213.
205   Goswami 2004.
206   Goswami 2004, p. 13.

understood as a formative part of a *global* 'spatial framework of power',[207] or, in hexagonal France, a veritably imperial state form.[208]

This insight moves us beyond both Fanon and Lefebvre. It helps both contextualise and concretise the transnational constellations one can find in Fanon's work (where the experience of racism and political violence in the imperial heartland is part and parcel of an imperial context of colonisation and neo-colonialism) and in Lefebvre's observations (about the world-wide links between peripheralised social spaces and modalities of state-sponsored spatial organisation). Lefebvre's hypothesis about the comparability of metropolitan Paris and colonial cities like Algiers both during Haussmannian times and under Fordism can thus be reconceptualised not only as a plea to understand the world-wide dynamics of urbanisation but also as an example of transnational state capacities, knowledge forms, and imaginaries that linked urban planning strategies in France with those in other parts of the empire. Thus rearticulated, the lineage Fanon-Lefebvre yields a conception of 'colonisation' as state-sponsored and racialised form of territorial hierarchisation which can be subject to comparison across national (and other territorial) boundaries. Here again, spatial strategies continue to be vital; if implemented, their longevity can transform colonial linkages into neo-colonial form, as even the Algerian case reminds us.[209] The following chapters will take up and develop this insight, among others.

4.4 ... and Opening Up Strategic Perspectives

The spatially mediated colonial relations analysed by Fanon no longer exist in the way he encountered them. In former or current colonies, colonial histories have been 'recomposed', that is, fused with newly invented, neo-colonial interventions and other aspects of social formations.[210] These complexities notwithstanding, Fanon need not be dissolved into the discourses and sensibilities of certain post-Marxist strands of postcolonial theory. Actualising the counter-colonial terms of Fanon's work is nonetheless a challenge because they need to account for both the historical and the comparative dynamics of transformation that have shaped (neo-)colonial relations, and capitalism

---

207 Goswami 2004, pp. 27, 31–40. Goswami makes her point also through an engagement with the classic argument by Hamza Alavi (1972) about the colonial and the postcolonial state.

208 For various perspectives on the imperial dimensions of the French state before and, more selectively, after the period of formal decolonisation, see Elsenhans 1974; Cooper 2005, pp. 153–203; Wilder 2003b, pp. 134–5; Le Cour Grandmaison 2009; Anderson 2018. For a re-casting of this analysis in relationship to the state in the metropole, see Chapter 5.

209 Henni 2017, p. 230; Rigouste 2020a, 2020b.

210 Khiari 2006.

more generally, since Fanon's time. There is no doubt that the historical and geographical recomposition of (neo-)colonial relations demand that Fanon's perspective be open to being recomposed also, and this in a comparatively variegated way. Fanon's life work was of course itself in a sense a statement about the interrelated comparative specificities of imperialism, colonialism and racism across the French empire, from Martinique to North and West Africa by way of the hexagone. The following chapters do, however, force us to confront not only Lefebvre (and urban Marxism) but also Fanon (and related counter-colonialisms) to situations where the problem of 'national liberation' has not been posed the way it was during the war of independence in Algeria.

In the hexagone, to which we will return in Chapter 5, a spatially refocused Fanon must confront a number of challenges, including the minoritarian status of those racialised as non-White, a close imbrication of racial and other social questions, and the fact that neo-colonial geographies are too chequered and porous to conform to a territorial binary (pitting European and against native quarters). In this context, Fanon lives best in political projects that have tried to do justice to these neo-colonial complexities with new political strategies. Among these, one can point to political anti-racisms that have the ambition to construct a political dynamic that is broad enough to mobilise various subaltern classes against neoliberalism and the spectre of fascism even while prioritising the struggle against neo-colonial features of life. To advance a shift in the relations of force adequate for this twin purpose, Sadri Khiari proposed a passive revolution with two interrelated moments: the moment of autonomy (of self-determined anti-racist practice defined by people of colour) and the moment of alliance (between these organisations and other left organisations, including parties and unions).[211] As Houria Bouteldja stressed, these two moments have an internationalist component; they should be linked to projects of building networks supporting anti-imperial practices in the global North.[212] This internationalist political anti-racism also demands that the left (metropolitan and anti-racist) be stretched once more. An important medium for such stretching purposes is the appropriation of space at all scales, from body and neighbourhood to nation and world order.

Given the imperial and neo-colonial dimensions of the Canadian social formation, some of these insights could, in modified form, also apply to Chapter 4. Yet, there, we will focus on an additional colonial question, one

---

211   Ibid.
212   Bouteldja 2016, p. 120.

that is missing in hexagonal France: the Indigenous question in a White settler colony. Settlement has of course been an important aspect of modern colonial endeavours in various parts of the world. For Fanon, it was clear that in Algeria, this 'settlers' colony' he compared to South Africa, the role of the settler population, while minoritarian, was decisive in shaping the character and intensity of (de-)colonisation.[213] His example shows that it would be wrong to build research on colonial realities on a simple dichotomy between colonialism and settler colonialism understood as ideal types. Still, the particular settlement dynamic in the White settler colonies of Canada, Australia, and the USA (where non-Indigenous settlement is both permanent and massively majoritarian) has had a peculiar influence on urbanisation patterns.[214] These facts require that Fanon be modified to sustain Indigenous liberation struggles, as Glen Coulthard has argued in *Red Skin, White Masks*.[215] Given the obstacles in the way of evicting the coloniser, and given the profound and insidious assimilatory pressures weighing on Indigenous nations, Fanon's conception of decolonisation as a double transformation (native and colonial society) must be adjusted to pay special attention to the thorny problem of 'tradition': the possibility of rescuing and reinventing the most important aspects of Indigenous modes of life (egalitarianism, open-ended, kinship-centred forms belonging, relational conceptions of land) for a project that combines decolonisation with anti-capitalism (and rejects both traditionalist and assimilationist paths to integrating into colonial society). As we will see, Indigenous strategies and imaginaries of appropriating and transforming space have proposed to cut across colonial divides (between 'city' and 'reserve') in order to mobilise and build alternatives. In this, they redirect Fanon's own habit of approaching colonial space-time as a whole, not just the colonial city or the colonial hinterland.

Coulthard's strategic vision is based on a recognition that colonialism (the colonial relation between the colonised and the coloniser embodied in the colonial state) is subject to comparative difference and historical change. Living as little in a post-colony as Indigenous peoples in Canada, Martinicans, too, have had to grapple with multiple social, economic, and political transformations of the colonial relation, first after abolition in 1848, then following the departmentalisation of the island in 1946. Fanon's analyses of comparative racialisation in *Black Skin, White Masks* and *West Indians and Africans*

213   Fanon 1965, pp. 28–9; 2011, pp. 10–11.
214   Hugill 2017.
215   Coulthard 2014, 2016.

show that he had a keen grasp of some of these changes. But with his energies absorbed by the Algerian War and his role in representing the FLN in
West Africa and within the emerging tricontinental networks of revolutionaries, Fanon's relationship to the Antilles was necessarily intermittent. He could
not do what he might have had he lived longer: focus his attention fully on
Martinique to produce a fine-grained analysis of the forces on the island that
helped reorganise, since 1848, the relationship between French state and capital, the old planter elites, the predominantly mulatto political class, and subaltern forces.[216] Arguably, these transformations produced a rare 'successful colonisation',[217] 'a system of hegemonic assimilationism'[218] based on a 'Republican
conception of colonialism'.[219] As Samir Amin said with respect to departmentalisation, the very success of the Antillean left in creating a terrain upon which
to wield a continuous struggle for equality within the French empire also generated new, deep forms of social and economic dependency.[220] It is this constellation of forces that helps us understand why Fanon's uncompromising and
internationalist anti-colonialism, while increasingly influential elsewhere,[221]
was often 'banned' and 'shunned',[222] or at least 'badly received by the intelligentsia' and the 'strategists of political assimilation' on the island.[223]

Needless to say, departmentalisation was a source of great disappointment
for Fanon.[224] Following the uprising in Fort-de-France in 1959, he remained
privately sceptical about the prospect of revolution there[225] even as he publicly expressed hope that the revolt would push the French Antilles to join the
British islands and the Cuban revolutionaries on a path to regional independence.[226] The cautiously optimistic public Fanon was right in one way. In the
wake of 1959, calls for independence flourished in various forms, with Fanon's
explicit support.[227] Fanon himself became an underground reference among
independentist, internationalist and far-left circles (before becoming more

---

216   Blérard 1988.
217   Glissant 1997, p. 189.
218   Blérald 1988.
219   Schmidt 2009, p. 19.
220   Amin 2011.
221   Gilly 1965; Wallerstein 2009; Amin 2011; Bouamama 2016, p. 162.
222   Manville 1992, pp. 245, 247.
223   Fallope 1986, pp. 311; also Macey 2000, pp. 12–15.
224   Fallope 1986, p. 302.
225   Macey 2000, pp. 419–22.
226   Fanon 1988, pp. 167–9; 2006, pp. 186–8.
227   In 1961, Fanon sent a message of support to the inaugural congress of the *Front des Antilles
      et de la Guyane pour l'Autonomie*, which was presided by Edouard Glissant (Manville 1984,
      p. 27).

widely recognised in the 1980s).[228] In response to aspirations for independence, Aimé Césaire and the *Parti Progressiste Martiniquais*, who had called for unity, not division after the 1959 revolt,[229] were compelled to modify their project a few times, redefining decolonisation as a quest for equality, dignity, and, then, autonomy within the French empire. This quest has continued to be a perennial struggle with shifting forms and moving targets. As we will see, it included efforts to revamp island geographies with agrarian reforms and urban policies. Thus 'cemented' territorially, the colonial relation withstood, isolated and absorbed demands for a genuine, regionally federated dynamic of decolonisation, within which Fanon's legacy would have flourished more freely. The absence of such a dynamic, which makes only 'non-sovereign futures' seem realistic,[230] makes it easier understand calls to transfigure Fanon with creole cultural and linguistic projects,[231] as well as, pace Fanon, grasp the limits of these very calls. Among these transfigurative ideas is 'creole urbanism', which we will discuss in the next chapter.

228   Pierre-Charles 2011, pp. 172–5; Manville 1992, p. 246. The partial rehabilitation of Fanon in Antillean intellectual life was in part due to the efforts of Marcel Manville and the *Cercle Frantz Fanon*. Both were inspired by a tricontinental conception of liberation and self-determination (Comité Frantz Fanon de Fort de France 1984; Manville 1984; Cercle Frantz Fanon 2002).

229   Aimé Césaire 2016 [1960], pp. 129–30.

230   Bonilla 2015.

231   Bernabé 2013.

Creolising the Urban Revolution? *Texaco* and Literary Imaginaries in Martinique

Whether a description of a social group, a name for a cultural process, or a term to denote a type of artistic or literary production, the meaning of creole and creolisation is comparatively varied, historically shifting, and socio-politically multiple, even contradictory. In this chapter, I do not provide an overall assessment of creole projects or competing approaches to interpreting creolisation across or beyond the linguistic, political or socio-economic regions of the Americas. Instead, I focus on one, Martinican contribution to the creole literary movement in the French Antilles: Patrick Chamoiseau's *Texaco*. I do this for two reasons. First, I treat this novel as a literary window into urbanisation and the colonial relation in Martinique. Second, I see it as an entry point to understanding the challenges creole intellectuals levelled at Frantz Fanon (as well as Aimé Césaire) and what this challenge tells us about the difficulty of keeping alive a Fanonian anti-colonialism within this still French part of the Antilles. As a literary creation, I hold *Texaco* and related texts to be highly generative for these purposes. I do so without claiming creole as a theoretical or political project, however. In fact, I take seriously insights produced by scholars of creole in the French, Spanish and English-influenced Caribbean.[1] I share the scepticism of those who have emphasised the frequently ambiguous if not tension-ridden relationship between, on the one hand, cultural-nationalist, liberal-cosmopolitan or left-wing proponents of creole culture, art and language, and, on the other, emancipatory projects against imperialism and (neo-)colonial rule, class-based, racially segmented and gendered relations of (re)production, and racialised relations among African/Black, Indian and Chinese diasporas (as well as Indigenous peoples). The lessons from these critical insights define my starting point, which is to insist on the need to situate creole claims (and processes of creolisation) in broader, geographically and historically variegated socio-political contexts.

When used generically, creole/creolisation often refers to a particular state or process of social mixing. Emphasising that cultural elements may dissolve

---

1 Bolland 1998; Chivallon 2013; Khan 2004; Price and Price 1997; Thomas 2004; Trouillot 1998; Wynter 1973.

in fusion (instead of staying apart), the terms creole/creolisation rival with hybridity/ hybridisation to offer alternatives to the terms of ethno-cultural group pluralism: diversity, multiculturalism. In imperial metropoles at least, they thus attest to a certain postmodernisation of life. Of course, whether creole and creolisation in Toronto, New York or London are emancipatory depends on how they relate to social violence,[2] the always impure character of subaltern social life,[3] and, last but not least, imperial and bourgeois urbanism.[4] This need to put creolisation in its historical and geographical place also holds for the much deeper creole debates in the Caribbean, and thus also the subject matter of this chapter: the creole (créole/kréyòl) linguistic, literary and intellectual movement that emerged in Martinique and the French dominated Antilles in the 1970s. Parallel to other creole currents in the Caribbean, this movement recast the multiform material culture that was produced by slavery and its aftermaths: forced population mixing and slave creativity at the 'edges' of plantation economies[5] and the racially stratified colonial class societies that were built after emancipation.[6] In Martinique, for example, claims and debates about creole must be related to a predominantly Black proletarian way of life that was formed after slavery and that was, depending on the period in question, banned, discouraged or frowned upon by the components of the post-abolition ruling bloc: French administrators, the descendants of slave-holding families (békés), and the political personnel recruited from the mulatto middle class.[7] As we will see in the fourth section of this chapter, the ways in which creole intellectuals transposed creole material culture into a movement concerned with Antillean cultural specificity and the general problem of cultural mixing offers theoretical and political challenges to the Martinican wing of the counter-colonial tradition outlined in Chapter 3, particularly Aimé Césaire's négritude and Frantz Fanon's partisan universal take on national liberation.

The main focus of this chapter will be on the historical geographies narrated by creole intellectuals, specifically the ways in which creole literature discusses urbanisation in relation to social and political life in Martinique (and to a lesser extent Guadeloupe). As we will explain further in the third section of the chapter, our focus will be on the spatial imaginaries that flourish in lit-

---

2   Walcott 2016, p. 50; 2015, p. 188.
3   Prashad 2001, pp. xi–xii, 56–65.
4   Goonewardena and Kipfer 2004, 2005.
5   Trouillot 1998.
6   Schnepel 1998; Bolland 1998; Khan 2004; Thomas 2004.
7   Gilberto Pago (2011) took careful stock of the social contours of post-emancipation Martinique, as it was revealed politically during the 1870–71 uprising.

erary works and that offer key insights into the relationship between everyday life and the larger institutions of colonial capitalism. Key for us will be the idea of creole urbanism in the work of Patrick Chamoiseau, specifically his award-winning book *Texaco*. Born in Martinique in 1953, Chamoiseau has been one of the main promoters of creole language and literature alongside Jean Bernabé and Raphaël Confiant. He has written an impressive range of plays, novels, screenplays, autobiographical accounts, children's tales, literary manifestos, political essays and columns since the early 1970s. Published in 1992, *Texaco* is a landmark in Caribbean and French literature and has been acclaimed much beyond the Creole-French world, including by Derek Walcott, Junot Díaz and Austin Clarke.[8] *Texaco* narrates postwar struggles against the clearance of a shantytown (Texaco) in Fort-de-France, Martinique to unearth a round of spatial imaginaries of resistance that reach back to the last years of slavery prior to 1848. In the novel, these spatial imaginaries are recomposed through creole urbanism, which Chamoiseau treats not only as a peculiarly mixed built form and everyday practice but also as a territorial compromise that helped transform Martinique into a department of France.

Texaco resonates with the previous chapters and their emphasis on the role of the production of space and urbanisation patterns (shot through with hierarchical, sometimes colonial territorial relations) in (dis)organising the social order. In fact, *Texaco* traces the historical transformations that have generated the urban revolution in Martinique. At the heart of *Texaco* are political and socio-spatial claims to central Fort-de-France and the broader processes (layered urbanisation included) that have made these claims possible in the first place. To understand *Texaco* properly we need to carefully translate (instead of unilaterally globalising) Lefebvre and Fanon to account for the particular ways in which Martinique relates to global and comparative dynamics of urbanisation and (anti-)colonial politics.[9] As we will delineate in the next section and elaborate in the core of the chapter, *Texaco* refracts globally articulated urbanisation patterns and their contradictions through the racially stratified social mixing characteristic of Antillean plantation economies. This underscores that the character of the urban in Martinique is, in comparative terms, coeval: contemporaneous and connected to world-wide, including French urbanisation but inflected with histories of town and plantation that are not to be confused with the historic distinctions between city and country that inform Lefebvre's starting point or that set the stage for Fanon's *Damned of the Earth*.

---

8 Knepper 2012, pp. 25–6.
9 For a warning against hasty ways of 'globalising' Lefebvrian insights, see Kipfer, Schmid, Goonewardena, and Milgrom 2008.

The coeval character of urbanisation in Martinique also gives us clues about the comparative specificities of colonial rule on the island. Even though 'creole urbanism' helps us see the 'solidity' of Martinique's colonial status as a French department, the form and content of *Texaco* alerts us to the continued salience of anti-colonial spatial imaginaries, and, thus, inadvertently, Fanon's counter-colonial orientation. As we will discuss in the last section of the chapter, the 2009 strike movement has kept alive elements of this orientation through the labour movement.

1   **The Urban Revolution and Uneven Urbanisation**

Let me begin with an excursus on Henri Lefebvre's conception of urban revolutions and how this conception needs to be stretched and transformed to account for urbanisation in the Antilles. I do so in order to set the historico-geographical stage for *Texaco* and to prepare the ground for a theoretical encounter between Lefebvre, Fanon and creole debates in the rest of this chapter. Lefebvre's 1970 book *The Urban Revolution* links the production of space to the production of the world. In his book, Lefebvre argued that society was in the process of being urbanised completely. He made this argument not only about national urban systems, within which much urban analysis was contained at that time. But he did not suggest either that the world as a whole was fully urbanised then. Lefebvre meant his claim about unleashed urbanisation as a hypothesis about a virtual reality, not a *fait accompli*. Urbanisation thus cannot be grasped adequately in objectivist (and nationally delimited) terms, with methods of analysis that want to pin down the empirical extent of actually existing urbanisation in a falsely concrete fashion, for example by tracking the statistical proportion of the population residing in settlement areas officially defined as urban. For Lefebvre, grasping urbanisation must avoid the pitfalls of unidirectional, deductive or inductive empirical research methods. It requires an iterative and dialectical method of transduction that can also link reality with possibility and imaginary.[10]

For Lefebvre, urbanisation represented a multifaceted field-in-formation-and-mutation. Urbanisation is not reducible to the physical extension and increasing demographic weight of existing settlements that happen to be described as 'urban'. Lefebvre's focus was on a multiplicity of qualitative processes – the expansion of the built environment, the relative weight of land

---

10   Lefebvre 2003a, p. 5.

rent in accumulation, and the industrialisation of agriculture. These processes all help disarticulate the integrity of seemingly evident spatial forms ('city' and 'countryside') that appear to contain social relations and demarcate them from nature. In contrast, Lefebvre holds that urbanisation is now a crucial, not a secondary medium through which social relations relate to nature. Issues often seen as crucial for matters of 'the countryside' such as agriculture remain of course crucial but should be investigated in their complex and historically variable relationship to urbanisation.[11] Indeed, Lefebvre's hypothesis pushes us to avoid lumping together agriculture, the peasantry and rural modes of life. Instead, it forces us to ask if, where and how agrarian life retains a relatively autonomous rural character built upon qualitatively distinct social relations.[12]

Of particular interest to Lefebvre was the phenomenon of centrality. For him, the capitalist version of urbanisation necessarily involves the production of centrality/difference as a fleeting spatial form that plays a crucial role in condensing and reshaping spatial peripheries. For him, the revolutionary quality of modern capitalist urbanisation lies in its tendency to undermine existing articulations of spatial and socio-political centrality and to recreate new such articulations by bringing together differences that come to serve as productive forces (for capital/the state) and resources (for oppositional social forces). As Brenner and Schmid have stressed in an early statement about 'planetary urbanisation', to which we will return in more detail in the next chapter, this dialectic of implosion and explosion of 'the city' can be grasped, in part, as a shifting interplay of spatial concentration and spatial extension, at various scales.[13] Whether in concentrated or extended form, the relations of centre and periphery that permeate the urban and urbanisation must also be stretched and recast, as Kanai has pointed out.[14]

---

11 Goonewardena 2014.

12 This question, which Lefebvre asked in his rural sociological work in the 1940s, set the tone for his urban investigations (1970d, pp. 38–40). As ongoing debates about the state of world agriculture indicate, the question is more crucial than ever. Provided one avoids equating agrarian life with the peasantry while also steering clear of linear-teleological perspectives on agrarian and other forms of life, one can see that imperial capitalism poses deep epistemological problems not only for urban studies but also for rural sociology and peasant studies. Two generations of uneven agricultural restructuring have forced researchers to differentiate agricultural from peasant and land questions and problematise the label 'rural' one often attaches to all three. See Araghi (1995, p. 358) and Bernstein (2006, p. 403).

13 Brenner and Schmid 2015.

14 Kanai 2014.

A crucial aspect of Lefebvre's analysis of urbanisation as a decomposition and recomposition of centralities is political. The most far-reaching aspect of Lefebvre's hypothesis is the insight that relationships of domination between centre and periphery cannot be subsumed under the categories that defined the terms of revolutionary theory when he wrote the *Urban Revolution* in 1970 (for instance, 'city', 'country', 'industry', 'agriculture'). For Lefebvre, territorial relations of domination can increasingly be found *within* amorphous urban fields. They help shape the distinct ways in which centrality brings together differences, alongside a range of spatial conceptions, practices and imaginaries that may rearticulate past historical geographies, urban, rural or otherwise. In light of this dynamic and ongoing socio-spatial sea change, revolutionary theory can thus no longer be conceptualised in classical terms without modification, whether as (1) an extension of urban-industrial-proletarian struggle, (2) an encirclement of cities by peasant movements, or (3) a united front linking 'city' and 'countryside' as if these were self-evident, pregiven entities. As we will see, moments like the 2009 strike wave in the French Caribbean, to which we will we return later in this chapter, no longer fit these three classic spatial imaginaries and spatialised political practices.

Lefebvre's discussion of riots, uprisings, and urban guerrillas late in *The Urban Revolution* underscores his concern that the explosion and implosion of the 'city' could recreate the conditions for new revolutionary mobilisations from multiple peripheries, old and new, in pursuit of new forms of social and spatial centrality. Lefebvre's text thus expressed and theorised the emergent global constellation of social movements that was '1968' in a provocatively new, specifically urbanised way. Theoretically, Lefebvre's twin understanding of the urban revolution – as both a process of transformation and revolutionary possibility – is articulated most powerfully through his language of 'levels'. For him, the urban as spatial form represented an intermediate level of analysis in a tension-fraught field, caught between the routines and aspirations of everyday life and the 'big' institutions of life, notably the state and capital. The ultimate importance of urban research, for Lefebvre, thus lies precisely in the fact that urbanisation in the modern world has been established as the main medium through which our everyday lives are connected to totality, the broader social order and its relations to nature. Without such an emphasis on the urban as level, Lefebvre believed, urban research will continue to be no more than a hyphenated subfield within the academic division of labour, one that remains subservient to 'high' theory, and that can be readily instrumentalised by statist forms of urbanism and modern planning apparatuses. Indeed, without reference to the urban as level, and its associated connections to both everyday life and the broader social order, urban politics is reduced to a merely local, municipal or city-regional concern.

Lefebvre's urban work – including his hypothesis of generalised urbanisation – offers challenges for comparative urban research. For Lefebvre, urbanisation cannot be confined to the study of urban regions and their inter-
relationships. It is a multi-scalar affair that includes but cuts across local,
regional, national and continental territorial configurations. Claims to the urban, fleeting or temporarily fixed articulations of centrality and difference can
also vary in their scalar reach. This, Lefebvre's multi-scalar vision also holds
for the question of 'colonisation'. As we have seen in Chapter 2, the term colonisation was originally a metaphor to sharpen the critique of everyday life
but ended up denoting, in Lefebvre's work, territorial relations of domination
between central and peripheral spaces at various scales, both in former colonies and in imperial heartlands. To put it differently, the form of centrality/differ-
ence that is the urban is itself shot through with territorial forms of domination,
some of which may be tied to imperial colonialism. As noted in Chapters 1 and
2, Lefebvre's insight has deep limits here. It must be stretched through forceful
critiques emanating from anti-colonial traditions. But this insight has relevance for the latter insofar as it insists that colonial or neo-colonial relations
of domination are increasingly mediated by a complex urban field that does
not correspond easily to historic divides between 'city' and whatever its others
might be in particular contexts.[15]

Methodologically, two implications follow for the comparative investigation
of urbanisation. First, Lefebvre's hypothesis regarding the boundary-defying
character of urbanisation implies a form of relational comparison that supersedes methodological nationalism and territorialism,[16] permitting socio-
spatial relations within the urban field to be compared without being neatly
confined to the typical scalar units of comparative analysis (nation, continent, First, Second or Third World). Second, Lefebvre's language of 'colonisation'
invites us to pay attention to how colonial history has shaped centre-periphery
relations in today's urbanising world. Provided we recast this invitation via
counter-colonial theory, it can lead to studies of racialised territorial relations
that are articulated to colonialism either indirectly ('colonisation' in post- and
neo-colonial contexts such as contemporary London or Paris, see Chapter 5) or
directly (persisting colonial occupation in Palestine, Indigenous North America, and France's overseas territories, the subject of this chapter).

We need to take Lefebvre's suggestions as just that and no more, as openings
towards more sustained global comparative analyses. For the force of his argu-

---

15   On a comparable point made rather early with reference to Latin America, see Quijano
      1967.
16   Hart 2002; Goswami 2004.

ment lies in the contrast he develops between boundary-defying, yet fractured modern urbanisation and the city-countryside divide characteristic of precapitalist Europe, where urban life stood in a relationship of 'internal exteriority' to feudalism.[17] In Lefebvre, this contrast takes him through a line of transformations from the 'political city' and the 'commercial city' to the 'industrial city' and, finally, to the contours of an urban reality under twentieth-century neocapitalism. In this neo-capitalist context, Lefebvre became cognisant of the boundary-dissolving tendency of capitalist urbanisation to implode and explode the centralities embodied in the historic city.[18] A key meaning of the urban revolution, in his framework, thus lies in process by which city and countryside are superseded as object-like markers of qualitatively distinct practices in European history. At the same time, claims to 'urban' and 'rural' life can persist in ideological, symbolic and imagined form *within* the emergent, amorphous urban field.[19]

Various limitations notwithstanding, Lefebvre's life work points beyond the linear-progressivist 'urbanism' that underlies various Eurocentrisms.[20] His rural sociological work was deeply aware of the historical variability of city-country relationships in Europe itself and gestured towards a global comparative approach to agrarian questions.[21] Lefebvre thus did not treat urbanisation as an evolutionary transition from rural life. But his urban work gives us little sense of how global urbanisation varies in relation to a much wider range of historical trajectories. In turn, it does not explore how Europe was formed in relation to other histories, including the multiform histories of 'city' and 'country', which, following Raymond Williams, we understand to be interconnected via imperialism, colonial and otherwise.[22] For such an understanding, we must extend and recast substantively Lefebvre's own basic procedure to link histories of space and urbanisation to transformations in modes of production. We need to focus on the comparatively distinct ways in which city-countryside relations emerged in *different* precapitalist, tributary social formations before being reshaped in *distinct ways* in articulation with merchant and industrial capitalism and the associated forces of colonialism and imperialism.[23]

---

17   Merrington 1975.
18   Lefebvre 2003a, pp. 9–16, 32–44.
19   Goonewardena 2014; Wachsmuth 2014.
20   Holton 1986.
21   Lefebvre 1970f., pp. 63–78.
22   Williams 1973.
23   Southalll 1998; King 1990.

Western Europe is not of course the only region in which the urban revolution has transformed histories shaped by clear if comparatively varied interplays of city and country. North African urbanisation is also impossible to understand without reference to the historical relationships between dynastic military and commercial urbanism, settled agriculture and tribal-nomadic networks, as already sketched by the famous fourteenth-century historian Ibn Khaldoun.[24] But such qualitative and social urban-rural contrasts did not inform precapitalist geographies everywhere. As we know from contemporary students of *desakota* urbanisation in Southeast Asia, and research about Chinese urban history, physical boundaries between settlement forms can hide urban-rural social continua organised by imperial administrations and other forces and institutions. Very different from the city-countryside divide of West European feudalism, such continua are essential reference points for understanding the most dynamic, currently ongoing urban revolutions in China as well as the twin processes of agricultural restructuring and mass migration that sustain them.[25]

Lefebvre's tentative historical and multi-scalar sketch of urbanisation in the *Urban Revolution* also obscures the degree to which city-country relationships are being revolutionised according to qualitatively distinct temporalities. While Lefebvre's *Rhythmanalysis* insisted that multiple rhythms – cyclical and linear – joined up differently in different, Atlantic and Mediterranean parts of urban Europe, his work does not extend this insight to paint a global comparative picture of such temporal multiplicity.[26] Yet we know that, in colonial contexts based on territorial systems of labour control (which tried to separate 'urban' production from 'rural' reproduction, as in British-dominated extractive economies in Africa), or on the incorporation-reproduction of tributary forms of agrarian production (in parts of Latin America and South Asia), city-country divides were materially (re-)*instituted* during modern capitalism rather than being subverted and transposed in the manner Lefebvre described for southern France, for example.[27] This problem – of city-non-city relationships being not so much superseded as recast or even created in the development of colonial-capitalist relations – is starkly evident on Caribbean sugar islands, Martinique included.

24   Khaldoun 2005; Abu-Lughod 1980, pp. 9–51.
25   McGee 1991; Tang 2014; Friedmann 2005. On the question of the relative autonomy of urban life in precolonial India and Africa, see Thapar 2003 and Coquery-Vidrovitch 1993.
26   Lefebvre 1992.
27   Freund 2007; King 1990, p. 52.

Important variations notwithstanding, Caribbean plantation economies led to common patterns of life in the region,[28] including creole material culture.[29] They also formed novel spatial divisions of labour between town and plantation. Claimed by the French in 1635 and built upon the marginalisation, decimation and ultimate deportation of the Arawak and Carib peoples, Martinique became an 'old' French colony defined by Black slavery (as codified by the *Code Noir* from 1685 until 1848). From Colbert's colonial planning efforts in the 1660s to the late eighteenth-century, slave-based production (focused increasingly on sugar) helped develop a distinct pattern of development centred on the plantation (*habitation*). In this basic 'cell unit' of slave production (Dale Tomich), relations of power and (re-)production were organised through spatial relations of proximity (to facilitate control and surveillance) and micro-separation (following the racialised class distinctions between owners, overseers, wage labourers, house slaves and field slaves). As Tomich put it,

> ... the social and spatial organisation of the *habitation sucrière* expressed both the technical imperatives of sugar production and the hierarchical character of social life and labour under slavery. The conditions of their combination gave each estate the appearance of a self-contained and autonomous social, economic, and administrative entity whose relations with the 'outside world' were controlled by the master.[30]

Tightly integrated internally, the plantation was spatially demarcated from small parish settlements and the two main island towns with the racially and legally coded mobility restrictions that were imposed on slaves. Crucial but small in size, towns functioned as classic colonial cities, as concentrations of imperial power (garrison and administration: Fort-de-France) and as way stations for colonial trade (ports, warehousing, trade and finance: Saint-Pierre) within a mercantilist, intra-imperial division of labour. Socially, island towns were too small for large-scale racial segregation. Compared to the plantations, they featured a more diverse and chaotic array of racially hierarchised social classes (including different categories of freed slaves, Black wage labourers, *petits blancs*, expatriates from the metropole, and, in the late slavery period,

---

28   On those common, if variegated patterns, see Tomich (2004, pp. 120–36); C.L.R. James (1989, pp. 391–2); King 1990, p. 31.
29   Trouillot 1998.
30   Tomich 2016, p. 164; see also Butel 2007, pp. 231–64.

a mulatto middle class). Somewhat more difficult to control than plantations, towns also attracted a share of the maroon population.[31]

The remarkable feature of the plantation-town relationship was not only that the predominance of the plantation on the island 'stunted the formation of town life'.[32] The relationship also defied basic assumptions about the very distinction between 'town' and 'country', as Katherine McKittrick also pointed out, with reference to the US-American context.[33] In Martinique, plantations integrated cane cultivation with sugar refining and, sometimes, rum production. They housed no peasants and were organised along quintessentially modern proto-industrial and proto-capitalist lines. Neither peasant-like nor clearly pre-capitalist, and certainly not strictly agrarian, they are difficult to describe as 'rural' spaces. True, at the 'edges' of the plantation famously invoked by Trouillot,[34] petty agricultural production emerged as slaves carved out provision grounds and fought for the time to cultivate them for subsistence and sale at local markets.[35] But it was only after the end of slavery in 1848 (and the concurrent socio-spatial dis-articulation of plantation activities: cane production and sugar refinery) that a 'countryside' of sorts emerged on the island. To invoke Sidney Mintz's thesis,[36] the end of slavery and the rise of a capitalism based on indentured and wage labour yielded a new, quintessentially modern, 'reconstituted' type of peasantry: smallholders whose intricate ties to an emerging agrarian working class were devoid of links to destructured tributary relations (such as those present in Algeria).[37] Nominally free, some former slaves formed an agricultural or industrial proletariat – on the fields or in the new sugar factories (*usines centrales*). Others (and sometimes the same people) pursued subsistence agriculture to limit economic coercion, supplement meagre wages and circumvent methods of enforcing key pillars of post-abolition social life: wage labour and married family life.[38] Claiming the slopes and mountains of

---

31   Butel 2007, pp. 225–6; Debien 1973, pp. 125–6.
32   Tomich 2016, p. 159.
33   McKittrick 2013, p. 8.
34   Trouillot 1998, pp. 25–6.
35   Tomich 2016, pp. 367–95.
36   Mintz 1974, pp. 61–2; Mintz 1989.
37   Thanks to Dale Tomich for stressing this point.
38   Chivallon 1990; Schmidt 2009; Pago 2011, pp. 34–5; Tomich 2004. Enforcing wage labour and reproductive family life was a way of creating the distinctions between productive and reproductive labour, paid work and domestic life slavery itself could not tolerate. Both were an attack on the historically inherited and violently enforced 'gender non-conformity of the Black community', as Saidiya Hartman put it in the US-American context (2016, p. 169).

the interior (or hiding in town), these former slaves gave new life to the spatial imaginaries of escape (*fuite*) that had informed *marronnage* as a practice of surviving and resisting slavery.

In a sense, then, colonial capitalism created peculiar town-country relations (in the period following abolition) *before* undermining these very relations again (in subsequent eras). The processes that undermined post-slavery town-country relations helped create, from the mid-nineteenth century into the post-war period, the spatial relations that come together in Chamoiseau's *Texaco*. What events and structural processes drove these dynamics of de-structuring? Periodic crises of the sugar economy since the late nineteenth century (and the consequent waves of rural-to-urban migration that neither spikes in rum production nor banana cultivation could stop permanently), the eruption of *Mont Pelée* (which destroyed Saint-Pierre in 1902 and forced many to move to Fort-de-France), and a new form of administrative-economic dependency organised after 1946 (when Martinique became a *département* of France). Tightly connected to the political reorganisation of colonial rule (in 1848 and in 1946), these dynamics of spatial de- and restructuring created the material and imagined territorial relationships that inform the landscapes of *Texaco*: the old colonial centre of *Fort-de-France*, the surrounding belt of initially informal and then renovated, 'solidified', working-class quarters, the hilltop enclaves of the White planter families, and the peculiar Fordist landscape spreading across the island starting in the postwar period.[39]

In comparative context, the French Caribbean example asks us to address the limitations in Lefebvre's comparative field of vision on the urban revolution.[40] To understand the meaning of urban revolutions in North and South,

---

39   Martouzet 2001, pp. 5–16, 43–5; Rey 2001, chapters 2, 3; Terral and Sélise 2018.
40   In current Anglo-American urban research, two avenues are on offer. As already mentioned, students of planetary urbanisation have built upon Lefebvre to map the extended dimensions of urbanisation, and on this basis to question thing-like conceptions of the city as bounded settlement (Monte-Mór 2004; Brenner 2014). We will return to planetary urbanisation selectively in this chapter and more systematically in the next chapter. In turn, authors who draw upon a range of influences, including strands of postcolonial, Southern and Black urban research, have emphasised the geographical biases in urban theory. In welcome challenges to Euro-American traditions of 'Metromarxism', including the work of Lefebvre, these critiques have recentred the geography of urban theory and begun to infuse research on the global North with sensibilities and analytic insights derived from studies of the urban South (Robinson 2006; Roy 2009a; Simone 2010). I have drawn on select insights from this tradition, too, particularly Robinson's attempt to stretch Benjamin for purposes of comparative analysis, which is comparable to Harry Harootunian's proposal to study modernity as a coeval form and minimal unity of the capitalist world. Insights in both sets of debates usefully cut across inherited divides of comparative research, albeit in distinctive ways and for different reasons.

I propose in this and the next chapter that we recast research and debates on planetary urbanisation to pay much greater attention to the ways in which the unevenness of the urban revolution is articulated in different spatio-temporal contexts under modern imperial capitalism. This approach – which builds upon Lefebvrean and Fanonian insights but also engages with other traditions – means that we cannot ignore the world-historical forces that have sustained and naturalised key spatial distinctions (for instance, between colonial and imperial spaces; and between first, second, and third worlds as well as between urban and rural environments) in previous rounds of comparative urban analysis. Embedded or reinvented in built environments, state forms, everyday practices and imaginaries, these forces continue to shape urban trajectories, despite the fact that transnational urbanisation has been cutting across inherited comparative geographies in novel ways. To account for such continuity-in-discontinuity, this chapter follows previous chapters by re-connecting Marxist and counter-colonial currents and drawing on select insights from research on colonial and Third World urbanisation in the 1970s and 1980s. After a brief discussion about the uses of fiction, I will do so first and foremost by learning from creole intellectual insights about the urban condition.

2   Literature and Spatial Imaginaries: Windows into Comparative Urbanisation

One entry point to comparative and global urban research is literature, poetry and prose. Whether cultivated by bourgeois society or generated and appreciated in subaltern circles, the fictional qualities of literary works force us to pay particular attention to the relationship between linguistic form and content.[41] Because of this very fictional quality, literary writing can mediate totality in ways that bring out the contradiction between potentiality and actuality, fantasy and historical reality in particularly sharp, and, to put it in Lefebvrean terms, transductive ways.[42] One may say that literature expresses social life, emanating from as well as surpassing in fantasy the realities of a given historical period or social situation.[43] In this context, criticism should be seen as an attempt to revisit the content and form of literary texts in order to bring to life –

---

41   On the specificity of literary texts, see Eagleton 2008, p. 9; 2013, pp. 3, 6–8.
42   On literature as mediation, see Jameson 1981.
43   Lefebvre 1955, pp. 19, 29.

and bring closer to our lives – the realities refracted in literature. As urban analysis, criticism should highlight the contradictions between reality and fantasy which literature includes in acute but not always intentional ways.

The promise of literature lies in its capacity to generate insight into aspects of totality through representations of everyday life. Focusing on the spatial forms articulated in literary texts thus may present us with insights into the relationship between large-scale historical forces and everyday routines and aspirations.[44] Placed in the context of the Black radical tradition, one can say that works of fiction offer a wealth of insight to understand spatial imaginaries, including Black ways of sensing place and rendering landscape poetically, to speak with Katherine McKittrick and George Lipsitz.[45] For Henri Lefebvre, too, literary creation allows one to follow how space is imagined, and thus produced. His exposition of the festival in Rabelais[46] allowed him later to trace the transposition of festivity from the early modern countryside to the major French urban revolutionary moments he analysed, 1871 and 1968. His work on Rabelais (an author whose linguistic exuberance holds appeal for advocates of creole as language and aesthetic form[47]) thus anticipated his basic claim that the urban revolution does not simply erase rural and urban life but recomposes city and countryside, symbolically and ideologically. Lefebvre makes this point by stressing the ways in which literature harbours spatial imaginaries that exceed the constraints set by dominant forces and the routines of daily life. This point, as well as McKittrick's and Lipsitz's, will be crucial when we encounter spatial imaginaries in creole literature further below.

The methods of comparative literature provide an opening for analyses of city and countryside across the North/South divide. This is true whether we insist on the idea of Third World literature or claim that we live in *one* world, albeit one where colonial-imperial histories continue to weigh.[48] For instance, the social realist treatment of metropolitan life and its broader articulations in the works of Emile Zola, Mulk Raj Anand and Ousmane Sembène could be compared provided one embeds such a comparison in careful historical and

---

44 As Kanishka Goonewardena (2005) has pointed out, following both Jameson and Lefebvre, mediation and totality as method may yield a form of 'cognitive mapping' different from cartographic visualisation. His insight also has profound implications for often misleading references to totality and totalisation in urban research today. See Goonewardena 2018.

45 McKittrick 2006, 2011; Lipsitz 2011.

46 Lefebvre 1955.

47 Chamoiseau 1992, p. 416.

48 For this contrast, see the classic exchange between Fredric Jameson (1986) and Aijaz Ahmad (1992, pp. 122–35; also Lazarus 2011, pp. 89–113).

geographical contexts. Neil Lazarus has argued that, along with considerations of land and environment, the literary treatment of city and countryside can shed light on urban-rural relationships in colonial contexts. In so doing, it can also illuminate the shock experience of old and new – modernity – in colonial and postcolonial metropoles.[49] He makes this point by discussing the works and insights of Raymond Williams, Marshall Berman, David Harvey, Lao She and Rohinton Mistry.

Lazarus's point invites us to connect debates in literary theory[50] to comparative urban research. His argument is to underscore that literary themes are comparable across contexts because they are neither absolutely relative in cultural terms nor universal in a strong, homogenising sense. Lazarus's claims jive with Harry Harootunian's take on the 'coeval' character of modernity.[51] Drawing on Walter Benjamin and Tosaka Jun as well as Henri Lefebvre, Harootunian's work on everyday life in interwar Japan suggests that modernity is not a product of diffusion from Europe (as modernisation theorists have it), nor is it incommensurate with the European modern (as one can gather from area studies and some strands of postcolonialism). As a regime of the new incorporating fragments of the past, the modern everyday represents a 'minimal unity' of the capitalist world that is always inflected with comparative specificity. We may thus hypothesise, with Lazarus and Lefebvre, that the urban as form of centrality/difference can be found simultaneously in multiple, interlinked contexts, literary and otherwise. As we pointed out in the introduction thanks also to Jennifer Robinson's Benjaminian insights about comparative analysis, this form cannot help but re-articulate specific historical-geographical content, including different histories of city and non-city. Articulating particularity and

---

49   Lazarus 2011, pp. 56–69.
50   Lazarus asserts a mode of criticism that eschews the one-sidedly deterritorialising orientation in postcolonial criticism (and its tendency to read the world of literature for signs of cultural flux and themes such as migrancy, hybridity, liminality, transnationality). He suggests that doing justice to urban and rural questions requires a sensitivity to themes that resonate in counter-colonial, materialist-feminist and Marxist registers – including mode of production, class, land, imperialism, state, patriarchy, national liberation, social revolution. He joins Priyamvada Gopal and Peter Hallward, among others, when he argues that the problem with postcolonialism does not lie in its debt to literary criticism, but in its penchant for deterritorialising literary themes. This penchant risks deflecting our attention from the territorial transformations wrought by imperial-capitalist urbanisation (see also Hallward 2011; Gopal 2005). In the following, I am recasting these arguments to suggest that Chamoiseau's *Texaco* reveals much more about colonial urbanism than one would expect if one only emphasised the neo-Deleuzian, rhizomatic allusions in the text.
51   Harootunian 2000, pp. 18, 61–2.

universality in relational fashion, Harootunian's idea of comparison is structurally open to countless partisan-universal entry points for research and action, to speak in Ato Sekyi-Otu's Fanonian register.[52]

3   Urbanising Creole, Creolising the Urban Revolution

The Creole literary movement (to which Patrick Chamoiseau belongs) and their predecessor and contemporary Edouard Glissant had a variegated and historically shifting relationship to Frantz Fanon and Aimé Césaire. For Glissant and the three authors of the Créole manifesto *Eloge de la créolité*, Chamoiseau, Raphaël Confiant and Jean Bernabé,[53] this is true both theoretically and politically. At a high level of abstraction, the intellectual shift is clear enough. These authors proposed a move from Fanon's and Césaire's perspectives on decolonisation as a situated revolutionary transformation (articulating particularity and universality in dialectical fashion) to an emphasis on theorising Antillean, indeed Caribbean specificity as the main task for Martiniquan intellectuals. In his *Discours antillais*, Glissant famously characterised Fanon's anti-colonial internationalism and Césaire's claim to négritude as detours from the path to *antillanité*, the regionally coherent and broadly cultural (if materially grounded) formation of which Martinique forms an integral part.[54] On their part, the creole intellectuals focused theoretical energies on the problematics of créolité and créolisation, the linguistic, cultural and philosophical complex of issues they thought Fanon and Césaire bypassed, underestimated or even denigrated[55] (and which, one should add, Glissant's *Discours* considered an intellectual detour, too).[56]

---

52   Sekyi-Otu 1996.
53   Bernabé, Chamoiseau, and Confiant 1989.
54   Glissant 1997, pp. 54–6.
55   Bernabé, Chamoiseau, and Confiant 1989, pp. 17–20. The creole critique of Fanon is sometimes made on the basis of the simply erroneous assumption that Fanon's work was based on dichotomous certainties and inadmissible simplifications regarding colonial rule and racial divides (Chamoiseau 1997, p. 221; Confiant 2006, p. 278). In his recently published fictional autobiography of Fanon, however, Confiant specifically disavows a range of caricatures of Fanon (as an apostle of violence, a fanatic, a traitor to Martinique), instead stressing what he considers the affinity between Fanon and the creolising move to always question fixed identities (2017).
56   Glissant 1997, p. 49. Glissant later changed his mind on this front, aligning himself with the creole movement and its dual conception of creolisation as Caribbean specificity and general human process (2008).

At this level, the charge against Fanon and Césaire is straightforward (though eminently arguable): having given short shrift to the cultural-linguistic peculiarities of the Antilles and exhibiting too great a readiness to frame anticolonialism in universalising ways.[57] The positions of the co-authors of *Eloge* on Césaire (and Fanon) have not been uniform or constant, mind you. They did not always stage an absolute break with them but moved between claiming their legacy (as Chamoiseau did with Césaire alongside Glissant and Perse)[58] and pointing to the paradoxes in their work (as Confiant did with Césaire).[59] Jean Bernabé, who founded the pathbreaking linguistic research project GÉREC (*Groupe d'Études et de Recherches en Espace Créole*) in 1973, put it in dialectical terms late in his life.[60] In a contribution to a workshop on Fanon held in Fort-de-France in 2011, he argued that the claims of créolité-créolisation offer a synthesis between the master's discourse (the thesis, negrophobia) and the response by the descendants of slavery (the anti-thesis, négritude). While Confiant inverted Césaire's saying to argue that 'Blackness (*négritude*) is a department of creolness (*créolité*)' rather than the opposite, as Césaire had it,[61] Bernabé suggested that the creole movement was big enough to house both Fanon and Césaire. Bernabé thought that the latter two failed to provide such a synthesis in their new humanist endeavours to transform the seemingly intractable fixities of a racialised world. In both cases, the creole project both affirms and demotes Blackness (whether understood as poetic discourse or proletarian material culture) to an element within a broader creole cultural formation.[62]

In their quest for creole as language and form of literary expression, Bernabé, Chamoiseau, and Confiant have vacillated between a situated opposition to France's falsely universal cultural imperialism (and the peculiar protocols of the French literary, linguistic and educational establishments), and open-

---

57   Glissant's famous concepts *relation* and *le divers* can be mobilised and recast to articulate specificity and totality, particularity and universality in relational fashion (see for example Shih 2013). In the formative *Discours*, however, Glissant's attempt to distance himself from 'universal' and 'generalising' habits in Fanon, Césaire and others (including advocates of 'class struggle') is unmistakable. While Glissant shares Fanon's and Césaire's critique of abstract humanism and the false, culturally assimilationist universalism of French colonialism (Wynter 1989, p. 645), he also represents a counterpoint to the dialectical humanism that one can find in Césaire's work and that permeates Fanon's situated internationalism.

58   Chamoiseau 2013.

59   Confiant 2006.

60   Bernabé 2013.

61   Confiant 2006, p. 284. All translations in the chapter are the author's.

62   Confiant in Watts 1998. On this point, see also Sylvia Wynter's early critical observation about creole criticism in the English-dominated Caribbean (1973).

ended calls for cultural mixing and epistemic complexification.[63] On the one hand, the authors have treated *creolité* as a specifically Antillean source of self not rooted in fixed racial hierarchy but permeated by a sense of cultural, linguistic, customary, religious and racial diversity. In this rendering, créolité is profound, situated, essential and sedimented, and may thus be expressed in 'thick' ecological metaphors ('magma', 'mangrove').[64] On the other hand, discussing creole as a form of becoming – *créolisation* – they describe a rather general process by which the world as a whole undergoes cultural diversification, from the Caribbean to the neighbourhoods of New York City.[65] Critics have suggested that this move from a regional or nationalist stance for cultural autonomy (or a cultural argument for regionally federated political independence) to a postmodern-cosmopolitan sensibility (or an otherwise welcome anti-identitarian and anti-essentialist observation about the 'non-fixity of peoples')[66] may not suffice when tackling persistent colonial realities, in the Antilles or elsewhere.[67] The tensions traversing the creole movement one also finds in Chamoiseau's *Texaco*, as we will see.

These remarks make it clear that Glissant and the creole intellectuals effect a qualitative shift in emphasis from Fanon's political conception of decolonisation (the idea that the liberation struggle plays a decisive part in forging new national cultures from the fragments of colonial and pre-colonial history) to a culturally rearticulated conception of the same project: a 'cultural

---

63   The ambiguities of the creole movement on this point are widely noted (Knepper 2011, pp. 25–30, 98–9; Majumdar 2007, pp. 151–5). Christine Chivallon points out that the ambiguities in the use of créolité and creolisation reveal contradictory meanings of the terms in question (2013).

64   Bernabé, Chamoiseau, and Confiant 1989, pp. 13, 20, 26–8.

65   Bernabé, Chamoiseau, and Confiant 1989, pp. 51, 30–1. This take on creolisation can have liberal undertones, as two books Chamoiseau co-authored with Glissant indicate. They levelled an appropriate critique at the mixophobic turn of racism in the Sarkozy government (and its talk of 'national identity') while also applauding the Barack Obama presidency as a hopeful step in the creolisation of the world (Glissant and Chamoiseau 2007, 2009).

66   Bernabé 2016.

67   Confiant took a hint from Césaire when he argued that *créolité* needed to be wrested from the White ruling class (Confiant 2006, p. 273). Yet 'conciliatory' notions of *créolité* and *créolisation* (Chivallon) as indeterminate maelstrom of complexity and cultural diversity are easy to find in creole texts (Bernabé et al. 1989, pp. 26–9, 51–5; Confiant 2006, p. 277; Chamoiseau 1997, pp. 281–317). In the Antilles themselves, excessively open-ended, if not generic conceptions of créolisation can be appropriated by dominant forces, békés included, to promote a colour-blind and folkloristic Martinique where everyone is creole and critics of racialised and colonial capitalism have no place (Chivallon 2012, pp. 514–23; Price and Price 1997).

reconquest' to ward off the threat of 'cultural genocide' that is cultural assimilation[68] and a quest to creolise life and modern literature of which popular sovereignty is considered not a cause and condition but a ramification.[69] Of course, none of our authors can be understood without the struggles that confronted Martinique's departmental status from the late 1950s to the 1970s. These struggles were put into sharp relief by the 1959 revolt against racist humiliation and economic stagnation that Chamoiseau retroactively interpreted as Martinique's modest, inconclusive contribution to anti-colonialism.[70] Even though the creole authors' views about the national question underwent change during their lifetimes, they were deeply shaped by the student and worker struggles in the 1960s and 1970s, to which they also contributed. For the Glissant of the *Discours*, independence remained 'vital' to *antillanité*,[71] decades after he co-founded the *Front des Antilles et de la Guyane pour l'Autonomie* and was banned from France for the act in the first half of the 1960s. Confiant has been consistent in favouring independence, as a member of MODEMAS (*Mouvement des démocrates et écologistes pour une Martinique souveraine*) or an independent sovereignist and environmentalist. For Chamoiseau, who eventually moved towards Césaire's governing *Parti Progressiste Martiniquais* (PPM), the anticolonial youth and student activism in the 1960s and the banana workers' strike in 1974 were formative influences as he entered the literary scene as a rebel theatre director and screenwriter in the 1970s.[72] Then, his theatrical work added to the charged times, helping to politicise the relationship between formal French, the language of the administrators and the assimilated middle class, and Creole, the working classes' oral language, then prohibited in school and derided by many.

Despite the cultural turn led by Glissant, Chamoiseau, Bernabé and Confiant, there thus remains an unexpected point of contact between their work and Fanon, who took the necessity of political independence for decolonisation for granted and was at least publicly hopeful about its prospects in the region following the 1959 revolt (and the Cuban revolution).[73] While Fanon's hopes clashed with Césaire the politician, for whom Fanon was too hot to

---

68   Glissant 1997, pp. 270, 297, 427.
69   Bernabé, Chamoiseau, and Confiant 1989, pp. 57–9.
70   Chamoiseau 2002.
71   Glissant 1997, p. 803.
72   Knepper 2012, pp. 10–17, 32–58.
73   In this hopeful argument for regionally federated and revolutionary independence, Fanon joined a range of contemporaries, including C.L.R. James (1989) and Daniel Guérin (1956). For a slightly expanded discussion of Fanon's relationship to Martinican politics, see the conclusion of Chapter 2.

handle,[74] Glissant and the creole intellectuals, too, were forced to engage with Césaire and his legacy not only at the level of theory but also in relationship to the departmentalisation project that Césaire never ceased to carry, his recurrent doubts, partial autocritiques and repeated reformulations notwithstanding.[75] Fundamentally, Césaire considered departmentalisation a form of political (not cultural) assimilation, that is to say a quest for economic, social and political equality that would continue, not abort, decolonisation. As he said in his comments about the legacy of abolitionist and republican colonialist Victor Schoelcher, Césaire thought that the promise of departmentalisation could be found in the fact that it could only further develop (instead of attenuating) the contradictions between political citizenship and the ongoing social and economic subordination of Martinique within France.[76] Needless to say, Césaire's dogged and pragmatic[77] pursuit of this project propelled him into the centre of the political class of Martinique, as deputy in the French National Assembly, mayor of Fort-de-France, and leader of the *Parti Progressiste Martiniquais* (PPM) after his resignation from the French Communist Party in 1956.

Strategically and self-consciously positioned within the contradictions of the French empire, Césaire and the PPM helped reorganise the colonial relation in Martinique by mediating and recasting, in a tension-ridden and dynamic fashion, the relationship between former slave-owning families (*békés*), the French state, multinational capital, and subaltern forces (including the labour unions and left-wing parties that took independist turns following the 1950s). While establishing a counterweight to the *békés* (and their own occasional designs for independence) and the French prefecture, Césaire and the PPM also absorbed independist aspirations (notably with their decision to claim

---

74 As Confiant reminds us, Césaire refused to preface Fanon's *Damned of the Earth* (Wajeman 2017).

75 Aimé Césaire 1956b, pp. 9–17; 2016c, pp. 321–31.

76 Aimé Césaire 2008, pp. 27–8.

77 Gary Wilder (2008; 2009a; 2009b; 2015) makes a theoretical virtue of this pragmatism, elevating it to a constitutive feature of Césaire's overall intellectual orientation. In this, his work parallels Bonilla's analyses of non-sovereignty, as we will see below. Whatever its merits, Wilder's approach (like Nesbitt's distinct alternative, for that matter) stops short of a full analysis of Césaire's political role in Martinique, his position within a broader constellation of forces that has reshaped and partly solidified the colonial relation in the course of departmentalisation (Wilder 2015, pp. 86–98; Nesbitt 2013, pp. 106–32). It thus underestimates the very tensions and fissures in Césaire's work to which Césaire himself alerted us. Of course, it paradoxically diminishes not just Fanon's critique of Césaire but also the revolutionary aspects of Césaire's work that have clearly clashed with Antillean realities since the postwar period. One does not have to dismiss Césaire's work as a form of 'betrayal' to understand these tensions in Césaire's life work.

'autonomy' within a French framework). They thus helped forge a peculiar modality of political practice that continues to bind the struggles (of agricultural labourers, public sector workers, and students, for example) against colonial discrimination and for equality and dignity ever closer to the French state, thus driving wedges between the social and the national question, between class struggles and claims to political and economic independence.[78]

Remarkable is the degree to which the political terrain of struggle which Césaire and the PPM helped build was in fact *built* through spatial strategies. Agricultural modernisation, land reforms and city building projects advanced departmentalisation by means of spatial reorganisation. Together, these interventions amounted to state-led urbanisation. As Bonilla pointed out, connecting Martinique to French (and then European) agricultural policy allowed the *béké* to rationalise their operations and diversify their holdings by investing in real estate and the import-export sector. This helped transform agricultural lands into an 'impressive infrastructure' of 'airports', 'schools, roads, hospitals and supermarkets', an 'impressive façade of prosperity for the underlying economic stagnation',[79] and, indeed, the material basis of a new economic dependency on imports controlled by multinationals and *béké*-controlled firms and paid for by public sector employment and transfer payments.[80] Césaire himself made it clear that he considered both land reform[81] and urban policy to be vital for the Martinican quest for equality within France. As he said in the French National Assembly in 1952, the absence of regular public housing corporations, mechanisms of housing finance, and official plans on the island were a form of colonial unequal treatment comparable to the gaps in salary and social service levels between the hexagone and Martinique.[82] He thus admonished his fellow parliamentarians as follows: 'Instead of moralising and scaremongering about the Antillean situation, erect housing for the people, cut streets and boulevards through the landscape, help them build conditions for a decent life'.[83]

The fact that Césaire, in contrast to Fanon, could help 'get people out of their slums'[84] and made a virtue out of the struggle to do so accentuates the importance of the urban question in assessing the significance of his life work (as well as the comparatively specific reorganisation of colonial relations in

78   Blérard 1988; Bruneteaux 2013, pp. 99–132; Jalabert 2007, pp. 34–41, 267–9.
79   Bonilla 2015, p. 25.
80   Jalabert 2007; Cabort Masson 1984; Martouzet 2001, chapter 3.
81   Césaire 2003b, pp. 149–55.
82   Césaire 2003a, p. 111.
83   Césaire 2003a, pp. 90–1.
84   Césaire 2004, p. 51.

Martinique).[85] Let me open a brief parenthesis here: there is much explore about the relationship between Césaire's role in urbanising Martinique, the urban and spatial dimensions of *négritude*, and the formation of creole literature. It is an open secret to underline that creole themes are already present in the moment of *négritude*. This is most directly the case with Suzanne Césaire, who in 1942 urged readers to move from a re-discovery of the African past to an affirmation of all the 'living forces' that combine to generate diversity and human intermixing in the Antilles.[86] For this purpose, which already pointed beyond *négritude*,[87] she did what Aimé Césaire also did in *Return to My Native Land* in 1939: mobilise images of island plant life to underscore the vital forces, the excessive exuberance and the dynamics of diversification that carry emancipation. Aimé contrasted plant metaphors embodying island vitality to the colonial city (Fort-de-France?), which he depicted as an inert space: devoid of fauna and flora, distanced from the hillsides (*mornes*), flat and stifled by geometry, silenced and stunted, with crowds of people that do not mix.[88] Rather than a force for emancipation and equality (as Césaire had it in the 1950s), or a compartmentalised stage for the battle between coloniser and colonised (as Fanon suggested), for the Césaire of *Return*, the urban embodies colonial thingification *in toto*.

Despite their differences, Suzanne and Aimé Césaire's early poetic works thus anticipate certain creole literary practices, including the deployment of organic landscape metaphors to capture Martinique's diverse living energies.[89] In turn, Creole literature and Patrick Chamoiseau have alerted us most forcefully to the spatial dimensions of creole culture and political departmentalisation. They are part of a line of Antillean literary works (from Joseph Zobel's *La Rue Case-Nègres* to Raphaël Confiant's *L'Allée des Soupirs* and Maryse Condé's *La Belle Créole*) that offer deep and multi-dimensional insights into the historical geographies of Martinique and Guadeloupe.

---

85   Blérard 1988, p. 116. Gidel (2016) highlights how these departmental urban strategies generated comparative differences between Fort-de-France and other Caribbean cities such as Port of Spain.

86   Suzanne Césaire 2009, p. 75; 2009a; 2009b.

87   Condé 1998.

88   Aimé Césaire 1983, pp. 7–11.

89   One cannot quite say the same thing about Fanon, despite the fact that the theoretically heterodox, stylistically multiform and eminently transdisciplinary character of his work has led Jane Gordon to suggest that Fanon helps us 'creolise' political theory in the generic sense of the term (Jane Gordon 2014; Lewis Gordon 2015, p. 73); and also despite the fact that Fanon's 'insurgent soul' pushed Confiant to read his life work in analogy to the idea of creolisation, as an opening to the world and a continuous questioning of identities (2017).

Chamoiseau himself attributes great significance to his childhood growing up in the old colonial centre of Fort-de-France.[90] Judging by his three-volume autobiography, town life was crucial for his creole becoming. In contrast to Guadeloupe's Maryse Condé, who grappled above all with the gendered, spatially fractured and always political class divide between her 'alienated' middle-class Black family and the Black proletariat (a divide which is also at the heart of Zobel's Martinique in *La Rue Case-Nègres*),[91] Chamoiseau reports having gone through two stages of development: 'considering his Blackness' before 'learning to be creole'.[92] He reports doing so in two ways: First, he rubbed off his schoolteachers (first the assimilationist for whom all civilisation was French and the French language, then the Césaire-like figure who took an oppositional, African stance but held onto the universal) just enough to succeed in school. In so doing, he left behind the Black proletariat, which appears in the figure of a Black creole (*créole-nègre*) schoolmate that is treated by the school as a quintessential outsider, a living reminder of plantation life because of his deep poverty, his creole language, and his bare living arrangements.[93] Second, Chamoiseau immersed himself in the hierarchised diversities of town life. A 'declared fiefdom of the mulatto ethnoclass',[94] the social life and built form of downtown Fort-de-France helped shape Chamoiseau's budding creole sensibilities. How? With its intricate insect life, its culinary curiosities, its multiple daily rhythms, its ethnic pluralities, and its complexly layered sound- and scent-scapes.[95]

Throughout his work Chamoiseau identifies the urban experience of diversity and creativity with emblematic characters (storytellers, hawkers and survival artists (*djobeurs*)), spirits and supernatural forces (*zombies, dorlis*). His novels (*Solibo Magnifique, Chronique des sept misères*, and *Texaco*) all discuss how these figures and their institutions (local markets, the creole language, oral history, self-built construction) confront the mortal dangers posed by the postwar urban revolution that was unleashed after Martinique became a *département* of France in 1946. As Glissant put it approvingly in his 1986 preface to *Chronique*,[96] Chamoiseau's characters are resistance figures defending cultural intermixing against the unmistakably statist, standardised and solidly concrete forms of

90   Knepper 2012, p. 21.
91   Condé 1999, pp. 105, 117, 127, 149; 2006, pp. 111, 153, 238–9, 289.
92   Chamoiseau 1996, p. 171.
93   Chamoiseau 1994, pp. 55–7, 117, 120–1, 164–6, 193–4.
94   Chamoiseau 2005, p. 200.
95   Chamoiseau 1994, 1996, 2005.
96   Glissant 2012, p. 4.

French Fordism swamping the Antilles. In *Ecrire en pays dominé*, Chamoiseau sums up the situation as follows:

> As the 1946 law started having wider effects, the country changed at great speed: concrete construction becomes king, glass windows, lamps, red lights, first television sets, automobile ecstasy, triumphant social housing blocks, sanitary plumbing, social assistance, family allowance payments, airplanes, roads and highways, schools, ready-to-wear clothing, stores, hotels, supermarkets, advertising.[97]

In this view, the urban tapestry being draped over Martinique threatened to 'sterilise' island life and 'invalidate' anti-colonial claims.[98] In his other work, Chamoiseau responded to departmental urbanisation in multiple ways, including revolt, nostalgia (or melancholy), and accommodation. *Texaco* testifies to all these responses, with a tendency towards the third, and a persistent emphasis on the articulation of standardised urbanisation processes with colonial pasts and presents. In so doing, one might say that *Texaco* condenses Chamoiseau's literary answer to the urban revolution in its specific Martinican form.

4   *Texaco*

> I wanted it to be sung from somewhere, for the ears of the future generations, that we fought with the town (*l'En-ville*) not in order to conquer it (it swallowed us, in fact) but to conquer ourselves through this new-found creole, which we had to name, in us and for us, to reach our full powers.[99]

> What is the town (*En-ville*), you ask? It is a tight spot where our histories join up. Temporalities, too. The plantation dissociated us. The hills (*mornes*) tied us down in an immobile drift. *L'En-ville* puts in motion, knots, moors, kneads, blends and mixes up at full speed.[100]

Named after a now regularised shantytown bearing the name of the oil company on whose ground it developed, *Texaco* zeroes in on the struggles of the

---

97   Chamoiseau 1997, pp. 69–70.
98   Chamoiseau 1997, pp. 74, 224.
99   Words by the narrator, Chamoiseau 1992, p. 498.
100   Words by the *vieux-nègre de la Doum*, Chamoiseau 1992, p. 375.

residents against the 'slum' clearance schemes proposed in postwar Fort-de-France. This literary critique of urban renewal does not take the form of a social realist counternarrative in the tradition of anti-colonial liberation novels. Instead, *Texaco* deploys the techniques of creole writing, which want to attest to how oral Creole inhabits and 'conquers' the French language.[101] As an oral form of literature (*oraliture*), it blurs genres and languages, infusing literary French with Creole vocabulary, figures of speech and oral rhythms. It also combines oral testimony with written historical documents and the narrator's commentary. The story of *Texaco* is told through multiple voices: the oral account of Marie-Sophie Laborieux, the Texaco inhabitant and activist; the memories of her late father, Esternome Laborieux, which are embedded in Marie-Sophie's own narrative; the commentaries by Christ, the *urbaniste*; and the interventions by the storyteller Chamoiseau. This collage-like form allows Chamoiseau to tie the relationship between Texaco residents and the middle classes and authorities housed in the historical centre of Fort-de-France to legacies of slavery, colonial violence and resistance.[102] This technique also makes it clear through the very form of the text that urban Martinique is a confluence of multiple rhythms and temporalities, all of which are refracted pervasively through language.[103] Infused by the struggles chronicled in the text, informal-creole shantytown Texaco, and with it formal-French Fort-de-France, embodies Marie-Sophie's voice: Texaco = *teks-a-ko* = text-future-body.[104]

It has been common to read *Texaco* as an illustration of the tensions of the creole movement, and, more specifically, the postmodern-postcolonial tendencies within this movement. Wendy Knepper has offered such a reading based on both formal and substantive grounds.[105] She has underlined how in *Texaco*, *oraliture* and the mixing of voices and linguistic forms (testimonies, reports, authorial narratives and so on) corresponds to a 'creole' vision of urban form as a bricolage of materials, habits and building types.[106] Christine Chivallon and Dorothy Blair also alert us to the ways in which *Texaco* links space and identity in postmodernising ways. They emphasise how the aforementioned problematics of *créolité* (being) and *créolisation* (becoming) return

---

101 Bernabé, Chamoiseau, and Confiant 1989, pp. 46–7.
102 For more on the form of *Texaco*, see Chivallon and Blair 1997 and Knepper 2012, pp. 112–29.
103 Chamoiseau 1992, pp. 370–7.
104 Knepper 2012, p. 128.
105 Knepper 2012, pp. 112–29.
106 This analogy between language and urban form is common in the creole tradition. Here is one of Confiant's affirmations of creolised urban space, 'the baroque, the extremely powerful grotesque qualities of Fort-de-France, the genius of the creole house that combines mud, wood, brick, fibrocement and concete' (1994, pp. 315–16).

in an interplay between three spatial imaginaries: (1) place-bound, coherent rootedness; (2) chaotic, confusing mobility; and finally (3) complex rhizomatic combinations of place and movement. The animating force in this triad is the rhizome, which for them prefigures and affirms, in postmodern fashion, chaos, uncertainty, elusiveness and disorder.[107] These readings dovetail with Peter Hallward's and Margaret Majumdar's critiques of the later Edouard Glissant and the French-language creole movement, which they both see as important examples of the postmodern-postcolonial, and in this case also Deleuzian, fixation on epistemic complexification and deterritorialisation.[108] Read in this way, Chamoiseau and *Texaco* appear as simple opposites to the Fanon-Lefebvre lineage sketched in Chapters 1 and 2.

After multiple re-readings of *Texaco*, these interpretations seem as partial as they were the first time I read the book. Chamoiseau's creole claims and their relationship to creole literary techniques are undeniable, explicit and insistent. But they are continuously overwhelmed by the depth and breadth of the historical and geographical materials he assembles; in fact, I think that the collage-like character of the book encourages this very formal and thematic abundance (in this, *Texaco* is of course not without parallel in literary modernism, which fractured the classic narrative novel, social realist or otherwise). What always struck me is how much one learns from *Texaco* about Martinique's colonial historical geography *in and through* the practices and imaginaries that shape postwar Texaco and its relationships to other parts of Fort-de-France. In particular, *Texaco* shows how the spatial relationships that come together in the capital of Martinique were instituted politically through struggle, and how they contributed in turn to the formation of a new colonial state in Martinique. Within the pages of *Texaco*, the impetus towards socio-spatial complexification, *horizontal* deterritorialisation, and epistemological ambivalence encounters weighty evidence that shows how in departmentalised Martinique, colonial forms of economic dependency, racialised class rule, and cultural assimilation have been created anew, in part through spatial strategies and *vertical* state-civil society relations. I think that *Texaco* poses the urban question in Martinique most insightfully through *this* tension (between creole project(s) and colonial realities as well as anti-colonial imaginaries).

Texaco is all about efforts to pursue 'the conquest of the city (*l'En-ville*)'[109] across a long historical arc, from the Saint-Pierre of late slavery times to the period circumscribed by the formation and consolidation of former shanty-

---

107   Chivallon and Blair 1997, pp. 329–32.
108   Majumdar 2007, pp. 53–4, 151–5; Hallward 2001, chapter 2.
109   Chamoiseau 1992, p. 45.

town Texaco at the edge of old Fort-de-France.[110] These efforts include individual practices, collective action and more diffuse hopes and aspirations. They are both objective and subjective; they pertain to social-spatial processes, political struggles and matters of subjectivity. In their explicit creole renderings, they are also existential in character. The target of the conquest, *l'En-ville* is not a thing (built form, a bounded area, downtown). As Chamoiseau explains, the creole term *En-ville* refers not to physical form but to content; it represents the city in movement, as a claim, an incursion, a project to exist.[111] Conquering *l'En-ville* is in fact a work of art (*oeuvre*),[112] the ultimate goal of which is conquering not 'the city' (as a thing out there) but 'ourselves'.[113] The initial resonances between Chamoiseau and the Lefebvre-Fanon lineage should be clear. Comparable to Lefebvre's notion of the city as a product of creative interventions, an *oeuvre*, conquering *l'En-ville* is not a one-time act of claiming a given object, thing or place. It is ongoing creative practice, an open-ended everyday endeavour that could include the kind of appropriation of space, body and self that Fanon thought women resistance fighters were practicing in late colonial Algiers.

In Chamoiseau's explicitly creole formulations, conquering *l'En-Ville* is not a matter of revolution, however. Unlike in Lefebvre's urbanised understanding of revolution and Fanon's spatially mediated take on anti-colonial liberation, it does not describe a punctual relationship between the occupation of space and the seizure of power; nor does it capture the longer-term processes (preceding and following revolutionary acts) through which multi-scalar territorial relations are transformed to accentuate fundamental social change and genuine decolonisation. The emphasis is not on the multi-temporal and multi-scalar – vertical and horizontal – interplay of wars of position and wars of movement (as in Fanon's and Lefebvre's Gramscian moments); it is more one-sidedly on the diffuse, horizontal, even subterranean processes of infusion and practices of transgression that cut across spatial divides, social separations, and urban forms just as a mangrove roots make their way across forests and waterways. Here, Chamoiseau's *Texaco* rejoins others where he stresses that the promise of diverse urban Martinique lies in a deterritorialising, chaotic life-force that permeates informal social spaces like Texaco, an errant 'drive' that holds traces of marooning slave resistance and invades the rationalism of the orderly Fort-de France proper. Alluding to Deleuze and Guattari's notion of the rhizome

---

110   Chamoiseau 1992, p. 205.
111   Chamoiseau 1992, p. 492.
112   Chamoiseau 1992, p. 205.
113   Chamoiseau 1992, p. 498.

here and elsewhere, he deploys the plant metaphor 'mangrove' to show how in Texaco, the multiple, complexly combined (creolised) and not-just human energies in Martinique history permeate urban life symbolically, swamp-like and in horizontal, lateral fashion.[114] These philosophically inflected visions led Chamoiseau to valorise self-help and other informal survival tactics. The efforts of shanty entrepreneurs and '*djobeurs*', who cobble together a subsistence living and invade Fort-de-France in search of marginal deals and petty jobs, play a role akin to *marrons* and other survival artists during earlier historical eras.[115]

Judging from Christ, the *urbaniste*, the planner and city-builder, it appears first as if the mangrove-like quality of 'creole urbanism' embodies an oppositional, threatening force, the impermanent, chaotic, diverse and ambivalent qualities (of informal Texaco) that obstruct 'modernisation' and 'civilisation', that is, 'Western' conceptions of a proper city built on solid, orderly, uniform, and rational grounds.[116] In his initial view, razing Texaco to the ground is necessary to advance the city proper, symbolised as it is by the stone foundations, poured concrete and grid layout of central Fort-de-France. However, as we keep reading, we come to understand that creole urbanism describes an unstable equilibrium between centre and periphery in Fort-de-France as a whole. In the course of the book, the *urbaniste* begins to see that creole urbanism expresses in fact an aesthetic duality, a sensory interdependence between central Fort-de-France and the ring of less-than-formal neighbourhoods surrounding it.

> In the old centre: a clear order, dominated, normalised. Around it: a bubbling ring of neighbourhoods, undecipherable, impossible, masked by misery and the obscure burdens of history. If the creole city were only about the order of its centre, it would be dead. It needs the chaos of its fringe. It is beauty full of horror, order enriched by disorder. Order trembling in horror, a secret order in the heart of disorder. Texaco is the disorder of Fort-de-France, the poetry of Order. The planner no longer chooses between order and disorder, beauty and ugliness.[117]

---

114   Chamoiseau 1997, pp. 279–94.
115   Chamoiseau 1992, pp. 304–5.
116   Chamoiseau 1992, pp. 19–20. Of course, to identify these qualities with Western urbanism is to ignore the much broader and longer histories of ordering and rationalising urban space in other parts of the world, in the Middle East, in China, in South and Southeast Asia, and in various regions of Africa and the Americas.
117   Chamoiseau 1992, pp. 235–6.

Why did the *urbaniste* have a change of heart? Throughout the book, his voice takes the measure of fluctuating political temperatures, thus tracing the spatial reorganisation of the colonial relation through struggle. In this regard, the *urbaniste* admits having learned from Marie-Sophie Laborieux, her presence, her struggles, her insights.[118]

Laborieux is the heart, soul and brain of *Texaco*. Her role foregrounds the gendered dynamics of island life in ways that differ from typically male-dominated texts in the creole tradition.[119] As the 'founder' of Texaco, Laborieux led co-inhabitants in a struggle to blur the boundaries between formal and informal Fort-de-France. How? By fighting against internal threats (slumlord-ism, petty exploitation, insecurity and gendered violence, including rape and physical assault), resisting external forces (demolition by bulldozer, eviction by police forces) and, crucially, encroaching onto the central city to survive (earn a salary, look for day jobs, sell wares, scavenge materials). In the process, two things happen. First, 'the town centre (*l'En-ville*) integrated the soul of Texaco'.[120] Second, Texaco was connected to the 'solidity' of the central city by means of roads and electricity lines. In this context of struggle, the *urbaniste* comes to think that the human and physical interpenetration of centre and periphery in Fort-de-France reflects a deeper dependence of each on the other's vitality and recognition.[121]

Here, Chamoiseau takes us far away from Fanon's politically charged contrast and struggle between the native and the European quarters of the colonial city as he saw it. How did we arrive at the cultural compromise that is creole urbanism? Answering this question gets us to what I think is most interesting about Texaco. In the first instance, informal Fort-de-France, Texaco included, is a product of three historical rounds of socio-spatial restructuring, resistance and spatial imaginary: the last years of slavery, the post-emancipation period, and the time of departmentalisation. As narrated in *Texaco*, Texaco 'lives' the spatial relations that mediated these three historical periods through the collective memories bundled by Marie-Sophie Laborieux's recollections and the memories of her father Esternome. Esternome was the son of a slave mother and the slaver owner who raped her. He grew up in the slave master's house and left the plantation nominally free. Esternome's stories are themselves tied up with those of his parents and those of the women in his life, including Laborieux's mother Idoménée. Seen through these gendered memor-

118   Chamoiseau 1992, p. 236.
119   Knepper 2012, p. 120; Condé 1993, pp. 129–30; Price and Price 1997, pp. 19–20.
120   Chamoiseau 1992, p. 487.
121   Chamoiseau 1992, p. 337.

ies, urban Martinique carries within itself both the violence of 'slavery, colonisation, racism'[122] and the possibility of survival, escape and struggle, including the intergenerational memory of 'urban conquests'.[123]

To demonstrate the spatial mediation of the colonial relation, Chamoiseau mobilises his deep interest in the morphology and built environment of Martinique, which also shapes other aspects of his work.[124] His text offers multiple insights into the memorialised territorial relations of slavery. 'Texaco remembers the interplay of power between slave dwelling (*case*) and slave masters' house (*Grand-case*), between the plantation and the village, between the rural village and town'.[125] In this complex of spatial relations, the micro-relations between *cases* and *Grand-cases* on the plantation are doubled by the larger territorial relationship between town and non-town (*habitation, bourg*). In this situation, 'the town (*l'En-ville*) was ... the master's house of masters' houses'.[126] As we have seen, during slavery, the colonial garrison and port towns (Saint-Pierre, Fort-de-France) and the plantations (*habitations*) were components of a single, integrated, always already modern colonial production system. Yet they were demarcated from each other with pass controls in order to facilitate supervision and labour control. Racialised spatial demarcation made even freed Blacks (who were nominally allowed to leave the plantation) subject to constant suspicion in the towns, which were dominated by a pigmentocratic hierarchy of French administrators, White slaveholders (*béké*), and assimilated mulatto inhabitants.

While not a slave, Esternome could still not experience Saint-Pierre as freedom.[127] In town, 'he learned to name each person according to their degree of Whiteness or their unfortunate shade of Blackness'.[128] This hostile, racially stratified character of town life pushed many plantation slaves' emancipatory aspirations towards the mountains, the refuge of marrons, fugitive slaves. From Esternome, who ended up giving in to the promise of the hills for a while,[129] we also learn that town life was not without opportunities, however. On Sundays, some plantation slaves were allowed to descend onto town, adding to the relative fluidity of town life that authorities perceived as a threat.[130]

---

122 Chamoiseau 1992, p. 192.
123 Chamoiseau 1992, pp. 48–9.
124 Milne 2006.
125 Chamoiseau 1992, p. 401.
126 Chamoiseau 1992, p. 107.
127 Chamoiseau 1992, p. 92.
128 Chamoiseau 1992, p. 94.
129 Chamoiseau 1992, p. 159.
130 Chamoiseau 1992, p. 204.

Saint-Pierre provided openings for escape because the mobility restrictions imposed on plantation slaves were not airtight and the social controls in towns were not absolute.[131] In the words of *le vieux-négre de la Doum*, the village elder who appears later in the text, marronnage cuts across spatial divides: 'whoever maroons up in the hills also maroons in town (*En-ville*)'.[132] At the end of slavery, the marrons' capacity to escape in multiple directions contributed to the contradictions of the slave economy and constituted a reservoir of collective resistance.[133] In 1848, this reservoir was tapped as people flocked to and converged in Prêcheur and Saint-Pierre to ensure the implementation of the decree of abolition.[134] After 1848, the *békés* (many of whom kept residing in retreats) never regained their sense of ease in town.[135]

The term urban marronnage, which Chamoiseau also deploys for Texaco inhabitants thus refracts a concrete historical practice which both permeated town life and created the conditions for collective claims to urban space and social power (centrality). Of course, marronnage also retains rurally inflected symbolisms (in Chamoiseau and many other sources, literary and colloquial).[136] In part, this is due to the lines of continuity one can draw between marronnage and post-slavery subsistence practices on the hillsides (*mornes*). These practices responded and contributed to the aforementioned destructuring of the slavery-era plantation economy and its spatial divide between town and plantation. As the sugar factories and the cane plantations confronted the early labour movement, these practices tried to hold against the economic coercion of wage labour (which was also enforced with decrees against 'vagabondage' and forced labour).[137] Memories from these tenuous and incomplete practices of *fuite* found their way to Fort-de-France through a new form of structural violence: rural-urban migration.[138] Caused by the repeated crises of

---

131   Chamoiseau 1992, pp. 83, 89–98.
132   Chamoiseau 1992, p. 374.
133   On slaves' struggle for autonomous time and petty agricultural production, see Tomich 2016, chapter 8. On the role of fugitives, see Blackburn 2011, pp. 496–8. On revolt and organised resistance, see Schmidt 2005.
134   Chamoiseau 1992, pp. 129–31; Schmidt 2005, pp. 229–30.
135   Chamoiseau 1992, p. 133.
136   As Bonilla points out also in relationship to the figure *nèg'marron*, the social and political symbolism of marronnage in the culture industry and popular culture is highly ambiguous, notably from the point of view of oppositional political organising; it includes pathologising images of petty delinquency (which follow from dominant uses of the term under slavery), unstructured, individual, and daily rebelliousness, and organised, even armed resistance (2015, pp. 42–62).
137   Chamoiseau 1992, pp. 146–57.
138   Chamoiseau 1992, p. 246.

the sugar economy and the difficulties of carving out semi-autonomous sub-sistence lives on marginal lands, this violence unleashed the forces that helped create, starting in the nineteenth century, a ring of settlements around the centre of Fort-de-France. There, many migrants found themselves without the livelihoods and steady employment they had hoped for.[139]

Those moving from plantations, hillsides (or, indeed, devastated Saint-Pierre) to the new neighbourhoods (Terres-Sainville, Trénelle, St. Thérèse, Morne Pichevin, Volga-Plage, Texaco and others) kept alive select aspects of their previous lives and dreams. Through Marie-Sophie Laborieux's memor-ies of Esternome and her mother Idoménée, the mornes descended onto town symbolically in the form of a spatial imaginary tied to hillside subsistence prac-tices. This imaginary, *Noutéka* ('nous des mornes'/'we, the hills') conjures up a sense of place and togetherness and a sense of cyclical, seasonal time[140] driven by a desire to keep at a distance town and plantation (i.e. wage dependency) through self-help and rotating cultivation.

> When we came, we brought with us the countryside .... We behaved as if we lived the life of *Noutéka* in the hills, which my *Esternome* had described to me at length, with its impeccably maintained open spaces next to the dwellings and a rhythm of life following the seasons, the rains and the winds. In the face of the city (*En-ville*), we wanted to live in the spirit of the hills.[141]

In informal Fort-de-France, fragments of Noutéka persist as practices of sur-vival, mutual aid and memories of hillside land. In so doing, they infuse the new undisputed capital of the island with multiple rhythms and collective social sensibilities.[142] To describe how these layers of the past are woven into the fab-ric of informal Fort-de-France, the *urbaniste* says that Texaco is neither town nor country but urban mangrove,[143] which is to say humanity[144] and 'vegetal soul'[145] all at the same time.

---

139 Chamoiseau 1992, p. 246.
140 Chamoiseau 1992, pp. 160–91.
141 Césaire 2003a, pp. 90–1.
142 *Lakou* is another social and spatial form of working-class life one can find in Antillean lit-erature, for example in Maryse Condé's *La Belle Créole*, set in Guadeloupe (2001). *Lakou* denotes a complex of spatial arrangements and social practices through which sociabilit-ies and imaginaries from the hillsides were transposed and recast in the informal neigh-bourhood that developed in Guadeloupe and Martinique (Rey 2001, pp. 193–8).
143 Chamoiseau 1992, pp. 336–7.
144 Chamoiseau 1992, p. 360.
145 Chamoiseau 1992, p. 373.

While sometimes melancholy in regard to Noutéka, Chamoiseau's composition is not anti-urban.[146] *Texaco* presents urban life as a profound contradiction between the promise of freedom and persistent racial hierarchy, between cosmopolitan openness and economic parasitism. Dependent on plantation production, imperial networks, and the labour of carpenters like Esternome, urban spaces are 'bulbs full of connections and accumulated layers' incorporating differences.[147] These embody forms of structural violence and yet facilitate creative interactions among an array of inhabitants. They are 'oxygen bubbles' for and against slavery and colonialism.[148] More open to the world than plantations[149] they make creolisation unfold.[150] These visions of the urban as a tension-filled confluence of human differences and multiple temporalities do resonate with Lefebvrean themes, notably the idea of the urban as multi-rhythmic confluence of differences (centrality). In fact, *Texaco* illustrates Chamoiseau's conviction, that, after the exhaustion of revolt during and after slavery, new political possibilities are most likely to emerge in and through urbanising spaces.[151] Through the voices he mobilises, Chamoiseau brilliantly shows how rural imaginaries of revolt and emancipation before and after 1848 exhausted themselves and were recast within an urban context shaped by new territorial relations.[152]

Texaco and other neighbourhoods thus represent a convergence of convergences, a re-combination of past nodal points of connection: restructuring, struggle and imaginary. As a result of the aforementioned structural forces, Fort-de-France crystallised into a new territorial relation between 'centre' (central Fort-de-France and béké hilltop retreats) and 'periphery' (the just described subaltern neighbourhoods, many of which were built along the ocean or on the slopes surrounding the flat central city). Reflecting upon the linkages cutting across the dualism of colonial centre and surrounding *fau-*

---

146   Given the long-standing romantic, sometimes even exoticising, symbolisms that permeate various strands of Antillean literature, the writing of Glissant and the creole intellectuals included (Condé 1993), the charge of anti-urbanism seems plausible also against Chamoiseau (Martouzet 2001, pp. 50–2, 55–6). I find this charge unconvincing. In *Texaco* and a broad range of other texts, Chamoiseau's promotes particular strands of urbanism even as he reflects upon broader dynamics of urbanisation.
147   Chamoiseau 1997, p. 196.
148   Chamoiseau 1997, p. 188.
149   Chamoiseau 1992, p. 89; Chamoiseau 1997, p. 187.
150   Chamoiseau 1997, p. 183.
151   Chamoiseau 1997, p. 182; Kassab-Charfi 2012, p. 77.
152   Chamoiseau 1992, pp. 218–23, 360, 401.

bourgs,[153] Marie-Sophie Laborieux makes it clear that this relationship is complex, combining avoidance and exclusion with exchange, domination with invisibility, separation with circulation:

> The old neighbourhoods joined up to surround and circumvent the town centre (*l'En-ville*), connected by families, tied together by exchange. We navigated around the centre, entered it to draw from its energies, subverted it in order to live.[154]

In her account, Laborieux relives this Fort-de-France territorial relationship as an employee of békés and middle-class mulattos (and, later, as a hawker of food) in the old colonial town, and as an occasional resident of informal neighbourhoods (le Quartier des misérables/Terres-Sainville, Morne-Abélard, and finally Texaco). She embodies and traverses the socio-spatial divides between centre and periphery through wage labour, violent sexual relations and rape suffered at the hand of her employers, and, finally, friendships and love affairs with other residents and workers.

Laborieux relays the political possibilities that this new centre-periphery constellation harboured. Some of these possibilities clearly overflow horizontal metaphors of deterritorialisation (mangrove) and the notion of creole urbanism (as open-ended physical and social mixing). The 1959 revolt pointed to one such possibility: the capacity of the new ring of subaltern spaces claiming central Fort-de-France not just fleetingly, for three days, but permanently, as part of an anti-colonial revolution. Marie-Sophie Laborieux does not claim to have assumed a role in the revolt akin to the women who contributed to the Battle of Algiers, for example. But she does recall that in the course of the events,

> The CRS [*Compagnies républicaines de sécurité*, French riot police] were routed by the crowds of Black people that burst out of *Sainte-Thérèse, Morne-Pichevin, Trénelle, Terres-Saintville, Morne Abélard, Rive Droite* ... Usually tied down outside of the city centre, these neighbourhoods went on the attack to express their pain and to shake off the shackles the city (*En-ville*) had put on them .... They destroyed the hotel *Europe* whose owner had called the police, they set on fire cars and police stations. At night, barricades went up. Bands of yelling demonstrators roamed freely,

---

153   Terral and Sélise 2018.
154   Chamoiseau 1992, p. 406.

thwarting any attempt by the CRS to pursue them. A strong fellow was hit
by a grenade and died. The city was on fire for two or three nights. The
prefect thought that he had a revolution on his hands.[155]

Despite its many limitations, the movement seemed to confirm what at least
some authorities had already conjured up earlier: the spectre of urban warfare
akin to Algeria and Vietnam.[156] In *Texaco*, Chamoiseau gives us only a glimpse
of what might have been Martinique's most well-known movement to the 'right
to the city', that is, a claim to power/centrality emanating from peripheralised
social spaces. The spatial dynamics of that movement and the bloody repression that ended it is however fully covered in Confiant's literary reconstruction
Allée des Soupirs,[157] which was published shortly after *Texaco* and can be seen
as a politically charged companion volume to *Texaco*.

What *Texaco* the book – and the story of the successful establishment and
solidification of Texaco the neighbourhood – does at a greater length is to
present us with a second set of arguments about the condition of possibility of
creole urbanism: a spatialised compromise resulting from relations of conflict
and cooperation between the main political forces gravitating around Fort-
de-France City Hall and the French prefecture. We thus gather that the main
beneficiaries of the new socio-spatial constellation of Fort-de-France were the
Communists and then the PPM under the leadership of Aimé Césaire. As Marie-
Sophie Laborieux reports:

> But Césaire, Black like us, brought us into politics. Like a Roman Emperor,
> he came to see us, in the *Quartier des Misérables*, in *Trenelle*, in *Rive-Droite*,
> in *Morne Abélard*, in *Sainte-Thérèse*. He was not afraid of getting his hands
> dirty; seeing him was exhilarating. We rushed in order to carry him across
> the dirty puddles and keep his shoes from getting stained. He convinced
> us we could become something else. To see this regular Black man in such
> high places, so powerful, gave us an enthusiastic image of ourselves. From
> now on, we were certain we could get ourselves out of trouble and con-
> quer the city (*En-ville*). When he asked us to vote for him, we did so in
> unison and sent him to City Hall, where no one will ever be able to remove
> him until I die.[158]

---

155 Chamoiseau 1992, pp. 400–1.
156 Chamoiseau 1992, pp. 391–2.
157 Confiant 1994.
158 Chamoiseau 1992, p. 320.

Césaire's electoral victory in 1945 sealed his controversial entry into the circles of political rule then dominated by assimilationist mulatto middle classes, which were deeply hostile both to his Blackness and to his communism, as Laborieux recounts.[159] Inhabitants descended onto the central city, the social space of merchants and middle classes. The ensuing mayhem signalled 'a revenge exacted upon the central city [*l'En-ville*], a genuine advance of our obscure conquest', according to Laborieux.[160] Ultimately, advancing upon *l'En-ville* was not just an electoral feat. It yielded a lasting socio-political bloc linking subaltern neighbourhoods to City Hall.

A big part of *Texaco* is devoted to the inhabitants' efforts to stay on swampy and hilly lands located next to the site of the American multinational (which was run by a local *béké*). These efforts centred on the manifold and daily 'horizontal' practices of 'quiet encroachement'[161] which are typical of informal politics in other places. But, under the leadership of Laborieux, who represents a type of female political leadership not found in the main texts by Fanon and Lefebvre, these daily (re-)productive practices fused with organised politics, collective actions to beat back efforts by the *béké* owner and the CRS to evict residents. Relative to these actions, Césaire and communist militants played a two-sided role. At one level, they were a mobilising force. Since they understood the informal neighbourhoods as a new social base, they organised them into a counterweight to békés and the national police under the prefect:

> With Césaire at their helm, the communists spoke up, threatened, denounced, and made a terrible racket. They had turned the people from the old neighbourhoods into a popular army. They had understood that this misery of wooden crates and fibrocement was ready to be summoned; the inhabitants were ready for action at the first sign of blood, eager to join any flag, any dream that would open the doors to the city (*En-ville*). The communists had understood that their old troops, those of the fields and the sugar factories, had left, taking the old colonial roads and leaving behind the mountain paths to settle down here, right at the entrance to the city (*En-ville*). A proletariat without factories, without workshops, without work, frantically looking for petty jobs, struggling to stay afloat, carving out an existence amongst smouldering ruins.[162]

---

159 Chamoiseau 1992, p. 318.
160 Chamoiseau 1992, pp. 322–3.
161 Bayat 2013.
162 Chamoiseau 1992, p. 402.

Yet, even as representatives of City Hall denounced colonialism and slavery and aided resistance with legal support, they also tried to deflect confrontations by working to convince residents to relocate to other neighbourhoods undergoing renovation.[163] *Texaco* thus underlines that Césaire, the Communists and the PPM did not challenge the ruling classes frontally. They mediated, and, in the process, helped reorganise, even consolidate the colonial relation on the island. The famous 'Césaire effect' limited the brutality and extent of evictions, yes.[164] But Césaire's City Hall redirected residents' political energies into strategies to 'harden' (*durcifier*) neighbourhoods like Texaco with materials and urban reforms: concrete, infrastructure, social housing, social security payments and financial support for self-built housing.[165]

5   After Texaco: Martinique between Dystopia and Revolt

The struggles for Texaco end with a concrete victory: a permanent Texaco and the relocation of the Texaco facility. The béké owner of this facility retreats to his White enclave, admitting to Laborieux of having lost the battle, but not the war.[166] Texaco's residents' efforts to have their housing regularised and their existence recognised (which Césaire selectively advocated for)[167] thus had larger, but also more ambiguous implications. They helped implement the urban strategies that forged a new power bloc and reorganised colonial hegemony on the island. *Texaco* itself is not consistently critical of 'papa Césaire' and his role as paternalist figure, engineer of political rule and moderniser of Martinique.[168] In its pages, the socio-political ambivalence of a reformed departmental Fort-de-France dovetails with the ambivalent promise of creole urbanism. In *Texaco*, neither the former nor the latter open to political independence or social revolution (even as they both embody struggles, aspirations, and imaginaries that exceed, in literary form, contemporary reality).

In a few parts of the book, darker clouds gather to overshadow its cautiously optimistic conclusion, however. Chamoiseau warns about an emerging threat

---

163   Chamoiseau 1992, pp. 394–5.
164   Chamoiseau 1992, pp. 452–5.
165   Chamoiseau 1992, pp. 454–5, 394–403. On the policies that related to these strategies, see
        Martouzet 2001, pp. 145–53.
166   Chamoiseau 1992, pp. 464–6.
167   Césaire 2016b.
168   Chamoiseau 1992, p. 454.

to the tenuous creole equilibrium embodied in Fort-de-France's territorial relations. He paints a picture of the city turned into overgrown hydrocephalus, a
monstrous babylon.

> But the city represents a danger, it becomes megalopolis and never stops;
> it petrifies and silences the countryside the way Empires used to suffocate
> their surrounding regions; on the ruins of the nation-state, it erects itself
> into a plurinational, transnational, supranational, cosmopolitan monster,
> a sort of demented creole, and becomes the one and only dehumanised
> frame for the human species.[169]

In returning to a long-standing concern, Chamoiseau cites his *urbaniste* to
express a critique of untrammelled, standardised urbanisation (automobilisa-
tion, sprawling urban deconcentration, central-city disinvestment) and what
he sees as its broader causes and consequences (import dependency, food
insecurity, superficially diverse cultural homogenisation).[170] Originating in the
postwar period, these forces link extended and concentrated urbanisation to
invert the historical geography built by the slave-based plantation economy.
They not only engulf the central and peripheral spaces captured in *Texaco*.
They threaten to explode and pave over the very bundled practices of creole
urbanism, the struggles that made them possible, and the memories they still
contain. As a result, creole and creolisation are reduced to mere local decor of
capitalist urbanism.

Texaco thus does more than trace an ambiguous victory. It also anticipates
the dystopian future Patrick Chamoiseau's details in a recent murder mystery.
Published in 2017, *J'ai toujours aimé la nuit* (I always like the night) paints a
grim picture of Martinique. Its main character is a serial killer who recounts
and rationalises his bloody exploits while holding a gun to the head of the
acting police commander. As the killer (*tueur*) narrates his efforts to avenge
the 'sins' of pimps, dealers and drug traffickers that he finds 'inadmissible' on
the island (along with the 'foreigners' from Haiti, the Dominican Republic, and
St. Lucia), it becomes clear that the killer experiences, imagines, and patholo-
gises urban life from the seclusion of his bungalow and the obsessively clean
interior of his car. For him, urban Martinique is not defined by particular places:
working-class neighbourhoods and housing estates, where he sees little but
addiction and gratuitous violence; and privileged enclaves, which express the

---

169   Chamoiseau 1992, p. 455.
170   Chamoiseau 1992, pp. 443–4.

colonial arrogance of the White descendants of slave owners (*békés*). For the killer, urban life announces itself by the roundabouts (*ronds-points*) and the billboards (*panneaux publicitaires*) along the arterial roads and highways that connect these places with industrial zones, warehouses and *hypermarchés*.[171] Moving around these landscapes, 'it is as if another world, or the world itself, opened up in the heart of our Martinique',[172] a world that has 'swallowed' the people who had arrived from the hills and plantations in the course of the twentieth century to settle in a ring of neighbourhoods surrounding the confines of the original colonial town of Fort-de-France.[173]

Chamoiseau's murder mystery takes in a dystopian direction the Antillean literary traditions that have provided sharp insights into the many historical and geographical layers of Martinique and its sister islands. Chamoiseau's recent literary statement captures a veritable socio-spatial inversion of Martinique's former plantation geography. While under slavery, life was dominated by the plantations that covered most of the island (and relegated town life to its physical edges), today Martinican lives exist in a gravitational force centred on the agglomeration of Fort-de-France that visibly dominates the built form, relays most activities across the island, supersedes the colonial town centre – faubourg relationship at the heart of *Texaco*, and grows demographically without major recourse to rural-urban migration, which was the characteristic driving force of urbanisation still in the mid-twentieth century.[174] Chamoiseau's vision of urban(ising) Martinique thus clearly resonates with Henri Lefebvre's hypothesis about the complete urbanisation of society, which we have argued must be recast with the help of Frantz Fanon's understanding of the role of spatial organisation in (de-)colonisation. With Texaco and his latest novel, Chamoiseau shows what it means to say that the urban field develops unevenly in part because it is fractured by historically shifting territorial relations between dominant, (central) and dominated (peripheral) social spaces. Through his work, we know how these shifting territorial relations refract earlier spatial divides between city and non-city, that is, in this case town and plantation, town and hillside, formal and informal social spaces.

While *Texaco* preserved radical spatial imaginaries in its otherwise ambiguous representation of urbanising Martinique, *J'ai toujours aimé la nuit* no longer offers any political openings, let alone the ones Lefebvre and Fanon gestured towards in the *Urban Revolution* and 'Algeria Unveiled', respectively.

---

171   Chamoiseau 2017, pp. 37–40.
172   Chamoiseau 2017, p. 38.
173   Chamoiseau 2017, p. 40.
174   Martouzet 2001, pp. 22, 125–31; Rey 2001, p. 58; Terral and Sélise 2018.

And yet the grim landscapes in Chamoiseau's murder mystery are the same landscapes that mediated the 2009 revolts and general strikes against high prices in Guadeloupe, Guyana, Martinique (as well as La Réunion). At the time, Chamoiseau himself underlined the significance of these movements. By politicising the indignities that flow from economic dependency and racially hierarchised class rule, these movements highlighted the colonial realities of life in overseas France.[175] In turn, the movements were also caught within socio-political constraints that seem to offer no way out of these realities. While key players (including some left labour activists, particularly in Guadeloupe) remained committed to independent Antillean futures, the social demands for equality, dignity and improved material conditions assumed the presence of the French state. In Martinique, certainly (but less in Guadeloupe), these demands overshadowed if not ignored the question of political status. This is why Chamoiseau, along with a number of other intellectuals, including Glissant, argued in a manifesto published during the events, that the 'prosaic' demands of the movements for basic necessities must be complemented by 'poetic' demands that could lay the foundation for socio-ecological and creole cultural alternatives to departmental dependency.[176]

Chamoiseau's work as a whole has thus not done what others have suggested: make a (postcolonial) theoretical virtue out of the considerable empirical social and political obstacles that block 'sovereign futures' in the Antilles.[177] In fact, reading the island landscapes depicted in *J'ai toujours aimé la nuit* in a less dystopian fashion gives us clues about the spatial dynamics through which the 2009 revolt developed. Not only in Guadeloupe (the epicentre of the movement) but also in Martinique, mobilisations tied occupations of traffic roundabouts to various types of blockades and central city mass demonstrations.[178] By transcending and recasting the relation between central city and surrounding neighbourhoods captured so well in *Texaco*, these mobilisations reshaped the meaning of the right to the city by producing new types of centrality out of the dispersed and disarticulated fragments of the islands' geographies. In so doing, the 2009 movements 'anticipated' by a

---

175   Chamoiseau 2010; see also Meylon-Reinette and Durpaire 2009.
176   Breleur 2009.
177   Yarimar Bonilla did just that when she moved from her sharp analyses of the 2009 movements in Guadeloupe (2015) to a project that embraces non-sovereignty as a theoretical programme informed by an anti-universalist version of postcolonial studies. As she herself admits (2017, p. 203), this move prolongs theoretically the limitations and contradictions of the 2009 movement, which otherwise did not uniformly abandon the problem of sovereignty and independence.
178   Odin 2019, pp. 220–72, 299–301.

decade the political geography of the yellow vest movement in France, both in the overseas territories and in the hexagone.[179]

To fully appreciate these spatial dynamics of mobilisation, one needs to do what neither Chamoiseau nor Fanon (nor Lefebvre) did: consider the *possibility* that in some, but of course not all historical situations, class struggle and anti-colonialism are articulated by labour movements, not the peasantry, the lumpenproletariat and the petty bourgeoisie. As Pierre Odin has demonstrated most recently, the 2009 revolt expressed a longer process through which such tension-ridden articulations were generated in the French Antilles, in Guadeloupe above all, but also in Martinique. There, the left and subaltern aspirations for independence of the 1960s were selectively carried into the labour movement and then recast – absorbed, submerged, redirected – through workers' struggles situated in various points of the socio-spatial landscape, in agriculture, in the ports, and in the public sector.[180] The role of the labour movement in selectively rearticulating Antillean anti-colonialism points to the fact that Fanon's treatment of the peasantry, the lumpen and workers in his political writings could not account for the ways in which the class struggle has 'traversed fields as well as streets' in the French Antilles,[181] where the historical relationship between peasantry and the proletariat developed in qualitatively different ways than in Algeria. The particular role of the labour movement also points to a certain social distance between intellectual treatments of creole (as Antillean cultural specificity articulated by figures representing informalised life) and working-class struggles (which emerge from creole subaltern lives but may not bother turning creole into a distinct, cultural terrain of struggle).

6   Conclusion: On the Coeval Character of the Urban

In *Texaco*, the urban holds the key to grasping the socio-spatial transformation of Martinique. Understood not as thing or a mere place but a project, a claim and a contradictory node of connections, Chamoiseau's notions of the urban helps us retrace the historical transfiguration of the peculiar divide between city and non-city (plantation, hillside) that shaped the history of the colonial relation in Martinique and the spatial imaginaries that form an integral part of that relation. In this respect, *Texaco* holds a number of lessons for urban

---

179   Kipfer 2019.
180   Odin's main focus is on the *Union Générale des Travaillers de la Guadeloupe* UGTG, the *Confédération Général du Travail Guadeloupe* (CGTG) and the CGT Martinique (CGTM).
181   Pierre-Charles 2011, pp. 89–90; Blérald 1984.

researchers. First, it shows how material and globally networked dynamics of urbanisation have complicated established understandings of urban geographies, while also remaining intimately bound up with stark territorial relations of domination, some of which rearticulate earlier historical geographies and spatial oppositions. Chamoiseau's literary work makes it clear that Martinique is being covered by the urban tapestry produced in part by French administrative practices, the tourist economy and circuits of mass consumption. It surely is a part of planetary networks of urbanisation. And yet, the island remains shaped by the deeply racialised relations between centres of decision-making and the spaces inhabited by slave descendants. These relations recompose, in the contemporary context, the particular entrenched spatial divides in Martinique's history as a plantation economy since the seventeenth century. The implication is clear: the boundary-defying dynamics of urbanisation must be investigated for the ways in which they mediate distinct historical geographies of rule.

Second, *Texaco* underlines the importance of spatial imaginaries in the political history of subjugated peoples, an importance that has been forcefully underlined in both Black radical and Marxist traditions. More specifically, it sheds light on how such imaginaries help produce space and relay comparatively distinct relationships between city and non-city in the urbanisation process. The book chronicles urbanisation as being mediated through twin processes of agricultural transformation and metropolitan expansion, inextricably tied to each other via intense processes of economic restructuring, migration and political struggle. In so doing, Texaco also represents the shifting symbolic terrains of political engagement. It demonstrates how the anti-urbanisms that informed some struggles against slavery and colonialism reached an impasse in the postwar period, during departmentalisation. Yet Texaco also powerfully underlines the persistence of land struggles in (neo-)colonial contexts, as Gillian Hart and Fernando Coronil have pointed out in relation to other globalised regions.[182] In *Texaco*, memories of anti-colonial conflict, both on the plantations and in the hills, continues to shape contemporary conflicts over land, recognition, and political power. They do so now *within* the urbanising fields of departmentalised Martinique, thus pushing beyond the city-countryside distinction that continued to shape Fanon's work (and that never had the same meaning in Martinique as it did in Western Europe or North Africa). Of course, in other contexts, land questions will be politically articulated differently in relationship to urbanisation. As we will see in the next chapter, Indigenous rad-

---

182   Hart 2002; Coronil 2000.

ical debates in Canada also foreground the land question, and this in ways that sometimes cut against the grain of colonial urban history. Research on comparative urbanisation must therefore proceed in a relational manner,[183] one that is attentive to the situated meaning and ongoing contestation of claims to city and countryside/non-city within the broader historical geographies of capitalist development.

Third, *Texaco* thus allows us to advance arguments about comparative urbanism. Following Harootunian (as well as Robinson and Benjamin), one can say that the urban(ising) world is coeval in ways similar to modernity, that regime of the new that embodies fragments of the past in enduringly distinct ways. It represents a form (of centrality/difference) that is infused with qualitatively distinct historical-geographical content. The urban is neither a result of European diffusionism nor a function of absolutely relative cultural traits. Urban Martinique is contemporaneous with imperial, including French urbanism; indeed, it is part of urban extensions that cross the Atlantic and the Caribbean seas. And yet *Texaco* shows that the symbolic meanings of town and non-town in Martinican urbanisation are strongly shaped by the colonial-capitalist dynamics that have transformed the urban/non-urban divides of its plantation economy as well as organised transnational urban networks. In Chamoiseau's Martinique the urban appears as a particular form of centrality/difference in a wider urbanisation process even as it is fraught with particular contradictions. In *Texaco*, tensions between real-existing differences and desires for a different urban life run through creole urbanism itself. They express themselves as a clash between transversal cultural mixing, the deep socio-spatial divides of racialised capitalism and the aspirations that exceed both.

Fourth, *Texaco* speaks to a theme that is central to what Ananya Roy has termed new geographies of urban theory: informality and informalisation.[184] In its fictional ways, *Texaco* does indeed deal with informalised work and informalised housing, or, what one might also call, with less reliance on the vocabulary of Development and with more emphasis on the inherent dynamics of capitalism, wageless life[185] and proletarian, popular or subaltern urbanisation.[186] In effect, Chamoiseau does so by cutting across key approaches to the problem. *Texaco* places informality at the interface of everyday practices,[187] globally articulated structural forces (agricultural restructuring, structural underem-

183   Hart 2018a.
184   Roy 2009a.
185   Denning 2010; also Azhar and Khan 2020.
186   Gallissot 2002; Streule 2018; Streule et al. 2020; Mukhopadhyay, Zérah, and Denis 2020.
187   Simone 2010.

ployment, rural-urban migration)[188] and spatialised forms of state intervention.[189] As a consequence, *Texaco* demonstrates the politically contradictory
character of informalised labour and urbanism. Everyday life in *Texaco* embodies profound tensions between courage and despair, agency and vulnerability, collective mobilisation and individual ruthlessness. The novel valorises as
heroic the efforts of survival artists and their capacity to destabilise 'solid'
Fort-de-France by invading it with fleeting, individualised, subsistence-driven
'quiet encroachements'.[190] Yet it is also clear about the role of the colonial state
and organised politics in inhabitant lives. It narrates how residents of Texaco
translate the tensions in their daily life into explicitly political – organised
and collective – forms of action that help restructure the colonial relation in
Martinique: transforming territorial relations (between central and peripheral
social spaces), changing the balance of political forces condensed in the extended state, and, finally, changing the meaning of creole urbanism as a fusion of
'formal' and 'informal' elements. A tale of a territorial compromise, *Texaco* in
effect evades one-sidedly celebratory or pessimistic treatments of (in)formal-
isation.[191] It forces us to move from easy presuppositions about the political
character of (in)formalised life to strategies of investigating how shantytown
dwellers become subjects of political mobilisation, whether in critical, radical
or reactionary fashion.

Finally, and paradoxically, *Texaco* demonstrates the continued relevance of
counter-colonial critique for urban analysis. As an exponent of the creole literary movement, Chamoiseau mobilises organic, flow-like metaphors against
colonial urban renewal. These metaphors resonate with Deleuze's and Guattari's rhizomatic, vitalist philosophy. Indirectly, *Texaco* thus allows us to make
some preliminary points about the neo-Deleuzian currents that have asserted
themselves in comparative urban research. Chamoiseau insists on the subversive character of informal urbanism, which he likens to a mangrove-like –
multi-rooted, complexly entangled – force. But in *Texaco* itself, the creolising
dynamics of informal urbanism cannot escape the complexly hierarchised confines of departmentalised Martinique; they are built on it and the struggles
that redefined the colonial relations on the island. They thus do not exhaust
Chamoiseau's own complex narrative and, indeed, the very creole/collage form
it takes. For purposes of comparative research, creolising or rhizomatic ontolo-

---

188   Portes, Castells, and Benton 1989; Davis 2006.
189   Castells 1983; Roy 2009b.
190   Bayat 2013.
191   Compare Mike Davis 2006 with Richard Pithouse 2008; Solomon Benjamin 2008 with
       Anurupa Roy 2016.

gies and their horizontal, deterritorialising tendencies are limited in two basic ways: they cannot, in and of themselves, grasp the specificities of the historical geographies (such as colonial capitalism) they cut across; and they do not tell us enough about how to transform actually-existing diversities, creolised or otherwise, with forms of political action that can challenge the multi-layered, also vertical relations of domination and exploitation that fracture these diversities.[192] In this context, neo-Fanonian quests to break with colonial rule remain pertinent. They keep alive the search for genuinely other possibilities (as *Texaco* also does, albeit only indirectly, by making resurface historical spatial imaginaries through its collage-like form). The 2009 revolt (and the supportive manifesto co-signed by Chamoiseau) also underscores, however, that such a search requires sustained reflections about the subaltern forces capable of advancing genuine decolonisation in, against and beyond colonial relations and ruling blocs in the Antilles.

192 For sharp notes on Marx and Deleuze, see Garo 2008 and Lecercle 2005. Work to bring into conversation Deleuze, Guattari, and Lefebvre has barely begun and remains unsatisfactory. See Lefebvre's musings in *Le temps des méprises* (1975, pp. 172–3, 209–10) and Attilio Belli 2012.

CHAPTER 4

Is This Pipeline Urban? Indigenous Resurgence and Extended Urbanisation in Canada

In this chapter, I bring the Lefebvre-Fanon lineage to what sometimes goes by Canada, or the Northern part of what in some Indigenous traditions is called Turtle Island. My initial focus will be on recent Indigenous and Indigenous-led mobilisations against extractive infrastructure projects, including pipelines. These struggles help us understand not only an Achilles heel of capitalist accumulation. Insofar as they are about Indigenous claims to land and jurisdiction, they also allow us to grasp a fundamental colonial dimension of Canadian capitalism and the Canadian state. This discussion will provide an opening to interpreting the 'place' of settler urbanisation in relationship to the colonial relation that continues to shape the Canadian social formation. A key focal point will be the spatial imaginaries that inform resistance and that one can also find in the writings of key Indigenous radicals from the period of Red Power in the 1960s and 1970s (Howard Adams, Lee Maracle, Maria Campbell) to the current period of Indigenous resurgence (Leanne Simpson, Audra Simpson, Glen Coulthard, Taiaiake Alfred, Rick Monture). These imaginaries dovetail with Fanonian insights about the violence and strategic opportunities generated by colonial territorial compartmentalisation in all its forms. In so doing, they push towards dynamic notions of place and network that put the land question at the centre of colonial historical geography as a whole. These notions resonate with dynamics of political mobilisation and challenge colonial time-space.

Before we get to these main sections, I will explore two conditions that make it possible to let both Fanon and Lefebvre travel to North America. First, I discuss points of contact between theories of Indigenous resurgence and other radical intellectual currents. In particular, I will focus on the Glen Coulthard's project to confront Indigenous radicalism with Marxian and tricontinental, including Fanonian, traditions of theory and practice. Reconstructing internationalist and left-wing lineages of Indigenous politics, Coulthard's contribution invites us to revisit current debates about settler colonialism and settler colonial urbanisation in and beyond the confines of Canadian political economy. Second, I will resume the discussion of extended and concentrated urbanisation in colonial context begun in Chapter 3, where we focused on creole urbanism as a particular mediation of the colonial relation in Martinique. Reviewing current debates on planetary urbanisation, I will suggest that a neo-Lefebvrean take on extended and concentrated urbanisation can be brought into contact with Indigenous anti-colonial perspectives provided that such an approach recognises that urbanisation and the urban are not everything. While of eminent, and growing material and strategic importance, urban questions do not exhaust social life as a whole but mediate the social order and everyday life. As such, they remain open to fundamental political and intellectual challenges, including those emerging from Indigenous anti-colonial vantage points.

From my perspective in Toronto, the need to link Marxian and Indigenous anti-colonial lineages with urban research is evident for biographical, political and intellectual reasons. The place where I learn and research, York University, is not only similar morphologically and socially to the University of Nanterre, the postwar expansion campus in suburban Paris where Henri Lefebvre held his lectures in the 1960s. While in close proximity to racialised and stigmatised working-class districts, the university is also located on Indigenous land and situated just one hundred metres north of Line 9, the pipeline that runs from Sarnia to Montreal through the Toronto area. From 2013 to 2015 in particular, the project faced intense resistance against the plans of energy company Enbridge to link the Alberta tar sands to Eastern oil refineries by reversing the flow of the pipeline. In the early 2010s, struggles around Line 9 and other pipelines were part of a broader political and intellectual Indigenous resurgence, including the *Idle No More* movement that got off the ground in 2012. This resurgence has left more traces even than the standoff between the Mohawk of Kanesatake and the Canadian army in 1990, which took place exactly at the time when I first learned in detail about the centrality of Indigenous questions in North America shortly after landing in Toronto in 1989. Needless to say, the political leadership exercised by *Idle No More*, as well as *Black Lives Matter*,[1] has also shaped my workplace, from student mobilisations to faculty politics. For this reason alone, linking historical materialism and Indigenous theory is more pertinent than ever.

---

1 On the multiple organisational and intellectual connections between *Idle No More* and *Black Lives Matter* in Canada, see Maynard and Simpson 2020; and Ware and Dias 2020. In some ways, these connections resume older linkages between Black and Indigenous politics, including the links between Black and Red Power in the 1960s and 1970s.

1   Indigenous Resurgence, Marxism and Settler Colonialism

For Indigenous nations to live, capitalism must die. And for capitalism to die, we must actively participate in the construction of Indigenous altern- atives to it.[2]

I firmly believe that the philosophy of my ancestors lines up quite tidily with the philosophy of communism.[3]

This oppression of the native people is so deeply rooted in the capitalist system that it cannot be completely eliminated without eliminating cap- italism itself.[4]

In their introduction to *Theorising Native Studies*, editors Audra Simpson and Andrea Smith lay out the intellectual terrain of critical Indigenous theory today. Describing the manifold connections between Indigenous radicalism and other intellectual traditions, they insist that there is political value in 'an engagement with intellectual work from ... other sites of struggle'.[5] To be clear, such an engagement is to take place on the terms of Indigenous intellectu- als and militants. Simpson and Smith wrote against the background of the *Idle No More* movement against the aggressive assimilationism and neoliberal extractivism of Prime Minister Stephen Harper's Conservative regime.[6] Indi- genous mobilisations (against the continuing murder of Indigenous women, new attempts to 'terminate' Indigenous peoples as distinct in law and prop- erty status, and countless dispossessive projects tied to resource extraction) underscored the power of self-determined Indigenous action. For many, it also foregrounded the task of 'rebuilding our own [Indigenous] house' above and beyond dismantling the master's.[7] In this context shaped by a renewed quest for Indigenous self-determination, Simpson and Smith's point simply under- lines that the imperative of autonomy is not to be confused with intellectual or political isolation.

Next to Leanne and Audra Simpson, Glen Coulthard's work represents an- other crucial contribution to 'Indigenous resurgence', this contemporary con-

---

2   Coulthard 2014, p. 173.
3   Maracle 1996, p. 120.
4   Adams 1975, p. 205.
5   Simpson and Smith 2014, p. 11.
6   Palmater 2015; Simpson 2016.
7   Simpson 2011, p. 32.

stellation of projects to articulate Indigenous art and scholarship with land-based practices and struggles for self-determination. In *Red Skin, White Masks* and subsequent work, Coulthard has developed a three-way dialogue between Indigenous authors (including Leanne and Audra Simpson as well as Taiai-ake Alfred), Marxian traditions (from Marx to Mao) and revolutionary anti-colonial currents (represented most prominently by Frantz Fanon). In so doing, Coulthard rejoins a long, if sometimes submerged lineage of political praxis that has stressed the crucial importance of Indigenous questions in the Americas for historical materialism while in turn considering Indigenous liberation in communist and internationalist terms. This lineage ranges from José Carlos Mariàtegui to Evo Morales in Latin America,[8] and from D'Arcy McNickle and Archie Phinney to Roxanne Dunbar-Ortíz and Nick Estes in the United States.[9] In Canada, where Cold War anti-Communism weighed slightly less heavily than in the USA, Coulthard's work rejoins Indigenous socialist currents in his Yellowknife Dene nation as well as intellectuals of the Red Power generation like Howard Adams and Lee Maracle, who appropriated insights from left-wing and other anti-colonial traditions for the purpose of Indigenous liberation.

Coulthard echoes these earlier voices when he urges the non-Indigenous left to take Indigenous resurgence and the realities of dispossessive settler colonialism most seriously.[10] For this purpose, his *Red Skin, White Masks* also levels a two-sided theoretical challenge to Marxian and Fanonian perspectives. First, he is adamant that Marx can only survive if the Marxian tradition divests itself of the developmentalist strands that have informed some of its currents. Drawing in part on Marx's comments on original accumulation, his letters to Vera Zasulich, and the articulation of modes of production debate in the 1970s, he insists that the formation of capitalism is not a linear-progressive development from one mode to another. In colonial contexts, the transition to capitalism represents a struggle-inflected, often protracted transformation of both colonial and colonised modes of life.[11] If one is to understand this dynamic, if eminently slanted process of transformation in colonies shaped by mass settlement, one must pay special attention to role of land dispossession in the construction of the colonial social relation. In turn, Coulthard reminds us, this dispossessive colonial relation remains an ongoing and active force shaping class relations and accumulation processes in settler colonies.

---

8   Mariàtegui 1971; Becker 2006; Dunbar-Ortìz 2007, 2009; Webber 2011.
9   Balthaser 2016a, 2016b; Dunbar-Ortìz 2014, 2016; Estes 2019a.
10   Coulthard 2017b.
11   Coulthard 2014, pp. 9–11, 187. Coulthard refers to Kulchyski 1992 and Foster-Carter 1977.

Second, Coulthard says that Fanonians, too, need to pay particular attention to the comparatively specific character of the colonial relation in White settler colonies, which imposes particular constraints on anti-colonial strategies. Coulthard mobilises various Fanonian insights for his critique of theorists of recognition from G.W.F. Hegel to Seyla Benhabib by way of Charles Taylor and Nancy Fraser. But, Coulthard argues, the permanence of settlement and the crushing weight of assimilation (from physical extermination to socio-cultural destructuring and legal-political recognition) faced by acutely minoritarian Indigenous nations in White settler colonies are such that Fanon's emphasis on the primacy of the liberation struggle in transforming native traditions and shaping new postcolonial cultures needs to be modified to effectively inform Indigenous *resurgence*: the project of recovering and reinventing land-related practices to develop Indigenous alternatives to colonial capitalism.[12] How so? By treating Indigenous traditions not as colonialism and its allies do, as folkloric caricatures, ossified relics from the past divorced from politics and material life. Instead of mimicking colonial culture, tradition must be considered as a creative, open-ended practice of handing down, that is a way of 'critically evaluating, reconstructing and redeploying Indigenous cultural forms in ways that seek to prefigure, alongside those with similar ethical commitments, radical alternatives to the structural and psychological facets of colonial domination'.[13]

Through such a reconstruction of egalitarian Indigenous currents, which loom larger than they do in traditions shaped by tributary societies,[14] it might be possible to see contours of Indigenous (and other) communist futures. Crucial here is, again, the land question. Coulthard wrote *Red Skin, White Masks* as the Conservative government was preparing to open the door to a private property right regime on Indigenous reserves in the very name of recognising Indigenous title and rights.[15] He reminds us that colonial dispossession is all about destroying Indigenous ways of living with and through the land. In this light, a proper challenge of settler colonialism involves more than reasserting control over land. Indigenous private property claims can also undercut the possibility of recreating Indigenous ways of life. Instead, regaining collective control over land requires an understanding of the social relations through

---

12   Coulthard 2014, pp. 148–9, 153.
13   Coulthard 2014, pp. 48–9. As Coulthard suggested in a response to Ciccariello-Maher 2016, links between his conception of tradition and Fanon's view about the relationship between promising and ossified aspects of colonised culture can be found in Fanon's 1956 address to the Congress of Black Writers and Artists in Paris entitled 'Racism and Culture' (Coulthard 2016; Fanon 1988, pp. 41–4).
14   Kulchyski 1992, 2017.
15   Pasternak 2015; Hall 2015.

which land is organised and acquires its very meaning: land 'as field of relationships of things [and people] to each other'.[16] Coulthard's point, that land
is a social relation and that egalitarian Indigenous traditions are tied to relational ethico-philosophical frameworks requires asking what Rick Monture, in
his work on Haudenosaunee debates at Grand River, says is a difficult question: 'What will we do with the land once we get it back?'[17] In Coulthard's view
of Indigenous resurgence, gaining land rights or winning the right to use the
'resources' of the land is essential but not sufficient for genuine decolonisation.

Echoing other dynamic, land-related, political and practice-oriented conceptions of Indigenous tradition,[18] Coulthard's redirection of Marx and Fanon
generates a most important point: the need to understand colonial relations as
forms of rule with changing characteristics. Rejecting developmentalist conceptions of capitalist development and revolutionary transformation, Coulthard urges us to study the colonially inflected articulation of modes of life by
analysing the terrain upon which this articulation has been organised in historically and geographically uneven ways: the modalities of struggle between
Indigenous nations and the colonial state. Discussing postwar Denendeh (the
five Dene regions in the North West Territories), he shows how through a generation of resistance and land claim negotiations there, 'recognition' (of Indigenous rights and titles) joined assimilation and dispossession in the contradictory
colonial relation permeating the Canadian state. The result: a partial but real
shift in the ideological and institutional terms in which Indigenous people
engage colonial society and understand themselves.[19] Combining continuity
and change, these shifting political realities explain the salience of Coulthard's
philosophical critique of recognition.[20] And they indicate that the stakes are
high for those who advance today a version of the autonomous, egalitarian, and
conservationist alternative development path the Dene proposed in the 1970s.

Of course, the settler colonial relation remains just that: a structurally violent relation of dispossession and assimilation that continues to be governed
to a significant extent by various forms of coercion. Ongoing efforts to destroy
Indigenous political arrangements by means of gendered violence, or 'settler
colonial misogyny' are particularly disturbing examples.[21] Nonetheless, prolif-

16   Coulthard 2014, p. 61.
17   Monture 2014, p. 213.
18   Alfred 2009a, pp. 197–8, 225, 247; Alfred 2009b, pp. 35, 39, 99–100, 117; Simpson 2011, pp. 17–
       20, 51; Monture 2015, pp. 11, 196; Lawrence 2012, p. 279; Estes 2019a, pp. 21–2, 167.
19   Coulthard 2014, pp. 77–8.
20   Coulthard 2014, pp. 25–49.
21   Simpson 2016. Coulthard concurs, drawing on Dory Nason, Patricia Monture, and Bonita
       Lawrence (2014, pp. 91–6, 101–2, 177–8).

erating legal-institutional forms of recognition have introduced a hegemonic element into the settler colonial relation: accommodation. As Coulthard says with reference to the Dene,

> I would suggest that one of the negative effects of this power-laden process of discursive translation [of negotiating land claims agreements] has been a reorientation of the meaning of self-determination for many (but not all) Indigenous people in the North; a reorientation of Indigenous struggle from one that was once deeply *informed* by the land as a system of reciprocal relations and obligations (grounded normativity), which in turn informed our critique of capitalism in the period examined above, to a struggle that is now increasingly *for* land, understood now as [property and] material resource to be exploited in the capital accumulation process.[22]

If anti-capitalist projects of Indigenous resurgence are contingent upon reconstructing links between land and modes of life, current claims for land and institutional recognition have a tendency to uncouple land from non-capitalist conceptions of tradition as mode of life. The limited hegemonic aspects of the settler colonial relation need not entail any active affirmation of colonial rule, of course. But they result from what Lawrence has called changes in the 'terms of struggle' that regulate Indigenous conceptions of land, nationhood, jurisdiction, and personhood.[23] Treating colonialism as a dynamic political relation helps us develop a basic insight: that Indigenous resistance changes along with colonialism itself.[24]

Coulthard's approach is an excellent way to frame a discussion of White settler colonialism, and this for at least two reasons. Insofar as Coulthard returns to the Dene struggles against the Mackenzie Valley pipeline in the 1970s, he not only explores an earlier historical conjuncture that brought together Indigenous aspirations with a range of other currents, including Black radicalism, tricontinental liberation struggles and Chinese and Tanzanian perspectives on socialism.[25] In revisiting these aspirations, marked most famously by the *Dene Declaration* for alternative and self-determined development (1975) and the subsequent *Dene Agreement in Principle* (1976),[26] he also revisits a minor

---

22 Coulthard 2014, p. 78.
23 Lawrence 2004, p. 42.
24 Estes 2019a, p. 21.
25 Coulthard 2018, 2020.
26 Coulthard 2014, pp. 65–70.

but nonetheless important point of contact between Indigenous politics and what was then a young and emerging field, the so-called 'new' Canadian political economy.[27] Although this point of contact has been ignored too often,[28] it helps us understand how researchers began to grapple with the realities of settler colonialism in Canadian history: the ways in which genocidal elimination and mass settlement combined with the privileged, and increasingly active role of the Canadian state within British and American empires to shape the development of Canadian capitalism and its various deeply racialised features, including class formation, territorial organisation, migration policy and state repression.[29]

Since the 2000s, the study of settler colonialism has become a highly visible field of its own. Intervening in an intellectual context then shaped by deconstructive postcolonial theory, students and critics of settler colonialism have rightfully insisting that decolonisation be analysed as a richly material, not only metaphorical project, particularly where colonialism cannot be qualified with the prefix 'post'.[30] They have also underscored the importance of subjecting colonialism to comparative analysis. This comparative imperative has generated powerful insights into the central features of colonialisms defined by permanent and White-dominated mass settlement: the conquest of land and the quest to eliminate Indigenous presence for the purpose of settler sovereignty and private property.[31] Theoretically multi-form, settler colonial studies have not been immune to pitfalls, however. There has been, for example, a tendency to distinguish (White) settler colonialisms from other colonialisms schematically. This had led some to treat the relationship between land and labour, assimilation and exploitation, settlement and other colonial imperatives in an ideal-typical, even categorical instead of a dynamic and relational fashion that ties the settler colonial relation to other aspects of imperialism and capitalist development.[32] In this context, Coulthard's twin proposal to (1)

---

27   Watkins 1977.

28   Coburn 2016a, 2016b.

29   For a review of the early debates about settler colonialism in Canadian political economy, see Abele and Stasiulis 1987; Stasiulis and Jhappan 1995. For more recent perspectives, including those that connect settler colonial with other imperial aspects of Canadian capitalism and the Canadian state, see, for example, Gordon 2010; Klassen 2014; Shipley 2020; Smith 2019; Hall 2019.

30   Tuck and Yang 2012.

31   Wolfe 2001, 2006, 2013; Veracini 2010.

32   Wolfe himself has addressed some but not all of these problems (2013). For constructive critiques of these pitfalls, that is, critiques that do not question the central role of land, assimilation, and settler sovereignty, see Kelley 2017; Day 2015; Smith 2019; Camfield 2019; Burrill 2019.

situate colonial settlement, land dispossession, and assimilation as decisive features of a politically regulated, historically shifting relationship between distinct modes of life/production; and to (2) understand Indigenous mobilisation in internationalist and tricontinental terms, that is in relation to fourth and third world liberation movements, is crucial to avoiding methodological pitfalls in the study of settler colonialism.[33]

Coulthard's intervention also resonates with what has been one of the richest sub-fields in historical geography, political economy and urban research since the mid-2000s: the study of settler colonial geographies, including the analysis of settler urbanisation and the spatial dynamics of Indigenous movements.[34] Coulthard's emphasis on the historically shifting relationship between land dispossession and the various ways in which Canadian colonialism has been organised spatially sums up a crucial preoccupation in this field. As he said when explaining the assumptions that inform the Dachinta Bush University project he has helped develop:

> The other distinction that tends to get made in discussion of land-based education is the one between urban and rural experiences in relation to decolonisation and colonisation. I think that needs to be broken down, not only because Indigenous lands are also cities but because the experience of colonisation has been, if you look at it in a larger historical view, very similar. Indigenous peoples were dispossessed from their territories. This was fundamental in the construction of cities and urbanisation. Once you are removed from the land, and once you are removed from your reserve land base, you have to migrate elsewhere – and that's often

---

33   In its broad emphasis on modes of life/production, Coulthard's work rejoins Howard Adams (1975), Ron Bourgeault (1986, 1988), Peter Kulchysky (1992, 2016), Terry Wotherspoon and Vic Satzewich (2000), all of whom offered versions of a mode of production analysis to understand the historically shifting dynamics of colonialism and dispossession in North America. Coulthard's own approach could be expanded to elaborate in greater detail the relationship between what he calls the colonial and capital relation, and, more specifically, the historically shifting relation between land dispossession and labour exploitation in the development of colonialism and capitalism (as well as Indigenous life). In turn, his discussion of Fanon could also be enlarged in a comparative sense to discuss land, settlement and assimilation/elimination in colonial contexts that are not (typically) grouped under the rubric of settler colonialism: the Caribbean, West Africa, and North Africa (above all Algeria).

34   Barman 2007; Blomley 2004; Edwards 2010, Freeman 2010; D'Arcus 2010; Harris 2003, 2004; Hugill 2017; Tomiak 2011, 2016, 2017; Stanger-Ross 2008; Perry 2016; Toews 2018; Dorries, Henry, Hugill, McCreary, and Tomiak 2019; Dorries, Hugill, and Tomiak 2019; Porter and Yftachel 2019; Blatman-Thomas and Porter 2018.

to urban centres that were built on your or someone else's stolen land. This was a constitutive feature of what Marx termed primitive accumulation, dispossession, proletarianisation, market creation – but also the geographical, spatial reorganisation of populations through subsequent urbanisation. And now that very colonial process (in Marx's own terms) is again devouring Indigenous spaces within cities through gentrification of neighbourhoods we inhabit. So, this constant cycle of dispossession and violence and dispossession and displacement has happened to Indigenous peoples as much in cities as in has in land-based contexts. And, indeed, they are structurally related. So, when we can start seeing that as Indigenous peoples, we can start building a more effective movement that recognises those similarities, that what we are fighting against is essentially the same thing.[35]

Coulthard's take on the geography of Indigenous decolonisation echoes earlier Indigenous insights. Today, it also expresses a growing tendency among researchers of settler colonial urbanisation, which is to consider settler cities as nodes within broader colonial geographies as well as places 'embedded in broader Indigenous networks and territorial relations'.[36] As I will suggest cautiously, and as others have also recognised,[37] this attempt to situate Indigenous claims to particular spatial forms (reserve, settler city or other unceded land) within vast colonial and anti-colonial geographies also resonates with Lefebvrean themes, provided of course that one relate these to Indigenous conceptions of time-space.

2   Politics and the Urban: From the Urban Revolution to Planetary Urbanisation

Research on planetary urbanisation has developed in definite relationships to Henri Lefebvre's hypothesis about complete urbanisation: the formation of urban forcefields that engulf or supersede 'city' and 'country'.[38] Researchers have extended Lefebvre's hypothesis to challenge current urbanist ideologies ('the urban age') and develop epistemological and methodological cri-

---

35   Coulthard 2017b, p. 60.
36   Tomiak, McCreary, Hugill, Henry, and Dorries 2019, p. 3.
37   On the production of space and the right to the city in contexts shaped by settler colonialism and Indigenous resistance, see Tomiak 2011; Tomiak 2019, p. 111; Grandinetti 2019.
38   Lefebvre 2003a.

teria to avoid city- and state-centric assumptions in urban research.[39] They
have worked to unearth the political promises of extended urbanisation[40]
while linking extended urbanisation to accumulation by dispossession,[41] socio-
natural metabolism,[42] urbicide and the right to the city,[43] spatial imaginaries and ways of seeing.[44] Given that researchers of planetary urbanisation
have translated Lefebvre's theory of the urban/urbanisation, a brief return to
the *Urban Revolution* can sharpen our sense of current debates. As stated in
Chapter 1 and in previous formulations,[45] my point of departure is that Lefebvre's Marxism defies the dichotomies (between political economy and cultural studies, universality and particularity, abstract and concrete) that have
shaped English readings of Lefebvre in the 1980s and 1990s and that some
want to recast now, often in neo-Heideggerian terms, to classify urban theory
in ways that counterpose Marxism to postcolonial concerns instead of articulating Marxist and counter-colonial lineages.[46]

In previous chapters, I have also taken the position that Lefebvre-inspired
work must – and can – be stretched to link up with counter-colonial concerns. The point of this chapter is to push neo-Lefebvrean work on planetary
urbanisation to the point where lines of connection to settler urbanism and
Indigenous politics are intelligible. In a spirit of immanent critique,[47] I propose that neo-Lefebvrean research on planetary urbanisation can be so pushed,

39   Monte-Mór 2004; Schmid 2006, Brenner and Schmid 2014, 2015; Brenner 2014; Brenner
     and Katsikis 2014; Kanai 2014.
40   Monte-Mór 2004; Castriota and Tonucci 2018; Merrifield 2013, Arboleda 2016b; Kanai 2014.
41   Sevilla-Buitrago 2014; Khan and Karak 2018.
42   Arboleda 2016a; Angelo and Wachsmuth 2014.
43   Lesutis 2020.
44   Angelo 2017.
45   Kipfer 1998, 2002, 2004; Kipfer, Goonewardena, Schmid, and Milgrom 2008.
46   Kate Derickson (2015) took this step most explicitly, and I would argue misleadingly, by
     grafting a distinction between urbanisation 1 and urbanisation 2 onto Dipesh Chakra-
     barty's distinction of History 1 and History 2 (which, its merits and nuances notwith-
     standing, stages a quasi-ontological encounter between Marx and Heidegger). In current
     debates (on comparative urbanism, planetary urbanisation, global cities, for example),
     which continue to be methodologically pragmatic and theoretically multiple, not every-
     one shares this distinction – *International Journal of Urban and Regional Research* (2016),
     Urban Studies (2015), *Dialogues in Human Geography* (2016). Most importantly, Derick-
     son's classification is based on faulty assumptions about the relationship between the
     particular and the universal and the link between the concrete and the abstract in social
     research. See also Goonewardena 2018; Hart 2018a; Angelo and Goh 2020.
47   See above all Goonewardena 2018; Hart 2016; Angelo and Goh 2020. For other constructive
     recent engagements and debates with planetary urbanisation, see Schmid 2018; Brenner
     2018; Castriota and Tonucci 2018; Khatam and Haas 2018; Ruddick et al. 2018.

upon three conditions. First, it must attend to politics and struggle, and thus centrality. Second, it has to pay particular attention to the temporal and spatial unevenness of urbanisation. And third, it must remain theoretically open-ended to the point of recognising challenges to the very scope of urban research itself.[48] This last task can be prepared by relating urban considerations to other levels of reality: everyday life and the 'large' social order. This multi-level contextualisation makes it clear that urban research is exactly not everything. Dealing with these three tasks will allow me to return, in the subsequent sections, to research on settler colonialism urbanisation and Indigenous politics, and thus tease out broader implications of infrastructure struggles in the Canadian context, something that cannot be done with a Lefebvrean approach alone. I end this chapter with an invitation to consider how Indigenous struggles and strategies have generated spatial imaginaries and sustained theories of time-space that defy on their own terms the abstract space and linear time of colonial capitalism.

2.1   Politics and Centrality

For Henri Lefebvre, the (structural) 'revolution' of urbanisation presents opportunities to reconsider the problematic of (political) revolution. While their recent work on planetary urbanisation did not start with considerations of struggle (or political revolution), Neil Brenner and Christian Schmid do mention the role of collective struggle in generating urban questions. They observe:

> ... a wide range of new urban practices and discourses are being produced in diverse places, territories and landscapes, often in zones that are geographically removed from large cities, but where new forms of collective insurgency are emerging in response to the patterns of industrial restructuring, territorial enclosure, and landscape reorganisation sketched above. From Nigeria, South Africa, India and China, new political strategies are being constructed by peasants, workers and Indigenous peoples and other displaced populations to oppose the infrastructuralisation and enclosure of their established forms of livelihood [...] The politics of anti-gentrification and resistance to corporate mega-projects in dense city cores can thereby be connected, both analytically and politically against land enclosures, large-scale infrastructures (dams, highways, pipelines, industrial corridors, mines) and displacement in seemingly 'remote' regions [...]. Rather than rejecting urban life, such mobilisations are often

---

48   Jazeel 2018.

demanding a more socially equitable, democratically managed and environmentally sane form of urbanisation than that being imposed by the forces of neoliberal capitalism.[49]

In other words, there is strategic value in thinking world-wide urbanisation as a contested interplay of extension and concentration.

The importance of broadening urban research from towns, cities, and conurbations to processes of extension is thus not only empirical. It is quite banal to say that dynamics of concentration – settlement and agglomeration – only constitute one side of the urban coin; the other being dynamics of spatial extension (the production of manifold networks and mobile geographies). But Lefebvreans also ask about the political implications of this insight. As Monte-Mór's formative study of the Amazon,[50] Kanai's research on Manaus in this Amazonian context,[51] and Lesutis's work on Lete, Mozambique show,[52] extended urbanisation forces us to recast and rescale our understanding of the relationship between peripheries and centralities in the urbanisation process. Politically, the peripheralising dynamics produced by extended urbanisation[53] can also yield new centralities, which result not just from structural dynamics (new spatial concentrations) but also a convergence of collective struggles in and against dynamics of extended urbanisation (amongst which are the Indigenous mobilisations we will encounter in the next section).[54] These arguments give us new insight into how the dialectic of implosion and explosion can give rise to the urban (centrality/difference) in unexpected ways,[55] on one condition: that we grant the possibility that these new centralities of struggle may also reject and refuse (instead of accepting or appropriating) the expansion of operational landscapes.[56]

Students of planetary urbanisation have insisted that grasping the precise political significance of urbanisation depends on a few assumptions. First, urbanisation does not exhaust but mediates the open totality of the world. Insofar as the urban is a level of analysis, research on extended urbanisation can highlight the links between the social order and everyday life, as Arboleda has

---

49 Brenner and Schmid 2015, p. 178.
50 Monte-Mór 2004, 2014a, p. 265b, 119; Castriota and Tonucci 2018.
51 Kanai 2014.
52 Lesutis 2020.
53 Kanai 2014.
54 Monte-Mór 2004, 2014.
55 Schmid 2005, 2006.
56 Lesutis 2020.

shown in his analysis of operational landscapes in the Chilean Andes.[57] Second, to understand the necessary specificities of urbanisation,[58] one should see the relationship between comparative differences and larger processes not simply in terms of variation but co-constitution.[59] As we have seen in relation to the Martinique case and the space-times of plantation production, the question is not only how meanings of 'city' and 'country' vary (if they exist at all as distinct material supports, spatial forms, or imaginaries), but also whether the relationship between city, country, and urbanisation is one of transformation, reproduction or reinscription. Third, answering such questions is impossible with linear-progressive conceptions of urbanisation as a unilateral move from 'country' to 'city'. Urbanisation is not only spatially uneven; it is also temporally multiple. Even extended urbanisation can yield encounters between multiple temporalities.[60] In part, this is because urbanisation is both staged and layered: each round of urbanisation re-casts previous rounds of extension/concentration.[61] In part, it is because the imaginaries of urbanity and rurality that emerge in or against urbanisation need not be temporally continuous with these.

In the last two sections of this chapter, I will return to these issues through a brief discussion of a particular aspect of urbanisation in Canada: pipelines. While contemporary contestations of oil and gas pipelines attest to the current role of extractive development in Canadian capitalism, pipeline politics also remind us of the central role the production of operational landscapes have played in Canadian urban history and the formation of the Canadian state. In fact, these landscapes bring into sharp relief a larger concern: the settler-colonial dimensions of urbanisation in Canada and literatures that allow us to understand these dimensions. Indigenous challenges to extractive infrastructure remind us of the importance of researching urbanisation without linear conceptions of history based on dichotomies of 'city' (civilisation) and 'non-city'/'country' (barbarism, *terra nullius*).[62] Where infrastructure projects face what intellectuals of Indigenous resurgence call 'generative refusal',[63] dialectical critics of urbanisation meet theoretical limits that challenge them to consider other relational conceptions of space/time. To get there, a few more words on the Lefebvrean aspects of research on extended-concentrated urbanisation are in order.

---

57   Arboleda 2015.
58   Schmid 2015.
59   Hart 2016.
60   Monte-Mór 2004.
61   Sevilla-Buitrago 2014; Schmid 2015.
62   See also Monte-Mór 2004.
63   Simpson 2017.

2.2   On the Discontinuous Character of (the) Urban Revolution(s)

The image of the country and the city acquired its material force precisely in the will of actors who, being human, could be appealed to politically on the grounds of their inherited mythical and associative structures of meaning.[64]

In a recent homage to Neil Smith, Timothy Brennan reminds us of a circuitous lineage in Marxism where 'city' and 'country' function as rich metaphors to capture the relationship between capitalism, imperialism and uneven development. This holds true in a peculiar way also for Henri Lefebvre's writings about urban, rural and spatial matters. A crucial access point to these matters, Lefebvre's *Urban Revolution* (UR) occupies a particular place in Lefebvre's 'spatial' work between the *Right to the City* and the *Production of Space*. Without returning to interpretative debates on the subject, one can say that Lefebvre's turn to 'space' in *Production* does not so much break with his urban considerations as redirect them.[65] As I have pointed out in Chapter 1, Lefebvre's urban work from the late 1960s to the early 1970s – UR included – played an important role in moving him from a metaphorical critique of everyday life as 'colonisation' (in the early 1960s) to an explicit engagement with theories of colonialism and imperialism (in some of his volumes on the state). This engagement does not make Lefebvre a sufficient source for research on matters imperial and colonial; it does, however, raise the possibility of articulating his work to counter-colonial traditions, a possibility we have pursued in Chapters 2 and 3.

In UR, the urban revolution refers not only to the (incomplete) process of urbanisation; it also alludes to the political possibilities that may emerge from the amorphous 'urban fields' of spatial practices, imaginaries and knowledge forms. In 1970, Lefebvre's UR moves beyond earlier Paris-specific arguments (that the Commune and May 1968 were 'urban revolutions') to paint a worldwide tableau of struggle: a constellation of centralities produced by 'near' and 'far' peripheries: French banlieues, Latin America barrios, African-American ghettos.[66] In painting this tableau, Lefebvre also picked up on themes from an earlier life, his discussions about agrarian and rural questions in the 1940s and 1950s. Lefebvre wrote PU in the late 1960s as debates about urban guerrilla movements[67] raised questions about the then dominant conception of

---

64   Brennan 2017, p. 16.
65   Stanek 2011.
66   Lefebvre 2003a, pp. 110–11, 145–50.
67   Marrighela 2009; Oppenheimer 1969.

revolution as peasant war.[68] His critique of Mao and Che urges us to revisit the spatial assumptions in theories of workers' and peasant revolution. For him, the Soviet, Chinese or Cuban revolutions teach us that it will not do to base political strategy on static views of city and country,[69] one that takes for granted without further investigation that the 'town-country dyad', which is 'so fundamental to social thought', continues to 'hold firm'.[70]

Like others in revolutionary traditions, Antonio Gramsci and Frantz Fanon included, Lefebvre treats 'city' and 'country' as more than spatial forms and material supports of social relations. He also sees them as myths, ideologies and imaginaries – lived space.[71] These may be persistent enough to live beyond the times that produced them.[72] Urbanisation thus does not follow a linear-developmentalist trajectory. On the one hand, it represents '*discontinuous* transformations',[73] a set of uneven processes (such as rural de- and restructuring) through which urbanisation can engulf historic city/country and absorb agricultural production while also recasting core-periphery relations.[74] On the other hand, urban and rural myths 'can come from a period other than the one in which they are reunited, reused or reworked'.[75] In what is a paradox only from a linear-progressivists perspective, urban myths can weigh in rural-agricultural societies[76] while non-urban imaginaries – 'myths, ideologies, utopias' – may (re-)surface in the urban field.[77] In this sense, city and country can outlive their eras and relate to core-periphery relations variably. Not necessarily anachronistic, they continue to produce space, also through nationalism, reactionary or otherwise.

Lefebvre's urban work is thus open to a multi-temporal conception of change where continuity and discontinuity relate to each other in tension. This is not surprising. Lefebvre's urban turn followed years of rural sociological research, which, albeit centred on the Pyrénées, aimed at a global comparative understanding of land rent, rurality and agriculture. The centrality of the land question has licensed strategies to mobilise Lefebvre for global comparative

---

68   Wolf 1969.
69   Lefebvre 2003a, pp. 112–13, 147–50.
70   Schrader 2018.
71   Lefebvre 1991.
72   Lefebvre 2003a, pp. 103–4.
73   Lefebvre 2003a, p. 2, original emphasis.
74   Lefebvre 2003a, pp. 1–7.
75   Lefebvre 2003a, p. 104.
76   Lefebvre 2003a, p. 106.
77   Ibid.

strategies.[78] And it allows us to understand better how Lefebvre's urban turn reconfigured the land question (instead of sidestepping it or treating it as the exclusive domain of rural sociology or agrarian studies). Of course, Lefebvre's urban work also returns to everyday life. Insisting that everyday life in an urbanising world is multi-temporal (as Lefebvre did in *Rhythmanalysis*)[79] allows us to see modernity and urbanity not so much as sequential (as developments away from to tradition) but as coeval (as comparatively distinct constellation of rhythms, linear or cyclical).[80] A comparative approach to urbanisation needs to pick up on Lefebvre's gestures and develop a multi-temporal as well as comparatively subtle, relational conception of city, country and urbanisation. This is particularly important in colonial and imperial contexts of urbanisation, which Lefebvre himself analysed insufficiently. These urban contexts often defy linear-developmentalist conceptions of space-time in particularly sharp ways and have been contested through imaginaries that refract anti-imperial or anti-colonial histories in sometimes unpredictable ways.

2.3   On Levels of Analysis and the Limits of Urban Research

In the context of Lefebvre's overall work, UR is an opening to an integral, non-specialist approach to urban questions. For Lefebvre the 'urban' is not everything; it is an intermediate level of analysis (M), that of spatial relations, centrality/difference and periphery. As such, the urban mediates other levels: the general level (G) (macro political economies) and the 'private' level (P) (the level of everyday life, of routine and utopian imaginary, of reality and possibility). The urban is neither a mere scale nor the counterpoint to the 'country'. Instead, the urban may emerge within the urban field, as a nodal point in multiscalar core-periphery relations. Understanding the urban as level and form traversed and produced by processes helps us relate Lefebvre's urban research (M) to other pillars of his work: theories of state (and, thus, capitalism and imperialism) (G), and reflections on everyday life (P).[81]

A multi-level approach to urban analysis has implications for the study of urbanisation.[82] As to level M, understanding the urban question not only as process[83] but also as form (centrality/difference) allows one to see most clearly the dialectical relationship between concentrated and extended urbanisation,

---

78   Hart 2016; Elden and Morton 2016.
79   Lefebvre 1992.
80   Harootunian 2000.
81   Kipfer 2009a; Goonewardena 2011; Schmid 2005, chapter 5.
82   See also Arboleda 2015.
83   Brenner and Schmid 2015, p. 165.

as well as the differential and political character of both. The *formal* problematic of centrality/difference alerts us to the *content* (including the comparatively distinct substantive *processes*) by which centralities may resurface, from above or from below, within the landscapes of urbanisation.[84] Centrality/difference here is not reducible to the central city, historic city types or other sociophysical concentrations; it can also be a product of an encounter, a convergence and mutual transformation of multiple mobilisations that may or may not leave a permanent imprint on urbanising landscapes. Politics is at the heart of the urban problematic, both in agglomerations, and along the extended tentacles of the urbanisation process, as we will see with reference to infrastructure and pipeline politics.

While everyday life appears both conceptually and empirically in the literature,[85] researchers of planetary urbanisation have so far paid less attention to level P than to political economies of state, capital and formal knowledge (level G). Linking urban analysis to critiques of everyday life, as Lefebvre proposed, remains vital, however, for various reasons.[86] For example, refusing to delink urban questions from everyday life is a precondition to understanding gendered relationships between the urban and the non-urban, particularly when these relationships are coterminous with private-public dichotomies and the neoliberalisation of social reproduction[87] that has superseded the Fordist domestication of social life Lefebvre observed in the postwar era. Also, without proper attention to the contradictory 'terrain' of banality and possibility, routine and imaginary that is everyday life in Lefebvre's conception, it is impossible to understand the relationship between uneven urbanisation processes and symbolic claims to the 'city' (or the 'non-city').

Picking up on the discussion of creole urbanism as a window to spatial imaginaries of struggle in Chapter 3, I will continue to emphasise the imagined side of daily life that stands in a complex, not derivative relationship to global and urbanising levels of reality. Discussing Indigenous claims made against projects that push forward infrastructural urbanisation in Canada, I focus on what Kristin Ross has called the lived spaces articulated in 'words spoken, attitudes adopted, physical actions performed' and 'memories elaborated' by insurgents.[88] In so doing, I want to push into a somewhat different direction the insights developed by Hilary Angelo, who alerts us to the

---

84   See Monte-Mór 2004, 2014a, 2014b; Arboleda 2016b.
85   Brenner and Schmid 2015, pp. 171–2; Arboleda 2015.
86   See also Buckley and Strauss 2016; Ruddick et al. 2018.
87   Mitchell et al. 2004.
88   Ross 2015, pp. 1, 92–3.

importance of studying the uneven relationship between spatial imaginaries and other aspects of planetary urbanisation.[89] It is obviously crucial to understand the imagined city – non-city binaries that help sustain dominant, even hegemonic knowledge forms, as Angelo does in relationship to Euro-American ideologies of nature. But it is equally important to understand how histories of subaltern experience and struggle have generated their own spatialised political imaginaries. To give these imaginaries their due is especially crucial when these emerge from struggles that had no choice but to confront urbanisation in its most violent dispossessive forms, those produced by imperial and colonial states.

Much work on planetary urbanisation has tied the urban question to the 'far' social order (level G). This is true for analyses of urban ideologies ('the urban age' thesis) and the role of the neoliberal state, capital and formal knowledge in increasing the intensity and scope of extended urbanisation. Thanks to the work of Monte-Mór, Arboleda, Sevilla-Buitrago, Khan and Karak, and Lesutis, greater emphasis has been put on the role of imperialism, (neo-)colonialism and North-South relations in shaping concentrated/extended urbanisation, past and present. Such a focus on such multi-layered imperial forces is essential if the comparative specificities of urbanisation are to be understood not only as variegations of contemporary processes (as Brenner and Schmid have argued) but also as transformations-reproductions of relationships between urbanisation, city and non-city. Such a deeper historical focus allows us to tie Lefebvre (and his basic proposition that each mode of production produces distinct forms of space) to comparative historical-materialist frameworks that insist that the meaning of city and countryside, their (non-) distinction and relationship is not just a variation of overarching processes but articulates distinct forms of social organisation: modes of production.[90] I will return to this point once again with reference to settler colonial urbanisation.

These comparative questions bring us back to an occasional Lefebvrean concern: the possibility that the 'urban revolution' opens up to a multi-polar, post-imperial world shaped intellectually by multiple sites of knowledge production.[91] This concern pushes us into a dialectical conception of the relationship between particularity and universality, concrete and abstract in comparative research.[92] My view is that visions of a multipolar world are related to (but

89   Angelo 2017.
90   Southall 1998.
91   Kipfer, Schmid, Goonewardena, and Milgrom 2008. From a distinct but related perspective, see also Sheppard, Gidwani, Goldman, Leitner, Roy, and Maringanti 2015.
92   Hart 2016; Schmid 2018.

not synonymous with) the demand that historical-materialist approaches to urban matters remain open to dialogues with other approaches to time and space.[93] As we will see with reference to Indigenous politics, such theoretical openness is vital for two reasons: to establish linkages between Lefebvrean approaches and research on settler colonialism, and, in order to understand self-determined struggles and autonomously defined Indigenous approaches that may eschew the language(s) of urban Marxism(s).

3   Infrastructure and Indigenous Politics: When Urbanisation Faces 'Refusal'

In North America today, geographically extensive infrastructure is politicised. The main reason: Indigenous-led opposition to mining operations, pipelines, and ports. One of the most publicised anti-pipeline protests in the 2010s was the struggle of Indigenous peoples and their allies against the Dakota Access Pipeline project to link shale oil fields in North Dakota to an oil terminal in Illinois. While this project was contested in numerous places, the most important site of resistance was at Standing Rock, in Oceti Sakowin territory. Reaching their high point during the impressive protest camp in 2016 and 2017, the Standing Rock mobilisations highlighted what one can also learn from other forms of resistance on the continent, past and present.[94] First, while these struggles articulate a range of concerns, they gravitate around Indigenous self-determination and Indigenous claims to land and territory in the face of the US-American and Canadian settler states. According to the Standing Rock Sioux, they are all about 'nation-to-nation relationships'.[95] Second, these struggles expose an 'infrastructural' or 'logistical' Achilles heel of capitalism: the strategic links between extractive and other forms of capitalist development and the difficulties of regulating these linkages territorially and otherwise.[96] As Pasternak and Dafnos pointed out with respect to the Canadian side of the continent, they indicate how the capillaries of capital (pipelines, waterways, roads, railways) are vulnerable to disruption.[97]

Third, these struggles are geographically complex. They can produce new centralities, points of spatial and political convergence as striking as the city-

93   See also Buckley and Strauss 2016.
94   Estes 2019a, pp. 1–65; *Cultural Anthropology* 2016.
95   Standing Rock Sioux Tribe 2016.
96   Labban 2008; Cowen 2014; Zalik 2016.
97   Pasternak and Dafnos 2017; Pasternak 2017a.

like resistance camp organised at Standing Rock in 2016 and 2017.[98] And they often link the most central places of mobilisation, occupations and blockades to other sites of resistance. Place-based, trans-local, and international at once, they show that Indigenous struggles escape the divide between city and non-city that is inscribed in layered histories of settler urbanisation. The parallels between the spatial dynamics of resistance against infrastructure projects and research on the political significance of operational landscapes and extended urbanisation are clear enough. But here I do not take these parallels as the empirical grounds upon which to build a conventional thesis exploring a particular subject (infrastructural development such as pipelines) through a pre-existing framework (planetary urbanisation). If in the last chapter, informal urbanisation allowed us to establish links between Lefebvre-inflected insights and spatial imaginaries in the creole literary movement, here, pipelines and infrastructure are a window through which to make connections between Marxist-influenced urban research (planetary urbanisation, for example) and Indigenous theories (including those shaping current research on settler urbanism, Indigenous politics and the geographies of Canadian political economy).

Following mobilisations against the Alberta tar sands and the Keystone XL pipeline, the opposition to the Dakota Access Pipeline that converged at Standing Rock was only one, albeit high-profile example of how, in the first two decades of the twenty-first century, resistance against oil and gas pipelines and other infrastructural projects across North America has been intense, often bringing together environmentalists, farmers, community organisations, and Indigenous groups. In our neoliberal age, Indigenous perspectives vary widely on how to approach infrastructure and extractive projects. Still, it is undeniable that Indigenous militants have been at the forefront resisting projects designed to facilitate 'resource' extraction and urban sprawl.[99] On the strategic political importance of pipelines, Awâsís Sâkíhítowín, an organiser against the project to reverse the flow of the Enbridge Line 9 pipeline said:

> The neo-colonial impacts of the tar sands disproportionately impact Indigenous communities, including the Aamjiwanaang, Mikisew Cree, Athabasca Chipewyan, Métis Nations, and more. The Enbridge terminal where the Line 9 reversal [in Sarnia, Ontario] would begin is on stolen land from Aamjiwnaang First Nation. The Mikisew Cree, Athabasca Chi-

---

98   Estes 2019a, pp. 57–63.
99   Preston 2015; Kulchyski and Bernauer 2014; Mulkewich and Oddie 2009.

pewyan, and Métis Nations are some of the communities living amidst the tar sands themselves [in Alberta]. In Toronto, 60 percent of the communities living along Line 9 are recent immigrants, most of whom are racialised. Low-income urban communities of colour and rural Native communities are at risk and heavily affected by the tar sands and accompanying pipelines.[100]

Resisting pipelines that link extraction sites to ports, metropoles and spaces in-between offers the advantage of connecting multiple struggles. Thus interlinked, these effectively or intentionally scale up the scope and visibility of each protest site. They bring into contact, if not conversation, various perspectives, from conservation to environmental justice and ecological socialism.[101]

Contestations of infrastructure and pipeline projects in Canada underscore the political salience of understanding extended and concentrated urbanisation as two sides of a dynamic that produces new centralities and makes it possible to see these centralities as a geographically stretched constellation of struggle. It would be wrong, however, to reduce this political dynamic of concentration and extension to a contestation only over the modalities of urbanisation, a demand for 'a more socially equitable, democratically managed, and environmentally sane form of urbanisation'[102] or a 'new model of urbanisation'.[103] While political orientations among Indigenous groups involved in infrastructure politics vary, no one would argue that they can be dissociated from issues of Indigenous self-determination and land control. As Shiri Pasternak says, blockades against infrastructure and resource extraction projects (such as those of the Algonquins of Barriere Lake against clear-cut logging) are 'where Canadian law meets modern Indigenous societies on the ground'.[104] Fundamental jurisdictional and land conflicts have also been central to the *Idle No More* movement, which in 2012 started to mobilise against the Conservative government under Prime Minister Stephen Harper. Just re-elected in 2011, the Harper government set out to radicalise the Canadian colonial state, deregulating the activities of extractive capital, terminating Indigenous claims to political independence and setting out to privatise property relations on reserve lands.[105]

---

100   Awâsís cited in Awâsís, Tokar, and Stevens 2013, p. 55.
101   Thomas-Müller n.d., *East End Against Line 9*.
102   Brenner and Schmid 2015, p. 178.
103   Brenner 2014, p. 28.
104   Pasternak 2017b, p. 33.
105   *Idle No More*, n.d.; Palmater 2015; Barker 2015; Hall 2015; Pasternak 2015.

In early 2020, Canada witnessed another intense round of mobilisation sparked by conflicts over extractive infrastructure. On 6 February, the Royal Canadian Mounted Police (RCMP) raided an Indigenous blockade on the traditional territory of the Wet'suwet'en to enforce a court injunction protecting the construction of the Coastal GasLink pipeline. This pipeline was first proposed in 2012 to link Dawson Creek to the Pacific Ocean at Kitimat in British Colombia. The hereditary leadership of the Wet'suwet'en (whose title over non-reserve lands were recognised by the 1997 Delgamuukw court case) had continued to resist the project, in contrast to the elected band council and a number of other Indigenous nations located along the natural gas pipeline.[106] In response to the RCMP raid, solidarity actions were quickly organised, interrupting railways, ports, bridges and highways across the country. During the month of February, Indigenous blockades (by the Mohawk at Tyendinaga in Ontario and the Gitxsan in Northern British Columbia, for example) combined with non-Indigenous solidarity actions (notably by climate justice organisations). Melding 'the power of Indigenous nationhood and Indigenous rights' with 'the power of young Canadians who are committed to the environment and social justice', as Taiaiake Alfred had it,[107] these actions disrupted vital supply and transportation lines for protracted periods of time with a view to 'shut down Canada', as protesters shouted. Highlighting the vulnerability of Canadian capitalism and the promise of bringing together Indigenous with other environmental justice mobilisations, this continent-wide geography of blockades was ultimately successful in forcing the federal government to negotiate with the traditional leadership of the Wet'suwet'en.[108]

While tied to the urban question in the Lefebvrean sense, mobilisations against infrastructure and extractive projects are thus at the same time a matter of *inter-national* relations: not only a struggle against capital and state as embedded in extended urbanisation, but also a struggle to (re-)establish and negotiate nation-to-nation relations between Indigenous peoples and the Canadian settler state. Needless to say, these international relations are themselves tied up in the struggle over future modes of life and the societal relations with nature these may embody.[109] This is hardly surprising. Subcontinental infrastructures (railways, canals, ports, dams, roads, pipelines) were part of the passive revolution that built the Canadian colonial nation-state. They helped rebuff subaltern aspirations by linking original and expanded reproduction

---

106   Office of the Wet'suwet'en 2014.
107   Alfred cited in Carlito 2020.
108   Cowen 2020.
109   Awâsís, Tokar, and Stevens 2013, p. 61.

through a web of metropole-hinterland linkages[110] and racialised forms of production that were both part of broader British imperial geographies.[111] These infrastructural networks have thus long been integral to forming and recasting the colonial relationship between settler state and Indigenous peoples. In the 1880s, for example, the transcontinental railway bundled the murderous forces that 'cleared the plains' for agrarian and industrial capitalism, Confederation, and colonial apartheid.[112] Since the 1970s, various struggles, including the ones fought by the Dene over the Mackenzie Valley Pipeline(s) in the Northwest helped forge a partial but real shift towards recognition and marketisation in the colonial relation between the Canadian state and Indigenous peoples, a shift that has also pushed Indigenous groups to recast their own conception of land, property and economic development.[113]

In the face of ongoing colonial-capitalist projects – and despite partial shifts in the colonial relation towards accommodation and recognition – some Indigenous groups continue to insist that operational landscapes like pipelines and the Alberta Tar Sands pose deep threats to their jurisdiction and modes of life.[114] For some, like the Unist'ot'en clan (and the traditional leadership) of the Wet'suwet'en in interior British Columbia, the focus of action is to protect unceded off-reserve land against pipeline projects in order to assert political sovereignty and reenergise modes of life based on matrilineal, kinship-centred and territorially fluid forms of jurisdiction.[115] Such struggles – and *Idle No More* – have defined an Indigenous politics of refusal.[116] While directed against both settler colonialism and the preference of some Indigenous leaders and nations to actively participate in colonial recognition, real-estate, extractive capitalism, and the extension of operational landscapes, this refusal is meant to be 'generative', to speak with Leanne Simpson.[117] It wants to rebuild the self-determined social relations that are vital for political autonomy and Indigenous daily practices.[118] As we will see, such generative refusal challenges all spatial and territorial relations of the colonial state and colonial capitalism.

---

110   Ryerson 1983, pp. 254–7.
111   Cowen 2019.
112   Daschuk 2013, pp. 127–86; Toews 2018, pp. 50–82.
113   Coulthard 2014, pp. 51–78; Altamiriano-Jiménez 2004; Radcliffe 2019; Bernauer 2018.
114   Adam 2012; *Yinka Dene Alliance* n.d.; *Indigenous Environmental Network* n.d.; McCreary and Millisan 2014; Rossiter and Wood 2015.
115   *Unist'ot'en* n.d.; Huson and Toghestiy 2015; McCreary and Turner 2018.
116   Simpson 2017.
117   Simpson 2017, pp. 243–5.
118   Simpson 2011, 2017; Coulthard 2014; Alfred 2009.

3.1   Settler-Colonial Urbanisation in Multi-level Context

To understand Indigenous engagements with operational landscapes, claims to Indigenous resurgence included, we cannot isolate urbanisation from the broader imperial, racialised and capitalist dynamics that permeate it and the Indigenous aspirations that challenge it from within and from without. To put it differently, and to insist on the mediating role of urban questions, we must place these in multi-level context and highlight the settler-colonial dimension that shape all levels, including the Canadian state and its imperial dimensions (level G). Provided one recognises the centrality of land in geographically mediated research,[119] proceeding in this manner allows us to see, in a distinct North American context, what José Carlos Mariátegui said in the Peru of the 1920s: that the Indigenous question in the Americas is not residual but central to historical materialism and revolutionary strategy. Tied to questions of land and social relations, it highlights the complex and uneven tensions, interdependencies, and protracted transformations between modes of production that meet in colonial conquest, domination and struggle.[120]

Historically, the Canadian social formation developed through multiple colonial processes. Disregarding for now the also formative British conquest of New France, these centre on the colonisation of Indigenous lands and peoples and the insertion of British North America into a privileged position within the British and American empires and their labour and migration regimes, as well as the ramifications of both: complexly racialised forms of state and class formation, slavery included.[121] To grasp even just the first colonial process, one must insist, as Indigenous radicals have, on multi-temporal conceptions of time in order to properly historicise the settler-colonial relation that underpins the nation-state.[122] Canada did not *evolve* from pre-capitalist modes of production to capitalism; it emerged from multi-dimensional, uneven and discontinuous changes in the *relationship* between (mostly communal, hunting-gathering-fishing or agrarian) Indigenous modes of life and mercantilist and capitalist modes of production. These changes have been infused with class-based and gendered transformations of (re-)production in and between Indigenous and European societies.[123] They have always been political, woven through and

---

119   Elden and Morton 2016, pp. 62–3.
120   Mariátegui 1971, pp. 22–76.
121   Abele and Stasiulis 1987; Stasiulis and Jhappan 1995; Dorries, Hugill, and Tomiak 2019; Toews 2018.
122   Coulthard 2014; Bourgeault 1986, 1988; Kulchysky 1992, 2017; Wotherspoon and Satzewich 2000.
123   Adams 1973, 1999, pp. 145–8; Bourgeault 1986, 1988; Carter 1999; Wotherspoon and Satzewich 2000; Lawrence 2012; Daschuk 2013; Hall 2019; Camfield 2019; Smith 2019; Toews 2018.

governed as they are by shifting terrains of struggle between settler state and Indigenous peoples, terrains that also helped form other dimensions of the Canadian historic bloc.[124]

The colonial relation was transformed by and helped institute the shift from merchant capitalism and the fur trade to *mass* settlement between the late eighteenth and, in the Canadian North, the mid-twentieth century.[125] Long, uneven, but ultimately totalising,[126] this shift towards full-fledged capitalist colonialism liberated colonisers from the dependencies they may have had on Indigenous labour, diplomacy and warfare capacities during the fur trade and the wars with the USA.[127] This shift thus recalibrated the relative weight of land and labour in colonisation and capital accumulation. In a capitalist world economy led by British imperialism, it favoured systematic land dispossession for the purpose of mass settlement, agricultural commodity production, and the creation of an internal market. This historical transformation was crucial not only for a reorganisation of capitalist-colonial time space; it was both a condition and a result for the creation of the modern Canadian state in the second half of the nineteenth century. In that period, it was organised by the genocidal apartheid system that helped build the Canadian nation-state-in-formation: a network of reserves, residential schools, pass controls and racist legal classification partly codified by the first Indian Acts, partly administered informally through hierarchical territorial relations between various levels of the Canadian state and a dizzying array of aboriginal band councils that facilitate divide and rule.

Modern Canadian urban history – level M – has mediated the formation of colonial capitalism in general and colonial policies in particular. As a result of two generations of research on settler colonial urbanisation, we know this better now than before. Apartheid rule formalised and consolidated the forced removal of Indigenous peoples from towns and cities to state-enforced spatial concentrations (reserves) as well as non-recognised, and less visible, dispersed informal social spaces. Among the latter were social spaces inhabited by Indigenous peoples without official Indian status[128] as well as Métis settlements on marginal agricultural lands and on the outskirts of towns.[129] Apartheid rule and

---

124   Coulthard 2014, 2016, pp. 77–8; Burrill 2019; Toews 2018.
125   See the references in footnote 123.
126   Kulchysky 1992.
127   Carter 1999.
128   Lawrence 2012.
129   Peters, Stock, and Werner 2018; McCreary in Dialogue with Anderson, Gaudry, and MacDougall 2019.

less formalised segregation have been studied most frequently with respect to the planning of cities such as Toronto, Ottawa, Winnipeg, Vancouver, Victoria and Thunder Bay,[130] city-centred efforts that wanted to create 'spatial reflections of the colonial relation'.[131] However, as we know from research such as Adele Perry's study of the Winnipeg Aqueduct, which has connected this urban region to Shoal Lake (and the Anishinaabeg First Nations present in that area) 150 km East of Winnipeg since the 1910s, extended urbanisation has also been profoundly bound up with settler colonial dynamics.[132] At a wider scale still, we can see clearly that continent-spanning operational landscapes like railways helped structure a vast landscape shaped by settler colonial divides between 'city' and 'non-city', including official reserves and Métis social spaces.[133]

An urban focus helps reveal the contradictions of settler colonialism. To sustain this point, Coulthard draws from Jean Barman as well as John Tobias's analysis of the tension between 'protection' (separate treatment) and 'civilisation' (assimilation) in Canadian Indian policy.[134] While the informally administered pass system that originated as a counterinsurgency measure to stop the 1884–85 North-West uprising from spreading helped keep Indigenous peoples out of towns and cities, the 1911 amendments to the Indian Act did, among other things, grant authorities the power to remove reserves from towns with at least 8,000 inhabitants. Coulthard highlights the contradictory implications of the 1911 policy change:

> This [policy] situated Indian policy in a precarious position, as by the turn of the nineteenth century the reserve system, originally implemented to isolate and marginalise Native people for the purpose of social engineering (assimilation), was increasingly being seen as a failure because of the geographical distance of reserves from the civilisational influence of urban centres. Here you have the economic imperatives of capitalist accumulation through the dispossession of Indigenous peoples' land come into sharp conflict with the white supremacist impulses of Canada's

---

130   Harris 2003, 2004; Blomley 2004; Barman 2007; Tomiak 2011, 2015; Edwards 2010, Stanger-Ross 2008; Hugill 2015; DeVries 2011; Comack et al. 2013; Talaga 2017; Toews 2018; Dorries, Henry, Hugill, McCreary, and Tomiak 2019; Dorries, Hugill, and Tomiak 2019.
131   Hugill 2019, p. 85.
132   Perry 2016.
133   This categorical distinction between pre-contact settlements (like Hochelaga) and European towns (those from the Renaissance, for example) had not been obvious to all early settlers (Viau 2012).
134   Barman 2007; Tobias 1991.

assimilation policy and the desire of settler society to claim 'the city for themselves – and only themselves'.[135]

While Coulthard affirms that urbanism is an integral part of the settler colonial project, he also emphasises that the production of urban settler space attests not only to the solidity but also the contradictions of colonialism and its two major goals with respect to Indigenous peoples: segregation and assimilation.

On the one hand, legal and territorial segregation in the late nineteenth and early twentieth centuries relegated Indigenous peoples, including Métis peoples to 'non-urban' spaces or settlements at the fringe of cities while symbolically erasing them from 'urban civilisation', indeed, 'history' itself.[136] Dispossessive, state-enforced private property regimes, urban planning and reserve-centred aboriginal administration did not eradicate but *instituted* this separation between 'cities' and 'native space'.[137] Parallel to other forms of racial segregation, including Canada's own Chinatowns and Jim Crow practices,[138] the segregationist plank of Canadian Indian policy did so with a view to 'disconnect and disappear Indigenous peoples, rights, and title from [concentrated] urban space'.[139] Enshrined in the Indian Acts between 1876 and 1985, this separation was deeply gendered, built on a territorialised and racialised conception of Indian status. This conception (and the ulterior, also dubiously racialised legal distinction between First Nations, Métis, and Inuit) inverted typically matrilineal, territorially fluid, clan-based forms of belonging in Indigenous nations. In a direct attack on Indigenous political organisations, many Indigenous women and their offspring thus lost their legal status at the same time as they were coerced into violent colonial-patriarchal systems of dependency and social reproduction.[140]

On the other hand, segregation has had to contend with its own effects – as well as with the other side of Canadian Indian policy: assimilation. The dispossession of Indigenous peoples from land and livelihood undermined their economic independence and pushed them, sometimes deliberately, into the margins of the capitalist labour market. This uneven and ongoing dynamic

135   Coulthard 2014, p. 174.
136   Freeman 2010; also Razack 2002; Tomiak 2011.
137   Harris 2002, 2004.
138   Anderson 1991; Reynolds 2016, pp. 35–68.
139   Tomiak 2019, p. 96.
140   Lawrence 2003, 2004; Simpson 2014, 2016; Stevenson 1999; Maracle 1996; Bourgeault 1986; Anderson 2015; Hall 2019.

reminds us of the intricate relationship between the colonial and the capital relation, shifting linkages between the commodification of land and labour in the process of capitalist accumulation, and, relatedly, transformations of pro-duction and social reproduction, waged or otherwise.[141] Furthermore, assim-ilation intended to shrink and eliminate, physically or culturally, Indigenous societies (with disease, starvation, residential schools, and, later, enfranchise-ment and children's aid societies).[142] As a result, Indigenous people often had to reach beyond the reserve to survive[143] or were forcibly 'integrated' into White society: stolen from their families, divested of their status, or coerced into the labour market. Despite segregation, Indigenous peoples were thus never absent from concentrated urban life. At least some of their spatial practices kept defy-ing colonial segregation, including the 'city' and 'reserve' divide.[144]

Mediated by urbanisation patterns, the contradictions of Canadian coloni-alism came to the fore in the postwar period. On the one hand, the 'city'–'non-city'/'reserve' dualism continued to shape colonial geography despite growing migration to towns and cities permitted by the petering out of pass controls and encouraged by urban aboriginal policies.[145] On the other, as a result of the expansionist dynamics of Fordist capitalism, central-city urban renewal, reserve-city migration, and the more permissive aspects of the 1951 Indian Act, it became clear more than ever that many Indigenous peoples led their lives in trans-local fashion, in and between reserves and off-reserve places of work, residence and activism. Along with an urban shift in Canadian aboriginal policy,[146] these dynamics put the 'urban aboriginal' problematic on the agenda of researchers.[147] These have often studied the 'urbanisation' of Indigenous lives with the typical 'city-centric' – and state-bound – statistical conceptions of the 'urban' (as settlements of at least 1,000 inhabitants with a minimum popu-lation density of 400 per square kilometre) to highlight the growing Indigenous presence in towns and cities.[148] Yet, next to this emphasis on aboriginal pres-ence in the 'settler city', they have also emphasised that Indigenous practices,

141   Adams 1973, 1999; Knight 1978; High 1996; Brownlie 2008; Harris 2004, pp. 265–6; Camfield 2019; Hall 2019.
142   Tobias 1991; Coulthard 2014; Lawrence 2003; Wotherspoon and Satzewich 2000; Daschuk 2013; Wolfe 2006; Murray 2017; Diabo 2017.
143   Harris 2004, pp. 274–5, 286–8.
144   Johnson 2013; Sanderson and Bobiwash 1997; Lawrence 2004.
145   See Tomiak 2011.
146   Peters 2002; Murray 2011; Tomiak 2011.
147   Peters and Anderson 2013.
148   Ibid.

conceptions, and imaginaries 'transcend the classic rural/urban binaries' established by colonial policy and dispossessive accumulation itself.[149]

3.2   *Between Node and Network: Anti-Colonial Indigenous Imaginaries*

We don't have to 'go back to the land'. We never left it.[150]

There is no necessary mutual incompatibility between indigeneity and
city.[151]

Indigenous peoples have always transgressed the boundaries imposed by
the settler state.[152]

The division between reserve and city is an artificial colonial division. We
are all related, and this is all Indigenous land.[153]

Aspirations and imaginaries emerging from everyday struggle (level P) refract
the other levels of colonial historical geography (G, M). In the last chapter,
we encountered Patrick Chamoiseau's literary treatment of creole urbanism
as a repository of spatial imaginaries situated within and against the perceived
and conceived dimensions of plantation geographies and their repeated transformations. As Mariátegui pointed out with respect to the relationship between
myth, Indigenous politics and communism in early twentieth-century Peru,[154]
subaltern imaginaries often relate to material historical geographies in ways
that defy progressivist accounts. In the North American context, the ways in
which 'city' and 'country' ('bush', 'land', 'reserve') have been mobilised symbolically in Indigenous struggles against colonialism have also tended to subvert
linear conceptions of urbanisation leading from country to city. Key texts from
the Red Power generation and the current period of Indigenous resurgence will
help us understand this point.[155]

As we have seen in the previous section, colonial apartheid has been a crucial
force in shaping modern urban history as well as Indigenous-settler relations. It

149   Anderson and Peters 2013, p. 382; Peters 2002, pp. 87–8.
150   Maracle 1996, p. 109.
151   Neigh 2012, p. 71.
152   Tomiak 2011, p. 177.
153   Simpson 2017, p. 81.
154   Mariátegui 1971.
155   For Red Power in Canadian and US-American contexts, see Fidler 1970; Palmer 2009; Estes
        2019a, pp. 169–97.

is not surprising, therefore, that the thematic of compartmentalisation looms large in the history of Indigenous radicalism. In his formative *Prison of Grass*, Howard Adams hit an eminently Fanonian note when he said that

> The results of this [colonial] mentality can be seen clearly in any reserve village whose population comprises both natives and whites. There are always two distinct communities ... The differences are more than eco-nomic and cultural, they are vividly racial. According to the whites, the native section is a place of lazy, diseased, and evil people incapable of doing anything for themselves, a breeding-ground for violence .... The fact is that the native villagers are hungry – hungry for food, for houses, for clothes, for power, and for whatever the whites take for granted .... In contrast, the colonisers' section is clean and beautiful. It has elec-tricity, plumbing, paved streets and garbage collection. It has beautiful modern houses with central heating and all public utilities. It has white authorities who draw handsome salaries because of the native people. These colonisers are privileged because they belong to the power struc-ture and they have physical comfort and luxury because they are white. They have opportunities and unlimited horizons because they are part of mainstream society. The law is on their side because they are administrat-ors. They are able to talk about the native world in 'rational and objective' terms because all the evidence is on their side.[156]

In this passage, Adams talks about spatial separation as an indicator of colonial ossification in a manner that could be taken straight from Frantz Fanon, who figured prominently in his library, along with Indigenous, African-American, anti-colonial and Marxian classics from Vine Deloria and Howard Cardinal to Frederick Douglass, Malcolm X, Karl Marx and Herbert Marcuse.[157] To make his point, Adams repeatedly discussed two distinct landscapes of segregation in Saskatchewan and other parts of Western Canada: official First Nations reserves and informal Métis ghettos.

To this deep reality of (settler) colonial compartmentalisation, various responses are possible. One obvious reaction is hostility, or at least scepticism of town and city life. As Lee Maracle said in *Bobbi Lee*, concentrated urban life can conjure up memories of the 'dehumanising process that urbanisation in a racist society is for us'.[158] In fact, she said that by moving 'back' to the

---

156   Adams 1975, p. 40; see also Adams 1999, p. 110; Adams 2005, pp. 3–50, 171.
157   Lutz 2005, p. 257.
158   Maracle 1990, p. 229.

city permanently, Indigenous people may face the unwelcome prospect of 'cultural integration into oppressor society'.[159] Maria Campbell concurs. For her, town and city life do embody aspirations for a better life. Yet, as she recounts frequently in her autobiography *Half-Breed*, these aspirations are easily disappointed by realities of poverty, segregation and settler violence, which force Indigenous peoples to keep their heads down in anticipation of possible taunts, sexist aggressions or other forms of physical violence.[160] Audra Simpson clarified and extended this point more recently in her *Mohawk Interruptus*. For Indigenous women without official Indian status, the 'city' can be a site of expulsion (where one goes after being told, on the reserve, to 'go back to the city') and a site of exclusion (where one hears settlers yell: 'go back to where you came from').[161]

Colonial segregation can also be an asset, both on the reserve and in segregated urban neighbourhoods. Appropriating segregated space can be the first step in resistance. The most well-known Red Power organisation in Canada, the *Native Alliance for Red Power* (NARP) made it clear in 1969 that self-determination was inconceivable without 'gaining power in our reservations and communities'.[162] In a continental context, Howard Adams argued against contemporaries such as Jack D. Forbes when he insisted on the importance of reserves and other segregated spaces as necessary land bases for Indigenous resistance.[163] Not only is there 'no alternative to segregation' for 'rank-and-file native people', Adams suggested.[164] Also, 'the ghetto does not have to mean continuous disintegration and political immobility', he said. 'Instead, it can serve as a base for civil-rights action and liberation'.[165] Of course, Adams proposed to appropriate segregated space not for localist purposes. For him, appropriating segregated space was a vital starting point, a way to create autonomous and self-determined socio-spatial bases to sustain broader mobilisations. These dynamics of liberation would include multiple social spaces in order to connect various radical 'red' nationalisms to each other as well as to other struggles such as anti-colonial mobilisations in the Third World and working-class struggles (Indigenous or otherwise) against global capitalism.[166] As Ron

159   Maracle 1996, p. 105.
160   Campbell 1973, pp. 34–7, 110–12, 131–5.
161   Simpson 2014, p. 164.
162   NARP 1969.
163   Dunbar-Ortíz 2005, pp. 255–6.
164   Adams 1975, p. 203.
165   Adams 1975, p. 204.
166   Adams 1975, pp. 194–6, 205–7, 209–11.

Bourgeault recounts, Adams saw 'locally-based struggles, where all contradictions are reduced, as the starting point for creating a revolutionary consciousness'.[167]

When Adams wrote first, in the 1970s, towns and cities had become more and more important targets for Indigenous projects of spatial appropriation. By then a growing number of Indigenous people had moved to concentrated urban spaces, the pass system was no longer administered systematically and some apartheid restrictions on cultural and political rights had been loosened by the 1951 amendments to the Indian Act. As a result, Indigenous ways to 'appropriate urban [city] space'[168] became more widespread and revealed a key contradiction of Indian urban policy.[169] Instead of assimilating Indigenous peoples by urbanisation, it helped (re-)create an Indigenous terrain of struggle, which, in turn, reshaped Canadian City politics in increasingly prominent ways during the postwar period. In this era and subsequent years, this relative geographical shift in Indigenous politics took various forms, from protests, blockades and 'urban' land claims, to street renaming projects, Indigenous housing and community development initiatives, and the creation of 'urban' reserves.[170] The substantial and durable increase in Indigenous populations in towns and cities since the postwar period has thus given rise to a critical mass of Indigenous practices and institutions that makes it easier to see – and say – that there is no inherent contradiction between (concentrated) urban

---

167   Bourgeault 2005, pp. 228–9.

168   Peters 2013.

169   Similar contradictions can be observed in the USA (Hugill 2015, 2019; D'Arcus 2010). As Estes pointed out with respect to the US-American policies of 'termination' and 'relocation': 'Originally envisioned as a means to dismantle Native communities by removing them from the land and integrating them into mainstream urban society, relocation in fact had the opposite effect. Indians didn't simply stop being Indians once they left the reservation. Relocation, for all its malicious intent, helped birth a new movement that arose from both poverty-stricken urban ghettos and rural reservations. Natives on relocation found each other in the cities and at universities, forming pan-Indigenous organisations such as the National Indian Youth Council, United Native Americans, AIM, and many more. Their concerns, however, were fundamentally no different than those of their reservation-based relatives. They merged their respective rural and urban experiences into one, and what emerged was a radical, explicitly anti-colonial political consciousness that took the world by storm. It viewed the federal system as a colonial structure rather than as a solution. And, unlike youthful generational protests of its day, Red Power looked to older generations, the traditional reservation leadership, for guidance – the elders who had rejected federal administration and kept alive the "old ways"' (2019a, pp. 170–1).

170   Tomiak 2011, 2017; Simpson 2011, p. 11; Comack, Dean, Morrissette, and Silver 2013, pp. 146–58; Craig and Hamilton 2015.

life, indigeneity, and Indigenous self-determination.[171] In fact, the combined force of Indigenous claims to urban space allows us to anticipate the contours of a 'non-racist city', a city that, instead of being 'built on human suffering', 'would provide the condition for the flourishing of Indigenous urban life'.[172]

Indigenous claims to town and city space are often part of multi-scalar geographies, as Julie Tomiak pointed out.[173] During the Red Power years, networked Indigenous spatial practices were vital in generating trans-local imaginaries. Howard Adams' locally rooted internationalism combined his knowledge of 'apartheid Saskatchewan'[174] with Prairie socialism and Québec nationalism as well as his experiences in Berkeley, where he made formative links with Black and Chicanx militants in the 1960s.[175] Adams's Métis contemporary Maria Campbell made similar experiences. Her place-based engagements also emerged from a range of geographical experiences in Saskatchewan, Vancouver, Calgary and Edmonton. In the afterword to the complete edition of *Half-Breed*, she recalls these years as follows:

> The 1960s were an exciting time in Indian country and like many young people of my generation I wanted change, not only for myself but for our people and especially for Indigenous women and children. The young people in that generation were inspired by what was happening within Black and Indigenous peoples' movements in the Americas as well as around the world. We were inspired that Indigenous peoples were standing up to their colonial oppressors and fighting to reclaim their cultures and lands. We devoured their writings and had long conversations with our people at home and across the country about our own situation and what we could do to change it. We travelled the country, talking and organising meetings, protests and demonstrations. We fundraised, wrote poetry and made art. We pumped out newsletters to keep our people informed. And for the first time in our colonial histories, our elders openly held meetings with us to share ceremonies and cultural knowledge that up to that point had been hidden because of government policies.[176]

---

171 Bobiwash 1997; Neigh 2012; Hoar 2014.
172 Dorries 2019, p. 41.
173 Tomiak 2016.
174 Adams 2005, p. 171.
175 Adams 1975, p. 176; 2005, pp. 163–5, 169; Pitsula 2005, pp. 230–5; Simmons 2002, pp. 7–8.
176 Campbell 2019, p. 191.

Campbell's lived and imagined geography placed geographical nodes in broader networks, as did Adams (with whom she otherwise disagreed, notably on grounds of gender).[177] Her acute sense of the importance of land-based struggles in central Saskatchewan was not weakened, but sharpened by her capacity to connect shifts in world politics and the political experiences she made in Canadian urban centres to the realities of spatial segregation, racist humiliation, class exploitation, male violence and, not the least, daily solidarity recounted in *Half-Breed*.[178]

More than Adams and Campbell, Lee Maracle centred her discussion of networked Indigenous practices and imaginaries explicitly on metropolitan spaces. She corroborated US-American accounts when she stressed how off-reserve contexts like Vancouver were crucial for the emergence of Red Power politics (exemplified by the *Native Alliance for Red Power* centred in Vancouver). These emerged from a growing Indigenous presence in Canadian cities[179] and the networks that made it possible for young Indigenous people there to 'feel connected' with each other as well as to other anti-colonial and left-wing radicals. As she put it in the epilogue to her *Bobbi Lee – Indian Rebel*:

> It was the beginning of the 1970 ... Youth was on a roll. Young Native people from all parts of the province and the country were coming together, tribalism, the village focus was breaking down. We are all Indians, one people with many cultures. Thinking of all sorts blossomed among us. A ground swell, a tide, everywhere in the country little groups of Red Power youth were springing up. I remember thinking what a miracle the Indian way of being was. All at once, every major city turned out Native youth who were talking about the same kinds of things. Sharpesville came alive for us. Vietnam brought out our poetic best ... somehow we all knew that this had everything to do with our own lives. Somehow we were all connected.[180]

Situated in between Vancouver, Toronto, Edmonton, Seattle, Visalia, Lake Labiche and Ashcroft, Maracle's *Bobbi Lee* showed how inter-personal Indigenous relations were shaped by various manifestations of settler racism, the necessity for intermittent 'shit work', sometimes violent family relations, countercultural experimentation and new political horizons. In turn, networks

---

177   Campbell and Heimbecker 2005.
178   Campbell 1973, pp. 167–70, 177–8.
179   Maracle 1996, p. 104.
180   Maracle 1990, pp. 208–9; see also Maracle 2017, pp. 89–90.

between reserves and off-reserve spaces brought various political influences to Indigenous communities.[181]

A range of Indigenous perspectives thus confirm that the 'unrest' of the 1960s and 1970s brought together many lines of influence, on and off reserve. It produced multiple, interconnected centralities in and across reserves, towns and big cities. Given this history, it makes eminent sense to hear Indigenous intellectuals today emphasise the need to embed land-based practices in movements that straddle the inherited colonial divide between city and reserve. Bonita Lawrence, Leanne and Audra Simpson, and Glen Coulthard argue that an effective geography of resistance against settler colonialism must build alliances between reserve-based Indigenous organisations and Indigenous people living in areas described as urban.[182] The point of such alliances is not only practical, helping to 'build movement'[183] by developing organisational capacities, sharing expertise and memories of struggle.[184] Indigenous 'reserve-city' resistance networks may also help subvert the real and imagined boundaries of colonial settlement. As Coulthard has it,

> ... the efficacy of Indigenous resurgence hinges on its ability to address the interrelated systems of dispossession that shape Indigenous peoples' experiences in *both* reserve- and urban-based Indigenous communities to reconceptualise Indigenous identity and nationhood in a way that refuses to replicate the 'colonial divisions' that contributed to the urban/reserve divide through racist and sexist policies like enfranchisement.[185]

While Coulthard uses a city-centred conception of the urban here, he indicates that a combination of place-based and trans-local Indigenous movements raises fundamental questions about the meaning of 'city' and 'non-city' on the North American continent.

I would suggest that these arguments resonate with Lefebvrean sensibilities: they allow us to see that trans-local Indigenous spatial practices do not just 'move' between the racialised fixities of 'city' and 'country' ('reserve', 'bush').

---

181   Stressing similar lines of influence, Rick Monture considered the Grand River reserve of the 1960s as a condensation of many influences. In part due to the connections between the reserve and the Haudenosaunee diasporas of Detroit, Toronto, Buffalo, and Rochester, the Six Nations reserve was a place embodying a 'wide array of perspectives regarding our history, cultural representation and future vision for the community' (2014, p. 142).
182   Lawrence 2004; Simpson 2017; Coulthard 2014.
183   Simpson 2017, p. 81.
184   Coulthard 2014, p. 176.
185   Ibid.

They are active, if subordinate forces in the production of space and centrality. However, non-urban imaginaries remain crucial in Indigenous politics, for
reasons that escape Lefebvre. This is in part because of the aforementioned
histories of racism and dispossession that permeate settler cities. And it is also
because the land question does not stop at the city border; it permeates all
social spaces, included concentrated urban space. As Lee Maracle said in *I
am Woman*, 'we don't have to "go back to the land". We never left it. We are
not reptiles and amphibians that lived in the sea and now wish to go back to
the land'.[186] Clearly, a reluctance to believe in false urban promises need not
yield anti-urbanism, particularly when this reluctance is based on relational,
not atomistic, fractured and dichotomous understandings of social life.[187] Just
as Indigenous lives more generally, Indigenous allegiances need not stop at the
edge of towns of cities either; they cut across the spatial divides of city and
reserve or bush.[188]

To put it differently, projects to rebuild Indigenous modes of life materially,
through place-sensitive, egalitarian, democratic and conservationist economies (which can involve a good measure of subsistence) may emerge in various
landscapes. Whether such projects involve a defence of remaining not-just-
capitalist modes of production (a 'bush mode of production',[189] or 'bush culture'),[190] a reconstruction of non-capitalist ways of life, or novel and heterodox
Indigenous socialist strategies, they can challenge instead of inverting colonial
dichotomies of city and non-city. Cognisant of the challenges that mass urbanisation (concentrated and extended) poses to Indigenous land, livelihood and
sovereignty, networked geographies of resistance and the 'politics of refusal'
advanced by Indigenous resurgence need not target cities per se but challenge
'colonial spatialities' as a whole.[191]

While Indigenous struggles embody various spatial imaginaries, as we have
seen, some current mobilisations offer overt challenges to colonial dichotomies
of 'city'/'non-city' or 'reserve'. Reflecting on the Wet'suwet'en blockade against
the Coastal GasLink pipeline in British Columbia, chief T'oghestíy thinks that

> a lot of First Nations people are ... realising that if they stay in their Indian
> reserves or urban centres and just exist in the system, nothing's going to

---

186   Maracle 1996, pp. 109–10.
187   Maracle 2017, pp. 109–15.
188   Ditidaht artist Tsaqwuasupp cited in Alfred 2009, pp. 173–4.
189   Coulthard 2014, p. 171; Kulchyski 1992.
190   Kulchyski 2013.
191   Simpson 2017, pp. 194–8.

change. But if they get onto their ancestral lands, they'll see exactly what's happening to them ....[192]

Claiming traditional lands off recognised reserves is one way to defy colonial territoriality. In the case of the Unist'ot'en clan of the Wet'suwet'en, this defiance reveals a clash between colonial-capitalist time-space (rooted in private property and the state), and spatially fluid, multi-layered and situational Indigenous conceptions of land, territory, and jurisdiction (generated by matrilineal and household- and kinship-centred practices of (re)production and decision-making).[193] This is the case also with the Carrier Sekani in interior British Columbia, who have mobilised dynamic, practiced and relational notions of time, space and territory against extractive infrastructure and the spatially extensive dynamics of urbanisation.[194]

Current Indigenous struggles thus corroborate the salience of Indigenous theories of time-space that foreground lines of connection across social practices, landscapes and memories in order to work against the ways in which colonial strategies of compartmentalisation 'disorganise tribal spaces' and 'erase Native presences on the land – both urban and rural'.[195] These Indigenous theoretical traditions are frequently based on differentiated and holistic ontologies that make it easy to articulate place-based with mobile conceptions of space. In *Dancing on Our Turtle's Back*, Leanne Simpson tells us that Nishnaabeg theories of space go beyond an ethics of place. They are based on relational ontologies that distinguish between spaces of movement, spaces of demographic density, and, between the two, boundary zones of transition.[196] In Nishnaabeg, 'Oodena' (the 'place where the hearts gather') is a term to capture the moment of socio-spatial concentration. Simpson calls it a dense, 'city-like' nexus bringing together broader relations.[197] Once one operates with this fluid and situational conception of territory, there is no reason to restrict geographies of self-determination to the confines of existing settlements, colonial or otherwise.

In her *Mohawk Interruptus*, Audra Simpson, too, emphasises that Mohawk, indeed Haudenosaunee, traditions of clan-based and confederate political and social organisation are built upon open-ended and relatively unbound concep-

---

192   Huson and Toghestiy 2015, p. 52.
193   McCreary and Turner 2018.
194   McCreary and Milligan 2014.
195   Goeman 2008, p. 301.
196   Simpson 2011, pp. 89–94.
197   Simpson 2011, p. 94.

tions of territory and citizenship. She underlines that these conceptions shifted and developed in the course of long struggles against colonialism. As Simpson says with reference to the Mohawk at Kahnawà:ke,

> Kahnawà:ke's history, hence, moves through several places and times as a single-nation community. It began as a Mohawk village in the Valley, some of whose people moved north to find temperance from alcohol, particip-ate in the fur trade, and seek respite from troubles in the Confederacy. The people within this village came north as Mohawks but also blen-ded with Abenaki, Huron, and other 'mission Indians' who were already in Sault St. Louis, the original seigniorial land grant. Eventually, the cul-ture that dominated there was Mohawk, and diplomacy was conducted according to Iroquois protocol. Their continued consciousness of being a nation, or a nation-like entity, within a reserve would be a sensible adapt-ation both the movements they made from the Valley as well as their distance from, yet relatedness to, the Confederacy. At the same time, this self-consciousness of being a reserve-nation was a sensible adaptation to what was happening to the south of them and to the colonial scene itself, which demanded, to a certain extent, the making of lists, the fixing of names, the rendering of 'legibility', and the congealment of identities around certain spaces.[198]

The dynamic space-time relayed by Audra Simpson has both antagonistic and immanent relationships to settler colonialism. It lends itself to confrontational and subtle political strategies in and against colonial rule. While cutting across the spatial dichotomy of 'city' and 'reserve', it may also challenge the hierarch-ical, patriarchal and homogenising features of colonial state-space per se. In fact, excavating Mohawk historical geographies subverts the very 'project of homogenising heterogeneity' embodied in racialised colonial citizenship and the state-like forms of band/tribal membership imposed by colonial states.[199]

---

198 Simpson 2014, p. 188.
199 Simpson 2014, p. 18. For Simpson, the relationship between Mohawk historical geograph-ies and the settler state also has implications for the experience of modernity in colonial context, an existential sense of uncertainty brutally intensified by the eliminatory force of settler colonialism. As she says: '"What is a Mohawk to oneself and to others?" A prosaic question, it is frighteningly modern ... "Who are we now; who shall we be for the future?" Retrospectively, these questions *are* deeply modern but signal a fear of disappearance, to be on the receiving end of an eliminatory story, disappearance at the hands of global cap-ital, and an ongoing settler project that attempts to move Indigeneity away, to eliminate it' (2014, p. 181).

4   Conclusion: Land and Urban Politics beyond Capitalism?

When I was among the *Qallunaat* [White people] first, I was amazed by
how property had an almost sacred air about it. And I perceived later that
they worked so hard as individuals to accumulate what they get in life that
they are quite vigilant about any perceived violation of the property that
they have.[200]

How can settler society, which possesses no fundamental ethical relationship to the land or its original people, imagine a future premised on
justice? There is no simple answer. But whatever the answer may be, Indigenous peoples must lead the way. Our history and long traditions of Indigenous resistance provide possibilities for futures premised on justice.[201]

Zebedee Nungak and Nick Estes remind us that Indigenous insight and intervention are of strategic importance. Situated in critical interstices of the accumulation process, Indigenous politics is well-placed to exercise leverage against
capitalist expansion. And, standing in long and dynamic traditions of resistance, Indigenous political and intellectual resurgence also constitutes an
essential reference point for anyone interested in egalitarian and ecological
politics in and beyond Indigenous communities themselves. Extending this
basic claim about the strategic importance of Indigenous radicalism, this
chapter has followed Indigenous theorists to stress that an analysis of settler colonial urbanisation gives us an acute sense of the contradictions that
permeate the colonial relation which regulates White settler colonialism in
North America. With reference to Indigenous spatial imaginaries, we have also
highlighted the importance of spatial (re-)appropriation for Indigenous anti-
colonialism, past and present. Strategies of spatial appropriation have targeted
various points in the landscape of settler colonialism, from segregated city
spaces to reserves and unceded traditional lands. However, they are often spatially multi-form. Projects of 'Indigenous resurgence and resistance are often
organised in networks that span urban and non-urban spaces'.[202] Generating
nodes and networks, Indigenous-led resistance against land-extensive infrastructure highlights the territorially fluid and multi-scalar character of Indigenous anti-colonialism in particularly sharp ways. In theory and practice, it

200   Zebedee Nungak, cited in Sandford 2006.
201   Estes 2019a, p. 256.
202   Tomiak, McCreary, Hugill, Henry, and Dorries 2019, p. 3.

can mobilise notions of land, time and space that challenge and cut across the compartmentalised and hierarchised fragments of colonial abstract space.

These insights allow us to return to the beginning of this chapter and out-line the conditions under which Lefebvre and Fanon can shed light on settler colonial dynamics. The first condition is to further historicise and spatialise the colonial relation by highlighting the comparative differences majoritarian and permanent settlement make to colonialism and its spatial organisation. Key here is an appropriate focus on the relationship between land dispossession, genocidal elimination, and socio-spatial segregation, and, in turn, dynamic conceptions of tradition in Indigenous political history. The second condition is to emphasise once more the discontinuous character of historical time. This becomes particularly crucial to understand the dynamic role of colonial *rela-tions* between settler and Indigenous formations in the emergence of mod-ern capitalism and the modern state. More specifically, dynamics of urban-isation should be understood in non-linear ways, as uneven and combined processes through which 'city' and 'country' were transformed, modified or reinstituted as socio-spatial forms. This helps us understand how, in the Canada since the nineteenth century, capitalist and colonial urbanisation did not so much replace city with country but developed new, deeply racialised distinc-tions between urban and non-urban social spaces. In turn, Indigenous presence within and in opposition to colonial urbanisation attests to the coeval charac-ter of the urban in a peculiar fashion.

Third, it is crucial to enlarge the scope of urban research while also recog-nising its limitations. Contestations of infrastructure show that research on extended and concentrated urbanisation features limits. Paying attention to extended urbanisation requires 'contextually specific and theoretically reflex-ive investigations', yes, of 'conditions within so-called "rural" or non-urban zones',[203] but also of qualitative challenges to the expansion of the urban field and the imaginaries (urban or not) that come along with such challenges. To recognise the limits of urban research conceptually it is important to treat urban questions not as all-encompassing but as mediations between everyday life and the 'large' social order. This allows us to link urban research to stud-ies of other settler-colonial dimensions of Canadian political economy. Doing so alerts us to the fact that struggles over concentrated and extended urban-isation raise (inter-)national questions that rest on Indigenous claims to self-determination. Once put into place, so to speak, historical-materialist urban research (Lefebvrean or not) can learn from Indigenous theories without swal-

203   Brenner and Schmid 2015, p. 174.

lowing these, just as it must do in relationship to traditions of struggle in other contexts, as we have argued in the last chapter on creole urbanism and Martinique. The relational conceptions of time-space that inform some Indigenous politics (in and beyond pipeline struggles) hold key lessons for urban research. But they do stand on their own. Self-defined yet not autarchic, they help ensure that claims to Indigeneity are not drowned out by 'stories of colonisation', even critical ones.[204]

My plea for theoretical openness suggests that urbanisation, that medium of (neo-)colonial capitalism, must remain both contestable *and* questionable. In Canada, insisting on the open-ended character of urban research is vital if the Indigenous question is not to be shoehorned into urban strategies that threaten to hegemonise colonial relations. Under pressure by Indigenous resistance, court decisions and legal requirements, such strategies include measures of consultation (and sometimes resource sharing and co-management) with Indigenous peoples, at least to manage the 'uncertainty' faced by all those who plan infrastructure projects and extractive investments.[205] These strategies now sustain a colonial relation that includes recognition and marketisation. More than in previous eras of settler colonialism, they are thus open to a degree of Indigenous entrepreneurial participation in capitalist development. But for this very reason, they leave no room for autonomous Indigenous futures. In fact, as with the case of Martinique, they indicate the manifold ways in which urban strategies can help re-organise, adapt and sustain colonial relations at multiple scales, and in comparatively and historically distinct ways.

In turn, those Indigenous struggles that continue to object to the expansion of the urban field and the resource frontier (as well as Indigenous ways of accommodating both) obstruct the expansion of Canadian capitalism, thus corroborating, again, the strategic importance of Indigenous questions still today. As some non-Indigenous intellectuals have learned since the 1960s in Canada,[206] critical Indigenous claims to land, livelihood and sovereignty hold promise for other left, environmental, feminist and anti-racist struggles against capitalism. More specifically, self-defined and resistant Indigenous praxis mounts welcome material and ideational pressures to reorganise *already existing* urban life, concentrated or extended, Indigenous or otherwise. How? Along red and green, de-commodified and non-capitalist lines that puncture the sacred aura of private property, embrace Indigenous demands for 'land back'[207]

---

204   Alfred and Corntassel 2005, p. 601, cited in Hugill 2017, p. 7.
205   Van Nostrand 2014.
206   Kulchyski 2016.
207   Yellowhead Institute 2019.

and accept Indigenous presence as basic 'anti-colonial common sense'.[208] Indigenous demands for 'land back' are especially explosive in concentrated urban spaces where colonial hegemony seems saturated, that is to say in the towns, cities and conurbations that seem settled for good and appear submerged forever under the abstract space and linear time embodied by the clock, real estate and the property line.[209] In the next chapter, we will return to this more conventional focus of urban research on the capitalist city. We will do so by leaving behind North American settler colonialism to focus on the Paris region and its manifold social, economic, institutional and political connections to the French colonies, formal and informal, past and present.

208   Estes 2019, p. 51.
209   Focusing on Vancouver, Vasudevan discusses the implications settler colonial history and
      Indigenous politics have for non-Indigenous anti-gentrification, housing and squatting
      movements in that city (2017, pp. 184–210).

Mixing It Up: Demolition and Counter-Revolution in Greater Paris

In the world of practising urbanists in the North, diversity planning and social mixing are equivalent to terms like diversity and multiculturalism in the broader social world. They emerged in response to comparatively varied political struggles and social histories at the end of the postwar period. Since the 1980s, they have proliferated as references in state-bound planning during periods characterised by intensified social inequality (including, sometimes, accentuated spatial segregation), renewed imperialism and rampant environmental degradation. This chapter offers a detailed analysis of French urban policy within which social mixing (and one of its nominal and putative objectives, de-segregation) has played a key role since the 1980s. The particular focus is on housing estate redevelopment in the Paris region. Deepening the Lefebvre-Fanon connection established in previous chapters, I interpret place-based policy and housing redevelopment as contradictory strategies to reorganise territorial relations in response to subaltern opposition, real or potential. I emphasise the racialised and specifically neo-colonial aspects of redevelopment projects, which are also shaped by complex dynamics of gentrification and neoliberalisation. Of course, these projects have broader ramifications, not the least for oppositional political strategies.

Previous chapters have prepared us to be sceptical about claims to mixity and diversity, particularly when they are made from positions of authority. In Chapter 3, we assessed claims to creole and creolisation in relationship to violent histories of slavery and colonialism in the still French-controlled part of the Antilles. There, we also learned that segregation is not the only medium through which exploitation, oppression and political rule can be organised. Physical proximity and forced mixing were the main techniques through which plantation production was organised, particularly during racial slavery.[1] In turn, the example of creole urbanism (which in Chamoiseau's *Texaco* appears as a territorial compromise that helped recast the colonial relation in Martinique) reminded us that desegregation (which social mixing projects claim to promote) is not necessarily emancipatory. In this chapter, we will see that

---

1 On this point in global comparative context, see also Nightingale 2012, pp. 52–3, 298.

while diversity and mixity can be components of egalitarian political projects, desegregation from above (social mix planning) is most likely to undermine, in effect or in intent, a crucial spatial basis of radical politics: the segregated social spaces that can constitute starting points for self-determined strategies of opposition, liberation, and revolution precisely because they lack the kind of social mix policy makers have in mind. We have encountered proposals to appropriate segregated space from below in urban Marxism (Chapter 2), dialectical anti-colonialism (Chapter 3), and red power and Indigenous resurgence (Chapter 4). From these perspectives, mixity may become emancipatory only if it is freed from the manifold, also propertied alienations, inequalities and oppressions that define their meaning in the here and now.[2] We will return to this strategic problem in the conclusion to this chapter.

1   Setting the Stage: Urban Policy and Political Anti-Racism

The noise [from the explosion] is frightening. It reminds me of Algeria's war of independence, when the army bombarded our houses.[3]

These are [demolition-reconstruction] projects that are targeted on the most 'sensitive' areas of the municipality, particularly *Les Indes*.[4]

On a Sunday morning in early June 2010, I took the suburban train to Sartrouville in the western Paris suburbs. I continued on foot to the housing estate *Les Indes* and, after 45 minutes, arrived just in time to witness the spectacular implosion of the three central residential towers there. Closely followed by television crews, the implosion had the feeling of a military operation. The local residents who watched the event from various sides were separated from the implosion site by barriers and many dozens of riot police from the infamous *Compagnies Républicaines de Sécurité* (CRS). When asked about what they felt about the implosion, bystanders – long-standing inhabitants and teenagers, mostly with African backgrounds – expressed a combination of sadness (about losing their places of residence and the memories associated with them) and mistrust (of politicians and their promises to tackle segregation). The inhab-

---

2   In the following, I push into a somewhat different direction the important distinction De Filippis and Fraser (2010) make between mixity in the current neoliberal and capitalist period and mixity under qualitatively different social and economic conditions.

3   Inhabitant of *Cité des 4000*, La Courneuve cited in Abdallah 2001, p. 160.

4   Interview 7, 14 February 2012.

itants' sense of resignation was hardly surprising. By 1991, when inhabitants took to the street after a security guard of a nearby supermarket killed resident Djamel Chettouh, *Les Indes* had already joined a considerable list of 'infamous' projects that symbolise the purported need of state intervention to restore order and prevent 'ghettos' from forming in France.

As the well-known documentary *Minguettes 1983 – Paix sociale ou pacification?* (1983) reminds us, spectacular public housing demolition had become part of the repertoire of state intervention to manage 'social disturbance' and 'valorise housing estates' already by the mid-1980s.[5] In *Les Minguettes*, the housing estate in Vénissieux, suburban Lyon, Mogniss Abdallah's interviewees – all local inhabitants – insisted that the targeted demolition of apartment towers was not an architectural necessity. It was a concerted intervention into a political situation defined by 'permanent confrontation between police and youth' (mostly from North African immigrant families) involving inhabitants squatting abandoned apartments, provocative police raids and resident responses: demonstrations, riots and hunger strikes. The film documents that demolition was part of a continuum of state violence that gave rise to the largest anti-racist mass mobilisations in postcolonial France: the *Marche pour l'égalité et contre le racisme* in 1983 (and its sister marches in 1984 and 1985),[6] the '1968' of the children of the immigrant workers who were themselves present during the actual moment of 1968.[7]

These two examples attest to two key realities in the historical geography of France. First, they highlight the importance of what is now called political anti-racism: a current committed to autonomous, self-determined praxis against the racialised dimensions of French capitalism.[8] This current is distinct both from 'moral' anti-racism (which sees racism as a function of individual behaviour only) and identitarian anti-racism (which eliminates the specificity of politics by reducing political strategy to a spontaneous function of ethno-racialised group identity). In the late 1960s and 1970s, it emerged from the workplace, housing and neighbourhood struggles of immigrant workers from the French colonies, who tried to carve out their own political space on the French (far) left. The most well-known example from that period was the *Mouvement des Travailleurs Arabes* (MTA) founded in 1972. The marches in the

---

5   Abdallah 2001, p. 16.
6   Abdallah 2008; Kawtari n.d.
7   Hajjat 2013, p. 17.
8   Bouamama, Sad-Saoud, and Djerdoubi 1994; Khiari 2006; Beaud and Masclet 2006; Abdallah 2008; Abdallah 2012; Boubeker and Hajjat 2008; Lessellier 2008; Bouamama 2011; Gordon 2012; Hajjat 2013; Hancock 2017; Azzouzi and Zerouala 2020.

early 1980s signalled the arrival on the political scene of a second generation, a growing proportion of whom was then growing up in functionalist housing projects. This generation helped produce the political repertoire of riot, revolt and uprising that would punctuate the history of political anti-racism from then on.[9] In the 1980s, revolt and mass mobilisation generated pressures for reform and co-optation (by the Mitterrand government, the Socialist *sos-Racisme* and municipal Communism). It also yielded efforts to re-embed anti-racism in self-organised political practices. In the 1990s and early 2000s, these latter efforts initiated a third generation of political anti-racism, one best represented by the *Mouvement de l'Immigration et des Banlieues* (MIB) and a successor initiative, the *Forum Social des Quartiers Populaires* (FSQP). Today, the banner of political anti-racism is carried by groups like the *Parti des Indigènes de la République* (PIR), the *Brigade Anti-Négrophie* (BAN), the *Front Uni des Immigrations et des Quartiers Populaires* (FUIQP), the *Comité Adama*, and *Femmes en Luttes 93*.

A few features of political anti-racism are worth highlighting. Political anti-racism is to a significant extent a translation of African and Caribbean anti-colonial politics, including the dialectical current we discussed in Chapter 2. While in every generation, debates took place about how to conceptualise anti-racist politics in relationship to colonial history (and, indeed, whether to frame anti-racism in anti-colonial terms at all), the very existence of political anti-racism highlights neo-colonial realities in French politics and its various historical mutations, including the shift to cultural or differential racism, the anti-terrorist and anti-Muslim turn, and the growing class differentiation among non-White residents. In addition, since the 1980s, political anti-racist movements have helped produce a new subaltern spatial imaginary, re-appropriating the terms *banlieue* and *quartiers populaires* from the Communist Party and the labour movement as well as the stigmatising connotations given to these subaltern social spaces by dominant forces. In so doing, they have pushed into new or different directions a long history of politicising the territorial relations through which rule is organised in France and, indeed, Paris.

Political anti-racism has been largely left or far left in practice. Its historical relationship to organised segments of the French left has been characterised by both tension and cross-fertilisation. While developing through a series of conflicts with Left institutions and intellectuals over organisational forms and the very political legitimacy of anti-racism and anti-colonialism, political anti-racism has for the most part redefined, not abandoned left concerns and strategic sensibilities, even when the term left is no longer claimed explicitly. Com-

---

9   Dikeç 2017, pp. 92–129.

mitted to a more broadly conceived egalitarian and subaltern politics, the history of political anti-racism is also a history of experiments building alliances across various segments of the working class against capitalism, neo-liberalism and neo-fascism. A fundamental part of this history is tied to the gendered ways in which (colonial) racism and its relationship to capitalism is organised. Recasting in neo-colonial context the gendered contradictions of colonial capitalism discussed in Chapters 2, 3, and 4, the history of political anti-racism in France is also a history of navigating two imperatives that sometimes clash: developing solidarity among those bearing the brunt of racism (which often treats patriarchy as a property of non-Whites or non-Europeans) while also nurturing struggles of liberation against real-existing forms of gender oppression.

Second, the initial anecdotes indicate that French urban policy represents, to a significant extent, an intervention against political threats emanating from social movements.[10] Researchers have highlighted different political threats. Those most focused on *la politique de la ville* since the late 1970s have foregrounded the role of the state in responding to anti-racist movements emanating from housing estates to argue that French urban policy is an answer to the challenge of decolonisation (notably the Algerian war of independence) and a strategy to contain populations with links to the French colonies.[11] In the theoretical register of political anti-racism developed by Sadri Khiari, urban policy is thus a part of a *colonial* counter-revolution.[12] This reading does not jive automatically with those who have suggested, borrowing from Henri Lefebvre, that the gentrification of central Paris and adjacent industrial suburbs is an *urban* counter-revolution: a response to the failed urban revolution of May 1968 that reinvents, with the help of a new urban intelligentsia with progressive, 'Lefebvrean' sensibilities, a much older ruling-class strategy to subdue the intransigence and potentially revolutionary character of working-class Paris.[13] However, by alluding to the language of revolution, both sets of analysts indicate that in imperial France, the possibility of revolt, if not revolution has loomed large historically. In fact, one may argue that both counter-revolutionary strands are part of a longer history of Paris as war against civil insurrection.[14]

Situated in debates about these two realities concerning the hexagone, this chapter traces the political meanings of the programme of demolishing, renov-

10   Butler and Noisette 1977; Bachmann and le Guennec 2002; Dikeç 2007.
11   Abdallah 2005, 2012; Bouamama 1993; 2009; Bouamama et al. 1994; Dikeç 2007.
12   Khiari 2008.
13   Garnier 2010, 2012; see also Hazan 2002, 2011; Clerval 2012.
14   Hazan 2003.

ating, reconstructing and redesigning housing estates across France overseen by the *Agence Nationale de la Rénovation Urbaine* (ANRU) between 2003 and 2014. Under this programme (which has been renewed since then) public housing demolitions are no longer undertaken sporadically, as they were in Minguettes in 1983, but in a nationally coordinated fashion. But they continue to tie physical redevelopment to the socio-political purpose of mixing up resident populations.[15] The chapter is focused on 18 redevelopment projects in 13 municipalities in Greater Paris.[16] This geographical focus highlights the strategic significance of Paris for the French state. It also makes it easy to understand redevelopment in its complexity in a region where the importance of social housing is disproportionate compared to the national average.[17] The projects are positioned differently relative to land and labour markets

15   Kirszbaum 2013.
16   The research was based on site visits, primary documents (legislation, newspaper articles and contracts (*conventions*) between municipalities and ANRU), and 15 open-ended interviews with planners, politicians, and activists conducted between 2008 and 2012. The projects were the following: Cité des 3000 (Aulnay-Sous-Bois), Croix-Petit (Cergy), Cités des Bosquets and Forestière (Clichy-Sous-Bois/Montfermeil), Cité des 4000 (La Courneuve), Le Luth and Les Grésillons (Gennevilliers), Val Fourré (Mantes-la-Jolie), Bel Air and Grands Pêchers (Montreuil), Goutte d'Or / Château Rouge (Paris), La Coudraie (Poissy), Francs-Moisins, St. Rémy, Floréal-La Saussaie, Pierre Sémard (Saint Denis), Les Lochères (Sarcelles), and Les Indes (Sartrouville). Selected by contacting municipal planning offices as well as by means of the snowball technique, interview partners were confronted with the same set of questions concerning the goals of redevelopment, the meaning of social mixity, the early effects of redevelopment, and the role of conflict in the planning process.
17   The relationship between ANRU projects, housing estates (*Grand Ensembles*) and social housing in France is complex. Most of the cases studied here are sizable or large housing estates built since the 1950s. Some, however, are focused on older, pre-functionalist neighbourhoods. Furthermore, in France, housing estates and social housing are not synonymous (Voldman 2015). Before redevelopment, housing estates were not all composed to 100 percent of social housing but included other tenure forms, including ownership housing in the form of bungalows (*pavillons*) and multi-residential condominiums (*co-propriétés*). Generally, redevelopment has reduced the proportion of social housing on site, but to varying degrees. Social housing itself contains a range of forms, from the units run by the public or non-governmental housing corporations HLM (*Habitat à loyer modéré*) to seniors' homes and workers' hostels. Social housing itself includes multiple categories of financial assistance, from construction finance to rental subsidies for a range of income groups. With the end of the era of *Grands Ensembles* and the relative shifts from social to market housing and from construction finance to personal rent subsidies since the 1970s, social housing has undergone internal fragmentation and is home to a greater proportion of precarious tenants. Yet it still houses a mix of people and remains less residualised (and financialised) than social housing in Britain and North America (as well as Germany) (Rowlands and Murie 2009, pp. 248–50).

in the region: in new towns (Cergy), outer suburbs (from the car manufacturing basin in western Mantes-la-Jolie and Poissy to Sartrouville, Sarcelles,
Aulnay-sous-Bois, Clichy-sous-Bois and Montfermeil), central Northern and
Eastern suburbs (Gennevilliers, St. Denis, Montreuil, La Courneuve), and central Paris (Goutte d'Or/Château Rouge in the eighteenth arrondissement). From
the small enclave La Coudraie in Poissy to the vast project in Sarcelles, they
vary in morphology and the socio-cultural weight they carry in their respective municipalities. Whether in former 'red' belt towns (St. Denis, Gennevilliers,
La Courneuve), symbolic centres of anti-colonial politics (Goutte D'Or) or epi-
centres of the 2005 uprising (Clichy-sous-Bois/Montfermeil), they embody distinct political histories. And they have been governed by different forces: the
bourgeois right (Mantes-la-Jolie, Montfermeil, Satrouville), alternating right
and left majorities (Aulnay, Poissy), the Socialists (Cergy, Clichy-sous-Bois, Sarcelles), Communists or reform Communists (Gennevilliers, La Courneuve, St.
Denis) or left coalitions (Paris, Montreuil).

Complementing empirical research with a comprehensive range of secondary French research, this chapter will demonstrate the relevance and limits
of the main Anglo-American theoretical currents that have been brought to
bear on equivalent cases of public housing redevelopment, place-based policy
and social mix planning.[18] It is certainly correct to interpret *ANRU* projects in
Paris as forms of state-led gentrification,[19] state rescaling,[20] territorial stigmatisation,[21] (re-)commodified collective consumption and (re-)privatised social
reproduction.[22] Yet, these interpretations are insufficient for two reasons. They
underestimate the role of redevelopment as a specifically *political* response
to subaltern mobilisations, as Anne Clerval's work on the gentrification of
Paris shows.[23] And they give short shrift to the racialised, ethnically absolutist,
and, in some cases, neo-colonial, dimensions of social mixing.[24] Condensing
insights from Chapters 1 and 2, the first section begins with a framework built
upon an articulation of Marxist and anti-colonial lineages (embodied in Henri
Lefebvre and Frantz Fanon) and complemented by a rich, heterodox literature
that has shed light on various neo-colonial aspects of French state interven-

---

18   Bridge, Butler, and Lees 2011; Arthurson 2012; Lees, Shin, and López-Morales 2016, pp. 128–
      33.
19   Hackworth and Smith 2001.
20   Brenner 2004.
21   Wacquant 2008.
22   Mitchell, Marston, and Katz 2004.
23   Clerval 2012.
24   These dimensions have also been stressed by Mele 2019; Chamberlain 2020; Addie and
      Fraser 2019.

tion since 1962. Upon this basis, I will show, in the main part of the chapter, that *Rénovation Urbaine* in the Paris region today links state, class and race by articulating urban with specifically neo-colonial forms of counter-revolution. Of course, redevelopment accentuates land-rent valorisation, which underscores the importance of defending social housing as decommodifed collective consumption.[25] But redevelopment helps reorganise territorial relations of domination in multiple, also racialised and concretely, not metaphorically neocolonial ways.[26] I conclude by commenting on the implications of this analysis for comparative research, the postcolonial state, and oppositional strategies.

2   State, Capital and Neo-colonialism in the Production of Space

It is in the city where the national border (the one that opposes nationals and foreigners) interferes with other divides, and where conflicts in Europe become ethnic.[27]

In *De l'Etat*, Lefebvre treats the modern state as a contradictory condensation of social relations, which, albeit hierarchical and centralised, also take on more diffuse, everyday dimensions. In conversation with economic theories like dependency theory, he underlined the centrality of modern state formation to the twin development of capitalism and imperialism. Crucial to both is the ongoing capacity of the state to enforce relations of equivalence necessary to generalise commodity exchange. In part this means facilitating primary accumulation: agricultural restructuring, the destruction-incorporation of precapitalist cities, transformations in the city-countryside relation, and colonial plunder.[28] This starting point helps us understand Lefebvre's more well-known point about the state's role in producing abstract – homogenous, fragmented, hierarchical – space by coordinating the flux of capital (in world fragmented by private property) while also organising domination through hierarchical territorial relations.[29] This emphasis on the role of the state in organising relations between dominant (central) and dominated (peripheral) spaces makes it

25   Madden and Marcuse 2016.
26   Here I take issue with those who call gentrification a 'new urban colonialism' without making substantial efforts to establish empirical and conceptual links between gentrification and colonial realities, past or present (Atkinson and Bridge 2005).
27   Gallissot 1995, p. 309.
28   Lefebvre 1976c, pp. 306–60; 1977, pp. 87–156.
29   Lefebvre 1991b.

clear that domination and accumulation are closely linked dimensions of state space. It also helps us understand that the form of the urban (centrality/difference) is itself infused by political relations between central and peripheral spaces.[30] These territorial relations need not be only coercive and conflictual but can include territorial compromises,[31] thus explaining the potentially hegemonic character of the production of space.[32]

Lefebvre's emphasis on the state's role in organising territorial hierarchies allows us to approach the problem of state scale from a somewhat different angle than the one proposed by Neil Brenner.[33] Calling the organisation of territorial relations of domination a form of 'colonisation', Lefebvre suggested that one can analyse it at multiple scales to shed light on geopolitical relationships between nations and macro-regions, forms of uneven development between regions within national-contexts, territorial relationships within cities and urban regions.[34] As we have seen in Chapter 1, Lefebvre's use of the term 'colonisation' is by no means only metaphorical. Shaped intellectually by the anti-colonialism of the 1960s and 1970s, Lefebvre's approach in *De l'Etat* posits a direct comparability of spatial organisation in the colonies proper with the territorial organisation of 'colonies' in the imperial core. 'Colonisation' is a phenomenon that straddles both the historical divide between colonial and postcolonial realities as well as the spatial distinction between colony and empire. As to 'colonisation' within urban regions, Lefebvre stresses that urban planning and city building projects like Haussmannisation in the nineteenth century and functionalism in the twentieth span the divide between imperial centre and colonial territory. They can be studied to compare not only Bordeaux and Lyon but also Paris and Algiers. This trans-scalar conception of 'colonisation' helps explain Lefebvre's understanding of urban revolution as a global convergence of struggles, a convergence long feared by counter-revolutionary strategists and architects of counterinsurgency against communism and Third World liberation.[35]

To the extent that Lefebvre's insights about 'colonisation' grew out of observations – and wishful thinking – about a convergence of struggle of workers, students and migrants in postwar France and inhabitants of shantytowns and ghettos in the Americas, one can extend his analyses to hypothesise that the

---

30   Lefebvre 2003a.
31   Schmid 2003.
32   Lefebvre 1991b, pp. 10–11.
33   Brenner 2004.
34   Lefebvre 1978, pp. 170–86.
35   Leroux 2013; Henni 2016; Rigouste 2017, 2020a; Saberi 2017b.

shift to post-functionalist urban interventions – including diversity planning and social mixing – responded in part to the struggles of the 'long' and world-wide '1968', partly with subsequent urban reforms (in which Lefebvre particip-ated[36]). They did so partly by reorganising territorial hierarchies along neo-colonial lines. For this insight to be fully developed (which Lefebvre did not, despite ample opportunities to do so in the 1980s),[37] I need to reorient Lefe-bvre with Fanon's insistence that racism is the 'most visible, the most day-to-day' element of the 'systematised oppression of a people' that is colonialism.[38] This reorientation is philosophically plausible given that despite their differ-ences, Lefebvre and Fanon shared a radical, dialectical humanist perspective. As Chapter 2 shows, it is useful to recall that for Fanon, racism as lived experi-ence of alienation (dehumanisation, homogenisation, inferiorisation) takes on a particularly ossified, caste-like form through various forms of spatial organ-isation: spatial separations in the colonial city, relations between city and coun-tryside in colonial territories, and inter-national relations under conditions of empire. For Fanon, these spatial forms are co-produced by colonial and imper-ial states: blocs of social forces and structurally violent institutions supplying the agents – soldiers, policemen, urban planners – who personify the lines of separation between colonised and coloniser. In this light, relations of territorial hierarchy can only be called properly colonial insofar as they are at least co-determined by racialised hierarchies, neo-colonial or otherwise. In turn, claims to the right to the city/difference can challenge colonisation only if they trans-form spatial forms of racialisation like segregation and other forms of bodily confinement.

Lefebvre's and Fanon's respective works were above all shaped by the exper-ience of vulgar – colonial and neo-capitalist – forms of modernism. Today, one can concretise their arguments with the help of theoretically multi-faceted traditions of empirical research on French political history that eschew nation-state centrism to point to the imperial dimensions of the French state, certainly before, but also after 1962 (the date of nominal Algerian independence).[39] Such insights also apply to urban policy, architecture and planning, which cannot be understood properly without reference to imperially networked institutions, ideologies and personnel. For example, the Haussmannian reconstruction of

---

36   Stanek 2014, pp. xi–xli.
37   Kipfer 2014.
38   Fanon 1988, pp. 32, 33; 2006, pp. 39, 41.
39   Elsenhans 1974; Sayyad 1991, 1999; Gallissot 2006; Gallissot et al. 1994; Cooper 2005; Wilder 2003a; Rosenberg 2006; Le Cour Grandmaison 2005, 2009; Abu-Lughod 1980; Wright 1991; Rabinow 1991.

Paris during the Second Empire and the Third Republic helped build a now decidedly capitalist resurgence of French colonial imperialism,[40] a resurgence largely ignored by formative scholarship on Haussmann's Paris.[41] Not only was 'Haussmann' an export product facilitating the reorganisation of property relations, infrastructure, gendered spatial relations and city-building principles elsewhere, including in colonial cities such as Algiers.[42] Haussmann's Paris (and its precondition, the bloody suppression of the 1848 revolution) was itself built upon colonial military expertise, including Marshall Bugeaud's doctrine of warfare against civilians, which he first developed during the conquest of Algeria in the 1830s and 1840s.[43]

In the twentieth century, the development of what Lefebvre called the 'model of isolated units' – functionalist architecture, zoning and master-planning – was influenced by colonial experiences in both early and late neo-capitalism (Fordism). Various parts of the new empire, notably Rabat, Casablanca, Marrakesh and Algiers were sites of experimentation for planners (such as Henri Prost) who became known as key exponents of French modernism between the two Wars.[44] Emerging from a conjuncture bracketed by the Battle of Algiers (1957), the Battle of Paris (1961) and other colonial massacres in mainland France,[45] postwar planning and mass housing were shaped by late colonial policy. Postwar security, policing, and immigration policy were influenced by colonial citizenship statutes and shaped by colonial personnel before being generalised after 1962.[46] Postwar urban planning, too, was developed in part through imperial networks. The clearance of 'slums' (*bidonvilles*) in the hexagone ran in tandem with slum clearance in Algeria. The housing forms in which shantytown dwellers and migrant workers were placed, policed and 'acculturated' separate from mainstream social housing (*HLM*) – migrant workers' hostels (*foyers*), and transitional social housing (*cités de transit*) – were run in part by lower-level personnel returning from the colonies.[47] Regional planning, including the conception of new towns in 1960s Paris, was shaped by Gaullist technocrats who had made a last futile attempt to modernise French rule in Algeria through the multi-faceted *Plan de Constantine*.[48]

---

40   Lafrance 2019; Mooers 1991.
41   Harvey 2003; Benevolo 1993; Hazan 2002.
42   Celik 1997; Picard 1996.
43   Bugeaud 1997; Le Cour Grandmaison 2005, pp. 310–32.
44   Abu-Lughod 1980; Wright 1991; Rabinow 1989; Hakimi 2005; Celik 1997.
45   Einaudi 1991; Amiri 2004; Kupferstein 2017.
46   Blanchard 2011.
47   Sayyad 1991; 1995; Henni 2017, pp. 165–75; Blanc-Chaléard 2016, pp. 57–204.
48   Elsenhans 1974; Fredenucci 2003b; Deluz-Labruyère 2004; Leroux 2014; Henni 2017, pp. 97–124, 205–32.

Through these imperial connections, urban strategies translated the 'colonial question into the urban question'[49] in France while simultaneously construct- ing neo-colonial linkages in places like Algeria that lasted much beyond formal independence.[50]

What about the period since the 1970s? The selective shift away from func- tionalism, *dirigisme*, and standardised housing production was of course not a mechanical reproduction of France's colonial past. The move to place-based planning, social mixing, decentralised 'governance' and creeping neoliberalism in the 1970s and 1980s, was shaped by a complex combination of responses to political struggle ('1968', radical struggles against urban renewal in the 1970s, and the Second Left) and structural contradictions (the crisis of Fordism, the impasse of Gaullist technocracy) that are not reducible to French imperial pasts and presents. Research has shown, however, that elements of French urban, spatial and housing policy have played a role in selectively reinvent- ing, adapting and renewing neo-colonial territorial relations. Crucial policy elements – social mixity, policing, architecture and physical planning – respon- ded in part to the 'destabilising', and sometimes effectively politicising incor- poration of migrants, particularly migrants of colour, into mainstream social housing in the 1970s. They did so through new repertoires of action to man- age colonial subjects in the 1950s and 1960s. As I have argued elsewhere,[51] the demonstration that French urban policy is far from being colour-blind is not contingent upon proving that French housing estates resemble US-American- style ghettos (or that French politics is increasingly shaped by American-style neoliberalism, law and order and insecurity, as Loïc Wacquant suggested, in collaboration with Pierre Bourdieu).[52] The sources of racialised, gendered and class-based spatial organisation in France are significantly homegrown and res- ult in part from a neo-colonial recomposition of institutions, practices and mentalities.[53]

49   Blanc-Chaléard 2016, p. 169.
50   Henni 2017, pp. 230, 284–7.
51   Kipfer 2012.
52   Wacquant 1999, 2008.
53   See also Tevanian 2003; Tissot 2007b.

3   *La Rénovation Urbaine* in Practice: Gentrification, State-Rescaling,
       and Neo-colonial Management

> [This] does not mean that we have left behind representations based
> on racial or ethnic presuppositions. On the contrary, they have been
> displaced. A good example, in my opinion, is the currently fashionable
> notion of social mixing [...] In municipalities which already have a high
> proportion of social housing [as opposed to rich ones] [...], the point is to
> modify the sociological composition of the social housing stock, that is, to
> diversify the now the majority poor inhabitant population to make room
> for the middle classes. In this logic, 'social mixing' becomes a euphemism
> for 'ethnic mixing' ... Consciously or not, this logic takes up the notion of
> tolerance threshold (*seuil de tolérance*), which led the communist mayor
> of Vitry-sur-Seine to bulldoze, in 1980, a hostel for immigrant workers
> where Malian workers had moved in ... I see another implicit justifica-
> tion for social mixing: that poor residents adopt, mimetically, the norms
> and ways of life of the middle classes.[54]

> It's the same logic as Haussmann's ... They create the space necessary so
> that the police can charge more rapidly.[55]

In August 2003, the Chirac government passed *La Loi d'orientation et de programmation pour la ville et la rénovation urbaine*.[56] Named the Borloo law after
the minister in charge, the legislation set up an agency, *Agence Nationale de
la Rénovation Urbaine* to oversee and coordinate the financing of projects to
reconstruct housing estates in select target districts (*Zones Urbaines Sensibles,
zus*). Implemented with contracts (*conventions*) with local authorities, *rénovation urbaine* was officially mandated to promote social mixing (*mixité sociale*)
and sustainable development by demolishing, rehabilitating, reconstructing,
and redesigning (*résidentialisation*) the physical form and diversifying tenure
forms by increasing market-rent and ownership housing on the redeveloped
sites. The Borloo law replaced the *Grand Projets de la Ville* policy from 1998,
which coordinated local redevelopment nationally at a more significant scale
than its predecessors, the *Grand Projets Urbains* (1991) and the experimental
Banlieue 89 (1983). Together with its immediate precursors, the Borloo law did

---

54   Abdallah 2001.
55   Interview 14.
56   Gouvernement de France 2003.

away with the 'taboo' of demolition[57] as a *general* strategy to pursue socio-political goals through physical planning and design.[58] In its focus on breaking up housing estates, this policy was the Right's response to the Socialist *Loi relative à la solidarité et au renouvellement urbain* (SRU) in 2000, which aims to redistribute social housing by obliging all but small municipalities to have at least 20 percent (starting in 2013, 25 percent) social housing.[59]

The Borloo Law consolidated France's move away from the functionalist 'model of isolated units' (Lefebvre) that dominated urban strategies from the 1950s to the 1970s. The *Programme Nationale de la Rénovation Urbaine* (PNRU) coordinated by ANRU confirmed the rise to the centre stage of housing redevelopment within France's post-functionalist *politique de la ville*.[60] From the 1980s to the late 1990s, public housing demolition/reconstruction and architectural redesign constituted a symbolically important, but secondary, experimental and often punctual element in wider place-based urban policies that have had the effect of territorialising social relations in an explicit fashion.[61] These territorialising strategies have targeted a range of policies (education, labour-market training, community policing, other social policies) on a patchwork of 'sensitive' zones defined by a dizzying, and frequently amended array of indicators (ranging, as in the designation of ZUS, from poverty and unemployment to citizenship). As housing redevelopment rose to prominence within French placed-based policy in the 2000s, other policies have been added to the arsenal of territorialised state intervention. During the Hollande Presidency, for example, equality between men and women has become a goal in place-based social policies. The assumption here is that gendered inequality is function not of French patriarchy but problems that inhere in social spaces inhabited mostly by workers of colour.[62]

Since the 1980s and 1990s, place-based policies were implemented through an increasingly complex patchwork of inter-governmental arrangements. They developed during a series of decentralisation reforms as well as European integration processes that have greatly complicated the scalar arrangements of the French nation-state. While France remains a unitary state, sub-national institutions have multiplied. They have become entangled with each other and

---

57   Driant 2012.
58   Baudin and Genestier 2006; Kirszbaum 2013.
59   Desponds 2010, p. 49.
60   Tranb 2005; Kirszbaum 2004.
61   Tissot 2007; Dikeç 2007.
62   Hancock, Blanchard, and Chapuis 2018; Blanchard and Hancock 2017; Coutras 2003; Guénif-Souilamas and Eric Macé 2006.

national-level institutions in increasingly arcane fashion. Given its nationally coordinated character and its nation-wide scope, the *Programme Nationale de la Rénovation Urbaine* (PNRU) was seen as a move to partially recentralise France's urban policy landscape, re-casting once more the relationship between national ministries, municipalities, and social housing providers.[63] In turn, given its bias towards market housing and physical planning (over social policy), demolition (over reconstruction), and security-conscious attempts to redesign and separate private from ill-defined public space, *PNRU* was considered deepening the neoliberal and revanchist policy turns of the 1990s.[64] While these interpretations still apply at the time of writing,[65] I will show that *ANRU* projects have also reinvented (neo-)colonial forms of state intervention going back to the 1950s and 1960s.

3.1   *'Valorisation' = Gentrification?*

'Valorisation' is an important, overarching goal of redevelopment. Consistent with the broader class-biased shift towards market and ownership housing underway since 1977,[66] 'valorisation' includes strategies of land-rent valorisation to facilitate market-oriented residential upgrading – gentrification in the classical sense of the term. Real-estate dynamics – and land developers – do play an important, if, in comparative terms, often limited and sometimes indirect role.[67] Strategies to exploit rent gaps are most obvious in places close to the existing gentrification frontier. This is true in the eighteenth arrondissement, where officials accept real-estate pressures as an inevitable background condition,[68] La Courneuve[69] or *Francs-Moisins* (St. Denis), next to the Canal St. Denis, across from the office districts next to the huge Stade de France, 'where even a rotten building is worth gold'.[70] It is also true in more remote areas that are linked to regional transit and already surrounded by white-collar employment and middle-class neighbourhoods (new town Cergy)[71] or where a high

63   Epstein 2012a; Viviano 2005.
64   Dikec 2007, pp. 120–4.
65   Under the Hollande and Macron Presidencies, the PNRU was extended in practice, with a second phase of the programme begun in 2015 (Gouvernment de France 2014). The main orientation of the policy has not changed, budgetary shrinkage and programmatic recalibrations notwithstanding.
66   Lambert 2015.
67   Lelévrier and Noyé 2012, pp. 188–99; Kirszbaum 2008, pp. 31–2.
68   Interview 8; Clerval 2012, pp. 92–112.
69   Belmessous 2007, p. 147.
70   Planner, Interview 4.
71   Epstein 2008.

degree of vacancy was seen as an opportunity to finance a large proportion of redevelopment with for-profit investment, thus massively shrinking the proportion of social housing tenants on the future site (*La Coudraie* in Poissy).[72]

The weight of land-rent-driven redevelopment is very uneven, however. On large, isolated estates or in municipalities with a very high proportion of social housing and precarious or unemployed working-class inhabitants, market housing development was initially limited to one or two market rental buildings (provided by payroll-tax-financed non-profit *Association Foncière Logement*) or enclaves of private ownership housing. This holds for *La Cité des 3000* (Aulnay-Sous-Bois) or *Val Fourré* (Mantes-la-Jolie), 50 km west of Paris, where, in the words of planners, 'real estate developers don't come the way they do in Nanterre' (adjacent to central business district *La Défense*).[73] In these cases, land-rent-oriented redevelopment is best understood as a way to build strategically placed beachheads that may provide the basis for future rounds of investment in market housing.[74] In such contexts, rapid transit connections have the potential to buttress land-rent-oriented redevelopment further in the future.[75] This is particularly the case with the *Grand Paris Express*, the automated subway that is being built to loop through various parts of the urban region.[76] Partly financed by receipts from future property development next to the new subway stations, this mega-subway project has been formally connected to various ANRU redevelopment projects, for example those in in Clichy-sous-Bois/Montfermeil and Aulnay-sous-Bois.[77]

'Valorisation' is not reducible to profit-oriented residential gentrification, however. It also describes, broadly, ways of 'upgrading' the character of social housing or providing the infrastructural, security-related or symbolic conditions for future private investment. Particularly in industrial suburbs with 'red' political pasts in the Northern and Eastern suburbs – St. Denis, Gennevilliers,

---

72   Fossey 2017.
73   Interview 9.
74   Bourdon and Noye 2016.
75   Tramways bring new connections to projects in Sarcelles, Sartrouville, Haut Montreuil, St. Denis, Gennevilliers, and La Courneuve.
76   Kipfer, Boudreau, Hamel, and Noubouwo 2017; Enright 2016.
77   Kipfer, Boudreau, Hamel, and Noubouwo 2017; Rigouste 2012, pp. 175–6; Lefebvre 2018, 2019; Lisi 2019. As a result of its developmental thrust, the *Grand Paris Express* project is facing various, sometimes networked local resistance campaigns against real-estate speculation, social housing demolition, the privatisation of planning and other democratic deficits, and, finally, the impacts of future development on ecology and agriculture. Some of these campaigns against *Grand Paris* are carried by social housing tenants (*Assemblée des Collectifs en lutte contre le Grand Paris* n.d.).

Montreuil – redevelopment is a part of municipal or inter-communal strategies to counter deindustrialisation and attract new employers (and workers) as well as new residents.[78] Also, in most cases, the bulk of housing-related 'valorisation' on housing estates takes place within the social housing sector itself. Institutionally complex, French social housing is still less residualised than its counterparts in Britain and North America, even though accumulated budget constraints are one factor pushing housing authorities towards redevelopment.[79] New units built by social housing providers tend to be in 'higher' categories: those that require fewer subsidies or those that make it possible for inhabitants to acquire their units by means of subsidised ownership (*accession sociale à la propriété*).[80] In these cases, design strategies (*résidentialisation*) mimic or anticipate private property lines by enclosing building envelopes or eliminating public space labelled as grey space (*terrain vague*). In the rare cases where redevelopment efforts take place in nineteenth-century districts with little social housing – the eighteenth district in Paris, Bas Montreuil next to Paris – new social housing units often displace what is called de facto social housing (*logement social de fait*): private rental units that house a higher number of low-income residents than regular social housing units. There, redevelopment aims at clarifying complex property claims to attract outside retail and residential investment. These cases demonstrate the decisive but multidimensional role the state plays in the gentrification process in Paris.[81]

3.2   *Recentralising State Intervention? Rescaling and Local Relations of Force*

Housing estate redevelopment signals a selective recentralisation of French urban policy, which, since the beginning of the decentralisation reforms of the

---

78   Bacqué and Fol 1997; Tissot 2007; Masclet 2006.

79   Tournon 2018.

80   Comité d'évaluation 2008. Further showcasing the institutional complexity of working-class housing in France, redevelopment on the estate straddling both *Clichy-Sous-Bois* and *Montfermeil* concentrates on devalorised multi-residential ownership housing (*co-propriétés*). Built by inexperienced speculators who benefited from low-interest loans under the programme *Logements économiques et familiaux* (*Logéco*) in the 1950s, this housing form has functioned as de facto rental housing for precarious households (Le Garrec 2014; Kechaou 2017).

81   Clerval 2012, pp. 43–60, 173–207; see also Clerval and Delage 2019; Clerval and Miot 2019. The fact that most redevelopment projects do not produce mass displacement and do not always attract new residents that fit the profile of typical central city gentrifiers does not mean there is no gentrification in estate redevelopment, as some have suggested (Lelévrier 2018). Gentrification – the restructuring of a social space that favours classes and social groups 'superior' to existing inhabitants, workers or consumers – can take various shapes and forms.

1980s had come to resemble a *mille-feuille* of cross-cutting lines of informal and contractual intra-state relations. The capacity of ANRU to leverage finance and engage localities in a competition for contracts has given it the power to harmonise and standardise local projects.[82] ANRU's template-like approach pushed left-leaning progressive municipalities to demolish more aggressively and prioritise physical reconstruction over social policy interventions than they otherwise might have. During my interviews, politicians and planners in municipalities like St. Denis, Gennevilliers, Poissy, and Montreuil corroborated that ANRU did indeed have these kinds of effects on their particular local approach to redevelopment.[83]

It is important to stress that ANRU's standardised approach is facilitated by a deeper, cross-partisan consensus about the basic assumptions and principles of redevelopment: the idea that social mixing is necessary because of the pathology that is concentrated poverty ('ghettos') and because the many real or perceived 'dysfunctionalities' of postwar physical planning, architecture and design. Planners and politicians in left-leaning municipalities sometimes cast their approach in a way that diverges somewhat from the right: as projects to produce socially cohesive communities in a territorially more equal and multi-polar urban region,[84] or as a way to build upon the existing 'social mix' in multicultural working-class districts,[85] not as projects to maximise demolitions, facilitate private investment, replace resident populations or subordinate all aspects of planning to the imperative of 'security'. Ultimately, these divergent arguments represent variations within a cross-partisan consensus about the imperative of 'mixing' qua reconstruction.[86]

If the upward rescaling of state strategies in France is made possible by a nation-wide consensus, it is also selective and uneven. Upward rescaling – and tendential scalar convergence – is mediated by local relations of force. Municipalities, and the mayor's office in particular, continue to play an important role in organising rule across an uneven political landscape otherwise governed by a unitary state. Both mayors and social housing providers remain crucial players in the development and implementation of ANRU contracts. As a result, local political realities matter in determining the modalities of public housing redevelopment, including the specific ways in which social mixing is defined and advanced. This is most evident in municipalities where electoral

82   Epstein 2012a, pp. 238–56, 304–34.
83   Interviews 1, 4, 5, 11, 13.
84   Interview 1.
85   Interviews 6, 8.
86   Epstein 2012b.

218

CHAPTER 5

majorities have alternated between the right and the left (Aulnay-Sous-Bois, Poissy) and different left formations (Montreuil). It is also true where redevelopment efforts predate *ANRU* (in almost all of our cases) or where they represented veritable 'laboratories' for subsequent national policies (as they did in La Courneuve and Mantes-la-Jolie).[87]

Grand ensembles were developed initially through locally differentiated experiments. National policies of mass housing and spatial planning were forged and consolidated through such experiments in the 1950s.[88] Not surprisingly, today's national policy to redevelop said estates is also refracted by local-regional political histories. One can identify two axes of differentiation within a broader political consensus about the necessity to 'redevelop' and 'mix'. First, the commitment to rebuilding (or expanding) social housing in varied Socialist or reform Communist municipalities like St. Denis, Sarcelles of Nanterre contrasts with strategies of squeezing the social housing stock on principle in right-wing cities like Mantes-la-Jolie and Sartrouville.[89] Second, local commitments to the 'Republican' imperative of mixing existing inhabitants with others on site and beyond vary.[90] In part, this is because the right-leaning mayors are more likely to culturalise social problems in ethno-racial ways.[91] However, advocates of ethnic dispersal (in Poissy, Sartrouville) as well as their conceptual opposites, defenders of communitarian or de facto multicultural management (in Mantes, Paris, Sarcelles), come in various party colours, as will become clear below.

3.3 Social Recomposition and Redesign as Conquest: Political Dynamics along Lines of Class and Race

They are in the process of cleansing the city.[92]

Starting tomorrow, we are going to subject the project to industrial cleansing.[93]

---

87   Interview 10.
88   Le Goullon 2014.
89   Interviews 4, 9.
90   Kirszbaum 1999, 2013.
91   Belmessous 2007, p. 154.
92   Activist with the *Forum Social des Quartiers Populaires*, Interview 3.
93   President Sarkozy during a visit to *La Cité des 4000*, La Courneuve 19 June 2005, cited in Hugues 2009.

Loïc Wacquant underscored that environmentally determinist arguments to justify place-based state intervention often rely on 'territorial stigmatisation': thick, institutionally reinforced assumptions about the 'problems' that supposedly inhere in the physical and cultural characteristics of particular types of places.[94] He sees this process, in Bourdieu-esque fashion, as an exercise of symbolic violence enacted by the state. In the French context, territorial stigmatisation is official policy – it is projected by the web of territorial targets and an array of maps by which the state focuses urban policies and thus conceives space in environmentally determinist ways.[95] Locally, territorial stigmata show their weight in the frequency by which decision-makers and planners invoke the need to 'change the image' of a particular project or municipality so as to turn them into 'normal' neighbourhoods or cities. As a long-standing planner in 'red', Communist-run Gennevilliers said, 'from the beginning in the 1970s, the main theme [of redevelopment] was to change the image of housing estate *Le Luth*, [and with it] the image of the *banlieue rouge*'. Why? To revalorise the territory for economic development and diversify housing tenure, and thus return to a 'traditional', 'European' city.[96] Territorial stigma thus emerge in contrast to assumed or desired norms. As planners, activists and politicians indicate, these norms can be framed variably, in terms of built form (street-related design, easier access to other neighbourhoods), mixed land-use (the presence of local businesses), attractiveness to new residents, tenure and social composition (average levels of social housing or immigrants), and 'civil' public space.[97]

Wacquant is also correct that territorial stigmata are comparatively variegated: they need not replay the particular racist culture of poverty in the USA. He is right to underline the importance of 'youth' as a category of stigmatisation in France.[98] But, as I will point out further below, the mobilisation of this category to justify a veritable 'reconquest' of stigmatised neighbourhoods and its inhabitants variously vilified by politicians as scum or uncivilised brutes (*racaille, sauvageons*), testifies not to the absence of racialisation in France but its comparative specificity. While Wacquant operates with a somewhat stylised conception of the African-American ghetto,[99] he also underestimates ethnically absolutist and racialised dimensions of territorial reorganisation in

94   Wacquant 2008, pp. 163–98.
95   Tranb 2005.
96   Interview 5.
97   Interviews 3, 4, 8, 9, 11, 12; ANRUa, ANRUb, ANRUd.
98   Wacquant 2008, pp. 188–90.
99   Gilbert 2010.

France.[100] Furthermore, he neglects the fact that these dimensions of French urbanism are largely homegrown; they are not a mere function of importing US-American neoliberalism and zero tolerance policing. They are entrenched in institutional practices of the French state and in imaginaries and ideologies of fear that rearticulate not only France's own history of class warfare but also various layers of its colonial past.[101] In this context, current dynamics of physical segregation, bodily confinement and daily humiliation can be understood in part by borrowing terms from earlier rounds of Francophone anti-colonialism.[102] This underscores the need to infuse and redirect a Lefebvrean critique of hierarchical spatial organisation with insights from Frantz Fanon in order to analyse the neo-colonial dimensions of social mixing qua redevelopment.

At the most basic level, racism works in unannounced ways, through the silent, structural effects of state strategies. Not only were ANRU projects originally designed for districts (*Zones Urbaines Sensibles*) that were statistically co-defined as areas with concentrations of immigrants and their French-born descendants far above the national or regional averages, reaching 64 percent in the Paris metropolitan region.[103] ANRU was also designed to target areas on ZUS where the proportions of immigrants, non-citizens, the unemployed and the low-waged are particularly high.[104] In the absence of other statistical indicators, immigrant or citizenship status measures ethno-racial composition only indirectly, possibly underestimating the prevalence of non-White residents. Certainly, the ANRU projects I visited at various times of the day target areas that are clearly dominated by various 'mixes' of people of colour (even though they are not homogenous in terms of class and race). Focusing

---

100   In her careful comparison of social housing unit allocation practices in Marseille and Birmingham, Valérie Sala Pala underlines the fluid boundaries between ethnically essentialist and explicitly racist frames of state-bound decision-making in both contexts (2013, p. 170).

101   Tevanian 2013, pp. 155–7; Tissot 2007; Kipfer 2012.

102   Lapeyronnie 2008.

103   ONZUS 2011. It is important to note, however, that the clear majority of migrants and their descendants in France do not live on ZUS (ONZUS 2011; Préteceille 2009). In France, the residential geography of racialisation is not reducible to the experience of living on large, segregated Fordist housing estates or in stigmatised low-rent districts dating from the eighteenth or nineteenth century. It extends to the private rental and property housing market, where immigrants of colour tend to live as demographic minorities (Lambert 2015; Belmessous et al. 2006). To put it differently, racialised micro-segregation is not only a result of public housing redevelopment; as spatial form, it predates such redevelopment or exists parallel to it.

104   Lelévrier 2010a, p. 132; Lelévrier and Noyé 2012, pp. 186–7; Lelévrier and Noyé 2018, p. 123.

reconstruction on areas with high poverty and unemployment thus dispro-
portionately affects inhabitants with immigrant backgrounds, as planners in
Montreuil, for example admitted.[105] This is also true for nineteenth-century
suburbs like *Bas Montreuil* and *Goutte d'Or/Château Rouge*. There planners
and politicians know that renovation has particular effects on non-European
undocumented workers (who do not qualify for replacement housing)[106] or
African and North African stores. In the eighteenth district of Paris, officials
do not consider these stores proper neighbourhood stores (*commerces de proximité*) even though they provide inhabitants – and not just visiting shoppers –
as much with necessities as the (more typically 'French') bakeries, wine stores,
and flower shops preferred by planners.[107]

In France, the notoriously vague policy category of social mixing (*mixité
sociale*) is often coded in ethnic or 'racial' terms.[108] Planners in left or right
municipalities hesitate discussing if the official goal of *mixité sociale* refers not
only to a mix of housing tenures, income groups, and labour-market status but
also to a veritable ethnic or 'racial' mix.[109] This hesitation can be explained
in part as a way to avoid legal sanction (ethnic or racial targeting is against
the law, and sometimes punished), in part as a way to render invisible racialised fractures in the indivisible Republic (which also helps explain the official
refusal to collect data on ethnicity and race). Yet the official – statistical and
legal – silence on ethnicity and race does get broken.[110] Official documents
occasionally refer to the 'weight' of the immigrant population as a problem
to be corrected by reconstruction.[111] In Poissy, a planner is adamant that the
ethno-racial interpretation of mixing is 'clearly in play; it is even quite explicit
in the [former] mayor's discourse'.[112] And in Montreuil, the local planner says
this about the *Rue de Paris*, an African-defined streetscape extending from *Rue
d'Avron* in the adjacent twentieth arrondissement of Paris:

> The general environment on *Rue de Paris* is pretty repulsive; in general it
> is a built form characteristic of *faubourgs* [nineteenth-century working-
> class suburbs]; it has always been an immigrant neighbourhood ... and
> today it is the neighbourhood [in Montreuil] with the highest proportion

---

105   Interviews 13, 14.
106   Interview 12.
107   Interview 8; ANRUa.
108   Belmessous 2006; Kirszbaum 2008.
109   Interviews 7, 13.
110   See also Kirszbaum 2013.
111   ANRUd; Portes 2007.
112   Interview 11.

of immigrants; this presents a bad image ... it is rather difficult to mix senior managers in suits and ties with immigrants living in a hostel ... The existing mix and ethnic concentration is the problem.[113]

In this Montreuil case, the residential and commercial concentration understood in immutably ethnic, if class-inflected categories – not only in terms of disrepair and fragmented ownership – is an obstacle to the goal of mixing up the area by attracting real estate investment and new residents.

Whether explicit or coded, the ethnically essentialist or racialised dimensions of social mixing are most concrete in two institutional state practices: the allocation of social housing units in the relocation process and security strategies. My research confirms the secondary literature that has documented how the commissions that decide who is (re-)housed in which housing units often argue against the concentration of 'social problems' in buildings or subdistricts in ways that effectively discriminate against low-income residents, single-parent families, and non-European inhabitants.[114] Planners in municipalities of divergent political colours confirm the bias of these commissions (and some of their most influential members: the mayor or the social housing provider) against the recreation of 'ghettos' or the concentration of 'large families' in rebuilt social housing.[115] One local facilitator working in *Bel Air* and *Grands Pêchers* estates in Montreuil is frank:

> Ethnic criteria are forbidden ... but they are used, we know that ... in a neighbourhood with a lot of people from Mali, they'll put fewer people from Mali ... We know because people are on these committees and tell us. It is not written down.[116]

In St. Denis, where the presence of immigrants of colour has been a key factor in decisions to renovate and demolish public housing since the 1980s,[117] the current project manager for renovation projects has this to say: 'In France, ethnic mixing is taboo ... [But] officials of social housing provider 3F, are going to be hyper-vigilant not to reconstitute a "village" in one section of an apartment block'.[118]

---

113   Interview 12.
114   Tanter and Toubon 1999; Simon 2003; Tissot 2005; Sala Pala 2013.
115   Interviews 5, 6, 7.
116   Interview 14.
117   David 2014, pp. 324–6.
118   Interview 4.

'Security' is also a major motivation – and a crucial micro-strategy – in the redevelopment of housing estates, some of which, like *Les Indes* in Sartrouville, are described by planners as veritable no-go areas for the police. One of the overarching priorities is to make projects 'open', 'legible', 'accessible' and 'permeable' for emergency services, particularly the police, which by law must be consulted before design plans are finalised.[119] The assumptions underlying 'insecurity' or 'sensitivity' are not socially neutral. They are coded in terms of class, race, and gender to, for example, describe the ways in which un- or underemployed or informally employed young men appropriate public space and thus become identified as a social threat to planners and politicians. While not reducible to a uniform 'racial' image, the spectre of loitering young men typically zeroes in on groups of racialised teenagers of African origin (which empirically may also include White proletarians).[120] In the *Grand Pêchers* estate in Haut Montreuil, for example, a project facilitator claims that the image of insecurity that was used to justify redevelopment was based on a few dozen young men that are used to occupying public space.[121] In Sarcelles, planners indicate that urban design is a tool to confront the habit of teenagers to 'occupy entrance halls' and engage in 'uncivil behaviour'.[122] In response, *residentialisation* includes measures to 'normalise' the residential character of projects by shrinking public space, enclosing entrances and demarcating private from public space with fences and other dividers. In these cases, the norm underlying this French version of defensible space planning (*prévention situationelle*) remains vague, referring to images of village life or Haussmannised sections of central Paris.[123]

As these examples of public space redesign indicate, there are explicitly political dimensions to racialised, gendered and class-based strategies of social mixing and physical redevelopment. Social mixing is often hoped to facilitate paternalistic control, ways of disciplining 'problem populations' by subordinating them to role models: the new inhabitants that arrive to bring the desired social mix. This paternalism has class, race, and gender dimensions, blaming social problems on those experiencing them: non-White, poor workers or single mothers. The expectation is that 'an unemployed person amidst tenants with jobs ... will be spontaneously pulled upwards'[124] or that people 'weighed down

---

119   ANRUe; Interviews 7, 11; *Le Parisien* 2009; Garnier 2012, pp. 26–33.

120   Abdallah 2012; Khiari 2008, pp. 194–8; Rigouste 2012, p. 12.

121   Interview 14.

122   Interview 6.

123   Lelévrier 2010a, p. 96.

124   Gilles Poux, mayor of *La Courneuve*, cited in Belmessous 2007, p. 146.

with social problems' such as single-parent families or people with the lowest incomes 'may show a little more responsibility towards the collectivity' once immersed in a 'mixed' environment.[125] Here existing inhabitants are deemed incapable of taking matters into their own hands without the presence of new, socially respectable – and morally and ethically 'responsible' – neighbours.

Demolition and social recomposition aim sometimes at undermining or preventing collective political resistance. As one activist from the *Forum Social des Quartier Populaires* says with the benefit of historical hindsight

> ... In certain neighbourhoods, certain struggles were organised, be that against police violence, against the *double peine* [deporting immigrants already convicted for committing a crime in France], around housing and work issues, against discrimination in housing and all that ... in a way, they are erasing these struggles ... The best way to erase them, to make sure that they don't emerge from these neighbourhoods, is to smash them; this is the goal of the *rénovation urbaine*, at least this is what we think .... They destroy the memory [of struggle], ... they destroy families ... it is violent.[126]

Certainly, in projects with a history of uprising (Val-Fourré, Mantes-La-Jolie, and Francs-Moisins, St. Denis after 1991), housing demolitions in the past tended to target the politically most riot-prone parts of the projects. On the Val-Fourré estate, a planner recalls that 'the first actions were demolitions, and they were linked to the riots that took place in 1991, they destroyed the buildings next to the skating rink, where the riots took place'.[127] A stark current case is Sartrouville, where memories of the 1991 riots in *Les Indes* explain in part why planners, politicians, developers and social housing providers want to 'radically change the image' of this most 'sensitive' project. How? By greatly shrinking the social housing stock to make room for market housing.[128] In Poissy, where residents quickly mobilised to stop what was originally planned to be the total demolition of their neighbourhood, *La Coudraie*, social mixing aims not only to disperse the existing concentration of French-Moroccan inhabitants. According to the planner, social mixing also wants to ensure that '*La Coudraie* [not] remain an isolated pocket of resisters'.[129]

---

125 Deputy mayor of the eighteenth arrondissement, Paris, Interview 8.
126 Interview 3.
127 Interview 9.
128 Interview 7; Tessier 2016; Piffaretti 2017.
129 Interview 11.

3.4   *Social Mixing as a Neo-colonial Project*

The social and physical reorganisation of housing estates is thus a multifaceted – also ethnicised and racialised – exercise to reorganise relations of domination territorially. Given my Fanon-Lefebvre line of analysis, I need to ask the following question: in what ways can the racialised dimensions of territorial reorganisation be called neo-colonial in the concrete historical sense of the term? There are at least three ways to answer this question. While fully developed only when immigrants (from the colonies and Southern Europe) started entering regular social housing in larger numbers (from the 1970s to the 1980s), social mixing in housing has a longer history. In the 1950s and 1960s, towns like Nanterre, Gennevilliers and Argenteuil started to experiment with 'quotas' and numerical thresholds tellingly called *seuils de tolérance*: attempts to limit the spatial concentration of immigrants (particularly Arab and Kabyle immigrants from Algeria) so as not to exceed the limited tolerance of local inhabitants. In this racist logic, immigrants are held responsible for 'native' French hostility, which is taken for granted, naturalised as an inevitable response. The term 'large families' was used already then as a code for immigrants, particularly those from the colonies.[130] In left-wing versions of this history, municipalities in the red, Communist belt of Paris like Gennevilliers, Nanterre or St. Denis wanted to redistribute social housing (particularly transitional housing for immigrants and the most subsidised social housing) across the Paris region. Instead of treating immigrant and precarious workers as part of their social base, these administrations treated them as a financial burden for local welfare states, and, with the rise of the *Front National* in the 1980s, also as an electoral liability.[131]

Understood as a strategy to limit, regulate or undo concentrations of non-White inhabitants, social mixing is gendered. In our discussion of Frantz Fanon in Chapter 2, we stressed the way in which urban policy in Algeria pursued a broader goal of 'unveiling' women: controlling Algerian households by making visible Algerian women. With the resurgence of anti-Muslim racism in the 2000s, the imperative of 'unveiling' women returned to the centre stage of French politics with laws banning headscarves from public schools and burqas from public space (during the Sarkozy era).[132] During the Hollande Presidency, this imperative was selectively incorporated into urban policy (*politique de la*

---

130   De Rudder 1991; De Barros 2005; Blanc-Chaléard 2012; Blanchard 2012; Masclet 2006, Belmessous 2015.

131   Masclet 2006, 2005; Tissot 2005; Stovall 2003; David 2014; Collet 2019, pp. 49–92.

132   Bouamama 2004; Chouder, Latrèche, and Tevanian 2008; Tevanian 2012; Hajjat and Mohammed 2013.

ville) to turn already targeted social spaces (*banlieues* and central city neighbourhoods inhabited by working-class people of colour) into places in need of
place-specific gender equality policies such as women audits of public space
and anti-harassment policies. While this new element of place-based urban
policy is not directly tied to housing estate reconstruction, it helps us understand the gendered aspects of *PNRU* projects. It suggests that one threatening
indicator of non-mixity (the dominance of non-White men in the public spaces
of target districts) reveals another one: the sexist forms of gender segregation
that are supposed to be typical of *African* households. As Claire Hancock has
shown, this policy is not only based on empirically flawed assumptions about
the daily (im)mobilities of non-White inhabitants, whether these are gendered
as men or women, boys or girls. It also resembles older civilising missions to
'emancipate' colonised women from above. As such, it indicates that the territorialised pursuit of social mixity recasts colonial traditions of state intervention
along both racialised and gendered lines.[133]

Current imperatives of mixing (breaking up existing housing estates, dispersing or resegregating their residents while 'unveiling' gender relations in
the projects) thus recast late colonial and early neo-colonial strategies. This
is also true for the third neo-colonial aspect of social mixing in *ANRU* projects: policing and counterinsurgency. As both documents and planners reveal,
redevelopment projects are often couched in military language, as *reconquests*
of areas that are officially called 'sensitive' in security terms.[134] This language
is not innocent. As a number of analysts have pointed out, it stands in a tradition of pacification and counterinsurgency that has always treated migrants
from the (former) colonies as political risks. Indeed, strategies to manage (or
dissolve) concentrated migrant settlements (in shantytowns (*bidonvilles*)), hostels (*foyers*), transitional housing (*cités de transit*), and regular social housing
(*HLM*) from the 1950s were informed by personnel, tactics, and population
classifications from the colonies, notably Algeria.[135] After 1962, these colonial
practices were adapted and diffused in order to control and 'civilise' migrants
through a number of state branches which at times worked with housing officials: those responsible for social security, immigration, citizenship, regional
planning, civil engineering, local policing, internal security and the military.[136]

133 Hancock 2017; Hancock and Mobillion 2019; Hancock, Blanchard, and Chapuis 2018; Blan-
     chard and Hancock 2017.
134 Interview 12; ANRUc; ANRUd.
135 De Barros 2005, 2012; Hmed 2007; Viet 1999; Blanc 1983; Ewane 2012; Cohen and David
     2012; Belmessous 2015; Henni 2017; Blanc-Chaléard 2016.
136 De Barros 2007; Blanchard 2011; Math 2000; Fredenucci 2003a, 2003b; Sacriste 2012;

In part, these state strategies responded to migrant struggles in workplaces, shantytowns, and housing projects before and after 1968: anti-eviction campaigns, strikes, rent strikes, and solidarity actions.[137]

The Goutte D'Or/Château Rouge neighbourhoods in the eighteenth district of Paris famously exemplify why it matters to insist on the neo-colonial – as well as the class-based and gendered – dynamics of current renovation projects. Anne Clerval's study of the gentrification of central Paris persuasively demonstrates how the class dynamics of gentrification in this still largely African neighbourhood have empirically strong ethnic and racialised dimensions – and must be understood in explicit political terms.[138] Building on this insight, one can also stress the specifically anti-racist and anti-colonial history that has shaped the area. For the Goutte D'Or has not only an explosive French working-class history going back to the nineteenth century (captured most famously in Emile Zola's *Assommoir*). Better known as Barbès, after the boulevard on its Western edge, the neighbourhood's importance for counter-colonial and anti-racist politics far exceeds its small size. The 1955 revolt there coincided with the declaration of the state of emergency in Algeria. It was met with concerted state repression that included assassination and torture and culminated in the 1961 massacre.[139] After 1968, this hub of then still mostly North African migration, was the site of the well-known mobilisations and hunger strikes against racist violence and murder in 1971. It came to house various crucial movement institutions, including the *Mouvement des Travailleurs Arabes*, which was founded in 1972.[140] Since the 1990s, the neighbourhood, parts of which had become settled by inhabitants from sub-Saharan Africa by then, was the heart of a new round of *sans papiers* mobilisations and a locally rooted squatting movement. In short, the political significance of destructuring the Goutte d'Or/Château Rouge cannot be grasped without accounting for – and conceptualising – this specific history of counter-colonial and anti-racist opposition.

The relationship between late colonial and early postcolonial state strategies and current security initiatives is best understood as a recomposition: a complex articulation of continuity and discontinuity. Current redevelopment projects (notably those in areas with recent histories of revolt like Clichy-sous-Bois, Villiers-le-Bel and Grenoble) have become points of experimentation not only

---

Laurens 2009; Spire 2005; Hajjat 2012; Rigouste 2012, pp. 21–49; Rigouste 2017; Belmessous 2014, 2015; David 2014; Blanc-Chaléard 2016.

137 Viet 1999; Hmed 2008b; Pitti 2008; Hervo 2012; Collet 2019.
138 Clerval 2012.
139 Taalba n.d.
140 Kawtari n.d.; Gordon 2012, pp. 120–32.

for securitised urban design but also for aggressive, racially profiled policing by highly autonomous mobile units (*Brigades Anti-Criminalités*, BAC) and paramilitary counterinsurgency methods aimed at keeping in check inhabitants and preventing links between local resistance and broader dynamics of mobilisation.[141] Counterinsurgency methods, which are used for urban warfare in non-European conflict zones, are based on state security doctrines that have shed their cold war anti-Communism but continue to treat people of colour as internal threats.[142] And the localised, hyper-masculinist practices of BAC units to provoke, chase and humiliate inhabitants redeploy late colonial policing methods that resemble, in effect, regimes of exception.[143] One can thus understand why the mobile police units are often perceived as occupying forces perpetuating a quasi-colonial form of state contempt and humiliation (*hogra*).[144] And one can see why spectacular demolitions by dynamite can evoke memories of colonial war among older residents[145] – or Gaza, the Sahel and West Africa among younger inhabitants. Fanon's insight holds: in a (neo-)colonial context, territorial hierarchies are organised in part through the stark, racialised lines of division drawn by the police and the military.

3.5   Don't Believe the Hype: The Contradictions of State Strategy

The *rénovation urbaine* is remaking the ghetto, just more tidily.[146]

They have demolished a lot here, and every time, the problems [drug trafficking] moved elsewhere.[147]

Rénovation Urbaine projects help break up stigmatised housing both physically and socially. They do this for the most part not by complete destruction and mass displacement but by shrinking the most subsidised housing stock, encouraging a differentiation of housing tenure (with selective additions of market or subsidised ownership units), and, in some cases, decentralising new construction. Yet evaluation reports and interviewees indicate that *PNRU*

---

141   Rigouste 2012; Belmessous 2010; see also Rigouste 2017.
142   Rigouste 2011.
143   Rigouste 2012, pp. 137–71; Blanchard 2011.
144   Belmessous 2010, p. 124; Abdallah 2012, p. 12.
145   Abdallah 2005, p. 160.
146   Yazid Sabeg, President of the *Comité d'évaluation et de suivi de l'Agence nationale de la rénovation urbaine*, 2012.
147   Abdel, resident of *Cité des 4000*, La Courneuve, cited in *Le Monde* 2012.

does not improve residents' economic conditions,[148] nor does it lead to social integration, political harmony, or a territorial equalisation of 'social problems'. Instead it produces social fragmentation, fine-grained re-segregation and differential residential mobilities. While some households are spatially reconcentrated in 'very social' (highly subsidised) housing, others may qualify for 'less social' housing or afford new market housing on or off redevelopment sites.[149] In the words of one planner, reconstruction encourages 'those with resources (be those financial or in the form of networks) [to leave]', thus undermining existing income mixes.[150] According to another planner, projects result in a 'certain kind of social sorting … between those who can afford the new housing [the less poor] and those how are rehoused in old apartments … [which] are always in the same place' [on existing or comparable sites].[151] Over-represented among those re-segregated people, spatially immobilised low-income households are large or single-parent families and households with an immigrant family history.[152]

Why this combination of resegregation and socially segmented (im-)mobility? First, the bias towards 'revalorised' – smaller and more expensive – social or market housing, the difficulty of attracting new residents to some sites, and the imperative of maintaining property values in capitalist land markets, real or simulated, all militate against fine-grained spatial proximity. Second, high land costs and mixophobia – racist or class-based resistance to social housing in other areas – can block the dispersal of the 'most social' [most subsidised] housing units, as planners in both left- and right-leaning parts of the region indicate.[153] Third, security-oriented redesign (*résidentialisation*) – gating new buildings, enclosing entrances, playgrounds and parking lots – undermines public space where inhabitants could actually 'mix' in real life. Called 'bunkerisation' by some,[154] securitised design symbolically and physically reinforces a culture of fear and an already existing tendency for current inhabitants and newcomers to avoid each other on site as well as in the school system.[155] As we know from the very history of the French *Grand Ensembles* (which also tried to prevent proletarian concentrations even though they are now deemed to lack

---

148   Jérôme 2012.
149   Lelévrier 2010a, 2010b; Lelévrier and Noyé 2012, 2018; Lelévrier 2015; Epstein 2012b; Oblet and Villechaise 2012; Faure 2006; Comité d'évaluation 2008.
150   Interview 14.
151   Interview 4.
152   Lelévrier 2010, p. 46; Lelévrier and Noyé 2012, p. 207.
153   Interviews 4, 9; Bacqué et al. 2010; Belmessous 2006.
154   Belmessous 2010.
155   Interviews 9, 14.

the *proper* social mix) the idea of the European city as a machine of integration does not hold up to closer scrutiny. What was true then still holds today: the spatial proximity of different social groups does not typically, let alone necessarily yield social integration.[156]

PNRU illustrates why analysts of place-based policy should refrain from taking for granted the intentions of public policy or the effectiveness of official discourses that circulate among policy makers in self-referential fashion. Following Lefebvre's and Fanon's dialectical perspectives on state and colonial policy, it makes more sense to pay closer attention to fissures within state strategies as well as contradictions between the conceptions of planners and politicians and daily spatial practices and imaginaries. In the French case, such a sensitivity to the contradictions of state intervention is vital also to grasp how local decision-makers differ in their interpretations of the central state objective of promoting Republican social integration by means of class-based social (and, by implication at least, ethno-racialised) mixing.[157] These differences recast, in a neo-colonial context, the long-standing contradictions between assimilation and segregation we have already encountered in relationship to Algeria (Chapter 2) and Canada (Chapter 4).

Municipalities like Poissy and Sartrouville are committed to breaking up existing concentrations of non-White inhabitants and the associated 'communitarian', that is to say, un-Republican image of housing estates. According to planners, they aim at dispersing significant numbers of existing inhabitants while refusing to build prayer spaces and mosques on the reconstructed sites, for example.[158] Others, however, have no such qualms with 'communitarian' management. In Mantes-la-Jolie, a left-wing local politician reports that

> for the racist right, the objective is not to mix; here, were are caught within a logic of ethnic management, ... a rather communitarian model [where] everybody stays amongst their own ... and the strategies attempt to encircle the Val-Fourré estate ... effectively adding to ethnic concentration.[159]

For the right-wing city government in Mantes, 'building mosques [on reconstructed Val-Fourré] ... is a way to buy social peace'[160] and prolong clientelist

156   Chamboredon and Lemaire 1970; Bernard 2009.
157   Kirzsbaum 1999, 2013.
158   Interviews 7, 11.
159   Interview 10.
160   Interview 9.

relationships with ethnically essentialised inhabitant groups without systematically dispersing them.[161] Social mixing is thus not only a function of rebuilding replacement housing in other areas and towns. It is also a result of reshuffling existing inhabitants based on income as those who can move into newly built ownership housing on site.[162] Meanwhile, in Socialist Paris, support for an Islamic prayer space in *Goutte d'Or/Château Rouge* allowed the City to differentiate itself from the populist and fascist right (which had mobilised against Muslim street prayers there, as well as elsewhere). In the words of the deputy mayor responsible for the district, the redevelopment symbolically affirms the 'working class and multicultural' 'mix' of the neighbourhood even as it wants to dilute the African character of existing retail, housing and public space.[163] These two cases show that seemingly colour-blind Republicanism can co-exist in practice with communitarian or multiculturalist state practices, as anti-racist intellectual Houria Bouteldja reminds us.[164]

3.6   *Demolition as Hegemonic Project? Structural Violence, Opposition and Incorporation*

Can the exercise of hegemony leave space untouched?[165]

The French experience suggests that urban movements do not survive if they only seek economic demands on collective consumption: they must represent something more or they fade.[166]

Inhabitants have resisted various forms of structural and symbolic violence advanced by reconstruction projects: the enclosure and commodification of social housing, the loss of home and memory, the fear of losing neighbours and

161   Interview 10; see also Kirszbaum 1999, p. 106.
162   Zappi 2015; Géraud 2014; Montesse 2015; Guémart 2017.
163   Interview 8.
164   Interview 2. Explicitly ethnicised strategies of managing immigrant workers' housing have a long history in the case of AFTAM (*Association pour la formation technique de base de travailleurs africains et malgaches*). In contrast to the *cités de transit*, this private association, which was originally organised in 1962 to house the first generation of workers from sub-Saharan Africa, did not follow a goal of dispersing and thus assimilating workers from the colonies. Today still, AFTAM workers' hostels continue to be run along ethno-racial lines, the national imperative of social mixing in this sector notwithstanding (Béguin 2014).
165   Lefebvre 1991b, pp. 10–11.
166   Castells 1983, p. 96.

social supports. While uneven and variegated, this resistance reminds us of a crucial insight in our Lefebvre-Fanon lineage: the idea that everyday resistance and collective action represent ways of (re-)appropriating space (and time). In our cases, resistance to housing redevelopment drew upon pre-existing, complexly gendered, repertoires of appropriating space in housing estates.[167] In diffuse or direct action forms, this meant refusing to leave units, throwing Molotov cocktails at construction sites,[168] or setting up camps for evicted residents.[169] Renovation seems to have increased participation in the 2005 riots, which were more intense in places with ANRU projects.[170] Most often, however, organised opposition took the form of what Castells called urban trade unionism: tenant organisations making partial demands – no needless demolition, more reconstructed social housing, less onerous relocation processes – to defend the integrity of social housing against mixing from above. As indicated by campaign materials and interviews with planners, these demands were carried by neighbourhood-specific or *département*-wide organisations, some of which with close links to the political infrastructure of the 'red' suburbs, including the *Confédération nationale du logement* (CNL).[171]

Mobilisations against the original plans to totally destroy *La Coudraie* in Poissy and the project to partially demolish the *Cité Rouge* in Gennevilliers were at the heart of an attempt to link local resistance movements in a broader network (*La Coordination anti-démolition des quartiers populaires*) and a nationwide umbrella organisation of stigmatised working-class neighbourhoods (the *Forum social des quartiers populaires*). Organised with the help from activists in long-standing movements – the housing advocates at *Droit au logement* (DAL) in the first case, the anti-racist *Mouvement de l'immigration et de la banlieue* (MIB) in the second – these two umbrella groups tried to overcome neighbourhood-based localism. As is evident from interviews with activists from both movements, campaign materials and discussions among militants, these groups conjured up the spectre of demolition as social cleansing (*épuration* or *nettoyage social/e*) and real estate speculation. They also analysed demolition and redevelopment as attacks on the banlieue as longstanding bases of life and opposition for working-class immigrants.[172] Seen

167   Bouamama 2009; Lapeyronnie 2008; Da Silva 2004.
168   Interview 4.
169   Muhammad 2011.
170   Epstein 2008, pp. 287–92; Lagrange 2008, p. 382.
171   Interviews 4, 5, 6, 11; *Collectif Logement Val D'Oise* 2007; *Yvelines En Lutte* 2007.
172   Interviews 3, 15; CAQP 2008; FSQP 2008a, 2008b; Kipfer 2009b; Berry-Chikhaoui, Chevalier, and Medina 2016, pp. 224–33.

together, these efforts at place-based but networked resistance articulated the long-standing collective consumption concerns of tenant organisations with anti-racist traditions of struggle embodied in a complex array of autonomous movements[173] and one of their historical products: neighbourhood organisations (*associations*).[174]

In Poissy or Gennevilliers, opposition had direct and concrete effects on rebuilding efforts, stopping complete demolition or reducing the number of demolished units, improving the relocation process and the quality of reconstructed units.[175] In Sartrouville, *anticipated* resistance limited the scale of demolition.[176] Indeed, there is little doubt that existing or potential opposition explains, in part, why demolition in the Paris region, in contrast to various cases in other countries, is almost always partial (reaching 100 percent only at Croix-Petit in Cergy).[177] However, it has been difficult to sustain collective opposition beyond particular, partial demands directed at individual projects. Why? Structurally, concerted redevelopment is hard to oppose *in toto* by organisations and inhabitants that are in permanent crisis mode coping with precarity.[178] Also the relocation process separates and individualises inhabitants, who either leave or try to stay on good terms with their housing provider to maximise their housing options.[179] Once atomised, inhabitants are easily divided into winners and losers.[180] In addition, reconstruction tends to tilt the local balance of power in favour of newcomers, particularly when these arrive in significant numbers. In the *Goutte D'Or/Château Rouge*, for example, gentrifiers have become a constituency supporting creeping social recomposition in ways that dovetail with public policy. They may selectively affirm diversity along lines of race and class but try to control it by calling for a 'calmer' public and residential life.[181]

In various ways, estate redevelopment helps fragment subaltern social spaces.[182] This fragmentation facilitates the capacity of politicians and planners to manage opposition with a mix of coercion, control and incorporation. In 'red' Gennevilliers, City Hall reactivated its long-standing paternalist rela-

---

173   Boubeker and Hajjat 2008; Bouamama 2011; Abdallah 2012; Gordon 2012.
174   Withold de Wenden and Leveau 2001.
175   Interviews 5, 11.
176   Interview 7.
177   While in Paris, my immediate reference point was Toronto (Kipfer and Petrunia 2009).
178   Abdallah 2005.
179   Deboulet 2006.
180   Oblet and Villechaise 2012.
181   Bacqué and Fijalkow 2011, pp. 127–31; Launay 2016; Chabrol and Launay 2016.
182   I am relaying Anne Clerval's observation about gentrification in central Paris (2012, pp. 208–28).

tionship to voters and tenant associations to convince activists to stay within the political family ('*la mairie-poule*').[183] In St. Denis, Sarcelles and Montreuil, consultations were tightly scripted, thus demoralising residents[184] or increasing planners' capacity to handpick a select few 'reliable' tenant representatives.[185] At *La Coudraie* in Poissy, a tenant leader joined the Mayor's office after helping to defeat the long-standing right-wing majority in 2008.[186] And, in Mantes-la-Jolie, an opposition politician argued that 'urban restructuring represented an opportunity' [for former mayor Bédier] to deepen clientelism by doling out contracts and fortifying links with local religious leaders.[187] ANRU projects thus demonstrate not only the contradictions of state action. They also attest to the role of urban specialists (*urbanistes*) in fostering subaltern passivity and reconstructing hegemony.[188] They did so in part by renewing with paternalistic assumptions and repertoires that deem workers and (neo-)colonised inhabitants incapable of historical agency or self-government.[189]

4   Conclusion: Mixity as Hegemonic Political Strategy?

In all regions of the urban world, the present moment is one of intense conflict over how cities are to be used and by whom. The notion that urbanisation is key to social integration probably doesn't mean much anymore, even as a popular myth ... Territorial and cultural proximities thus do not facilitate collaboration and negotiation.[190]

In this chapter, I have foregrounded the specifically political aspects of housing estate redevelopment in the Paris region. Drawing on Henri Lefebvre, Frantz Fanon and research on neo-colonial state intervention in France, I have suggested that these projects cannot be captured only as examples of urban neoliberalism.[191] To some extent, they can be understood as attempts to rescale state intervention in order to facilitate accumulation through land-rent valorisation and economic development. They often do extend the frontier of gentrification

183   Interview 5.
184   Interview 14.
185   Interview 6.
186   Interview 11.
187   Interview 10.
188   Lefebvre 2003a, pp. 184–6.
189   Memmi 1985, p. 114.
190   Simone 2010, pp. 314–15.
191   See also Morel Journel and Sala Pala 2011.

or prepare the ground to do so later. And yet, these projects also recast relations of domination territorially in a particular, racialised and neo-colonial fashion. Partly in response to local and national traditions of struggle or in anticipation of future social conflict, they propose to reorganise social relations of class and race through spatial relations of physical proximity, micro-segregation and functional integration.

To the extent that social mixing and post-functionalist physical planning recast state repertoires developed in the wake of anti-colonial struggles, the long 1968 and anti-racist movements since the 1980s, they represent strategies of 'recolonisation' not only in the metaphorical but also in the racialised and specifically neo-colonial senses of the term. Of course, the effects of redevelopment projects are riddled with contradictions. Recasting an older colonial tension between assimilation and segregation, they lead to re-segregation and micro-segmentation, not social integration (let alone social peace). However, by changing the property form and restructuring the social and physical composition of housing estates, these projects contribute do a broader de- and recomposition of subaltern groups, including inhabitants of colour.[192] They thus raise broader questions about the prospects for claims to the right to the city to open to a dialectic of struggle.[193] Can the 'banlieues' continue to serve as bastions of popular mobilisation and sites of decommodified collective consumption, as generations of left-wing and anti-racist organisers in France have assumed? Will these segregated social spaces remain starting points for broader dynamics of convergence and transformation, as Lefebvre and Fanon hoped, along with other radical intellectuals from Steve Biko (in relationship to the township)[194] to Eldridge Cleaver (with respect to the ghetto)?[195] And: given social mixing as a state strategy from above, can desegregation still promise emancipation on the terms of the segregated, as both Lefebvre and Fanon thought it would?

As AbdouMaliq Simone's quotation indicates, housing estate redevelopment in Paris is not an isolated story. Despite their differences, spatially nuanced projects of 'slum' clearance/rehabilitation, housing redevelopment, gentrification, military urbicide, anti-terrorism, and states of emergency in

---

192 Lambert 2015, pp. 28–32.
193 The antagonism between public housing redevelopment as social mixing and more modest conceptions of the right to the city (as a claim to participatory, use-value based social spaces) is also clear, as Jones and Popke (2010) have pointed out for the US-American HOPE VI projects.
194 Gerhardt 2008, pp. 40–2; Biko 1986; Gibson 2011a, pp. 43–70.
195 Cleaver 1968, pp. 115, 121–8; Douglas 2007; Tyner 2006; Heynen 2009.

these and other parts of the world also show that state-bound strategies of forcibly breaking up, de- and re-segregating subaltern spaces do not bring emancipation but new forms of political domination in an era of intensified socioeconomic polarisation.[196] My emphasis on the politically charged character of urban redevelopment in Paris in part reflects the role of revolutionary history in France and its (former) colonies in politicising state spatial strategies, a role that reminds us of the specifically counter-revolutionary meaning of pacification in this particular imperial context. However, it would be misleading to see state spatial strategies as merely derivative of a French 'model'. This is not only because French Republicanism is contradictory and shot through by uneven sub-national paths of struggle and state intervention.[197] It is also because French urban policy stands in a symbolic and institutional relationship to other current imperial contexts. It developed in part in response to the perceived threat posed by the African-American 'ghetto' (and its supposed British equivalents, Brixton and Toxteth). In turn, it continues to be an export model, serving both as negative foil (the now racialised danger of the 'banlieue') and a positive reference point for pacification projects in various parts of the world, including in historically less revolution-prone contexts of Europe and North America.[198] This chapter is thus less a study of the French case and more an opening for relational comparison.[199]

Drawing on Lefebvre and Fanon, my analysis of neo-colonial state strategies attests to the role of urban policy in organising bourgeois rule as consent and coercion. This has various implications for further research. One such implication is the need to further develop research on the post or neo-colonial aspects of contemporary capitalism, particularly the state. It is well-known that the term postcolonial was used to refer to the concrete realities of post-independence state formation[200] years before it became a code word for a specific deconstructive way of theorising (neo-)colonialism. This chapter indicates the need to reinvigorate research not only on (post-)colonial states in the global South[201] but also on the neo-colonial dimensions of the state form and state space in the imperial North, an underexplored aspect of Euro-American state theory. Such research can contribute to the materialist turn of postcolonial research, including the research traditions on the French imperial state

---

196   Kipfer and Goonewardena 2007; Saberi 2019; Mechai and Hergon 2020.
197   Amiraux 2010.
198   Ronneberger and Tsianos 2009; Saberi 2017a, 2017c; Chamberlain 2020.
199   Hart 2006; Kipfer 2012; Kipfer and Goonewardena 2014.
200   Alavi 1971.
201   Elsenhans 1984; Amin-Khan 2012; Goswami 2004.

that I have drawn upon for the purpose of this chapter, which can help inform materialist and dialectical theoretical approaches to (neo-)colonial realities. A focus on the state's role in hierarchical territorial organisation can show that postcolonial realities are reinventions of colonial pasts that stand in variegated relationships to class- and gender relations. In turn, such a focus may help illuminate the degree to which Nicos Poulantzas's well-known insight – that subaltern groups can be present in state strategies 'from a distance', as a real or potential threat, without being fully incorporated[202] – must be infused with counter-colonial theory.

Counter-colonial traditions also allow us to recast Poulantzas's neo-Gramscian strategy of articulating struggles for autonomy (self-organisation) with the quest to radically transform and democratise the state.[203] It is useful to recall that the traditions of political anti-racism in the French metropole outlined in the introduction have faced a persistent dilemma. According to Saïd Bouamama, the recurrent question has been how to insist on 'the necessity of political, economic, ideological, and organisational autonomy' while also facing the difficulty of 'defining the contours and functions of said autonomy'.[204] This dilemma has led Sadri Khiari and Houria Bouteldja to suggest that political anti-racist strategy is best understood as a multi-layered dialectic of autonomy and mixity, a continuously shifting attempt to adjust and re-calibrate the relationship between autonomous self-organisation and alliance-formation.[205] Mixity here is not to be confused with social or cultural diversity, or related ethnicised terms such as hybridity, creolisation or *métissage*. It is also distinct from state policy: efforts to advance de-segregation from above and impose forms of social mixing that may well be undesired by the targets of state intervention.[206] In the context of political anti-racism, mixity is a struggle concept, a strategic category that revisits Gramsci's conception of the war of position in neo-colonial context and on the self-determined and self-organised terms of the (neo-)colonised.

Once understood as a category of struggle and political strategy, mixity highlights the difficulty of challenging and, perhaps, transforming, the real but complex and usually porous lines of racialised demarcation running through metropolitan working classes. In the first instance, it raises the problem of

202   Poulantzas 2013, pp. 207–8.
203   Poulantzas 2013, pp. 347–67. See also Sotiris 2017.
204   Bouamama 2011, p. 43.
205   Khiari 2006, pp. 140–1; Khiari 2012, pp. 59–78; Bouteldja 2018. An early commentary is Kipfer 2011b.
206   See also Delphy 2008a, 2012.

how to construct alliances along class and race that are based on and nurture
instead of undermining the goal of self-organisation: autonomy. Sustaining as
well as complicating this first aspect of mixity as struggle concept, there is also
a second, gendered dimension to mixity and autonomy understood as twin
political strategy against racialised and imperial capitalism.[207] This dimension advances egalitarian gender relations in and through strategies committed
to solidarity within racially oppressed groups and non-White fractions of the
working class. In so doing, the feminist side of political anti-racism returns
to a long-standing problem encountered already in previous chapters: how to
grapple strategically with the twin burdens and dual traps generated by patriarchy and racism in (neo-)colonial capitalism.

In a post- or neo-colonial metropolitan context like France, where decolonisation cannot mean political independence understood as territorial integrity,
the dialectic of mixity and autonomy makes us think territory relationally, as
spatial practice and spatial imaginary tied to traditions of struggle. Echoing the
spatial imaginaries we have encountered in the French-dominated Caribbean
and in Indigenous North America, Sadri Khiari suggests the following about the
relationship between territory and decolonisation in metropolitan heartlands
like France:

> Territory is also a social relation, a mediation between humans. It is the
> site of 'living together' in history. Territory is a social bond which is con-
> structed in space but equally in time, with previous generations, ancest-
> ors, history; temporal relations are themselves mediations of social rela-
> tions in space. They are the still active history of these relations. Under-
> standing the role of territory is to understand how the conquest of territ-
> ory remains in some ways imperative for immigrants to France, who are
> excluded from history and civic life and asked to integrate into a different
> history while forgetting their own.[208]

According to Khiari, to appropriate territory is thus also to remember, indeed to
re-activate the rhythms and imaginaries of struggle that are condensed in particular social spaces.[209] Relating territory to traditions of struggle and political
imagination offers crucial insights into the times and spaces of decolonisation

---

207   Collectif des feministes indigènes 2012; Bouteldja and Delphy 2007; Delphy 2008a, 2008b,
       2012; Bouteldja 2016, pp. 71–97; Guénif-Souilamas and Macé 2006; Hancock 2017; Kipfer
       2011b, pp. 1168–71.
208   Khiari 2006, p. 116.
209   Khiari 2006, pp. 142–3.

today. It is also crucial in order to reimagine the right to the city, that is to say the relationship of struggle of the peripheralised against dominant spaces in neo-colonial contexts.[210]

Today, the broader importance of appropriating mixity as one side of a strategic dialectic of struggle is easy to grasp. It is one way to think of building political capacities among various subaltern groups and working-class fragments (as well as 'their' various peripheralised social spaces) against a contradictory combination of forces: neoliberalism and neo-fascism. Despite their disagreements, these dominant forces converge in projects to advance authoritarian rule in and beyond the state. They also intensify already existing class-based, gendered, racialised processes that individualise, segment, and disorganise subaltern groups.[211] In our age of sanitary and ecological crisis, such disorganisation is a recipe for death and disaster. In response, the strategic couple mixity and autonomy is promising also because it helps us reframe the meaning of the united front as a temporally and spatially uneven formation within which counter-colonial considerations can flourish and expand. In imperial heartlands such as France, a dialectic of mixity and autonomy might help connect subaltern social spaces and political histories to each other as well as to (neo-)colonised worlds in the global South.

---

210   Hancock, Blanchard, and Chapuis 2018; Hancock 2017.
211   Monzat 2016; Kipfer and Dikeç 2019; Kipfer 2019.

Conclusion

What would Fanon have done with the ideas that he had?
C.L.R. JAMES[1]

∴

In this book, I was centrally concerned with the role the production of space plays in the organisation and destabilisation of the social order. I have paid particular attention to the ways in which the hierarchical organisation of territorial relations, which constitutes one aspect of capitalist state-space, structures colonial and neo-colonial situations, and thus also shapes anti- and counter-colonial traditions. Furthermore, I have suggested that understanding the spatial and territorial ways of (dis-)organising rule and its (neo-)colonial dimensions is of profound significance for urban research, urban theory and urban politics. To understand this significance, and thus to grasp the (neo-)colonial aspects of urbanisation processes properly, I have proposed that we consider urban research as one important meeting point of Marxist and anti-colonial currents of theory and practice. In this spirit, I have established linkages between Henri Lefebvre and Frantz Fanon, particularly the aspects of their respective works that gravitated around Paris and Algiers. I then subjected Lefebvre and Fanon to closer scrutiny, confronting them with creole debates in the French-dominated Antilles, radical Indigenous debates on Turtle Island, and political anti-racist traditions in mainland France. The terrains for these additional theoretical encounters were creole urbanism in Martinique, settler colonial urbanisation in Canada, and urban redevelopment and social mix planning in Paris.

Before bringing this conclusion to an end, a brief disclaimer is in order. Considering the state of the world in 2020, my focus on the (neo-)colonial aspects of urban politics and social theory may appear to some as counter-intuitive, if not altogether anachronistic. Today, imperialism is alive and kicking in all its tension-ridden violence, but it is not typically organised in directly colonial fashion, that is to say through direct and formal types of territorial control. While the US-American empire is fraught more than ever by limits and con-

---

1   James 1979.

traditions, and while the contours of world order are uncertain in the near to mid-term future, the largely indirect and territorially supple modalities of imperial rule developed under US-centred imperialism in the twentieth century (in part by modifying experiments in the British-dominated nineteenth century) remain, for the most part, operative.[2] In this light, it is clear that social totality and world order are not adequately, let alone fully, encapsulated by colonial terminology. I have tried to avoid colonial hyperbole (*le tout colonial*) by foregrounding colonial questions in concrete situations: where the exercise of colonial rule remains intact (in the French Caribbean and settler colonial Canada) and where colonial histories have demonstrably been recomposed and reinvented within a larger, no longer strictly colonial world (in neo-colonial Algeria and imperial France).

Once placed in broader contexts, neo-colonial realities and recomposed colonial legacies remain important forces in imperial capitalism today. These forces need to be understood also spatially, for example through the territorial relations and urban strategies that help organise them. As I am writing these lines, in the middle of the COVID-19 pandemic in 2020, the fact that (neo-)colonial realities pervade the production of space has become clear in a new way. The spread of the novel coronavirus provides an excellent opportunity to understand the fundamental unsustainability of capitalism. More specifically, it also illustrates the concrete and variegated ways in which colonial pasts and presents matter today. One can see, for example, that the ways in which the COVID-19 pandemic is managed politically through strategies of spatial separation ('social distancing') and confinement ('lock-down') have recast and amplified the (neo-)colonial dimensions of today's world. Here are a few examples that expand upon the historico-geographical situations encountered in the book.

– In Algeria, the pandemic provided opportunities to the ruling regime to repress the *Hirak* movement. Exponents and journalists were arrested or put under closer surveillance as the movement entered a state of demobilisation due to the sanitary crisis and as emergency measures (lock-downs and curfews) were put in place during the first wave of the pandemic in the spring of 2020.[3] Under way since February 2019, the *Hirak* mobilisations had been called by some (for example the icon of the liberation struggle Djamila Bouhired) a movement for a second independence.[4] The *Hirak* developed from a wave of protest against President Abdelaziz Bouteflika's decision

---

2 Smith 2003.
3 Zerrouky 2020.
4 Ayad 2019; Hamouchene 2020.

to run for another term into a movement opposing various aspects of the politico-military ruling bloc as a whole. Crucial foundations of this bloc were built in the early 1960s in order to confiscate the mobilisations and popular aspirations at that time.[5] Following Chapter 2 on Fanon's conception of time and space and his critique of false decolonisation, we are in a good position to grasp the significance of calls for a second, this time genuine, form of independence. Keeping in mind both Lefebvre and Fanon (in Chapters 1 and 2), we also understand how pandemic crisis management in Algeria tells us a few things about the (always contradictory and incomplete) role state spatial strategies and their (neo-)colonial dimensions play in disorganising subaltern capacities to act collectively.

– In the French-dominated Antilles, Eli Domota, the secretary-general of the *Union Générale des Travailleurs de la Guadeloupe* (UGTG), called the response of the French state to the pandemic a form of 'colonial crisis management'. Why? Partly because the pandemic revealed the particular, and uneven, ways in which the French state had underdeveloped health services in its overseas territories; partly because its ways of organising the lockdown were reinforced by a sanitary state of emergency and the presence of military helicopter-carrier *Dixmuth*, which not only brought medical supplies but also signalled to inhabitants: stand down with your political demands.[6] At the end of Chapter 3, we briefly encountered the UGTG in the context of the 2009 strike movement against high prices in the Antilles. Politicising colonialism and neoliberalism all at once, the movement selectively reinvented (in Guadeloupe more than in Martinique) the prospect of political independence in situations where colonial rule (as modernised in the decades following departmentalisation in 1946) seemed to have been secured for good. As Domota suggested in 2020, the crying incompetence of French pandemic crisis management served as a reminder that the legitimacy of French rule is limited, and that a socio-economically different, truly independent future for the Antilles remains possible.[7]

– In Indigenous Canada, the pandemic revealed once more the stark ways in which colonialism exposes Indigenous people on and off reserves to a series of health-compromising conditions that make them vulnerable to the spread of the novel coronavirus: absent, minimal or distant health services as well as insufficient sanitary infrastructure such as safe and drinkable

---

5 Rigouste 2020b.
6 Domota 2020; Odin 2020. On Martinique, see Confiant 2020. On Mayotte and La Réunion, see Marchal 2020.
7 Domota 2020.

water supply on many reserves; and a striking overrepresentation of Indigenous peoples among populations in deep poverty, among prisoners and shelterless people.[8] In turn, pandemic crisis management helped put to rest the nation-wide, geographically multi-form movement we encountered in Chapter 4: the protests and blockades that developed in February 2020 in solidarity with the struggles of the Wet'suwet'en against the attempts of the federal government to enforce colonialism by pipeline on their traditional territory. In response to the pandemic, many Indigenous nations decided to close access to their reserves and territories in order to avert a new phase in the genocidal history of settler colonialism, which has decimated Indigenous populations also due to illnesses imported from Europe. In so doing, Indigenous nations were obliged to enforce the colonial fault line between reserve and settler space, a divide that is otherwise shot through with contradictions, cross-cutting connections and countervailing political practices, as we have also seen in Chapter 4.

– In the Paris region, the pandemic has brought to light realities that are common across Euro-America. It has reinforced pre-existing inequalities along lines of class, race and gender. In the *Ile-de-France*, these inequalities have placed working classes, and in particular precarious and non-White fractions of the working class, in conditions that expose them in acute fashion to the virus and the mortal effects of infection. Among these conditions: pre-existing health conditions, insufficient access to health care, accentuated crises of social reproduction, working poverty, precarity and unemployment, overcrowded housing conditions, and over-representation in 'essential' economic sectors.[9] In turn, pandemic crisis management in France has shed light on and intensified neo-colonial dimensions of urban policy. During the first wave of the pandemic, the lock-down was enforced unevenly, handing opportunities to police forces to target with renewed vigour already over-policed, stigmatised and segregated neighbourhoods,[10] including the places subject to the urban redevelopment strategies analysed in Chapter 5. In a few places, inhabitants responded with riots and revolts.[11] Moreover, the sanitary state of emergency added to already existing emergency provisions, which were normalised, that is, inscribed into regular legislation, following

---

8   Yellowhead Institute 2020; Borrows and Mackintosh 2020; Starblanket and Hunt 2020; Menleson 2020.

9   Couvelaire et al. 2020; Gilbert 2020; Mariette and Pitti 2020.

10 Gilbert 2020.

11 Ramdani 2020.

the state of emergency in place from 2015 to 2017. If so normalised, the sanitary state of exception threatens to intensify, in an ever-more intimate and corporeal fashion, the racialised and class-based ways in which inhabitants are surveilled and regulated.[12]

These snapshots of a world shaken by the COVID-19 pandemic underline the need to always historicise and spatialise colonial and neo-colonial realities. Chapters in this book haven taken to heart Glen Coulthard's suggestion: that to fully understand the role of colonial relations in the modern capitalist world, one must treat it as a historically shifting and comparatively varied terrain of struggle. While Coulthard made this point to highlight recent shifts in the settler colonial relation in Canada, one can also make it in relationship to departmentalised Martinique after 1946 and imperial France following the wave of independence in the 1950s and 1960s. Indeed, a main objective of this volume has been to show that shifts in (neo-)colonial realities can be understood particularly well if one pays attention to the territorial relations and urbanisation patterns that help organise the terrain of struggle that is the colonial relation. Chapters 1, 2, and 5 insist that the shift from Haussmannian to functionalist and post-functionalist urbanism in Paris and Algiers created terrains of struggle that, while distinct, can only be understood through the imperial networks that have connected them since 1830. The conventional focus of these chapters on urban regions is complicated in Chapters 3 and 4 on Martinique and Canada. There, comparative urban analyses of the colonial relation, including anti-colonial strategies and imaginaries, are pushed further to take into account both concentrated and extended urban forms and processes, the two crucial sides of planetary urbanisation.

I would like to finish by touching upon two insights that emerged in the course of writing these texts and that open up to further work. The first is that comparison is both a methodological must and a political imperative. This becomes clear by following the fate of Frantz Fanon's internationalism throughout the chapters of this book. Extending C.L.R. James's question that opens this conclusion, one can ask not only whether Fanon would have struggled for a genuinely postcolonial future in the Caribbean had he had the chance (of course he would have, C.L.R. James answered in the late 1970s)?[13] We can also ask: what kind of analyses and strategies would Fanon have developed had he lived to continue his struggle for national liberation in the various contexts he knew, in the Maghreb, West Africa, and the French Caribbean?

12   Mechaï and Hergon 2020.
13   James 1979.

There is no doubt that to keep alive his internationalism, that is to say his conception of national liberation as a partisan universal (Ato Sekyi-Otu) entry point to tricontinental revolution, Fanon would have been forced to confront the (neo-)colonial relations in the places we 'visited' in this book in all their comparative specificity, historical dynamism, and geographically interrelated character. Fanon would have been compelled to engage in a form of relational comparison (Gill Hart) if only in order to understand the obstacles that stand in the way of internationalism. Paying particular attention to the role of territorial relations, urban strategies and spatial imaginaries, we have encountered some of these obstacles on our journey from Algeria to Paris, Martinique and North America. These encounters offer excellent starting points to unpack the links between comparative method and political strategy.

The obstacles that stand in the way of Fanon's internationalism (as well as the Fanon-Lefebvre lineage more specifically) point us to another insight running through these pages: the fact that the question of hegemony matters in (neo-)colonial contexts. Due to the economic imperatives and the racialised separations that structure (neo-)colonialism, (neo-)colonial relations obstruct the development of expansive forms of hegemony. From this basic insight, which formed our Fanonian starting point in Chapter 2, one cannot, however, conclude that (neo-)colonial rule is a form of domination demarcated from the exercise of hegemony. In fact, the question of hegemony (which for Antonio Gramsci always represented a combination of coercion and consent, never just a matter of consent) re-imposed itself in the composition of these essays. The authors encountered here (starting with both Fanon and Lefebvre) and the varied situations covered in this book all push us to pay attention to the problematic of hegemony when tackling (neo-)colonial questions and their urban mediations. Whether in Algeria, Martinique, Canada, or France, (neo-)colonial relations cannot be understood by separating considerations of consent from realities of coercion. In fact, the specific examples I explored in various chapters – social mix planning, creole urbanism, infrastructural urban strategies – indicate clearly that (neo-)colonialism and anti-colonialism should be considered as spatially organised hegemonic projects. Needless to say, probing the relationship between (anti-)colonialism and hegemony also invites us to reintegrate Gramsci into the Lefebvre-Fanon lineage while recognising Gramsci's place in dialogues among Marxism and anti-colonialism more generally.[14] These twin political and theoretical currents have combined to shape

---

14   Kipfer 2004, 2013, 2018; Kipfer and Hart 2013; Kipfer and Mallick forthcoming.

tricontinental political traditions for some time now.[15] They remain essential for anyone searching for a plural and truly liveable planet liberated from both capitalism and imperialism.

15   Mehdi Ben Barka, cited in Bouamama 2016, p. 9.

Bibliography

Abane, Belaïd 2011, 'Frantz Fanon and Abane Ramdane: Brief Encounter in the Algerian Revolution', in *Living Fanon*, edited by Nigel Gibson, London: Palgrave.

Abdallah, Mogniss H. 2001, 'Banlieue Show – oder das Politikspektakel der Sprengung abgewirtschafteter cités', in *Bigness. Size Does Matter. Image/Politik. Städtisches Handeln*, edited by Jochen Becker, Berlin: b_books.

Abdallah, Mogniss H. 2005, 'Face au "banlieue-show" à la française. Pour un renouveau de l'action collective dans les quartiers d'habitat social', http://fsqp.fr/Face-au-Banlieue-show-a-la.html last accessed 17 December 2014.

Abdallah, Mogniss H. 2008, '1983: La marche pour l'égalité', http://indigenes-republique.fr/1983-la-marche-pour-legalite-2/

Abdallah, Mogniss H. 2012, *Rengainez – on arrive! Chroniques des luttes contre les crimes racistes ou sécuritaires contre la hagra policière et judicaire des années 1970 à aujourd'hui*, Paris: Libertalia.

Abele, Frances, and Daiva Stasiulis 1987, 'Canada as a "White Settler Colony"', in *The New Canadian Political Economy*, edited by Wallace Clement and Glen Williams, Kingston: McGill-Queen's University Press.

Abu-Lughod, Janet 1980, *Rabat: Urban Apartheid in Morocco*, Princeton: Princeton University Press.

Abu-Lughod, Janet 1987, 'The Islamic City – Historic Myth, Islamic Essence, and Contemporary Relevance', *International Journal of Middle East Studies* 19, 2: 155–76.

Abu-Lughod, Janet 1999, *New York, Chicago, Los Angeles: America's Global Cities*, Minneapolis: University of Minnesota Press.

Abu-Lughod, Janet, and Richard Hay (eds) 1977, *Third World Urbanisation*, Chicago: Maaroufa.

Adam, Allan 2012, 'Gateway Pipeline Threatens Our Way of Life', *Climate and Capitalism* https://climateandcapitalism.com/2012/05/08/gateway-pipeline-threatens-our-way-of-life/ accessed 1 March 2016.

Adamczak, Bini 2017, *Beziehungsweise Revolution: 1917, 1968 und kommende*, Frankfurt: Suhrkamp.

Adams, Howard 1975, *Prison of Grass*, Toronto: General Publishing.

Adams, Howard 1999, *Tortured People*, revised edition, Penticton BC: Theytus Books.

Adams, Howard 2005, *Otapawy! The Life of Métis Leader in his own words and in those of his contemporaries*, Saskatoon: Gabriel Dumont Institute of Native Studies and Applied Research.

Addie, Jean-Paul, and James Fraser 2019, 'After Gentrification: Social Mix, Settler Colonialism, and Cruel Optimism in the Transformation of Neighbourhood Space', *Antipode* 51, 3: 1369–94.

Ahmed, Sara 2007, 'A Phenomenology of Whiteness', *Feminist Theory* 8, 2: 149–68.

Ahiska, Meltem 2005, 'Orientalism/Occidentalism: The Impasse of Modernity', in *Waiting for the Barbarians: A Tribute to Edward Said*, edited by Müge Gürsoy Sökmen and Basak Ertür, London: Verso.

Ahman, Aijaz 1992, *In Theory: Classes, Nations, Literatures*, London: Verso.

Ajari, Norman 2019, *La dignité ou la mort. Ethique et politique de la race*, Paris: La Découverte.

Alavi, Hamza 1972, 'The State in Post-Colonial Societies: Pakistan and Bangladesh', *New Left Review* 74, 1.

Alfred, Taiaiake 2009a, *Wasàse: Indigenous Pathways of Action and Freedom*, Toronto, University of Toronto Press.

Alfred, Taiaiake 2009b, *People, Power, Righteousness: An Indigenous Manifesto*, Oxford: Oxford University Press.

Alfred, Taiaiake 2017, 'It's All About the Land', in *Whose Land is it Anyway: A Manual for Decolonisation*, edited by Peter McFarlane and Nicole Schabus, Vancouver: Federation of Post-Secondary Educators of BC.

Alfred, Taiaikae, and Jeff Corntassel 2005, 'Being Indigenous', *Government and Opposition* 40, 4: 597–614.

Almi, Saïd 2002, *Urbanisme et Colonisation: Présence française en Algérie*, Mardaga: Sprimont.

Altamarino-Jiménez, Isabel 2004, 'North American First Peoples: Slipping up into Market Citizenship?' *Citizenship Studies* 8, 4: 349–65.

Amin, Samir 1989, *Eurocentrism*, London: Zed Books.

Amin, Samir 2011, *Global History: A View from the South*, Cape Town, Pambazuka Press.

Amin, Samir 2013, 'Frantz Fanon en Afrique et en Asie', in *Frantz Fanon, un héritage à partager*, edited by Cercle Frantz Fanon, Paris: l'Harmattan.

Amin-Khan, Tariq 2012, *The Post-Colonial State in the Era of Capitalist Globalisation*, London: Routledge.

Amiraux, Valérie 2010, 'Crisis and New Challenges? French Republicanism Featuring Multiculturalism', in *European Multiculturalism Revisited*, edited by Alessandro Silj, London: Zed Books.

Amiri, Linda 2004, *La Bataille de France: La Guerre d'Algérie en Métropole*, Paris: Robert Laffon.

Anderson, Chris 2015, *Métis: Race, Recognition, and the Struggle for Indigenous Peoplehood*, Vancouver: UBC Press.

Anderson Chris, and Evelyn Peters 2013, 'Indigenising Modernity or Modernising Indigeneity?' in *Indigenous in the City*, edited by Evelyn Peters and Chris Anderson, Vancouver: UBC Press.

Anderson, Grey 2018, *La guerre civile en France, 1958–1962: Du coup d'Etat gaulliste à la fin de l'OAS*, Paris: La Fabrique.

Anderson, Kay 1991, *Vancouver's Chinatown: Racial Discourse in Canada*, Montreal: McGill-Queen's University Press.

Anderson, Kevin 1995, *Lenin, Hegel, and Western Marxism*, Chicago: University of Illinois Press.

Angelo, Hillary 2017, 'From the City Lens Toward Urbanisation as a Way of Seeing: Country/city Binaries on an Urbanising Planet', *Urban Studies* 54, 1: 158–78.

Angelo, Hillary, and Kian Goh 2020, 'Out in Space: Difference and Abstraction in Planetary Urbanisation', *International Journal of Urban and Regional Research* online first.

Angelo, Hillary, and David Wachsmuth 2014, 'Urbanising Urban Political Ecology', *Implosions/Explosions*, edited by Neil Brenner, Berlin: Jovis.

ANRUa (Agence National de la Rénvation Urbaine) 2007, *Convention ANRU ZUS Goutte Goutte d'Or Paris 18eme arrondissement.*

ANRUb 2007, *Montreuil Bel Air et Grands Pêchers Projet de Rénovation Urbaine et Sociale Convention Pluriannuelle 2007–2012.*

ANRUc 2005, *Convention de la Rénovation Urbaine La Courneuve Quartiers Ouest, Quartiers Nord, Centre Ville.*

ANRUd 2004, *Clichy-Sous-Bois Montfermeil Convention parternariale pour la mise en œuvre du projet de renovation urbaine de Clichy-Sous-Bois – Montfermeil.*

ANRUe 2006, *Le Plâteau – Cité des Indes. Dossier de convention financière.*

Antipode Editorial Collective 2019, *Keywords in Radical Geography: Antipode at 50*, London: Wiley.

Anievas, Alexander, and Kerem Nisancoglu 2015, *How the West Came to Rule: The Geopolitical Origin of Capitalism*, London: Pluto.

Aouragh, Miriyam 2019, '"White Privilege" and Shortcuts to Anti-Racism', *Race and Class* 61, 2: 3–26.

Araghi, Farshad A. 1995, 'Global Depeasantisation, 1945–1990', *Sociological Quarterly* 36, 2.

Arboleda, Martín 2015, 'Financialisation, Totality and Planetary Urbanisation in the Chilean Andes', *Geoforum* 67: 4–13.

Arboleda, Martín 2016a, 'In the Nature of the Non-City', *Antipode* 48, 2: 233–51.

Arboleda, Martín 2016b, 'Spaces of Extraction, Metropolitan Explosions', *International Journal of Urban and Regional Research* 40, 1: 96–112.

Armah, Ayi Kwei 1984, 'Masks and Marx', *Présence Africaine* 131: 35–65.

Armstrong, Warwick, and T.G. McGee 1985, *Theatres of Accumulation*, New York: Methuen.

Arthurson, Kathy 2012, *Social Mix and the City*, Collingwood: CSIRO Publishing.

Artières, Philippe, and Michelle Zancarini-Fournel (eds) 2008, *68: Une histoire collective*, Paris: La Découverte.

Assemblée des Collectifs en lutte contre le Grand Paris, n.d. https://grandparisdesluttes.wordpress.com/

Atkinson, Rowland, and Gary Bridge (eds) 2005, *Gentrification in a Global Context: The New Urban Colonialism*, London: Routledge.

Aureli, Pier Vittorio 2008, *The Project of Autonomy: Politics and Architecture Within and Against Capitalism*, New York: Princeton Architectural Press.

Aureli, Pier Vittorio (ed.) 2016, *The City as a Project*, Berlin: Ruby Press.

Awâsís, Sa?kihitowin, Brian Tokar, and Kat Stevens 2013, 'Anti-Pipeline Organising Across Turtle Island. An Interview', *Upping the Anti* 15: 53–82.

Ayad, Christophe 2019, 'Djamila Bouhired: l'aura intacte de Djamila Bouhired, héroïne de l'indépendance algérienne', *Le Monde Mag*, 19 August.

Azhar, Sharam, and Danish Khan, 2020, 'Rethinking Informal Labour in Peripheral Capitalism: The Dynamics of Surplus, Market and Spatiality', *Labour History* online.

Azzouzi, Rachida, and Faïza Zerouala 2020, 'Le comité Adama, héritier de 50 ans de combats invisibilisés', *Médiapart*, 5 July.

Bachmann, Christian, and Nicole Le Guennec 2002, *Violences Urbaines*, Paris: Hachettes.

Bacqué, Marie-Hélène, and Yankel Fijalkow 2011, 'Social Mix as the Aim of a Controlled Gentrification Process: The Example of the Goutte d'Or District in Paris', in *Mixed Communities: Gentrification by Stealth?* edited by Gary Bridge, Tim Butler, and Loretta Lees, Bristol: Policy Press.

Bacqué, Marie-Hélène, Yankel Fijalkow, Amélie Flamand, and Stéphanie Vermeersch 2010, '"Comment nous sommes devenus HLM" Les opérations de mixité sociale à Paris dans les années 2000', *Espaces et Sociétés* 140–1, 1–2: 93–109.

Bakan, Abigail 2014, 'Marxism and Anti-Racism: Rethinking the Politics of Difference', in *Theorizing Anti-Racism: Linkages in Marxism and Critical Race Theories*, edited by Abigail Bakan and Enakshi Dua, Toronto: University of Toronto Press.

Bakan, Abigail, and Enakshi Dua (eds) 2014, 'Introducing the Questions, Reframing the Dialogue', in *Theorizing Anti-Racism: Linkages in Marxism and Critical Race Theories*, Toronto: University of Toronto Press.

Balandier, Georges 1947, 'Le noir est un homme', *Présence Africaine* 1: 31–6.

Balandier, Georges 1951, 'La situation coloniale: approche théorique', *Cahiers Internationaux de Sociologie* 11: 44–79.

Balandier, Georges 2002, 'La situation coloniale: ancien concept, nouvelle réalité', *French Politics, Culture, and Society* 20, 2: 4.

Baldwin, James 1984 [1955], *Notes of a Native Son*, Boston: Beacon.

Baldwin, James 1993 [1963], *The Fire Next Time*, New York: Vintage.

Baldwin, James 2014, *The Last Interview and Other Conversations*, Brooklyn: Melville House.

Balthaser, Benjamin 2016a, 'Colonies and Capital', *Jacobin* https://www.jacobinmag.com/2016/11/native-americans-marxism-colonialism-nodapl-archie-phinney-means-nez-perce

Balthaser, Benjamin 2016b, *Anti-Imperialist Modernism: Race and Transnational Radical Culture from the Great Depression to the Cold War*, Ann Arbor: University of Michigan Press.

Banaji, Jairus 2011, *Theory as History: Essays on Modes of Production and Exploitation*, Chicago: Haymarket.

Bannerji, Himani 1995, *Thinking Through: Essays on Feminism, Marxism and Anti-Racism*, Toronto: Women's Press.

Bannerji, Himani 2011, *Demography and Democracy: Essays on Nationalism, Gender and Ideology*, Toronto: Canadian Scholars' Press.

Bannerji, Himani 2014, 'Marxism and Anti-Racism in Theory and Practice: Reflections and Interpretations', in *Theorizing Anti-Racism: Linkages in Marxism and Critical Race Theories*, edited by Abigail Bakan and Enakshi Dua, Toronto: University of Toronto Press

Bannerji, Himani 2015, 'Building from Marx: Reflections on "Race", Gender and Class', in *Marxism and Feminism*, edited by Shahrzad Mojab, London: Pluto.

Bannerji, Himany, Shahrzad Mojab, and Judith Whitehead (eds) 2001, *Of Property and Propriety*, Toronto: University of Toronto Press.

Barker, A.J. 2015, 'A Direct Act of Resurgence, a Direct Act of Sovereignty', *Globalisations* 12, 1: 43–65.

Barman, Jean 2007, 'Erasing Indigenous Indigeneity in Vancouver', *BC Studies* 155: 3–30.

Barnes, Trevor J., and Eric Sheppard 2019, *Spatial Histories of Radical Geography: North America and Beyond*, Hoboken, NJ: Wiley.

Bartolovich, Crystal 2002, 'Introduction: Marxism, Modernity and Postcolonial Studies', in *Marxism, Modernity and Postcolonial Studies*, edited by Crystal Bartolovich and Neil Lazarus, Cambridge: Cambridge University Press.

Bartolovich, Crystal, and Neil Lazarus (eds) 2002, *Marxism, Modernity and Postcolonial Studies*, Cambridge: Cambridge University Press.

Baudin, Gérard, and Philippe Genestier 2006, 'Faut-il vraiment démolir les grands ensembles?' *Espaces et Sociétés* 2–3: 207–22.

Bayat, Asaf 2013, *Life as Politics: How Ordinary People Change the Middle East*, 2nd edition, Stanford: Stanford University Press.

Beaud, Stéphane, and Olivier Masclet 2006, 'Des marcheurs de 1983 aux émeutiers de 2005', *Annales* 61, 4: 809–45.

Becker, Marc 2006, 'Mariátegui, the Comintern and the Indigenous Question in Latin America', *Science and Society* 70, 4: 450–79.

Béguin, Hélène 2014, 'Des "Africains Noirs" à la "mixité sociale". Usages paradoxaux des catégories ethniques dans les foyers de travailleurs migrants (AFTAM)', in *Le peuplement comme politique*, edited by Fabien Desage, Christine Morel Journel, and Valérie Sala Pala, Rennes: Presses Universitaires de Rennes.

Belli, Attilio 2012, 'Differential Space and Hospitality: Starting from a Nietzschean Lefebvre', *Crios* 4: 41–51.

Belmessous, Fatiha 2014, 'Catégorisation et discrimination des Algériens dans les politiques du logement à Lyon', in *Le peuplement comme politique*, edited by Fabien Desage, Christine Morel Journel, and Valérie Sala Pala, Rennes: Presses Universitaires de Rennes.

Belmessous, Fatiha 2015, 'La tolérance s'arrête au seuil. Traitements spécifique et pratique ségrégatives du logement des immigrés (1950–1970)', in *En finir avec les banlieues? Le désenchantment de la politique de la ville*, edited by Thomas Kirszbaum, Paris: L'Aube.

Belmessous, Fatiha, et al. (eds) 2006, *Les minorisés de la République: la discrimination au logement des jeunes générations d'origine immigrée*, Paris: La Dispute.

Belmessous, Hacène 2006, *Mixité sociale: une imposture*, Nantes: Atalante.

Belmessous, Hacène 2007, *Maire de Banlieues: La politique à l'épreuve du réel*, Paris: Editions du Sextant.

Belmessous, Hacène 2010, *Opération Banlieues: Comment l'Etat prépare la guerre urbaine dans les cités françaises*, Paris: La Découverte.

Ben Barka, Bachir (ed.) 2007, *Mehdi Ben Barka en héritage: de la Tricontinentale à l'altermondialisme*, Paris and Casablanca: Syllepse/Tarik.

Benevolo, Leonoardo 1993, *The European City*, Oxford: Blackwell.

Benjamin, Solomon 2008, 'Occupancy Urbanism: Radicalising Politics and Economy beyond Policy and Programs', *International Journal of Urban and Regional Research* 32, 3: 719–29.

Benjamin, Walter 1980, *Moskauer Tagebuch*, Frankfurt: Suhrkamp.

Benjamin, Walter 1982, *Das Passagenwerk*, edited by Rolf Tiedemann, Frankfurt am Main: Suhrkamp.

Benoit, Yves 2004 [1987], *La Révolution française et la fin des colonies*, Paris: La Découverte.

Bensaïd, Daniel 2002, *Marx For Our Times*, translated by Gregory Elliott, London: Verso.

Berman, Marshall 1982, *All That is Solid Melts into Air*, New York: Simon and Schuster.

Berman, Marshall 1997, 'Justice/Just Us: Rap and Social Justice in America', in *The Urbanisation of Injustice*, edited by Andy Merrifield and Erik Swyngedouw, New York: New York University Press.

Berman, Marshall 2006, *On the Town*, London: Verso.

Bernabé, Jean 2013, 'Eléments pour une lecture postmoderne de Peau Noire Masques Blancs', in *Frantz Fanon: une héritage à partager*, edited by Cercle Frantz Fanon et Fondation Marcel Manville, Paris: L'Harmattan.

Bernabé, Jean 2016, *La Dérive Identitariste*, Paris: Harmattan.

Bernabé, Jean, Patrick Chamoiseau, and Raphaël Confiant 1989, *Eloge de la Créolité*, Paris: Gallimard/Presses Universitaires Créoles.

Bernal, Martin 1987, *Black Athena: The Afroasiatic Roots of Classical Civilisation, Volume 1: The Fabrication of Ancient Greece*, London: Free Association Books.

Bernard, Marc 2009, *Sarcellopolis*, Paris: Finitude.

Bernasconi, Robert 1996, 'Casting the Slough: Fanon's new Humanism for a New Humanity' in *Fanon: A Critical Reader*, edited by Lewis Gordon, Denean Sharpley-Whiting, and R.T. White, London: Blackwell.

Bernasconi, Robert 1997, 'Philosophy's Paradoxical Parochialism: The Reinvention of Philosophy as Greek', in *Cultural Readings of Imperialism: Edward Said and the Gravity of History*, edited by Keith Ansell-Pearson, Benita Parry, and Judith Squires, New York: St. Martin's Press.

Bernasconi, Robert 2002, 'The Assumption of Negritude: Aimé Césaire, Frantz Fanon, and the Vicious Circle of Racial Politics', *Parallax* 8, 2: 69–83.

Bernasconi, Robert, with Sybil Cook (eds) 2003, *Race and Racism in Continental Philosophy*, Bloomington: Indiana University Press.

Bernauer, Warren 2018, *Extractive Hegemony in the Arctic: Energy Resources and Political Conflict in Nunavut, 1970–2017*, PhD Thesis, Department of Geography, York University.

Bernstein, Henry 2006, 'Once were/Still are Peasants? Farming in a Globalising South', *New Political Economy* 11, 3.

Berry-Chikhaoui, Isabelle, Dominique Chevalier, and Lucile Medina, 2016, 'Le Quartier du Petit-Bard dans la rénovation urbaine: La double peine de la discrimination ethnique et territoriale', in *Discriminations Territoriales*, edited by Claire Hancock, Christine Lelévrier, Fabrice Ripoll, and Serge Weber, Paris: L'oeil d'or.

Bhabha, Homi 1994, *The Location of Culture*, London: Routledge.

Bhabha, Homi 1999, 'Remembering Fanon: Self, Psyche, and the Colonial Condition', in *Rethinking Fanon: The Continuing Dialogue*, edited by Nigel Gibson, New York: Humanity.

Bhabha, Homi 2004, 'Foreword: Framing Fanon', in Frantz Fanon, *Wretched of the Earth*, New York: Grove.

Bhattacharya, Tithi 2017, 'Introduction: Mapping Social Reproduction Theory', in *Social Reproduction Theory: Remapping Class, Recentring Oppression*, edited by Tithi Bhattacharya, London: Pluto.

Biko, Steve 1986, *I Write What I Like*, edited by Aelred Stubbs, San Francisco: Harper and Row.

Biondi, Jean-Pierre 1992, *Les anticolonialistes (1881–1962)*, Paris: Albert Laffont.

Blackburn, Robin 2011 [1988], *The Overthrow of Colonial Slavery 1776–1848*, London: Verso.

Blanc, Maurice 1983, 'Le logement des travailleurs immigrés en France: après le taudis, le foyer, et aujourd'hui le h.l.m.', *Espaces et Sociétés* 42: 129–40.

Blanc-Chaléard, Marie-Claude 2012, 'Les quotas d'étranger en HLM: un héritage de la guerre d'Algérie? Les Canibouts à Nanterre (1959–1968)', *Métropolitiques*, 16 mars http://www.metropolitiques.eu/spip.php?page=print%id_article=301.

Blanc-Chaléard, Marie-Claude 2016, *En finir avec les bidonvilles: immigration et politique du logement dans la France des Trente Glorieuses*, Paris: Sorbonne.

Blanchard, Emmanuel 2011, *La Police Parisienne et les Algériens (1944–1962)*, Paris: Nouveau Monde.

Blanchard, Emmanuel 2012, 'La police et les "médinas algériennes" en métropole', *Métropolitiques*, 8 février http://www.metropolitiques.eu/spip.php?page=print&id_article=279

Blanchard, Sophie, and Claire Hancock 2017, 'Enjeux de genre et politiques urbaines: les enseignments d'une recherche à Aubervilliers', *Géocarrefour* 91, 1.

Blatman-Thomas, Naama, and Libby Porter 2018, 'Placing Property: Theorizing the Urban From Settler Colonial Cities', *International Journal of Urban and Regional Research* 43, 1: 30–45.

Bledsoe, Adam 2017, 'Marronage as a Past and Present Geography in the Americas', *Southeastern Geographer* 57, 1: 30–50.

Bledsoe, Adam, and Willie Jamaal Wright 2019, 'The Pluralities of Black Geographies', *Antipode* 51, 2: 419–36.

Blérard, Alain-Philippe 1984, 'Culture et Politique en situation coloniale dans l'œuvre de Frantz Fanon', in *Mémorial International Frantz Fanon*, edited by Comité Frantz Fanon de Fort de France, Paris and Dakar: Présence Africaine.

Blérard, Alain-Philippe 1988, *La Question Nationale en Guadeloupe et en Martinique*, Paris: L'Harmattan.

Blomley, Nicholas 2004, *Unsettling the City*, London: Routledge.

Bobiwash, Rodney 1997, 'Native Urban Self-Government and the Politics of Self-Determination', in *The Meeting Place: Aboriginal Life in Toronto*, edited by Heather Howard-Bobiwash and Frances Sanderson, Toronto: Native Canadian Centre.

Boggio Ewanjé-Epée, Félix, and Stella Magliani-Belkacem 2012, *Les feministes blanches et l'empire*, Paris: La Fabrique.

Boggio Ewanjé-Epée, Félix, and Matthieu Renault 2013, 'Que faire des Postcolonial Studies?' *Revue des Livres* 13: 35–43.

Boggio Ewanjé-Epée, Félix, Stella Magliani-Belkacem, Morgane Merteuil, and Frédéric Monferrand (eds) 2017, *Pour un féminisme de la totalité*, Paris: Amsterdam.

Bogues, Anthony (ed.) 2006, *After Man, Towards the Human: Critical Essays on Sylvia Wynter*, Kingston: Ian Randle.

Bolland, Nigel O. 1998, 'Creolisation and Creole Societies: A Cultural Nationalist View of Caribbean Social History', *Caribbean Quarterly* 44, 1/2: 1–32.

Bonilla, Yarimar 2015, *Non-Sovereign Futures: French Caribbean Politics in the Wake of Disenchantment*, Chicago: University of Chicago Press.

Bonilla, Yarimar 2017, 'Freedom, Sovereignty and Other Entanglements', *Small Axe* 21, 2: 201–8.

Bosteels, Bruno 2013, 'The Mexican Commune', http://www.cronistas.org/wp-content/uploads/2016/08/The-Mexican-Commune-Bostells.pdf

Bouamama, Saïd 1993, *De la galère à la citoyenneté: Les jeunes, la cite, la société*, Paris: Desclée de Brouwer.

Bouamama, Saïd 2004, *L'affaire du foulard islamique: la production d'un racisme respectable*, Paris: Geai Bleu Editions.

Bouamama, Saïd 2009, *Les Classes et quartiers populaires: paupérisation, ethnicisation et discrimination*, Paris: Éditions du Cygne.

Bouamama, Saïd 2011, 'L'expérience politique des Noirs et des Arabes en France. Mutations, invariances et récurrences', in *Race Rebelle: Luttes des quartiers populaires des années 1980 à nos jours*, edited by Rafik Chekkat and Emmanuel Delgado Hoch, Paris: Syllepse.

Bouamama, Saïd 2014, *Figures de la révolution africaine: de Kenyatta à Sankara*, Paris: La Découverte.

Bouamama, Saïd 2016, *La Tricontinentale. Les peuples du tiers-monde à l'assaut du ciel*, Paris: Syllepse.

Bouamama, Saïd, Hadjila Sad-Saoud, and Mokhtar Djerdoubi 1994, *Contribution à la mémoire des banlieues*, Paris: Volga.

Boubeker, Ahmed, and Abdellali Hajjat (eds) 2008, *Histoire politique des immigrations (post)coloniales en France, 1920–2008*, Paris: Amsterdam.

Bourdieu, Pierre, and Abdemalek Sayad 1964, *Le déracinement: la crise de l'agriculture traditionelle en Algérie*, Paris: Editions de Minuit.

Bourdon, Daniel, and Christophe Noyé 2016, 'L'impact des projets de rénovation urbaine: mixité sociale et mobilité des ménages', *La revue fonçière* 11, 13–16.

Bourgeault, Ron G. 1986, 'The Indian, the Métis and the Fur Trade', *Studies in Political Economy* 12: 45–80.

Bourgeault, Ron G. 1988, 'Race and Class Under Mercantilism', in *Racial Oppression in Canada*, edited by Bolaria B. Singh and Peter S. Li, Toronto: Garamond.

Bourgeault, Ron G. 2005, 'An Appreciation of the Late Howard Adams', in *Otapawy! The Life of Métis Leader in his own words and in those of his contemporaries*, Saskatoon: Gabriel Dumont Institute of Native Studies and Applied Research.

Bouteldja, Houria 2016, *Les blancs, les juifs et nous: vers une politique de l'amour révolutionnaire*, Paris: La Fabrique.

Bouteldja, Houria 2018, 'Beaufs et Barbares: comment converger?' www.indigenesrepublique.fr, 2 December.

Bouteldja, Houria, and Christine Delphy 2007, 'Soumise à l'ordre postcolonial', *Politis*, 28 June.

Bouvier, Pierre 2010, *Aimé Césaire Frantz Fanon: Portraits de décolonisés*, Paris: Les Belles Lettres.

Breleur, Ernst et al., 2009, 'Manifeste pour les produits de haute nécessité', *Le Monde*, 16 February.

Brennan, Timothy 1997, *At Home in the World: Cosmopolitanism Today*, Cambridge, MA: Harvard University Press.

Brennan, Timothy 2002, 'Postcolonial Studies between the Wars: An Intellectual History', in *Marxism, Modernity and Postcolonial Studies*, edited by Crystal Bartolovich and Neil Lazarus, Cambridge: Cambridge University Press.

Brennan, Timothy 2006, *Wars of Position*, New York: Columbia University Press.

Brennan, Timothy 2014, 'Subaltern Stakes', *New Left Review* 89: 67–87.

Brennan, Timothy 2017, 'On the Image of the "Country and the City"', *Antipode* 49, 51: 34–51.

Brenner, Neil 2001, 'State Theory in the Political Conjuncture: Henri Lefebvre's "Comments on a New State Form"', *Antipode* 33, 5: 49–62.

Brenner, Neil 2004, *New State Spaces: Urban Governance and the Rescaling of Statehood*, Oxford: Oxford University Press.

Brenner, Neil (ed.) 2014, *Implosions/Explosions*, Berlin: Jovis.

Brenner, Neil 2018 'Debating Planetary Urbanisation: For an Engaged Pluralism', *Environment and Planning D* 36, 3: 570–90.

Brenner, Neil, and Stuart Elden 2009, 'Introduction: State, Space, World: Lefebvre and the Survival of Capitalism', in *Henri Lefebvre, State, Space, World: Selected Essays*, edited by Neil Brenner and Stuart Elden, Minneapolis: University of Minnesota Press.

Brenner, Neil, and Nikos Katsikis 2014, 'Is the Mediterranean Urban?' in *Implosions/Explosions*, edited by Neil Brenner, Berlin: Jovis.

Brenner, Neil, and Christian Schmid 2014, 'The Urban Age in Question', in *Implosions/Explosions*, edited by Neil Brenner, Berlin: Jovis.

Brenner, Neil, and Christian Schmid 2015, 'Towards a New Epistemology of the Urban?' *City* 19, 2–3: 151–82.

Breton, André 1947, 'Un grand poète noir', Preface to *Cahier d'un retour au pays natal*, by Aimé Cesaire, Paris and Dakar: Présence Africaine.

Brewer, Anthony 1980, *Marxist Theories of Imperialism: A Critical Survey*, second edition, London: Routledge.

Bridge, Gary, Tim Butler, and Loretta Lees (eds) 2008, *Mixed Communities: Gentrification by Stealth*, Bristol: Policy Press.

Brownlie, R.J. 2008, '"Living the Same as the White People": Mohawk and Anishinabe Women's Labour in Southern Ontario, 1920–1940', *Labour/Le Travail* 61: 41–68.

Bruneteaux, Patrick 2013, *La Colonisation oubliée: de la zone grise plantationnaire aux élites mulâtres à la Martinique*, Vulaines sur Seine: Editions du Croquet.

Buckley, Michelle 2013, 'Locating Neoliberalism in Dubai: Migrant Workers and Class Struggle in the Autocratic City', *Antipode* 45, 2: 256–74.

Buckley, Michelle, and Adam Hanieh 2014, 'Diversification by Urbanization', *International Journal of Urban and Regional Research* 38, 1: 155–75.

Buckley, Michelle, and Kendra Strauss 2016, 'With, Against and Beyond Lefebvre', *Environment and Planning A* 34, 4: 617–36.

Buck-Morss, Susan 1986, 'The Flaneur, the Sandwichman, and the Whore: The Politics of Loitering', *New German Critique* 39: 99–140.

Buck-Morss, Susan 1989, *The Dialectics of Seeing: Walter Benjamin and the Arcades Project*, Cambridge, MA: MIT Press.

Buck-Morss, Susan 2002, *Dreamworld and Catastrophe: The Passing of Mass Utopia in East and West*, Cambridge, MA: MIT Press.

Bugeaud, Maréchal 1997, *La Guerre des rues et des maisons*, Paris: Jean-Paul Rocher.

Burkhard, Bud 2000, *French Marxism Between the Wars: Henri Lefebvre and the 'Philosophies'*, New York: Humanity.

Burrill, Fred 2019, 'The Settler Order Framework: Rethinking Working-Class History', *Labour/Le Travail* 83: 175–97.

Borrows, John, and Constance Mackintosh 2020, 'Indigenous Communities are Vulnerable in Times of Pandemic', *The Globe and Mail*, 18 April.

Butel, Paul 2007, *Histoire des Antilles françaises*, Paris: Perrin-Tempus.

Butler, Rémy, and Patrice Noisette 1977, *De la cité ouvrière au grand ensemble: la politique capitaliste du logement sociale 1875–1975*, Paris: François Maspéro.

Cabort Masson, Guy 1984, *Les puissances d'argent en Martinique. L'Etat francais, la caste béké et les autres*, Laboratoire de recherches de l'AMEP.

Cabral, Amilcar 1973, *Return to the Source: Selected Speeches of Amilcar Cabral*, edited by Africa Information Service, New York: Monthly Review Press.

Camfield, David 2019, 'Settler Colonialism and Labour Studies in Canada: A Preliminary Exploration', *Labour/Le Travail* 83: 147–72.

Campbell, Maria 1973, *Half-Breed: The Powerful Life Story of a Woman whose Courage and Strength You Will Never Forget*, Halifax: Formac Publishing.

Campbell, Maria 2019 [1973], *Half-Breed: The Powerful Life Story of a Woman whose Courage and Strength You Will Never Forget*, Toronto: McClelland and Stewart.

Campbell, Maria, and Donna Heimbecker 2005, 'The Man That We Knew', in *Otapawy! The Life of Métis Leader in his own words and in those of his contemporaries*, by Howard Adams, Saskatoon: Gabriel Dumont Institute of Native Studies and Applied Research.

Carlito, Pablo, 'Wet'suwet'en Protests a Revolutionary Moment in Canada: Mohawk Scholar Gerald Taiaiake Alfred', *The Georgia Straight*, 13 February, https://www.straig ht.com/news/1360101/wetsuweten-protests-revolutionary-moment-canada-moha wk-scholar-gerald-taiaiake-alfred

Carter, Sarah 1999, *Aboriginal People and the Colonisers of Western Canada to 1900*, Toronto: University of Toronto.

Cassano, Jay 2013, 'The Right to the City Movement and the Turkish Summer', *Jadaliyya*, 1 June, http://www.jadaliyya.com/pages/index/11978/the-right-to-the-city-moveme nt-and-the-turkish-sum

Castells, Manuel 1978, *City, Class and Power*, London: Macmillan.

Castells, Manuel 1977, *The Urban Question*, London: Edward Arnold.

Castells, Manuel 1983, *The City and the Grassroots*, Berkeley: UCLA Press.

Castriota, Rodrico, and João Tonucci 2018, 'Extended Urbanisation in and from Brazil', *Environment and Planning D* 36, 3: 512–28.

Çelik, Zeynep 1996, 'Gendered Spaces in Colonial Algiers', in *The Sex of Architecture*, edited by Diana Agrest, Patricia Conway, and Leslie K. Weisman, New York: Harry N. Abrams.

Çelik, Zeynep 1997, *Urban Forms and Colonial Confrontations: Algiers under French Rule*, Berkeley: University of California Press.

Cercle Frantz Fanon 2002, *Les Nouvelles Tropiques, Bulletin Fanonien* Numéro 1 and Numéro 2.

Césaire, Aimé 1955, *Discours sur le colonialisme*, Paris: Présence Africaine.

Césaire, Aimé 1956a, 'Culture et colonisation' *Présence Africaine* 8–10: 190–205.

Césaire, Aimé 1956b, 'Introduction', in *Les Antilles décolonisées*, Daniel Guérin, Paris: Présence Africaine.

Césaire, Aimé 1959, 'L'homme de culture et ses responsabilités', *Présence Africaine* 24–5.

Césaire, Aimé 1961a, *Toussaint Louverture: La révolution française et le problème colonial*, Paris: Présence Africaine.

Césaire, Aimé 1961b, 'La révolte de Frantz Fanon', *Jeune Afrique*, 13–19 December.

Césaire, Aimé 1983 [1939], *Cahier d'un retour au pays natal*, Dakar and Paris: Présence Africaine.

Césaire, Aimé 2003a [1952], 'Reconstruction et Urbanisme', in *Ecrits Politiques 1945–1983*, Paris: Jean Michel Place.

Césaire, Aimé 2003b [1961], 'Réformes Agricoles', in *Ecrits Politiques 1945–1983*, Paris: Jean Michel Place.

Césaire, Aimé 2004, *Conversation avec Aimé Césaire*, edited by Patrice Louis, Paris: Arléa.

Césaire, Aimé 2005, *Nègre je suis, nègre je resterai. Entretiens avec Françoise Vergès*, Paris: Albin Michel.

Césaire, Aimé 2008 [1948], 'Introduction', in Victor Schoelcher, *Esclavage et Colonisation*, Paris: Presses Universitaires de France.

Césaire, Aimé 2016a [1960], 'En finir avec les querelles subalterne', in *Ecrits Politiques 1957–1971*, Paris: Jean-Michel Place.

Césaire, Aimé 2016b [1967], 'A propos des mal lotis de Texaco', in *Ecrits Politiques 1957–1971*, Paris: Jean Michel Place.

Césaire, Aimé 2016c [1971], 'Entretien avec Lilian Kesteloot' (Présence Africaine), in *Ecrits Politiques 1957–1971*, Paris: Jean Michel Place.

Césaire, Suzanne 2009 [1942], 'Malaise d'une civilisation', in *Le grand camouflage. Ecrits de dissidence (1941–1945)*, Paris: Seuil.

Césaire, Suzanne 2009a [1943], '1943: Le surréalisme et nous', in *Le grand camouflage. Ecrits de dissidence (1941–1945)*, Paris: Seuil.

Césaire, Suzanne 2009b [1945], 'Le grand camouflage', in *Le grand camouflage. Ecrits de dissidence (1941–1945)*, Paris: Seuil.

Chabrol, Marie, and Lydie Launay, 'Résider dans un quartier en gentrification', in *Gentrifications*, edited by Marie Chabrol, Anaïs Collet, Matthieu Giroud, Lydie Launay, Max Rousseau, and Hovig Ter Minassian, Paris: Amsterdam.

Chakrabarty, Dipesh 2000, *Provincializing Europe*, Princeton: Princeton University Press.

Chamberlain, Julie 2020, 'Experimenting on Racialized Neighbourhoods: Internationale Bauausstellung Hamburg and the Urban Laboratory in Hamburg-Wilhelmsburg', *Environment and Planning D: Society and Space*, online.

Chamboredon, Jean-Claude, and Madeleine Lemaire 1970, 'Proximité spatiale et distance sociale. Les grands ensembles et leur peuplement', *Revue française de sociologie* 11, 1: 3–33.

Chamoiseau, Patrick 1992, *Texaco*, Paris: Gallimard.

Chamoiseau, Patrick 1994, *Une enfance créole II: Chemin d'école*, Paris: Gallimard.

Chamoiseau, Patrick 1996 [1990], *Une enfance créole I: Antan d'enfance*, Paris: Gallimard.

Chamoiseau, Patrick 1997, *Ecrire en pays dominé*, Paris: Gallimard.

Chamoiseau, Patrick 2002, *La Biblique des derniers gestes*, Paris: Gallimard.

Chamoiseau, Patrick 2005, *Une enfance créole III: au bout d'enfance*, Paris: Gallimard.

Chamoiseau, Patrick 2010, 'Nous avons intériorisé l'infériorité', *Le Monde Hors Série*, January and February, 26–7.

Chamoiseau, Patrick 2012 [1986], *Chronique des sept misères*, Paris: Gallimard.

Chamoiseau, Patrick 2013, *Césaire, Perse, Glissant: Les liaisons magnétiques*, Paris: Philippe Rey.

Chamoiseau, Patrick 2017, *J'ai toujours aimé la nuit*, Paris: Sonatine.

Cherki, Alice 2002, 'Préface à l'édition de 2002', in *Les damnés de la terre*, Frantz Fanon, Paris: La Découverte.

Cherki, Alice 2006, *Frantz Fanon: A Portrait*, translated by Nadia Benabid, Ithaca: Cornell University Press.

Cheyette, Bryan 2006, 'Fanon et Sartre: Noirs et Juifs', *Les Temps Modernes* 61, 635–6: 159–74.

Chibber, Vivek 2013, *Postcolonial Theory and the Spectre of Capital*, London: Verso.

Chivallon, Christine 2012, *L'esclavage: du souvenir à la mémoire*, Paris: Karthala.

Chivallon, Christine 2013, 'Créolisation universelle ou singulière? Perspectives depuis le Nouveau Monde', *L'Homme* 207–8.

Chivallon, Christine, and Dorothy Blair 1997, 'Images of Creole Diversity: A Reading of Patrick Chamoiseau's *Texaco*', *Cultural Geographies* 4, 3: 318–36.

Chouder, Ismahane, Malika Latrèche, and Pierre Tevanian 2008, *Les filles voilées parlent*, Paris: La Fabrique.

Ciccariello-Maher, George 2014, '"So Much the Worse for the Whites": Dialectics of the Haitian Revolution', *Journal of French and Francophone Philosophy* 22, 1: 19–39.

Ciccariello-Maher, George 2016, 'Dispossession without Labour: Bridging Abolition and Decolonisation', *Historical Materialism* 24, 3: 62–75.

Ciccariello-Maher, George 2017, *Decolonising Dialectics*, Durham, NC: Duke University Press.

Clapp, Alexander 2018, 'Below the Acropolis', *New Left Review*, 114: 67–96.

Cleaver, Eldridge 1968, *Soul on Ice*, New York: Delta.

Clerval, Anne 2012, *Paris sans le peuple: la gentrification de la capitale*, Paris: La Découverte.

Clerval, Anne, and Matthieu Delage 2019, 'L'embourgeoisement différencié de l'Est parisien aujourd'hui', in *Vivre à l'est de Paris: Inégalités, mobilités et recompositions socio-spatiales*, edited by Anne Clerval and Matthieu Delage, Paris: L'œil d'or.

Clerval, Anne, and Yoan Miot 2019, 'Conditions de logement et inégalités sociales', *Vivre à l'est de Paris: Inégalités, mobilités et recompositions socio-spatiales*, edited by Anne Clerval and Matthieu Delage, Paris: L'œil d'or.

Cohen, Muriel, and Cédric David 2012, 'Les cités de transit: le traitement urbain de la pauvrété à l'heure de la décolonisation', *Métropolitiques*, 29 February.

Collectif des Féministes Indigènes 2012 [2007], 'Stop au féminisme néocolonial et paternaliste', in *Nous sommes les Indigènes de la République*, Houria Bouteldja and Sadri Khiari, Paris: Amsterdam.

Collectif Logement Val D'Oise 95 Est 2007, No title, 14 October 2007, antidemolition .blogspot.com/search/label/ville%20sarcelles. Accessed 1 May 2010.

Collet, Victor 2019, *Nanterre, du bidonville à la cité*, Marseille: Agone.

Comack, Elizabeth, Lawrence Dean, Larry Morrissette, and Jim Silver 2013, *Indians Wear Red: Colonialism, Resistance and Aboriginal Street Gangs*, Halifax: Fernwood.

Comité d'évaluation de de suivi de l'ANRU 2008, *Rénovation urbaine 2004–2008*, Paris: La documentation française.

Comité Frantz Fanon de Fort de France (ed.), *Mémorial International Frantz Fanon*, Paris and Dakar: Présence Africaine.

Condé, Maryse 1993, 'Disorder, Freedom, and the West Indian Writer', *Yale French Studies*, 83, 2: 121–35.

Condé, Maryse 1998, 'Unheard Voice: Suzanne Césaire and the Construct of Caribbean Identity', in *Winds of Change: The Transforming Voices of Caribbean Women Writers and Scholars*, New York: Peter Lang.

Condé, Maryse 1999, *Le Cœur à rire et à pleurer: contes vrais de mon enfance*, Paris: Robert Laffont.

Condé, Maryse 2001, *La Belle Créole*, Paris: Gallimard.

Condé, Maryse 2006, *Victoire, Les saveurs et les mots*, Paris: Folio.

Confiant, Raphaël 1994, *L'Allée des Soupirs*, Paris: Gallimard.

Confiant, Raphaël 2006, *Aimé Césaire: une traversée paradoxale du siècle*, Paris: Ecrire.

Confiant, Raphaël 2017, *L'insurrection de l'âme: Frantz Fanon, vie et mort du guerrier-silex*, Le Lamentin et le Petit-Bourg: Caraibéditions.

Confiant, Raphaël 2020, 'Soliloque de Confiné', *Montray Kréyol*, https://montraykreyol
.org/article/soliloque-de-confine-4.

Cooper, Frederick 2005, *Colonialism in Question: Theory, Knowledge, History*, Berkeley:
University of California Press.

Coordination anti-démolition des quartiers populaires (CAQP) 2008, 'Manifeste de
la Coordination anti-démolition des logement HLM: Démolitions violentes et non
concertées des quartiers: non!!!' http://marseille2008.novox.org/spip.php?article49
&lang=fr last accessed 1 May 2008.

Coquery-Vidrovitch, Catherine 1993, *Histoire des villes d'Afrique noire des origines à la
colonisation*, Paris: Albin Michel.

Cornell, Drucilla 2001, 'The Secret behind the Veil: A Reinterpretation of "Algeria Unveiled"', *Philosophia Africana* 4, 2: 27–35.

Cornell, Drucilla 2015, 'Afterword', in *What Fanon Said*, Lewis Gordon, New York: Fordham University Press.

Coronil, Fernando 1996, 'Beyond Occidentalism: Toward Nonimperial Geohistorical
Categories', *Cultural Anthropology* 11, 1: 51–87.

Coronil, Fernando 1997, *The Magical State: Nature, Money and Modernity in Venezuela*,
Chicago: The University of Chicago Press.

Coronil, Fernando 2000, 'Towards a Critique of Globalcentrism: Speculations on Capitalism's Nature', *Public Culture* 12, 2: 351–74.

Coulthard, Glen 2014, *Red Skin, White Masks: Rejecting the Colonial Politics of Recognition*, Minneapolis: University of Minnesota Press.

Coulthard, Glen 2016, 'Response', *Historical Materialism* 24, 3: 92–103.

Coulthard, Glen 2017a, 'From Recognition to Decolonisation', Interview by Karl Gardner
and Devin Clancy, *Upping the Anti*, online, http://uppingtheanti.org/journal/article/
19-from-recognition-to-decolonisation/

Coulthard, Glen 2017b, *Whose Land is it Anyway: A Manual for Decolonisation*, edited
by Peter McFarlane and Nicole Schabus, Vancouver: Federation of Post-Secondary
Educators of BC.

Coulthard, Glen 2018, 'Global Red Power', Public Lecture, Department of Political Science, University of Toronto, 9 March.

Coulthard, Glen 2020, 'Once Were Maoists: Third World Currents in Fourth World Anti-
Colonialism', Public Lecture, Jackman Humanities Institute, University of Toronto,
6 March.

Coutras, Jacqueline 2003, *Les peurs urbaines et l'autre sexe*, Paris: l'Harmattan.

Couvelaire, Louise, Mathilde Costil, Delphine Papin, Sylvie Gittus, Eugénie Dumas, and
Eric Dédier 2020, 'Coronavirus: une surmortalité très élevée en Seine-Saint-Denis',
Le Monde 17 May.

Cowen, Deborah 2014, *The Deadly Life of Logistics*, Minneapolis: University of Minnesota Press.

Cowen, Deborah 2019, 'Following the Infrastructures of Empire: Notes on Cities, Settler Colonialism and Method', *Urban Geography*, online, November.

Cowen, Deborah 2020, '#SHUTCANADADOWN: Anti-colonial Counterlogistics for Indigenous Sovereignty', *The Funambulist* 28, 2–4.

Craig, Tyler, and Blair Hamilton 2015, 'In Search of Mino-Bimaadiziwin', in *Poor Housing*, edited by Josh Brandon and Jim Silver, Halifax and Winnipeg: Fernwood Publishing.

Cultural Anthropology 2016, 'Standing Rock, #NoDAPL, and Mni Wiconi', special online issue, https://culanth.org/fieldsights/1010-standing-rock-nodapl-and-mni-wiconi

Cusset, François 2005, *French Theory: Foucault, Derrida, Deleuze et Cie. Et les mutations de la vie intellectuelle aux Etats-Unis*, Paris: La Découverte.

Dacy, Ely (ed.) 1986, *L'actualité de Frantz Fanon. Actes du Colloque de Brazzaville* (12–16 décembre 1984), Paris: Karthala.

D'Arcus, Bruce 2010, 'The Urban Geography of Red Power: The American Indian Movement in Minneapolis-Saint Paul', *Urban Studies* 47, 6: 1241–55.

Daschuk, James 2013, *Clearing the Plains*, Regina: University of Regina Press.

Da Silva, Marina 2004, 'Quand les femmes des quartiers sortent de l'ombre', *Le Monde Diplomatique*, September, 8–9.

David, Cédric 2014, 'Faire du logement social des "immigrés" un problème de peuplement. Configuration politico-administratives et usages des catégories ethno-raciales (St. Denis)', in *Le peuplement comme politique*, edited by Fabien Desage, Christine Morel Journel, and Valérie Sala Pala, Rennes: Presses Universitaires de Rennes.

Davis, Diane E. 2005, 'Cities in Global Context: A Brief Intellectual History', *International Journal of Urban and Regional Research* 29, 1: 92–109.

Davis, Mike 1986, *Prisoners of the American Dream*, London: Verso.

Davis, Mike 1990, *City of Quartz*, London: Verso.

Davis, Mike 1998, *Ecology of Fear*, New York: Metropolitan.

Davis, Mike 2000, *Magical Urbanism*, London: Verso.

Davis, Mike 2001, *Late Victorian Holocausts*, London: Verso.

Davis, Mike 2004, 'The Urbanization of Empire: Megacities and the Laws of Chaos', *Social Text* 22, 4: 9–15.

Davis, Mike 2006, *The Planet of Slums*, London: Verso.

Day, Iyko 2015, 'Being or Nothingness: Indigeneity, Anti-Blackness, and Settler Colonial Critique', *Critical Ethnic Studies* 1, 2: 102–21.

De Andrade, Mario 1984, 'Fanon et l'Afrique combattante: témoignage', in *Mémorial International Frantz Fanon*, edited by Comité Frantz Fanon de Fort de France, Paris and Dakar: Présence Africaine.

De Barros, Françoise 2005, 'Des "franco-musulmans" aux "immigrés": l'importation de classification coloniale dans les politiques du logement en France', *Actes de la recherche en sciences sociales* 159, 4: 26–53.

De Barros, Françoise 2007, 'Contours d'un réseau administratif "algérien" et construction d'une competence en "affaires musulmanes". Les conseillers techniques pour
les affaires musulmanes en métropole (1952–1965)', *Politix* 76: 97–117.

De Barros, Françoise 2012, '"Bidonvilles": From Colonial Policy to the Algerian War',
Métropolitiques 21 March.

De Filippis, James, and Jim Fraser 2010, 'Why Do We Want Mixed-income Housing and
Neighbourhoods?' in *Critical Urban Studies*, edited by Jonathan Davies and David
Imbroscio, Albany: SUNY Press.

De Rudder, Véronique 1991, '"Seuil de tolerance" et cohabitation pluriethnique', in
Face au racisme tome 2: analyses, hypotheses, perspectives, edited by Pierre-André
Taguieff, Paris: La Découverte.

Debien, Gabriel 1973, 'Marronnage in the French Caribbean', in *Maroon Societies: Rebel
Slave Communities in the Americas*, edited by Richard Price, New York: Anchor
Books.

De Simoni, Simona 2014, 'La "vie quotidienne": une analyse féministe', *Période* 31 March,
revueperiode.net

De Sousa Santos, Boaventura 2009, 'A Non-Occidentalist West? Learned Ignorance and
Ecology of Knowledge', *Theory, Culture and Society* 26, 7–8: 103–25.

Dear, Michael, and Allen Scott (eds) 1981, *Urbanisation and Urban Planning in Capitalist
Society*, London: Methuen.

Debord, Guy 1990 [1988], *Comments on the Society of the Spectacle*, London: Verso.

Debord, Guy 1977 [1967], *The Society of the Spectacle*, Detroit: Black and Red Books

Debord, Guy 1981a [1955], 'Introduction to a Critique of Urban Geography', in *Situationist International Anthology*, edited by Ken Knabb, Berkeley: Bureau for Public
Secrets.

Debord, Guy 1981b [1959], 'Situationist Theses on Traffic', in *Situationist International
Anthology*, edited by Ken Knabb, Berkeley: Bureau for Public Secrets.

Debord, Guy 1981c [1966], 'The Decline and Fall of the Spectacle-Commodity Economy',
in *Situationist International Anthology*, edited by Ken Knabb, Berkeley: Bureau for
Public Secrets.

Debord, Guy 1981d [1961], 'Perspectives for Conscious Alterations in Everyday Life', in
Situationist International Anthology, edited by Ken Knabb, Berkeley: Bureau for Public Secrets.

Deboulet, Agnès 2006, 'Le résident vulnérable. Questions autour de la démolition',
Mouvements 47–48: 4–5.

'Déclaration sur le droit à l'insoumission dans la guerre d'Algérie', available at: www
.lecri.net/liste_noire/manifeste_121.html.

Delphy, Christine 2008a, 'La non-mixité, une nécessité politique: domination, ségrégation et auto-émancipation', *Les mots sont importants*, https://lmsi.net/La-non-mixite
-une-necessite.

Delphy, Christine 2008b, *Classer, dominer: qui sont les 'autres'?* Paris: La Fabrique.

Delphy, Christine 2012 [2006], 'De la non-mixité', in *Nous sommes les Indigènes de la République*, Houria Bouteldja and Sadri Khiari, Paris: Amsterdam.

Deluz-Labruyère, Joëlle 2004, 'Les Grands Ensembles et l'Impuissance de l'Utopie. L'exemple d'Alger', in *Le Monde des Grands Ensembles*, edited by Annie Fourcaut, Paris: Créaphis.

Denning, Michael 2010, 'Wageless Life', *New Left Review* 66, 79–97.

Derickson, Kate D. 2015, 'Urban Geography 1: Locating Urban Theory in the Urban Age', *Progress in Human Geography* 39, 5: 647–57.

Desai, Radhika 2013, *Geopolitical Economy: After US Hegemony, Globalisation and Empire*, London: Pluto.

Desponds, Didier 2010, 'Effets paradoxaux de la loi Solidarité et renouvellement urbain (SRU) et profil des acquéreurs de biens immobiliers en Ile-de-France', *Espaces et sociétés* 140–1, 1–2: 37–58.

DeVries, Laura 2011, *Conflict in Caledonia*, Vancouver: UBC Press.

Dewitt, Philippe 2008, 'Les mouvements nègres', in *Histoire politique des immigrations (post)coloniales en France, 1920–2008*, edited by Ahmed Boubeker and Abdellali Hajjat, Paris: Amsterdam.

Diabo, Russell 2017, 'The Indian Act: The Foundation of Colonialism in Canada', in *Whose Land is it Anyway: A Manual for Decolonisation*, edited by Peter McFarlane and Nicole Schabus, Vancouver: Federation of Post-Secondary Educators of BC.

Dialogues in Human Geography 2016, Article forum on 'Can the Straw Man Speak? An Engagement with Postcolonial Critiques of "Global Cities Research"', edited by Michi van Meeteren, Ben Derudder, and David Bassens, 6, 3.

Dikeç, Mustafa 2007, *Badlands of the Republic: Space, Politics, and Urban Policy*, London: Blackwell.

Dikeç, Mustafa 2017, *Urban Rage: The Revolt of the Excluded*, New Haven: Yale University Press.

Dirlik, Arif 1996, 'Chinese History and the Question of Orientalism', *History and Theory*, 35, 4: 96–118.

Dirlik, Arif 2007, *Global Modernity: Modernity in the Age of Global Capitalism*, Boulder: Paradigm.

Djebar, Assia 1985, *L'Amour-la Fantasia*, Paris: J.C. Lattès.

Djebar, Assia 2002, *La Femme sans Sépulture*, Paris: Albin Michel.

Domota, Eli 2020, 'Nou konfiné nou ka kontinyé luté', Interview with Mireille Fanon Mendès-France, 8 avril, *Fondation Frantz Fanon* https://www.facebook.com/FondationFrantzFanon/videos/212370870066811/

Dorries, Heather 2019, 'Welcome to Winnipeg', in *Settler City Limits: Indigenous Resurgence and Colonial Violence in the Urban Prairie West*, edited by Heather Dorries, Robert Henry, David Hugill, Tyler McCreary, and Julie Tomiak, Winnipeg: University of Manitoba Press.

Dorries, Heather, David Hugill, and Julie Tomiak 2019, 'Racial Capitalism and the Production of Settler Colonial Cities', *Geoforum* online, July.

Dorries, Heather, Robert Henry, David Hugill, Tyler McCreary, and Julie Tomiak (eds) 2019, *Settler City Limits: Indigenous Resurgence and Colonial Violence in the Urban Prairie West*, Winnipeg: University of Manitoba Press.

Douglas, Emory 2007, *Black Panther: The Revolutionary Art of Emory Douglas*, edited by Sam Durant, New York: Rizzoli.

Drapeau, Thierry 2019, 'The Roots of Karl Marx's Anti-Colonialism', *Jacobin*, 4 January, https://www.jacobinmag.com/2019/01/karl-marx-anti-colonialism-ernest-jones

Driant, Jacques 2012, 'Défaire les grands ensembles', in *A quoi sert la rénovation urbaine*, edited by Jacques Donzelot, Paris: Presses Universitaires de France.

Duarte, Adriano Luiz 2016, 'The Right to the City in Two Moments: The Bus and Tram Riots in São Paulo City in 1947 and 2013', *Historical Materialism* 24, 3: 147–83.

Dubey, Madhu 1998, 'The "True Lie" of the Nation: Fanon and Feminism', *differences* 10, 2.

Dubois, Laurent 2006, 'An Enslaved Enlightenment: Rethinking the History of the French Atlantic', *Social History* 31, 1: 1–14.

Du Bois, W.E.B. 1967 [1899], *The Philadelphia Negro: A Social Study*, New York: Schocken.

Dunbar-Ortíz, Roxanne 2005, 'Howard Adams at UC Davis and DQU', in *Otapawy! The Life of Métis Leader in his own words and in those of his contemporaries*, by Howard Adams, Saskatoon: Gabriel Dumont Institute of Native Studies and Applied Research.

Dunbar-Ortíz, Roxanne 2007, 'Indigenous Peoples and the Left in Latin America', *Monthly Review* 59, 3.

Dunbar-Ortíz, Roxanne 2009, 'Indigenous Resistance in the Americas and the Legacy of Mariátegui', *Monthly Review* 61, 4.

Dunbar-Ortíz, Roxanne 2014, *An Indigenous Peoples' History of the United States*, Boston: Beacon.

Dunbar-Ortíz, Roxanne 2016, 'The Relationship between Marxism and Indigenous Struggles and Implications of the Theoretical Framework for International Indigenous Struggles', *Historical Materialism* 24, 3: 76–91.

Duncan, Simon, and Mark Goodwin 1988, *The Local State and Uneven Development*, Cambridge: Cambridge University Press.

Dussel, Enrique 1993, 'Eurocentrism and Modernity', *boundary* 2, 20, 3: 65–76.

Eagleton, Terry 2008, *Literary Theory*, Minneapolis: University of Minnesota Press.

Eagleton, Terry 2013, *How to Read Literature*, New Haven: Yale University Press.

East End against Line 9 (n.d.) available at: https://eastendnotar.org/about, accessed 1 March 2016.

Edwards, Penelope 2010, 'Unpacking Settler Colonialism's Urban Strategies', *Urban History Review* 38, 2: 4–20.

Einaudi, Jean-Luc 1991, *La bataille de Paris. 17 Octobre 1961*, Paris: Seuil.

Ekers, Mike, and Scott Prudham 2017a, 'The Metabolism of Spatial Fixes: Capital Switching, Spatial Fixes and the Production of Nature', *Annals of the American Association of Geographers* 107, 6: 1370–88.

Ekers, Mike, and Scott Prudham 2017b, 'The Socio-Ecological Fix: Fixed Capital, Metabolism and Hegemony', *Annals of the American Association of Geographers* 108, 1: 17–34.

Ekers, Mike 2013, 'Gramsci and the Erotics of Labour: More notes on "The Sexual Question"', in *Gramsci: Space, Nature, Politics*, edited by Mike Ekers, Gillian Hart, Stefan Kipfer, and Alex Loftus, London: Wiley-Blackwell.

Ekers, Mike, Gillian Hart, Stefan Kipfer, and Alex Loftus (eds) 2013, *Gramsci: Space, Nature, Politics*, London: Wiley-Blackwell.

Elden, Stuart, and Adam David Morton 2016, 'Thinking Past Henri Lefebvre: Introducing "The Theory of Ground Rent and Rural Sociology"', *Antipode* 48, 1: 57–66.

Elsenhans, Hartmut 1974, *Frankreichs Algerienkrieg 1954–1962: Entkolonisierungsversuch einer kapitalistischen Metropole. Zum Zusammenbruch der Kolonialreiche*, Munich: Carl Hanser.

Elsenhans, Hartmut 1984, *Abhängiger Kapitalismus oder bürokratische Entwicklungsgesellschanft: Versuch über den Staat in der Dritten Welt*, Frankfurt: Campus.

Eluther, Jean-Paul 1984, 'Processus et modèles de développement dans la pensée de Frantz Fanon', in *Mémorial International Frantz Fanon*, edited by Comité Frantz Fanon de Fort de France, Paris and Dakar: Présence Africaine.

Enright, Theresa 2016, *The Making of Grand Paris: Metropolitan Urbanism in the Twenty-First Century*, Cambridge, MA: MIT Press.

Epstein, Renaud 2008, *Gouverner à distance: la rénovation urbaine, démolition-reconstruction de l'appareil d'Etat*, Thèse de Doctorat, Ecole Normale Supérieur de Cachan.

Epstein, Renaud 2012a, *La rénovation urbanie: démolition-reconstruction de l'Etat*, Paris: Les Presses Sciences Po.

Epstein, Renaud 2012b, 'ANRU: Mission Accomplie?' in *A quoi sert la rénovation urbaine*, edited by Jacques Donzelot, Paris: Presses Universitaires de France.

Estes, Nick 2019, 'Anti-Indian Common Sense', in *Settler City Limits: Indigenous Resurgence and Colonial Violence in the Urban Prairie West*, edited by Heather Dorries, Robert Henry, David Hugill, Tyler McCreary, and Julie Tomiak, Winnipeg: University of Manitoba Press.

Estes, Nick 2019a, *Our History is the Future*, London: Verso.

Ewane, Elongbil Emilie 2012, 'La guerre d'Algérie à Lyon: la bataille pour le contrôle de l'habitat' *Métropolitiques*, 22 February.

Fallope, Josette 1986, 'Analyse fanonienne du monde antillais', *L'actualité de Frantz Fanon*, edited by Elo Dacy, Paris: Karthala.

Fanon, Frantz 1952, *Peau noire, masques blancs*, Paris: Seuil.

Fanon, Frantz 1963 [1961], *The Wretched of the Earth*, translated by Constance Farrington, New York: Grove Weidenfeld.

Fanon, Frantz 1965 [1959], *A Dying Colonialism*, translated by Haakon Chevalier, New York: Grove.

Fanon, Frantz 1967 [1952], *Black Skin, White Masks*, translated by Charles Lam Markmann, New York: Grove Press.

Fanon, Frantz 1970 [1961], *Les damnés de la terre*, Paris: François Maspéro.

Fanon, Frantz 1988 [1964], *Toward the African Revolution*, translated by Haakon Chevalier, London: Grove.

Fanon, Frantz 2004 [1961], *The Wretched of the Earth*, translated by Richard Philcox, London: Grove.

Fanon, Frantz 2006 [1964], *Pour la révolution africaine*, Paris: La Découverte.

Fanon, Frantz 2011 [1959], *L'an v de la révolution algérienne*, Paris: La Découverte.

Fanon, Frantz 2015, *Ecrits sur l'aliénation et la liberté*, Paris: La Découverte.

Fanon, Frantz 2018 [2015], *Alienation and Freedom*, translated by Steven Corcoran, London: Bloomsbury.

Faure, Sylvia 2006, 'De quelques effets sociaux des démolitions d'immeubles d'un grand ensemble HLM à Saint-Etienne', *Espaces et Sociétés* 2–3: 191–206.

Fernandes, Edésio 2007, 'Constructing the "Right to City" in Brazil', *Social and Legal Studies* 16, 2: 201–19.

Ferguson, James 1999, *Expectations of Modernity: Myths and Meanings of Urban Life on the Zambian Copperbelt*, Berkeley: California University Press.

Fidler, Richard 1970, *Red Power in Canada*, Toronto: Vanguard Publications. Available at https://www.socialisthistory.ca/Docs/1961-/Red%20Power/Red_Power_1970.htm, accessed on 16 July 2020.

Fonseca, Claudia Alfaro 2018, *The Land of the Magical Maya: Colonial Legacies, Urbanisation and the Unfolding of Global Capitalism*, Doctoral Dissertation, Department of Urban Studies, Malmö.

Forum Social des Quartiers Populaires (FASQP) 2008a *Quartiers en lutte*: une publication hors série du Forum des Quartiers Populaires et de la Coordination antidémolition des quartiers populaires.

Forum Social des Quartiers Populaires (FASQP) 2008b, 'Logement: J'y suis! J'y reste', *Le Journal 3* http://www.fsqp.fr/last accessed 17 December 2014.

Fossey, Yves 2017, 'Poissy: deux barres de la Coudraie bientôt rasées', *Le Parisien* 5 March.

Foster-Carter, Aidan 1978, 'The Modes of Production Controversy', *New Left Review* 107: 47–77.

Fredenucci, Jean-Charles 2003a, 'L'émergent colonial des ingénieurs des Pont et Chaussées dans l'urbanisme des années 1950–1970', *Vingtième Siècle* 79, 3: 79–91.

Fredenucci, Jean-Charles 2003b, ' "L'urbanisme d'Etat": nouvelles pratiques, nouvelles acteurs', *Ethnologie française* 37: 13–20.

Freeman, Victoria 2010, 'Toronto Has No History!' *Urban History Review* 38, 2: 21–35.

Freund, Bill 2007, *The African City*, New York: Cambridge University Press.

Friedmann, John 2005, *China's Urban Transition*, Minneapolis: University of Minnesota Press.

Friedman, Michael Todd, and Cathy Van Ingen 2011, 'Bodies in Space: Spatialising Physical Cultural Studies', *Sociology of Sport Journal* 28: 85–105.

Friendly, Abigail 2013, 'The Right to the City: Theory and Practice in Brazil', *Planning Theory and Practice* 14, 2: 158–79.

Front de Libération Nationale 2004 [1956], 'La Plate-Forme de la Soummam: 20 août 1956 (extraits)', in *Le FLN: Documents et Histoire*, edited by Mohammed Harbi and Gilbert Meynier, Paris: Fayard.

Gallissot, René 1995, 'Maghreb-Europe. La ville bourgeoise, la ville coloniale et l'urbanisation prolétaire: ségrégation nationale et ségrégation sociale', in *Les quartiers de la ségrégation: Tiers monde ou quart monde?* edited by René Gallissot and Brigitte Moulin, Paris: Karthala.

Gallissot, René 2002, 'Urbanisation prolétaire et paupérisation culturelle', *Sarl Naqd* 16, 1: 149–64.

Gallissot, René 2005, 'Mehdi Ben Barka et la Tricontinentale', *Le Monde Diplomatique*, October.

Gallissot, René 2006, *La République française et les indigènes: Algérie colonisée, Algérie algérienne*, Paris: Éditions de l'Atelier.

Gallissot, René 2009, *Henri Curiel: Le mythe mesuré à l'histoire*, Paris: Riveneuve.

Gallissot, René 2016 [1969], 'Classes sociales en Algérie. Au-delà de Bourdieu et Sayad', http://revueperiod.net

Gallissot, René, Nadir Boumaza, and Ghislaine Clément 1994, *Ces Migrants qui font le prolétariat*, Paris: Méridiens Klincksieck.

Galonnier, Juliette 2012, 'Le droit à la ville en Inde, un monopole des classes moyennes au détriment des minorités?' *Métropolitiques*, 1 June.

Gandesha, Samir 2019, 'Insurgent Universality', *Radical Philosophy* 2, 4: 89–93.

Garnier, Jean-Pierre 1973, *Une ville, une révolution: La Havane. De l'urbain au politique*, Paris: Anthropos.

Garnier, Jean-Pierre 2010, *Une violence éminemment contemporaine*, Marseille: Agone.

Garnier, Jean-Pierre 2011 *Un espace indéfendable: L'aménagement urbain à l'heure sécuritaire*, Paris: Le monde à l'envers.

Garo, Isabelle 2008, 'Deleuze, Marx and Revolution', in *Critical Companion to Contemporary Marxism*, edited by Jacques Bidet and Stathis Kouvelakis, Leiden: Brill.

Gaviria, Mario 1974, *España a go-go: turismo charter y neocolonialismo del espacio*, Madrid: Ediciones Turner.

Géraud, Alice 2014, 'Le Val-Fourré "restera une zone d'habitat social"', *Libération*, 17 June.

Gerhardt, Gail 2008, 'Interview with Steve Biko', in *Biko Lives*, edited by Andile Mngxit-ama, Amanda Alexander, and Nigel Gibson, Palgrave: New York.

Gibson, Nigel (ed.) 1999, *Rethinking Fanon: The Continuing Dialogue*, New York: Human-ity.

Gibson, Nigel (ed.) 2003a, *Fanon: The Postcolonial Imagination*, Cambridge: Polity.

Gibson, Nigel (ed.) 2003b, 'Losing Sight of the Real: Recasting Merleau-Ponty in Fanon's Critique of Mannoni', in *Race and Racism in Continental Philosophy*, edited by Robert Bernasconi with Sybil Cook, Bloomington: Indiana University Press.

Gibson, Nigel (ed.) (ed.) 2011a, *Living Fanon: A Global Perspective*, London: Palgrave.

Gibson, Nigel (ed.) (ed.) 2011b, *Fanonian Practices in South Africa*, Scottsville: University of KwaZulu-Natal Press.

Gibson, Nigel, and Roberto Beneduce 2017, *Frantz Fanon: Psychiatry and Politics*, Lon-don: Rowman and Littlefield.

Gidel, Mélanie 2016, 'Discrimination territoriale et bricolage institutionnel: les tra-jectoires contrastées des quartiers populaires dans deux villes de la Caraïbe', in *Discriminations Territoriales*, edited by Claire Hancock, Christine Lelévrier, Fabrice Ripoll, and Serge Weber, Paris: L'oeil d'or.

Gidwani, Vinay 2008, 'The Subaltern Moment in Hegel's Dialectic', *Environment and Planning A* 40: 2578–87.

Gilbert, Melissa 2010, 'Place, Space and Agency: Beyond the Homogenous Ghetto', *Urban Geography* 31, 2: 148–52.

Gilbert, Pierre 2020, 'Le Covid-19, la guerre et les quartiers populaires', *Métropolitiques*, 16 April, https://www.metropolitiques.eu/Le-Covid-19-la-guerre-et-les-quartiers-po pulaires.html

Gilly, Adolfo 1965, 'Frantz Fanon et la révolution en Amérique latine', *Partisans*, Novem-ber, 41–8.

Gilmore, Ruth Wilson 2007, *Golden Gulag: Prisons, Surplus, Crisis and Opposition in Globalising California*, Berkeley: University of California Press.

Gilroy, Paul 1993, *The Black Atlantic: Modernity and Double Consciousness*, Cambridge, MA: Harvard University Press.

Girard, Youssef 2008, 'Assimilation et séparatisme dans le mouvement nationaliste algérien au milieu des années 1930', in *Histoire politique des immigrations (post)colo-niales en France, 1920–2008*, edited by Ahmed Boubeker and Abdellali Hajjat, Paris: Amsterdam.

Glissant, Edouard 1997 [1981], *Le Discours Antillais*, Paris: Gallimard.

Glissant, Edouard 2008 [1995], 'Creolisation in the Making of the Americas', *Caribbean Quarterly* 54, 1/2: 81–9.

Glissant, Edouard 2012 [1986], 'Un marqueur de paroles', in Patrick Chamoiseau, *Chro-nique des sept misères*, Paris: Gallimard.

Glissant, Edouard, and Patrick Chamoiseau 2007, *Quand les murs tombent: L'identité nationale hors-la-loi?* Paris: Galaade Editions.

Glissant, Edouard, and Patrick Chamoiseau 2009, *L'intraitable beauté du monde: Adresse à Barack Obama*, Paris: Galaade Editions.

Global Platform for the Right to the City, http://www.righttothecityplatform.org.br

Godlewska, Anne, and Neil Smith (eds) 1994, *Geography and Empire*, London: Blackwell.

Goebel, Michael 2017 [2015], *Paris, capitale du tiers monde: comment est née la révolution anticoloniale (1919–1939)*, translated by Pauline Stockman, Paris: La Découverte.

Goeman, Mishuana 2008, '(Re)Mapping Indigenous Presence on the Land in Native Women's Literature', *American Quarterly* 60, 2: 295–302.

Goerg, Odile, and Xavier Huetz 2003, *La ville coloniale*, Paris: Seuil.

Goonewardena, Kanishka 2005, 'The Urban Sensorium: Space, Ideology and the Aestheticization of Politics', *Antipode* 37, 1: 46–71.

Goonewardena, Kanishka 2011, 'Henri Lefebvre', in *New Blackwell Companion to Major Social Theorists*, edited by George Ritzer and Jeff Stepnisky, Oxford: Blackwell.

Goonewardena, Kanishka 2014, 'The Urban Revolution in the Country and the City', in *Implosions/Explosions*, edited by Neil Brenner, Berlin: Jovis.

Goonewardena, Kanishka 2018, 'Planetary Urbanization and Totality', *Environment and Planning D* 36, 3: 456–73.

Goonewardena, Kanishka, and Stefan Kipfer 2004, 'Creole City: Culture, Capital, and Class in Toronto', in *The Contested Metropolis: Six Cities at the Beginning of the 21st Century*, edited by INURA (International Network of Urban Research and Action), Basel, Boston, Berlin: Birkhäuser.

Goonewardena, Kanishka, and Stefan Kipfer 2005, 'Spaces of Difference: Reflections from Toronto on Multiculturalism, Bourgeois Urbanism and the Possibility of Radical Urban Politics', *International Journal of Urban and Regional Research* 29, 3.

Gopal, Priyamvada 2005, *Literary Radicalism in India: Gender, Nation and the Transition to Independence*, London: Routledge.

Gopal, Priyamvada 2013, 'Concerning Maoism: Fanon, Revolutionary Violence, and Postcolonial India', *South Atlantic Quarterly* 112, 3: 115–28.

Gopal, Priyamvada 2019, *Insurgent Empire: Anticolonial Resistance and British Dissent*, London: Verso.

Gordon, Daniel 2012, *Immigrants and Intellectuals: May 68 and the Rise of Anti-Racism in France*, London: Merlin.

Gordon, Jane Anna 2014, *Creolising Political Theory: Reading Rousseau Through Fanon*, New York: Fordham University Press.

Gordon, Lewis 1995, *Fanon and the Crisis of European Man*, London: Routledge.

Gordon, Lewis 1996, 'The Black and the Body Politic: Fanon's Existential Phenomenological Critique of Psychoanalysis', in *Fanon: A Critical Reader*, edited by Lewis Gordon, Denean Sharpley-Whiting, and R.T. White, London: Blackwell.

Gordon, Lewis 2000, 'Africana Thought and African Diasporic Studies', *The Black Scholar* 30, 3–4: 25–30.

Gordon, Lewis 2005, 'Through the Zone of Nonbeing: A Reading of *Black Skin, White Masks* in Celebration of Fanon's Eightieth Birthday', *The C.L.R. James Journal* 11, 1: 1–43.

Gordon, Lewis 2007, '*Through the Hellish Zone of Nonbeing*: Thinking through Fanon, Disaster, and the Damned of the Earth', *Human Architecture: Journal of the Sociology of Self-Knowledge* 5: 5–12.

Gordon, Lewis 2008, *An Introduction to Africana Philosophy*, New York: Cambridge University Press.

Gordon, Lewis 2012, 'Essentialist Anti-Essentialism, with Considerations from Other Sides of Modernity', *Quaderna* 1.

Gordon, Lewis 2013, 'Africana Philosophy and Philosophy in Black', *The Black Scholar* 43, 4: 46–51.

Gordon, Lewis 2015, *What Fanon Said: A Philosophical Introduction to His Life and Thought*, New York: Fordham University Press.

Gordon, Lewis 2018, 'Re-Imagining Liberations', *International Journal of Critical Diversity Studies* 1, 1: 11–29.

Gordon, Lewis, Denean Sharpley-Whiting, and R.T. White (eds) 1996, *Fanon: A Critical Reader* London: Blackwell.

Gordon, Todd 2010, *Imperialist Canada*, Winnipeg: Arbeiter Ring Publishing.

Goswami, Manu 2004, *Producing India: From Colonial Economy to National Space*, Chicago: Chicago University Press.

Goswami, Manu 2002, 'Rethinking the Modular Nation Form: Towards a Sociohistorical Conception of Nationalism', *Comparative Studies in Society and History* 44, 4: 770–99.

Gouvernement de France 2003, *La Loi d'orientation et de programmation pour la ville et la rénovation urbaine*, http://www.legifrance.gouv.fr/affichTexte.do?cidTexte=JORFTE XT000000428979.

Gouvernement de France 2014, *Loi de programmation pour la ville et la cohesion urbaine*, http://www.legifrance.gouv.fr/affichTexte.do?cidTexte=JORFTEXT000028636804& categorieLien=id

Gradhiva 2009, Special Issue: *Présence Africaine. Les conditions noires: une généalogie des discours*, 10.

Gramsci, Antonio 1971, *Selections from the Prison Notebooks*, edited and translated by Quintin Hoare and Geoffrey Nowell Smith, New York: International Publishers.

Grandinetti, Tina 2019, 'Urban aloha 'aina: Kaka'ako and a Decolonised Right to the City', *Settler Colonial Studies* 9, 2: 227–46.

Gregory, Derek 1994, *Geographical Imaginations*, Oxford: Basil Blackwell.

Gregory, Derek 2004, *The Colonial Present*, Oxford: Blackwell.

Gregory, Derek, and John Urry (eds) 1985, *Social Relations and Spatial Structures*, London: Macmillan.

Guémart, Loris 2017, 'Démolitions – reconstructions: la grande valse des logements sociaux', *La Gazette en Yvelines*, 4 January.

Guénif-Souilamas, Nacira, and Éric Macé 2006, *Les Féministes et le Garçon Arabe*, Paris: Editions de l'Aube.

Guérin, Daniel 1956, *Les Antilles Décolonisées*, Paris: Présence Africaine.

Guilbaud, Pierre, Henri Lefebvre, and Serge Renaudie 2009 [1986], 'International Competition for the New Belgrade Urban Structure Improvement', in *Autogestion, or Henri Lefebvre in New Belgrade*, edited by Sabine Bitter and Helmut Weber, Vancouver: Fillip Editions.

Ghulyan, Husik 2019, 'Lefebvre's Production of Space in the Context of Turkey: A Comprehensive Literature Survey', *SAGE Open* 9, 3: 1–14.

Haas, Oded 2020, 'Lefebvre in Palestine: Anti-colonial Re-colonisation and the Right to the City', in Habitat International Coalition 2019, *The Right to City: #Cities are Listening*, https://www.hic-net.org/wp-content/uploads/2019/10/Righ-to-the-City_Policy Paper.pdf

Hackworth, Jason, and Neil Smith 2001, 'The Changing State of Gentrification', *Tijdschrift voor Economische en Sociale Geografie* 92, 4: 464–77.

Haddour, Azzedine 2001, 'Remembering Sartre', in Jean-Paul Sartre, *Colonialism and Neocolonialism*, translated by Azzedine Haddour, Steve Brewer, and Terry McWilliams, London: Routledge.

Haddour, Azzedine 2006, 'Foreword: Postcolonial Fanonism', in Frantz Fanon, *The Fanon Reader*, edited by Azzedine Haddour, London: Pluto.

Hadjri, Karim, and Mohamed Osmani 2004, 'The Spatial Development and Urban Transformation of Colonial and Postcolonial Algiers', in *Planning Middle Eastern Cities*, edited by Yasser Elshehtawy, London: Routledge.

Haider, Asad 2018a, *Mistaken Identity: Race and Class in the Age of Trump*, London: Verso.

Haider, Asad 2018b, 'Eight Theses on Identity', *Salvage* 6: 145–50.

Hajjat, Abdellali 2012, *Les frontières de l'identité nationale*, Paris: La Découverte.

Hajjat, Abdellali 2013, *La Marche pour l'égalité et contre le racisme*, Paris: Amsterdam.

Hajjat, Abdellali, and Marwan Mohammed 2013, *Islamophobie: Comment les élites françaises fabriquent le 'problème musulman'*, Paris: La Découverte.

Hakimi, Zohra 2005, 'Le développement de "l'urbanisme de plan" à Alger durant la période coloniale', in *Villes coloniales aux XIXe–XXe siècles*, edited by Hélène Vacher, Paris: Maisonneuve et Larose.

Hall, Rebecca Jane 2015, 'Divide and Conquer: Privatising Indigenous Land Ownership as Capital Accumulation', *Studies in Political Economy* 96: 23–46.

Hall, Rebecca Jane 2019, 'A Feminist Political Economy of Indigenous-State Relations in Northern Canada', in *Change and Continuity: Canadian Political Economy in the New Millennium*, edited by Mark Thomas, Leah Vosko, Carlo Fanelli, and Olena Lyubchenko, Montreal and Kingston: McGill and Queen's University Press.

Hall, Stuart 1996, 'Gramsci's Relevance for the Study of Race and Ethnicity', in *Stuart Hall: Critical Dialogues in Cultural Studies*, edited by Kuan-Hsing Chen and David Morley, London: Routledge.

Hall, Stuart 2003, 'Marx's Notes on Method: A "Reading" of the "1857 Introduction"', *Cultural Studies* 17, 2: 113–49.

Hallward, Peter 2001, *Absolutely Postcolonial: Writing Between the Singular and the Specific*, Manchester: Manchester University Press.

Hamon, Hervé, and Patrick Rotman 1979, *Les porteurs de valises. La résistance française à la guerre d'Algérie*, Paris: Albin Michel.

Hamouchene, Hamza 2020, 'La révolution algérienne: la lutte pour la décolonisation continue', *Contretemps*, 15 April.

Hancock, Claire 2017, 'Feminism from the Margin: Challenging the Paris/*Banlieues* Divide', *Antipode* 49, 3: 636–56.

Hancock, Claire, Sophie Blanchard, and Amandine Chapuis 2017, '*Banlieusard.e.s* Claiming a Right to the City of Light: Gendered Violence and Spatial Politics in Paris', *Cities* 76: 23–38.

Hancock, Claire, and Viriginie Mobillion 2019, '"I want to tell them, I'm just wearing a veil, not carrying a gun!" Muslim Negotiating Borders in Femonationalist Paris', *Political Geography* 69, 1–9.

Harbi, Mohammed 1980, *Le FLN: Mirage et réalité*, Paris: editions j.a.

Harbi, Mohammed 2008, 'Frantz Fanon et messianisme paysan', *Tumultes* 31: 11–15.

Hardt, Michael, and Antonio Negri, *Empire*, Cambridge, MA: Harvard University Press.

Harootunian, Harry 2000, *History's Disquiet: Modernity, Cultural Practice and the Question of Everyday Life*, New York: Columbia University Press.

Harootunian, Harry 2005, 'Some Thoughts on Comparability and the Space-Time Problem', *boundary 2* 32, 2: 23–52.

Harootunian, Harry 2015, *Marx After Marx: History and Time in the Expansion of Capitalism*, New York: Columbia University Press.

Harris, Cole 2002, *Making Native Space*, Vancouver: UBC Press.

Harris, Cole 2004, 'How Did Colonialism Dispossess?' *Annals of the Association of American Geographers* 94, 1: 165–82.

Hart, Gillian 2001, 'Development Critiques in the 1990s', *Progress in Human Geography* 25, 4.

Hart, Gillian 2002, *Disabling Globalisation: Places of Power in Post-Apartheid South Africa*, Berkeley: University of California Press.

Hart, Gillian 2006, 'Denaturalising Dispossession: Critical Ethnography in the Age of Resurgent Imperialism', *Antipode* 38, 5: 977–1004.

Hart, Gillian 2018a, 'Relational Comparison Revisited: Marxist Postcolonial Geographies in Practice', *Progress in Human Geography* 42, 3: 371–94.

Hart, Gillian 2018b, 'Becoming a Geographer: Massey Moments in a Spatial Education', in *Doreen Massey: Critical Dialogues*, edited by Marion Werner, Jamie Peck, Rebecca Lave, and Brett Christophers, New York: Columbia University Press.

Harvey, David 1982, *Limits to Capital*, Chicago: University of Chicago Press.

Harvey, David 2001a [1975], 'The Geography of Capitalist Accumulation: A Reconstruction of the Marxian Theory', in *Spaces of Capital*, London: Routledge.

Harvey, David 2001b [1985], 'The Geopolitics of Capitalism', in *Spaces of Capital*, London: Routledge.

Harvey, David 2003a, *The New Imperialism*, Oxford: Oxford University Press.

Harvey, David 2003b, *Paris, Capital of Modernity*, London: Routledge.

Hatherley, Owen 2015, *Landscapes of Communism*, London: Allen Lane.

Haug, Frigga 1992, *Beyond Female Masochism: Memory-Work and Politics*, London: Verso.

Haug, Frigga 2003, 'Alltagsforschung', in *Historisch-Kritisches Wörterbuch des Feminismus Volume 1*, edited by Frigga Haug, Hamburg: Argument Verlag.

Haug, Frigga 1994, 'Alltagsforschung als zivilgesellschaftliches Projekt', *Das Argument* 206: 6–13.

Haug, Frigga et al. 1999 [1983], *Female Sexualisation: A Collective Work of Memory*, London: Verso.

Haug, Wolfgang Fritz 1987, *Pluraler Marxismus: Beiträge zur politischen Kultur*, Berlin: Das Argument.

Hayden, Dolores 1981, *The Grand Domestic Revolution*, Cambridge, MA: MIT Press.

Hayes, Brent Edwards 2003, *The Practice of Diaspora: Literature, Translation and the Rise of Black Internationalism*, Cambridge, MA: Harvard University Press.

Hazan, Eric 2002, *L'Invention de Paris*, Paris: Seuil.

Hazan, Eric 2003, *Chronique de la guerre civile*, Paris: La Fabrique.

Hazan, Eric 2011, *Paris sous tension*, Paris: La Fabrique.

Henni, Samia 2016, 'On the Spaces of Guerre Moderne: The French Army in Northern Algeria', *Footprint: Spaces of Conflict* Winter: 37–56.

Henni, Samia 2017, *Architecture of Counterrevolution: The French Army in Northern Algeria*, Zurich: GTA.

Herod, Andrew 2001, *Labor Geographies: Workers and the Landscapes of Capitalism*, New York: Guilford.

Hervo, Monique 2012, *Nanterre en guerre d'Algérie. Chroniques du Bidonville: 1959–62*, Paris: Actes du Sud.

Hess, Rémi 1988, *Henri Lefebvre et l'aventure du siècle*, Paris: Metailie.

Heynen, Nik 2009, 'Bending the Bars of Empire from Every Ghetto for Survival: The Black Panther Party's Radical Antihunger Politics of Social Reproduction and Scale', *Annals of the American Association of Geographers* 99, 2: 406–22.

High, Steven 1996, 'Native Wage Labour and Independent Production during the "Era of Irrelevance"', *Labour/Le Travail* 37: 243–64.

Hitz, Hansruedi et al. (eds) 1995, *Capitales Fatales: Urbanisierung und Politik in the Finanzmetropolen Frankfurt und Zürich*, Zurich: Rotpunktverlag.

Hmed, Choukri 2007, ' "Tenir ses hommes": la gestion des étrangers isolés dans les foyers Sonacotra après la guerre d'Algérie', *Politix* 76, 11–30.

Hmed, Choukri 2008, 'Des mouvements sociaux "sur une tête d'épingle": le rôle de l'espace physique dans le processus contestataire à partir de l'exemple des mobilisations dans les foyers de travailleurs migrants', *Politix* 145–65.

Hoar, Aedan 2014, *Beyond the Politics of Recognition*, Master's Major Research Paper, Faculty of Environmental Studies, York University, Canada.

Holton, R.J. 1986, *Cities, Capitalism, Civilisation*, London: Allen & Unwin.

hooks, bell 2000, *Feminist Theory: From Margin to Center*, 2nd edition, Boston: South End Press.

Howlett, Marc-Vincent, and Romuald Fonkoua 2009, 'La maison Présence Africaine', *Gradhiva* 10: 107–30.

Heynen, Nik, Maria Kaika, and Erik Swyngedouw (eds) 2006, *In the Nature of Cities: Urban Political Ecology and the Politics of Urban Metabolism*, London: Routledge.

Hubbard, Phil, and Teela Sanders 2003, 'Making Space for Sex Work: Female Street Prostitution and the Production of Urban Space', *International Journal of Urban and Regional Research* 72, 1: 75–89.

Hudis, Peter 2015, *Frantz Fanon, Philosopher of the Barricades*, London: Pluto.

Hudis, Peter 2017, 'Frantz Fanon's Contribution to Hegelian Marxism' *Critical Sociology* 43, 6: 865–73.

Hudis, Peter 2018, 'Racism and the Logic of Capital: A Fanonian Reconsideration', *Historical Materialism* 26, 2: 199–220.

Huffer, Lynne 2006, 'Derrida's Nostalgeria', in *Algeria and France: Identity, Memory, Nostalgia*, edited by Patricia M.E. Lorcin, Syracuse: Syracuse University Press.

Hugill, David 2015, *The Urban Politics of Settler Colonialism*. Phd Thesis, York University, Canada.

Hugill, David 2017, 'What is a Settler Colonial City?' *Geography Compass* 11, 5.

Hugill, David 2019, 'Comparative Settler Colonial Urbanisms', in *Settler City Limits: Indigenous Resurgence and Colonial Violence in the Urban Prairie West*, edited by Heather Dorries, Robert Henry, David Hugill, Tyler McCreary, and Julie Tomiak, Winnipeg: University of Manitoba Press.

Hugues, Bastien 2009, 'D'Argenteuil à Bobigny, les visites de Sarkozy en banlieue', *Le Figaro*, 24 November, http://www.lefigaro.fr/politique/2009/11/24/01002--2009112 4ARTFIG00435-d-argenteuil-a-bobigny-les-visites-de-sarkozy-en-banlieue-.php accessed on 27 November 2014.

Huson, Freda, and T'oghestíy 2015, 'Indigenous Sovereignty Fuels Pipeline Resistance: An Interview', *Upping the Anti* 17: 46–59.

Ibrahimi, Khaoula Taleb 2004, 'Les Algériennes et la guerre de libération nationale:

l'émergence des femmes dans l'espace public et politique au cours de la guerre et l'après-guerre', in *La guerre d'Algérie*, edited by Benjamin Stora and Mohammed Harbi, Paris: R. Laffont.

Idahosa, P.L.E. 2004, *The Populist Dimension to African Political Thought: Frantz Fanon, Amilcar Cabral, and Julius Nyerere*, Trenton and Asmara: Africa World Press.

Idle No More n.d., www.idlenomore.ca last accessed last in July 2020.

Indigenous Environmental Network n.d., available at: http://www.ienearth.org/ accessed in March 2016.

Irele, F. Abiola 2011, *The Negritude Moment: Explorations in Francophone African and Caribbean Literature and Thought*, Trenton: Africa World Press.

Jalabert, Laurent 2007, *La Colonisation Sans Nom: La Martinique de 1960 à nos Jours*, Paris: Les Indes Savantes.

James, C.L.R. 1979 [1978], 'Fanon and the Caribbean', in *International Tribute to Frantz Fanon: Record of the Special Meeting of the United Nations Special Committee Against Apartheid*, New York City, United Nations Centre against Apartheid, available at: www.marxists.org.

James, C.L.R. 1989 [1938], *Black Jacobins: Toussaint L'Ouverture and the San Domingo Revolution*, second edition, New York: Vintage.

Jameson, Fredric 1981, *The Political Unconscious: Narrative as a Socially Symbolic Act*, Ithaca: Cornell University Press.

Jameson, Fredric 1986, 'Third-World Literature in the Era of Multinational Capitalism', *Social Text* 15: 65–88.

Jameson, Fredric 1990, 'Modernism and Imperialism', in *Nationalism, Colonialism, and Literature*, edited by Terry Eagleton, Fredric Jameson, and Edward W. Said, Minneapolis: University of Minnesota Press.

Jazeel, Tariq 2018, 'Urban Theory with an Outside', *Environment and Planning D* 36, 3: 405–19.

Jérôme, Béatrice 2012, 'La Cour des comptes dresse un bilan sévère de dix ans de rénovation urbaine', *Le Monde*, 18 July.

Jiang, Hongsheng 2014, *La Commune de Shanghai et La Commune de Paris*, Paris: La Fabrique.

Johnson, Jon 2013, 'The Indigenous Environmental History of Toronto', in *Urban Explorations*, edited by Anders Sandberg, Hamilton: L.R. Wilson Institute for Canadian History.

Jones, Katherine, and Jeff Popke 2010, 'Re-envisioning the City: Lefebvre, HOPE VI, and the Neoliberalisation of Urban Space', *Urban Geography* 31, 1: 114–33.

Kahn, Bonnie 1987, *Cosmopolitan Culture: The Gilt-edged Dream of a Tolerant City*, New York: Atheneum.

Kaiwar, Vasant 2013, *L'Orient postcolonial: sur la 'provincialisation' de l'Europe et la théorie postcoloniale*, Paris: Syllepse.

Kamran, Matin 2011, 'Redeeeming the Universal: Postcolonalism and the Inner Life of Eurocentrism', *European Journal of International Relations* 19, 2: 353–77.

Kanai, Juan Miguel 2014, 'On the Peripheries of Planetary Urbanisation: Globalising Manaus and Its Expanding Impact', *Environment and Planning D* 32: 1071–87.

Kassab-Charfi, Samia 2012, *Patrick Chamoiseau*, Paris: Institut Français.

Katznelson, Ira 1981, *City Trenches*, Chicago: University of Chicago Press.

Katznelson, Ira 1993, *Marxism and the City*, Oxford: Clarendon.

Kechaou, Jean-Riad 2017, *93370: Les Bosquets, un ghetto français*, Paris: Melting Book.

Keil, Roger 1993, *Weltstadt – Stadt der Welt: Internationalisierung und lokale Politik in Los Angeles*, Münster: Westfälisches Dampfboot.

Kelley, Robin D.G. 1999, 'A Poetics of Anticolonialism', *Monthly Review* 51, 6.

Kelley, Robin D.G. 2017, 'The Rest of Us: Rethinking Settler and Native', *American Quarterly* 69, 2: 267–76.

Khaldoun, Ibn 2005, *The Muqaddimah: An Introduction to History*, translated by F. Rosenthal, Princeton: Princeton University Press.

Khalfa, Jean 2009, 'Naissance de la Négritude', *Les Temps Modernes* 656: 38–63.

Khalfa, Jean, and Robert Young 2015, 'Introduction', in Frantz Fanon, *Ecrits sur l'aliénation et la liberté*, Paris, La Découverte.

Khan, Aisha 2004, 'Sacred Conversions: Syncretic Creoles, the Indo-Caribbean, and "Cultures-in-Between"', *Radical History Review* 89: 165–84.

Khan, Danish, and Anirban Karak 2018, 'Urban Development by Dispossession: Planetary Urbanisation and Primitive Accumulation', *Studies in Political Economy* 99, 3: 307–30.

Khatam, Azam, and Oded Haas 2018, 'Interrupting Planetary Urbanisation: A View from Middle-Eastern Cities', *Environment and Planning D* 36, 3: 439–55.

Khiari, Sadri 2006, *Pour une politique de la racaille: immigré-e-s, indigènes et jeunes de banlieues*, Paris: Textuel.

Khiari, Sadri 2008, *La contre-révolution coloniale en France: de de Gaulle à Sarkozy*, Paris: La Fabrique.

Khiari, Sadri 2012 [2007], 'L'Indigène discordant. Autonomie et convergences', in Houria Bouteldja and Sadri Khiari, *Nous Sommes les Indigènes de la République*, Paris: Amsterdam.

King, Anthony 1990a, *Urbanism, Colonialism, and the World Economy*, London: Routledge.

King, Anthony 1990b, *Global Cities: Post-Imperialism and the Internationalisation of London*, London: Routledge.

Kinkaid, Eden 2019, 'Re-encountering Lefebvre: Toward a Critical Phenomenology of Social Space', *Environment and Planning D: Society and Space* 38, 1: 167–86.

Kipfer, Stefan 1995, 'Globalisation, Hegemony, and Local Politics: The Case of Zurich, Switzerland', in *A New World Order? Global Transformation in the Late 20th Century*, edited by Joszef Böröcz and David A. Smith, Westport, CT: Greenwood, pp. 181–99.

Kipfer, Stefan 1998, 'Urban Politics in the 1990s: Notes on Toronto', in *Possible Urban Worlds*, edited by Hansruedi Hitz et al., Basel/New York, Birkhäuser.

Kipfer, Stefan 2002, 'Everyday Life, Urbanisation, and the Survival of Capitalism: Lefebvre, Gramsci, and the Problematic of Hegemony', *Capitalism, Nature, Socialism*, June: 117–49.

Kipfer, Stefan 2004, *Urbanisation, Everyday Life and Difference: Lefebvre, Gramsci, Fanon and the Problematic of Hegemony*, Doctoral Dissertation, Department of Political Science, York University, Toronto.

Kipfer, Stefan 2007, 'Fanon and Space: Colonisation, Urbanisation and Liberation from the Colonial to the Global City', *Environment and Planning D: Society and Space* 25, 4: 701–26.

Kipfer, Stefan 2008, 'How Lefebvre Urbanised Gramsci: Hegemony, Difference and Everyday Life', in *Space, Difference, Everyday Life: Reading Henri Lefebvre*, edited by Kanishka Goonewardena, Stefan Kipfer, Richard Milgrom, and Christian Schmid, New York: Routledge.

Kipfer, Stefan 2009a, 'Why the Urban Question Still Matters', in *Towards a Political Economy of Scale*, edited by Roger Keil and Rianne Mahon, Vancouver: UBC Press.

Kipfer, Stefan 2009b, 'Tackling Urban Apartheid: The Social Forum of Popular Neighbhourhoods in Paris', *International Journal for Urban and Regional Research* 33, 4: 1058–66.

Kipfer, Stefan 2011a, 'The Times and Spaces of (De-)colonisation: Fanon's Counter-Colonialism, Then and Now', in *Living Fanon*, edited by Nigel Gibson, New York: Palgrave, pp. 93–104.

Kipfer, Stefan 2011b, 'Decolonisation in the Heart of Empire: Some Fanonian Echoes in France Today', *Antipode* 43, 4: 1155–80.

Kipfer, Stefan 2012, 'Ghetto or Not Ghetto: Quelques remarques sur la "race", l'espace et l'Etat à Paris', in *Race et Capitalisme*, edited by Félix Boggio Ewanjé-Epée and Stella Magliani-Belkacem, Paris: Syllepse, pp. 125–46.

Kipfer, Stefan 2013a, 'City, Country, Hegemony: Gramsci's Spatial Historicism', in *Gramsci: Nature, Space, Politics*, edited by Mike Ekers, Gillian Hart, Stefan Kipfer, and Alex Loftus, London: Blackwell.

Kipfer, Stefan 2013b, 'Urbanisation et racialisation: déségrégation, émancipation, hégémonie', in *Penser l'émancipation: offensives capitalistes et résistances internationales*, edited by Hadrien Buclin, Joe Daher, Christakis Georgiou, and Pierre Raboud, Paris: La Dispute.

Kipfer, Stefan 2014, 'Lefebvre's Metamorphosis: 1989–2006–2014', *Society and Space* open site http://societyandspace.com/material/discussion-forum/forum-on-henri-lefebvre-dissolving-city-planetary-metamorphosis/stefan-kipfer-lefebvres-metamorphosis-1989--2006--2014/

Kipfer, Stefan 2018, 'Quel Gramsci décolonial? Plaidoyer pour une piste Fanon-Gramsci', in *Rosa Luxemburg, Antonio Gramsci actuels*, edited by Marie-Claire Caloz-Tschopp, Romain Felli, and Antoine Chollet, Paris: Kimé.

Kipfer, Stefan 2019, 'What Colour is Your Vest? Reflections on the Yellow Vest Movement in France', *Studies in Political Economy* 100, 3: 209–31.

Kipfer, Stefan, and Kanishka Goonewardena 2007, 'Colonisation and the New Imperialism: On the Meaning of Urbicide Today', *Theory and Event* 10, 2: 1–39.

Kipfer, Stefan, Christian Schmid, Kanishka Goonewardena, and Richard Milgrom 2008a, 'Globalising Lefebvre?' in *Space, Difference, and Everyday Life: Reading Henri Lefebvre*, edited by Kanishka Goonewardena, Stefan Kipfer, Richard Milgrom, and Christian Schmid, New York: Routledge.

Kipfer, Stefan, Kanishka Goonewardena, Christian Schmid, and Richard Milgrom 2008b, 'On the Production of Henri Lefebvre', in *Space, Difference, and Everyday Life: Reading Henri Lefebvre*, edited by Kanishka Goonewardena, Stefan Kipfer, Richard Milgrom, and Christian Schmid, New York: Routledge.

Kipfer, Stefan, and Jason Petrunia 2009, '"Colonisation" and Public Housing in the Competitive City: A Toronto Case Study', *Studies in Political Economy* 83: 111–39.

Kipfer, Stefan, and Kanishka Goonewardena 2013, 'Urban Marxism and the Postcolonial Question: Henri Lefebvre and "Colonisation"', *Historical Materialism* 21, 2: 76–117.

Kipfer, Stefan, and Kanishka Goonewardena 2014, 'Henri Lefebvre and "Colonisation": From Reinterpretation to Research', in *Urban Revolution Now: Henri Lefebvre in Social Research and Architecture*, edited by Łukasz Stanek, Christian Schmid, and Ákos Moravánsky, Farnham: Ashgate.

Kipfer, Stefan, and Gillian Hart 2013, 'Translating Gramsci in the Current Conjuncture', in *Gramsci: Nature, Space, Politics*, edited by Mike Ekers, Gillian Hart, Stefan Kipfer, and Alex Loftus, London: Blackwell.

Kipfer, Stefan, Julie-Anne Boudreau, Pierre Hamel, and Antoine Noubouwo 2017, '*Grand Paris*: The Bumpy Road Towards Metropolitan Governance', in *Governing Cities Through Regions: Canadian and European Perspectives*, edited by Roger Keil, Pierre Hamel, Julie-Anne Boudreau, and Stefan Kipfer, Waterloo: Wilfrid Laurier Press.

Kipfer, Stefan, and Mustafa Dikeç 2019, 'Peripheries Against Peripheries? Against Spatial Reification', in *Massive Suburbanisation: (Re-)Building the Global Periphery*, edited by Murat Güney, Roger Keil, and Murat Üçoğlu, Toronto: University of Toronto Press.

Kipfer, Stefan, and Ayyaz Mallick forthcoming, 'Which Gramsci for (Post)Colonial Times? For a Fanon-Gramsci Lineage', in *Gramsci nel mondo nord-americano*, edited by Renate Holub, Francesco Giasi, and Giuseppe Vacca, Bologna: Il Mulino.

Kirszbaum, Thomas 1999, 'Les Immigrés dans les politiques de l'habitat: variations locales sur le thème de la diversité', *Sociétés Contemporaines* 33–34: 87–110.

Kipfer, Stefan, and Ayyaz Mallick forthcoming, 'Which Gramsci for (Post)Colonial Times? For a Fanon-Gramsci Lineage', in *Gramsci nel mondo nord-americano*, edited by Renate Holub, Francesco Giasi, and Giuseppe Vacca, Bologna: Il Mulino.

Kirszbaum, Thomas 2004, 'Discours et pratiques de l'intégration des immigrés: la période des grands projets de la ville', *Les annales de la recherché urbaine* 97, 12: 51–8.

Kirszbaum, Thomas 2008, *Mixité sociale dans l'habitat*, Paris: La documentation française.

Kirszbaum, Thomas 2013, 'La rénovation urbaine comme politique de peuplement: Les Etats-Unis et la France entre classe et "race"', *Métropoles* 13.

Klassen, Jerome 2014, *Joining Empire: The Political Economy of the New Canadian Foreign Policy*, Toronto: University of Toronto Press.

Knepper, Wendy 2011, *Patrick Chamoiseau: A Critical Introduction*, Jackson: University Press of Mississippi.

Knight, Rolf 1978, *Indians at Work*, Vancouver: New Star Books.

Knox, Paul, and Peter Taylor 1995, *World Cities in a World System*, Cambridge: Cambridge University Press.

Kopp, Anatole 1970, *Town and Revolution: Soviet Architecture and City Planning 1917–1935*, translated by T. Burton, New York: George Braziller.

Kruks, Sonia 1996, 'Fanon, Sartre, and Identity Politics', in *Fanon: A Critical Reader*, edited by Lewis Gordon, Denean Sharpley-Whiting, and R.T. White, Oxford: Blackwell.

Kulchyski, Peter 1992, 'Primitive Subversions: Totalisation and Resistance in Native Canadian Politics', *Cultural Critique* 21: 171–96.

Kulchyski, Peter 2013, *Aboriginal Rights Are Not Human Rights*, Winnipeg: ARP Books.

Kulchyski, Peter 2016a, '50 Years in Indian Country', in *Canada Since 1960*, edited by Cy Gonick, Toronto: James Lorimer.

Kulchyski, Peter 2016b, 'Hunting Theories: Totalisation and Indigenous Resistances in Canada', *Historical Materialism* 24, 3: 30–44.

Kulchyski, Peter 2017, 'Theses on Indigenous Challenges to Dominant Structures', Lecture, GERG Revolutions Conference, University of Manitoba, Winnipeg.

Kulchyski, Peter, and Walter Bernauer 2014, 'Modern Treaties, Extraction, and Imperialism in Canada's Indigenous North', *Studies in Political Economy* 93: 3–23.

Kupferstein, Daniel 2017, *Les Balles du 14 Juillet 1953: Le massacre policier oublié de nationalistes algériens à Paris*, Paris: La Découverte.

Kusno, Abidin 2000, *Behind the Postcolonial: Architecture, Urban Space and Political Cultures in Indonesia*, New York: Routledge.

Kuymulu, Mehmet Baris 2013, 'Reclaiming the Right to the City: Reflections on the Urban Uprisings in Turkey', *City* 17, 3: 274–8.

Kwatari, Tarek n.d., 'Années 70, L'âge d'or de Barbès', http://fsqp.fr/IMG/pdf/BARBES _AGE_D_OR.pdf last accessed 17 December 2014.

Labban, Mazen 2008, *Space, Oil and Capital*, London: Routledge.

Lafrance, Xavier 2019, *The Making of Capitalism in France: Class Structures, Economic Development, the State and the Formation of the French Working Class, 1750–1914*, Leiden: Brill.

Lagrange, Hugues 2008, 'Emeutes, ségrégation et aliénation', *Revue française de science politique* 58, 3: 377–401.

Lambert, Anne 2015, *Tous Propriétaires: L'envers du décor pavillonnaire*, Paris: Seuil.

Lapeyronnie, Didier 2008, *Ghetto urbain*, Paris: Laffont.

Lapierre, Georges 2008, *La Commune d'Oaxaca: Chroniques et considérations*, Paris: Rue des Cascades.

Launay, Lydie 2016, 'Négocier la diversité au quotidien: des rapports de voisinage et des choix scolaires sous contrôle', in *Gentrifications*, edited by Marie Chabrol, Anaïs Collet, Matthieu Giroud, Lydie Launay, Max Rousseau, and Hovig Ter Minassian, Paris: Amsterdam.

Laurens, Sylvain 2009, *Une politisation feutrée: les hauts fonctionnaires et l'immigration en France (1962–1981)*, Paris: Belin.

Lawrence, Bonita 2003, 'Gender, Race, and the Regulation of Native Identity in Canada and the United States: An Overview', *Hypatia* 18, 2: 3–31.

Lawrence, Bonita 2004, *'Real' Indians and Others*, Vancouver: University of British Columbia Press.

Lawrence, Bonita 2012, *Fractured Homelands*, Toronto: University of Toronto Press.

Lawson, James 2019, 'Colonialism, Indigenous Struggles, and the Ontario State', in *Divided Province: Ontario Politics in the Age of Neoliberalism*, edited by Greg Albo and Bryan M. Evans, Montreal and Kingston: McGill/Queen's University Press.

Lazarus, Neil 2002, 'The Fetish of "the West" in Post-Colonial Theory', in *Marxism, Modernity and Postcolonial Studies*, edited by Crystal Bartolovich and Neil Lazarus, Cambridge: Cambridge University Press.

Lazarus, Neil (ed.) 2004, *The Cambridge Companion to Postcolonial Literary Studies*, Cambridge: University Press.

Lazarus, Neil (ed.) 2011, *The Postcolonial Unconscious*, Cambridge: Cambridge University Press.

Lazarus, Neil, and Rashma Varma 2008, 'Marxism and Postcolonial Studies', in *Critical Companion to Contemporary Marxism*, edited by Jacques Bidet and Stathis Kouvelakis, Leiden: Brill.

Lazarus, Neil, Steven Evans, Anthony Arnove, and Anne Menke 1995, 'The Necessity of Universalism', *differences* 7, 1: 75–99.

Leadbeater, David 2019, 'Northern Ontario and the Crisis in Development and Democracy', in *Divided Province: Ontario Politics in the Age of Neoliberalism*, edited by Greg Albo and Bryan M. Evans, Montreal and Kingston: McGill/Queen's University Press.

Leary-Ohwin, Michael E., and John P. McCarthy (eds) 2020, *The Routledge Handbook of Henri Lefebvre, The City and Urban Society*, London: Routledge.

Lecercle, Jean-Jacques 2005, 'Deleuze, Guattari, and Marxism', *Historical Materialism* 13, 3: 35–55.

Le Cour Grandmaison, Olivier 2005, *Coloniser exterminer: Sur la guerre et L'Etat colonial*, Paris: Fayard.

Le Cour Grandmaison, Olivier 2009, *La République impériale: Politique et racisme d'Etat*, Paris: Fayard.

Le Garrec, Sylvaine 2014, 'Bulles spéculatives et copropriétés en difficulté: Les leçons de l'histoire du grand ensemble de Clichy-Montfermeil', in *Logement et politique(s): un couple encore d'actualité*, edited by Fatiha Belmessous, Loic Bonneval, Lydia Coudray de Lille, and Nathalie Ortar, Paris: L'Harmattan.

Le Goullon, Gwenaëlle 2014, *Les grands ensembles en France: Genèse d'une politique 1945–1962*, Paris: Editions du comité de travaux historiques et scientifiques.

Le Monde 2010, 'Histoire du quartier (3): L'espoir éphémère des années 80', 23 July.

Le Parisien 2009, 'Les Tours des Indes seront démolies en 2010', 19 May.

Lees, Loretta, Hyun Bang Shin, and Ernesto López-Morales 2016, *Planetary Gentrification*, Cambridge: Polity.

Lefebvre, Henri 1955, *Rabelais*, Paris: Les éditeurs français réunis.

Lefebvre, Henri 1965, *La proclamation de la commune*, Paris: Gallimard.

Lefebvre, Henri 1968a, *L'irruption. De Nanterre au sommet*, Paris: Anthropos.

Lefebvre, Henri 1968b [1965], *The Sociology of Marx*, translated by Norbert Guterman, New York: Vintage Books.

Lefebvre, Henri 1970a [1960], *Du rural à l'urbain*, Paris: Anthropos.

Lefebvre, Henri 1970b [1960], 'Les nouveaux grands ensembles', in *Du rural à l'urbain*, Paris: Anthropos.

Lefebvre, Henri 1970c [1960], 'Introduction à la psycho-sociologie de la vie quotidienne', in *Du rural à l'urbain*, Paris: Anthropos.

Lefebvre, Henri 1970d [1949], 'Problèmes de sociologie rurale', in *Du rural à l'urbain*, Paris: Anthropos.

Lefebvre, Henri 1970e [1951], 'Les classes sociales dans les campagnes', in *Du rural à l'urbain*, Paris: Anthropos.

Lefebvre, Henri 1970f. [1953], 'Perspectives de la sociologie rurale', in *Du rural à l'urbain*, Paris: Anthropos.

Lefebvre, Henri 1970g [1956], 'Théorie de la rente foncière et sociologie rurale', in *Du rural à l'urbain*, Paris: Anthropos.

Lefebvre, Henri 1970h, *Le manifeste différentialiste*, Paris: Gallimard.

Lefebvre, Henri 1971a [1957], 'Le romantisme révolutionnaire', in *Au-delà du structuralisme*, Paris: Antropos.

Lefebvre, Henri 1971b [1961], 'Marxisme et Politique', in *Au-delà du structuralisme*, Paris: Anthropos.

Lefebvre, Henri 1971c [1968], *Everyday Life in the Modern World*, translated by S. Rabino-vitch, London: Penguin.

Lefebvre, Henri 1972a, *La pensée marxiste et la ville*, Paris: Casterman.

Lefebvre, Henri 1972b [1965], *Soziologie nach Marx*, translated by Beate Rehschuh and Peter Anton von Arnim, Frankfurt a/M: Suhrkamp.

Lefebvre, Henri 1972c, 'La bourgeoisie et l'espace', in *Le droit à la ville suivi de Espace et Politique*, Paris: Anthropos.

Lefebvre, Henri 1972d, 'La classe ouvrière et l'espace', in *Le droit à la ville suivi de Espace et Politique*, Paris: Anthropos.

Lefebvre, Henri 1973, *La somme et le reste*, Paris: Bélibaste.

Lefebvre, Henri 1975, *Le temps des méprises*, Paris: Stock.

Lefebvre, Henri 1976a [1973], *The Survival of Capitalism*, translated by Frank Bryant, London: Alison and Busby.

Lefebvre, Henri 1976b, *De l'état I: L'état dans le monde moderne*, Paris: Union générale d'éditions.

Lefebvre, Henri 1976c, *De l'état II*, Paris: Union générale des éditions.

Lefebvre, Henri 1976d, 'Une Interview d'Henri Lefebvre', *Autogestion et Socialisme* 33/34.

Lefebvre, Henri 1977, *De l'état III: Le mode de production étatique*, Paris: Union générale d'éditions.

Lefebvre, Henri 1978, *De l'état IV*, Paris: Union générale des éditions.

Lefebvre, Henri 1980, *Une pensée devenue monde: faut-il abandoner Marx?* Paris: Fayard.

Lefebvre, Henri 1991a [1947], *Critique of Everyday Life*, Volume 1, translated by John Moore, London: Verso.

Lefebvre, Henri 1991b [1974], *The Production of Space*, translated by Donald Nicholson-Smith, New York: Blackwell Publishing.

Lefebvre, Henri 1992, *Eléments de rhythmanalyse: Introduction à la connaissance des rhythmes*, Paris: Syllepse.

Lefebvre, Henri 1995 [1962], *Introduction to Modernity*, translated by John Moore, London: Verso.

Lefebvre, Henri 1996 [1968, 1972], *Writings on Cities*, translated by Eleonore Kofman and Elisabeth Lebas, Oxford: Wiley-Blackwell.

Lefebvre, Henri 1997 [1965], *Métaphilosophie*, Paris: Syllepse.

Lefebvre, Henri 2002a, 'Lefebvre on the Situationists', Interview with Kristin Ross in *Guy Debord and the Situationist International*, edited by Tom McDonough, Cambridge, MA: MIT Press.

Lefebvre, Henri 2002b [1961], *Critique of Everyday Life*, Volume 2, translated by John Moore, London: Verso.

Lefebvre, Henri 2003a [1970], *The Urban Revolution*, Minneapolis: University of Minnesota Press.

Lefebvre, Henri 2003b [1962], 'Myths in Everyday Life', in *Henri Lefebvre: Key Writings*, edited by Stuart Elden, Elizabeth Lebas, and Eleonore Kofman, New York: Continuum.

Lefebvre, Henri 2003c [1977], 'Space and the State', translated by Alexandra Kowalski-Hodges, Neil Brenner, Aaron Passell, and Bob Jessop, in *State/Space*, edited by Neil Brenner, Bob Jessop, Martin Jones, and Gordon MacLeod, Oxford: Blackwell.

Lefebvre, Henri 2003d [1966], 'Theoretical Problems of *Autogestion*', in *State, Space, World: Selected Essays*, edited by Neil Brenner and Stuart Elden, Minneapolis: University of Minnesota Press.

Lefebvre, Henri 2003e [1970], 'Reflections on the Politics of Space', in *State, Space, World: Selected Essays*, edited by Neil Brenner and Stuart Elden, Minneapolis: University of Minnesota Press.

Lefebvre, Henri 2003f. [1970], *The Urban Revolution*, translated by Robert Bononno, foreword by Neil Smith, Minneapolis: University of Minnesota Press.

Lefebvre, Henri 2008 [1981], *Critique of Everyday Life*, Volume 3, London: Verso.

Lefebvre, Henri 2009a [1986], 'Revolutions' (from *Le Retour de la Dialectique*), in *State, Space, World: Selected Essays*, edited by Neil Brenner and Stuart Elden, Minneapolis: University of Minnesota Press.

Lefebvre, Henri 2009b [1939], *Dialectical Materialism*, translated by John Sturrock, preface by Stefan Kipfer, Minneapolis: University of Minnesota Press.

Lefebvre, Henri 2009c, *State, Space, World*, edited by Neil Brenner and Stuart Elden, Minneapolis: University of Minnesota Press.

Lefebvre, Henri 2014, *Toward an Architecture of Enjoyment*, edited by Łukasz Stanek and translated by Robert Bononno, Minneapolis: University of Minnesota Press.

Lefebvre, Isabel-Rey 2018, 'Enquête sur les exclus du Grand Paris', *Le Monde*, 5 April.

Lefebvre, Isabel-Rey 2019, 'Le pari perdu de la mixité sociale', *Le Monde*, 1 July, 18.

Lelévrier, Christine 2010a, *Action publique et trajectoires résidentielles: un autre regard sur la politique de la ville*, Habilitation, Université de Paris-Est, Marne-la-Vallée.

Lelévrier, Christine 2010b, 'La mixité dans la rénovation urbaine: dispersion ou ré-concentration', *Espaces et sociétés* 140–1, 1–2: 59–74.

Lelévrier, Christine 2015, '"Casser le ghetto, chasser les pauvres?" Les effets paradoxaux de la rénovation urbaine', in *En finir avec les banlieues? Le désenchantment de la politique de la ville*, edited by Thomas Kirszbaum, Paris: L'Aube.

Lelévrier, Christine 2018, 'Rénovation urbaine et trajectoires résidentielles: quelle justice sociale?' *Métropolitiques*, 12 March.

Lelévrier, Christine, and Christophe Noyé 2012, 'La fin des grands ensembles?' in *A quoi sert la rénovation urbaine*, edited by Jacques Donzelot, Paris: Presses Universitaires Françaises.

Lelévrier, Christine, and Christophe Noyé 2018, 'Rénover les banlieues populaires: quelle "égalité territoriale" pour la Seine-Saint-Denis?' in *Banlieues Populaires: ter-*

ritoires, sociétés, politiques, edited by Marie-Hélène Bacqué, Emmanuel Bellanger, and Henri Rey, Paris: L'Aube.

Leroux, Denis 2013, 'Promouvoir une armée révolutionnaire pendant la guerre d'Algérie', *Vingtième Siècle* 120.

Lessellier, Claudie 2008, 'Mouvements et initiatives des femmes des années 1970 au milieu des années 1980', in *Histoire politique des immigrations (post)coloniales en France, 1920–2008*, edited by Ahmed Boubeker and Abdellali Hajjat, Paris: Amsterdam.

Lewis, Holly 2016, *The Politics of Everybody: Feminism, Queer Theory and Marxism at the Intersection*, London: Zed.

Levasseur, Thierry 2008, 'Les vietnamiens en France du milieu des années 1920 au milieu des années 1950', in *Histoire politique des immigrations (post)coloniales en France, 1920–2008*, edited by Ahmed Boubeker and Abdellali Hajjat, Paris: Amsterdam.

Liauzu, Claude 2004, 'Ceux qui ont fait la guerre à la guerre', in *La guerre d'Algérie: la fin de l'amnésie*, edited by Benjamin Stora and Mohammed Harbi, Paris: Robert Laffont.

Liauzu, Claude 2007, *Histoire de L'anticolonialisme en France. Du xvie siècle à nos jours*, Paris: Armand Colin.

Lichtner, Maurizio 2010 [1991], 'Translations and Metaphors in Gramsci', in *Gramsci, Language, and Translation*, edited by Peter Ives and Rocco Lacorte, Plymouth: Lexington.

Lindner, Kolja 2010, 'L'Eurocentrisme de Marx: pour un dialogue du débat marxien avec les études postcoloniales', *Actuel Marx* 48, 2: 106–28.

Lipsitz, George 2011, *How Racism Takes Place*, Philadelphia: Temple University Press.

Lisi, Cosimo 2019, 'La Révolution est en Marche: un défi au colonialisme néoliberal français', in *Villes Radicales: Du Droit à la Ville à la Démocratie Radicale*, edited by Collectif 'Engagée', Paris: Eterotopia, pp. 77–83.

Liss, Jon 2012, 'The Right to the City: From Theory to Grassroots Alliance', *Cities for People, Not for Profit: Critical Urban Theory and The Right to the City*, edited by Neil Brenner, Peter Marcuse, and Margit Mayer, New York: Routledge.

Lutz, Hartmut 2005, 'Howard Adams, Radical Métis (Inter-)Nationalist', in Howard Adams *Otapawy! The Life of Métis Leader in his own words and in those of his Contemporaries*, Saskatoon: Gabriel Dumont Institute of Native Studies and Applied Research.

Madden, David, and Peter Marcuse 2016, *In Defense of Housing*, London: Verso.

McCann, Eugene J. 1999, 'Race, Protest and Public Space: Contextualising Lefebvre in the US City', *Antipode* 31, 2: 163–84.

McClintock, Anne 1995, *Imperial Leather: Race, Gender and Sexuality in the Colonial Context*, New York: Routledge.

McCreary, Tyler A., and Richard A. Milligan 2014, 'Pipelines, Permits and Protests', *Cultural Geographies* 21, 1: 115–29.

McCreary, Tyler, and Jerome Turner 2018, 'The Contested Scales of Indigenous and Set-tler Jurisdiction: Unist'ot'en Struggles with Canadian Pipeline Governance', *Studies in Political Economy* 99, 3: 233–45.

McCreary, Tyler, in dialogue with Chris Anderson, Adam Gaudry, and Brenda MacDou-gall 2019, in *Settler City Limits: Indigenous Resurgence and Colonial Violence in the Urban Prairie West*, edited by Heather Dorries, Robert Henry, David Hugill, Tyler McCreary, and Julie Tomiak, Winnipeg: University of Manitoba Press.

McGee, T.G. 1971, *The Urbanisation Process in the Third World*, London: Bell.

McGee, T.G. 1991, 'The Emergence of Desakota Regions in Asia: Expanding a Hypo-thesis', in *The Extended Metropolis: Settlement Transition in Asia*, edited by N.J. Gins-burg, B. Koppel, and T.G. McGee, Honolulu: University of Hawaii Press.

McKittrick, Katherine 2006, *Demonic Grounds: Black Women and the Cartographies of Struggle*, Minneapolis: University of Minnesota Press.

McKittrick, Katherine 2011, 'On Plantations, Prisons, and a Black Sense of Place', *Social and Cultural Geography* 12, 8: 947–63.

McKittrick, Katherine 2013, 'Plantation Futures', *small axe* 42: 1–15.

McKittrick, Katherine (ed.) 2015, *Sylvia Wynter on Being Human as Praxis*, Durham, NC: Duke University Press.

McLeod, John 2007, *The Routledge Companion to Postcolonial Studies*, New York: Rout-ledge.

McLeod, Mary 1997, 'Henri Lefebvre's Critique of Everyday Life', in *Architecture of the Everyday*, edited by Steve Harris and Deborah Berke, New York: Princeton Architec-tural Press.

McMichael, Philipp 1999, 'The Global Crisis of Wage Labour', *Studies in Political Eco-nomy* 58: 11.

McNally, David 2001, *Bodies of Meaning Studies on Language, Labour and Liberation*, Albany: SUNY Press.

McNally, David 2017, 'Intersections and Dialectics', in *Social Reproduction Theory: Re-mapping Class, Recentring Oppression*, edited by Tithi Bhattacharya, London: Pluto.

Macey, David 2000, *Frantz Fanon: A Life*, London: Granta.

Malm, Andreas 2015, 'The Anthropocene Myth', *Jacobin* https://www.jacobinmag.com/2015/03/anthropocene-capitalism-climate-change/

Majumdar, Margaret 2007, *Postcoloniality: The French Dimension*, New York: Berghahn.

Mamdani, Mahmood 2004, *Good Muslim, Bad Muslim: America, The Cold War, and the Roots of Terror*, New York: Doubleday.

Manuel, Arthur 2017, 'From Dispossession to Dependency', in *Whose Land is it Anyway: A Manual for Decolonisation*, edited by Peter McFarlane and Nicole Schabus, Van-couver: Federation of Post-Secondary Educators of BC.

Manville, Marcel 1984, 'Discours d'ouverture', in *Mémorial International Frantz Fanon*, edited by Comité Frantz Fanon de Fort de France, Paris and Dakar: Présence Afri-caine.

Manville, Marcel 1988, 'Périssent les colonies', *Le Monde Diplomatique*, April.

Manville, Marcel 1992, *Les Antilles sans fard*, Paris: l'Harmattan.

Maracle, Lee 1990, *Bobbi Lee – Indian Rebel*, Toronto: Women's Press.

Maracle, Lee 1996, *I Am Woman*, second edition, Vancouver, B.C.: Press Gang Publishers.

Maracle, Lee 2017, *My Conversations with Canadians*, Toronto: Book Thug.

Marchal, Manuel 2020, 'Coronavirus à Mayotte: le néocolonialisme français en pleine crise', https://www.temoignages.re/politique/actualites/coronavirus-a-mayotte-le-neocolonialisme-francais-en-pleine-crise,97968

Mariátegui, José Carlos 1971, *Seven Interpretive Essays on Peruvian Reality*, translated by Marjory Urquidi, Austin: University of Texas Press.

Mariette, Audrey, and Laure Pitti 2020, 'Covid-19 en Seine-Saint-Denis (1/2): quand l'épidémie aggrave les inégalités sociales de santé', *Métropolitiques*, 6 July.

Marrighela, Carlos 2009 [1970], *Manuel du Guérillero Urbain*, Paris: Libertalia.

Martín-Criado, Enrique 2008, *Les deux Algéries de Pierre Bourdieu*, Paris: Editions du Croquant.

Martouzet, Denis 2001, *Fort-de-France, ville fragile?* Paris: Anthropos.

Masclet, Olivier 2005, 'Du bastion au ghetto: le communisme municipal en butte à l'immigration', *Actes de la recherche en sciences sociales* 4: 10–25.

Masclet, Olivier 2006, *La Gauche et les Cités: Enquête sur un rendez-vous manqué*, Deuxième Edition, Paris: La Dispute.

Maspéro, François 1962, 'Hommage à Frantz Fanon', *Présence Africaine* 40.

Massey, Doreen 1984, *Spatial Divisions of Labour: Social Structures and the Geography of Production*, New York: Routledge.

Massey, Doreen 1991, 'A Global Sense of Place', *Marxism Today* 38, 24–9.

Massey, Doreen 1994, *Space, Place and Gender*, Minneapolis: University of Minnesota Press.

Math, Antoine 2000, *Les allocations familiales et l'Algérie coloniale: A l'origine du FAS et de son financement par les régimes de prestations familiales*, Paris: GISTI. http://www.gisti.org/doc/presse/1998/math/allocations.html, last accessed September 2015.

Matin, Kamran, 2011, 'Redeeeming the Universal: Postcolonalism and the Inner Life of Eurocentrism', *European Journal of International Relations* 19, 2: 353–77.

Mayer, Margi 2012, 'The "Right to the City" in Urban Social Movements', in *Cities for People, Not for Profit: Critical Urban Theory and The Right to the City*, edited by Neil Brenner, Peter Marcuse, and Margit Mayer, New York: Routledge.

Maynard, Robyn, and Leanne Betasamosake Simpson 2020, 'Towards Black and Indigenous Futures on Turtle Island: A Conversation', in Rodney Diverlus, Sandy Hudson, and Syrus Marcus Ware, *Until We are Free: Reflections on Black Lives Matter in Canada*, Regina: University of Regina Press.

Maximin, Daniel 2009, 'Suzanne Césaire, fontaine solaire', in Suzanne Césaire, *Le grand camouflage. Ecrits de dissidence (1941–1945)*, Paris: Seuil.

Mbembe, Achille 2001, *On the Postcolony*, Berkeley: University of California Press.

Mbembe, Achille 2003, 'Necropolitics', *Public Culture* 15, 1.

Mbembe, Achille 2007, 'De la scène coloniale chez Frantz Fanon', *Rue Descartes* 58: 30–54.

Mbembe, Achille 2016, *Politiques de l'intimité*, Paris: La Découverte.

Mechaï, Hassina, and Flora Hergon, 2020, '"Make yourself at home": The French State of Emergency and Home Searches in 2015–2017', *Funambulist* 29: 38–43.

Mele, Christopher 2019, 'The Strategic Uses of Race to Legitimize "Social Mix" Urban Redevelopment', *Social Identities* 25, 1: 27–40.

Memmi, Albert 1971, 'La vie impossible de Frantz Fanon', *Esprit* September: 248–73.

Memmi, Albert 1985, *Portrait du colonisé, portrait du colonisateur*, Paris: Gallimard.

Mendieta, Eduardo 2008, 'The Production of Urban Space in the Age of Transnational Mega-urbes', *City* 12, 2: 148–52.

Menleson, Rachel 2020, 'Vulnerable First Nations Brace for COVID-19's Spread', *Toronto Star*, 9 April.

Mennozzi, Filippo 2019, 'Inheriting Marx: Daniel Bensaïd, Ernst Bloch and the Discordance of Time', *Historical Materialism* 28, 1: 147–82.

Merrifield, Andy 2002a, *Metromarxism: A Marxist Tale of the City*, New York: Routledge.

Merrifield, Andy 2002b, *Dialectical Urbanism*, New York: Monthly Review Press.

Merrifield, Andy 2013, *The Politics of the Encounter*, Atlanta: University of Georgia Press.

Merrington, John 1975, 'Town and Country in the Transition to Capitalism', *New Left Review* 93.

Meszaros, Istvan 1970, *Marx's Theory of Alienation*, London: Merlin.

Meylon-Reinette, Stéphanie, and François Durpaire 2009, 'Les Ferments d'une Révolution', in *La Révolution Antilllaise*, edited by François Durpaire, Paris: Eyrolles.

Miège, J.L. 1985, 'Algiers: Colonial Metropolis (1830–1961)', in *Colonial Cities*, edited by Robert Ross and Gerard J. Telkamp, Dordrecht: Martinus Nijhoff.

Milne, Lorna 2006, *Patrick Chamoiseau: Espaces d'une écriture antillaise*, Amsterdam: Rodopi.

Mintz, Sidney 1974, 'The Caribbean Region', in *Slavery, Colonialism and Racism*, edited by Sidney Mintz, New York: Norton.

Mintz, Sidney 1989 [1974], *Caribbean Transformations*, New York: Columbia University Press.

Misselwitz, Philipp, and Eyal Weizman 2003, 'Military Operations as Urban Planning', in *Territories*, curated by Aselm Franke, Berlin: Institute for Contemporary Art.

Mitchell, Katharyne, Sallie Marston, and Cindi Katz, 2004, *Life's Work*, Chichester: Wiley.

Mongia, Radhika 2007, 'Historicising State Sovereignty: Inequality and the Form of Equivalence', *Comparative Studies in Society and History* 49, 2: 384–411.

Monte-Mór, Roberto Luís de Melo 2004, *Modernities in the Jungle*, PhD Thesis, University of California, Los Angeles.

Monte-Mór, Roberto Luís de Melo 2014a, 'What is the Urban in the Contemporary World?', in *Implosions/Explosions*, edited by Neil Brenner, Berlin: Jovis.

Monte-Mór, Roberto Luís de Melo 2014b, 'Extended Urbanisation and Settlement Patterns in Brazil', in *Implosions/Explosions*, edited by Neil Brenner, Berlin: Jovis.

Montesse, Juliette 2015, 'Au Val-Fourré, le retour timide des classes moyennes', *Le Point*, 27 January.

Monture, Rick 2014, *Teionkwakhashion Tsi Niionkwariho:ten*, Winnipeg: University of Manitoba Press.

Monzat, René 2016, 'La Gauche peut-elle dire 'nous' avec Houria Bouteldja?' *Contretemps.fr*, 22 April.

Mooers, Colin 1991, *The Making of Bourgeois Europe: Absolutism, Revolution and the Rise of Capitalism in England, France and Germany*, London: Verso.

Moore, Jason 2017, 'The Capitalocene Part I: On the Nature and Origins of Our Ecological Crisis', *Journal of Peasant Studies* 44, 3: 594–630.

Moran, Marie 2018, 'Identity and Identity Politics: A Cultural-Materialist History', *Historical Materialism* 26, 2: 21–45.

Morel, Journel, Christelle, and Valérie Sala Pala 2011, 'Le peuplement, catégorie montante des politiques urbaines neolibérales? Le cas de Saint-Etienne', *Métropoles* 10.

Morfino, Vittorio, and Peter D. Thomas (eds) 2017, *The Government of Time: Theories of Plural Temporality*, Leiden: Brill.

Morton, Adam David 2018, 'The Urban Revolution in Victor Serge', *Annals of the American Association of Geographers* 108, 6: 1554–69.

'Motion d'un groupe de marxistes' [at the second congress of Black writers and artists in Rome] 1959, *Présence Africaine* 24–5.

Müller, Jost 2001, 'Alltagsleben – Rassistische Diskriminierung und Kritisches Denken', *Jungle World – Subtropen* 5, 6: 9–11.

Muhammad, Marwan 2011, 'Le combat des réfugiés de la Tour Balzac', http://www.foulexpress.com/2011/11/le-combat-des-refugies-de-la-tour-balzac/ last accessed November 2011.

Mukhopadhyay, Partha, Marie-Hélène Zérah, and Eric Denis 2020, 'Subaltern Urbanisation: Indian Insights for Urban Theory', *International Journal for Urban and Regional Research* 582–98, online.

Mulkewich, Jane, and Rich Oddie 2009, 'Contesting Development, Democracy and Justice in the Red Hill Valley', *Environmental Conflict and Democracy in Canada*, edited by Laurie Adkin, Vancouver and Toronto: UBC Press.

Murphy, David 2007, 'Materialist Formulations', in *The Routledge Companion to Postcolonial Studies*, edited by John McLeod, London: Routledge.

Murray, Karen Bridget 2017, 'The Violence Within: Canadian Modern Statehood and the

Pan-Territorial Residential School Ideal', *Canadian Journal of Political Science* 50, 3: 747–72.

Murray, Karen Bridget 2011, 'The Silence of Urban Aboriginal Policy in New Brunswick', in *Urban Aboriginal Policy-Making in Canadian Municipalities*, edited by Evelyn Peters, Montreal and Kingston: McGill and Queen's University Press.

Nardal, Jeanne 2002a [1928], 'Exotic Puppets', in *Negritude Women*, edited by Denean Sharpley-Whiting, Minneapolis: University of Minnesota Press.

Nardal, Jeanne 2002b, 'Black Internationalism', in *Negritude Women*, edited by Denean Sharpley-Whiting, Minneapolis: University of Minnesota Press.

Nardal, Paulette 2002, 'The Awakening of Race Consciousness among Black Students', in *Negritude Women*, edited by Denean Sharpley-Whiting, Minneapolis: University of Minnesota Press.

Native Alliance for Red Power (NARP) 1969, *Indian Control of the Indian Communities*, https://indigenousarchive.wordpress.com/2018/11/22/indian-control-of-the-indian-communities-narp-program/ accessed July 2020.

Ndiaye, Pap 2009, 'Présence Africaine avant "Présence Africaine": La subjectivation politique noire en France dans l'entre-deux-guerres', *Gradhiva* 10: 65–80.

Negri, Antonio 2018, *From the Factory to the Metropolis*, Cambridge: Polity Press.

Neigh, Scott 2012, 'Urban Colonisation and Resistance: Roger Obonsawin and Kathy Mallett on Building Space for Indigeneity in Canadian Cities', in *Resisting the State*, edited by Scott Neigh, Halifax: Fernwood.

Nesbitt, Nick 2013, *Caribbean Critique: Antillean Critical Theory from Toussaint to Glissant*, Liverpool: Liverpool University Press.

Nightingale, Carl 2012, *Segregation: A Global History of Divided Cities*, Chicago: University of Chicago Press.

Nizan, Paul 1931, *Aden Arabie*, Paris: Rieder.

Oblet, Thierry, and Agnès Villechaise 2012, 'Les leçons de la rénovation urbaine', in *A quoi sert la rénovation urbaine*, edited by Jacques Donzelot, Paris: Presses Universitaires de France.

Odin, Pierre 2019, *Pwofitasyon: Luttes syndicales et anticolonialisme en Guadeloupe et en Martinique*, Paris: La Découverte.

Odin, Pierre 2020, '"Un coup d'avance?" Des mobilisations anticolonialistes face au Covid-19', *Silomag* 10, April, https://silogora.org/un-coup-davance-des-mobilisations-anticolonialistes-face-au-covid-19/

Office of the Wet'suwet'en 2014, *Wet'suwet'en Title and Rights and Coastal Gas Link. Submission to: BC EAO and Coastal GasLink Pipeline*, http://www.wetsuweten.com/files/Wetsuweten_Title_and_Rights_report_to_EAO_for_Coastal_GasLink_Application.pdf last accessed in July 2020.

Okoth, Kevin Ochieng 2020, 'The Flatness of Blackness: Afro-Pessimism and the Erasure of Anti-Colonial Thought', *Salvage* 7, 16 January.

Olaloku-Teriba, Annie 2018, 'Afro-Pessimism and the (Un)logic of Anti-Blackness', *Historical Materialism* 26, 2: 96–122.

ONZUS (*Observatoire national des zones urbaines sensibles*) 2009, *Rapport 2009*.

ONZUS (*Observatoire national des zones urbaines sensibles*) 2011, *Rapport 2011*.

Oppenheimer, Martin 1970, *The Urban Guerrilla*, Chicago: Quadrangle Books.

Pago, Gilbert 2011, *L'Insurrection de Martinique, 1870–1871*, Paris: Syllepse.

Palmater, Pamela 2015, *Indigenous Nationhood*, Halifax and Winnipeg: Fernwood.

Palmer, Bryan D. 2009, *Canada's 1960s: The Ironies of Identity in the Rebellious Age*, Toronto: University of Toronto Press.

Parnreiter, Christof 2013, 'The Global City Tradition', in *Global City Challenges*, edited by Michele Acuto and Wendy Steele, New York: Palgrave, pp. 15–32.

Parry, Benita 2002, 'Liberation Theory: Variations on Themes of Marxism and Modernity', in *Marxism, Modernity and Postcolonial Studies*, edited by Crystal Bartolovich and Neil Lazarus, Cambridge: Cambridge University Press.

Pasternak, Shiri 2015, 'How Capitalism Will Save Colonialism: The Privatisation of Reserve Lands in Canada', *Antipode* 47, 1: 179–96.

Pasternak, Shiri 2017a, *Grounded Authority*, Minneapolis: University of Minnesota Press.

Pasternak, Shiri 2017b, 'Blockade: A Meeting Place of Law', in *Whose Land Is It Anyway: A Manual for Decolonisation*, Edited by Peter McFarlane and Nicole Schabus, Vancouver: Federation of Post-Secondary Educators of BC.

Pasternak, Shiri, and Dafnos T. 2017, 'How Does a Settler State Secure the Circuitry of Capital?' *Society and Space* 36, 4: 739–57.

Pelletier, Jean 2015 [1959], *Alger 1955: Essai d'une géographie sociale*, présentation actualisée et commentée par Rachid Sidi Boumedine, Alger: Editions Apic.

Perry, Adele 2016, *Aqueduct*, Winnipeg: ARP Books.

Perry, Elizabeth 1999, 'From Paris to the Paris of the East and Back: Workers as Citizens in Modern Shanghai', *Comparative Studies in Society and History* 41, 2: 348–73.

Peters, Evelyn 2002, ' "Our City Indians": Negotiating the Meaning of First Nations Urbanisation in Canada, 1945–1975', *Historical Geography* 30: 75–92.

Peters, Evelyn 2013, ' "I Basically Mostly Stick with My Own Kind" ', in *Indigenous in the City*, edited by Evelyn Peters and Chris Anderson, Vancouver: UBC Press.

Peters, Evelyn, and Chris Anderson (eds) 2013, *Indigenous in the City*, Vancouver: UBC Press.

Peters, Evelyn, Matthew Stock, and Adrian Werner 2018, *Roostertown: The History of an Urban Métis Community (1901–1961)*, Winnipeg: University of Manitoba Press.

Persaud, Richard 1997, 'Frantz Fanon, Race, and World Order', in *Innovation and Transformation in International Studies*, edited by Stephen Gill and James Mittelman, Cambridge: Cambridge University Press.

Picard, Aleth 1996, 'Colonie de peuplement et aménagement du territoire. Algérie

(1830–1880)', in *Colonies, territoires, sociétés: L'enjeu français*, edited by Alain Saus-
sol and Joseph Zitomersky, Paris: L'Harmattan.

Pierre-Charles, Philippe 2011, *Frantz Fanon, l'Héritage*, Fort-de-France: K. Editions.

Piffaretti, Alain 2017, '15 ans pour redorer la cité des Indes', *Les Echos*, 4 January.

Pile, Steve 2000, 'The Troubled Spaces of Frantz Fanon', in *Thinking Space*, edited by
Michael Crang and Nigel Thrift, London: Routledge.

Pithouse, Richard 2008, 'A Politics of the Poor: Shack Dweller's Struggles in Durban',
Journal of Asian and African Studies 43, 1: 63–94.

Pithouse, Richard 2010, 'Abahlali baseMjondolo and the Popular Struggle for the Right
to the City in Durban, South Africa', reprinted by *Habitat International Coalition*,
http://www.hic-net.org/articles.php?pid=3460

Pitsula, James 2005, 'Howard Adams and the Revival of Métis Nationalism', in Howard
Adams, *Otapawy! The Life of Métis Leader in his own words and in those of his con-
temporaries*, Saskatoon: Gabriel Dumont Institute of Native Studies and Applied
Research.

Pitti, Laure 2008, 'Travailleurs de France: voilà votre nom: les mobilisations des ouvri-
ers étrangers dans les usines et le foyers durant les années 1970', in *Histoire politique
des immigrations (post)coloniales*, edited by Ahmed Boubeker Abdellali Hajjat, Paris:
Amsterdam.

Porter, Libby, and Oren Yftachel, 2019, 'Urbanising Settler Colonial Studies: Introduction to the Special Issue', *Settler Colonial Studies* 9, 2: 177–86.

Portes, Alejandro, Manuel Castells, and Lauren A. Benton (eds) 1989, *The Informal Economy: Studies in Advanced and Less Developed Countries*, Baltimore: Johns Hopkins
University Press.

Portes, Thierry 2007, 'A 50 ans Sarcelles rêve d'une nouvelle jeunesse', *Le Figaro*.

Poulantzas, Nico 2013, *L'Etat, le pouvoir et le socialisme*, Paris: Les prairies ordinaires.

Prashad, Vijay 2001, *Everybody was Kung-Fu Fighting*, Boston: Beacon.

Prashad, Vijay 2007, *The Darker Nations: A People's History of the World*, New York: The
New Press.

Preston, Jen 2015, 'La guerre des pipelines', *Nouveaux Cahiers du Socialisme* 13: 55–64.

Préteceille, Edmond 2009, 'La ségrégation ethno-raciale a-t-elle augmenté dans la métropole parisienne?' *Revue Française de Sociologie* 50, 3: 489–519.

Price, Richard, and Sally Price 1997, 'Shadowboxing in the Mangrove', *Cultural Anthropology* 12, 1: 3–36.

Quijano, Aníbal 1967, 'La urbanización de la Sociedad en Latinoamérica', *Revista Mex-
icana de Sociología* 29, 4: 669–703.

Rabaka, Reiland 2010, *Forms of Fanonism: Frantz Fanon's Critical Theory and the Dialectics of Decolonisation*, Lexington: Lanham.

Rabinow, Paul 1989, *French Modern*, Cambridge, MA: MIT Press.

Radcliffe, Sarah A. 2020, 'Geography and Indigeneity III: Co-Articulation of Colonialism and Capitalism in Indigeneity's Economies', *Progress in Human Geography* 44, 2: 374–88.

Ramdani, Ilyes 2020, 'A Villeneuve-la-Garenne, retour sur une colère raisonnée', *Bondyblog*, 25 April, https://www.bondyblog.fr/societe/a-villeneuve-la-garenne-retour-sur-une-colere-raisonnee/

Razack, Sherene (ed.) 2002, *Race, Space, and the Law*, Toronto: Between the Lines.

Rebucini, Gianfranco 2017, 'Etat intégral, bloc historique et homonationalisme en France: une analyse gramscienne des politiques des droits', in *Pour un féminisme de la totalité*, edited by Félix Boggio Ewanjé-Epée, Stella Magliani-Belkacem, Morgane Merteuil, and Frédéric Monferrand, Paris: Amsterdam.

Renault, Matthieu 2011a, ' "Corps à corps": Frantz Fanon's Erotics of National Liberation', *Journal of French and Francophone Philosophie* 19, 1: 49–55.

Renault, Matthieu 2011b, *Frantz Fanon: De l'anticolonialisme à la critique postcoloniale*, Paris: Amsterdam.

Renault, Matthieu 2014, 'Le genre de la race: Fanon, lecteur de Beauvoir', *Actuel Marx* 55, 1: 36–48.

Renault, Matthieu 2017a, *L'Empire de la Révolution: Lenine et les Musulmans de Russie*, Paris: Syllepse.

Renault, Matthieu 2017b, 'Alexandra Kollontaï et le dépérissement de la famille … ou les deux verres d'eau de Lénine', in *Pour un féminisme de la totalité*, edited by Félix Boggio Ewanjé-Epée, Stella Magliani-Belkacem, Morgane Merteuil, and Frédéric Monferrand, Paris: Amsterdam.

Rex, John 1973, *Race, Colonialism and the City*, London: Routledge and Kegan Paul.

Rey, Nicolas 2001, *Lakou et Ghetto: Les quartiers péripheriques aux Antilles françaises*, Paris: Harmattan.

Reynolds, Graham 2016, *Viola Desmond's Canada: A History of Blacks and Racial Segregation in the Promised Land*, Halifax and Winnipeg: Fernwood.

Rigouste, Mathieu 2011, *L'ennemi intérieur*, Paris: La Découverte.

Rigouste, Mathieu 2012, *La domination policière: une violence industrielle*, Paris: La Fabrique.

Rigouste, Mathieu 2017, 'Des massacre oubliés de mai 1967 en Guadeloupe aux prémices de l'ordre sécuritaire moderne dans les quartiers', *basta!* 29 May, https://www.bastamag.net/Des-massacres-oublies-de-mai-1967-en-Guadeloupe-aux-premices-de-l-ordre

Rigouste, Mathieu 2020a, *Un seul héros, le peuple: La contre-insurrection mise en échec par les soulèvements algériens de décembre 1960*, Paris: Premiers matins de novembre.

Rigouste, Mathieu 2020b, 'Un seul héros, le peuple', interview with Selim Nadi, *Contretemps*, 26 May.

Robinson, Cedric 1993, 'Appropriating Frantz Fanon', *Race and Class* 35, 1: 79–91.

Robinson, Jennifer 2006, *Ordinary Cities: Between Modernity and Development*, London: Routledge.

Robinson, Jennifer 2013, 'The Urban Now: Theorising Cities Beyond the New', *European Journal of Cultural Studies* 16, 6: 659–77.

Robinson, Jennifer, and Ananya Roy 2016, 'Debate on Global Urbanism and the Nature of Urban Theory', *International Journal of Urban and Regional Research* 40, 1: 181–6.

Ronneberger, Klaus, and Vassilis Tsianos 2009, 'Panische Räume: Das Ghetto und die "Parallelgeselllschaft"', in *No Integration? Kulturwissenschaftliche Beiträge zur Integrationsdebatte in Europa*, edited by Sabine Hess, Jana Binder, and Johannes Moster, Berlin: Transcript.

Rosenberg, Clifford 2006, *Policing Paris: The Origins of Modern Immigration Control between the Wars*, Ithaca: Cornell University Press.

Ross, Kristin 1995, *Fast Cars, Clean Bodies: Decolonisation and the Reordering of French Culture*, Cambridge, MA: MIT Press.

Ross, Kristin 2002, *May '68 and its Afterlives*, Chicago: University of Chicago Press.

Ross, Kristin 2015, *Communal Luxury*, London: Verso.

Ross, Robert, and Gerard J. Telkamp (eds) 1985, *Colonial Cities*, Dordrecht: Martinus Nijhoff.

Ross, Robert, and Kent Trachte 1990, *Global Capitalism: The New Leviathan*, Albany: SUNY Press.

Rossiter, David A., and Patricia B. Wood 2015, 'Neoliberalism as Shape-Shifter', *Society and Natural Resources* 29, 8: 900–15.

Rowlands, Rob, and Alan Murie 2009, 'Whose Regeneration: The Spectre of Revanchist Regeneration', in *Mass Housing in Europe*, edited by Rob Rowlands, Sako Musterd, and Ronald van Kempen, Houndmills: Palgrave.

Roy, Ananya 2009a, 'The 21st-Century Metropolis: New Geographies of Theory', *Regional Studies* 43, 6: 819–30.

Roy, Ananya 2009b, 'Why India Cannot Plan Its Cities: Informality, Insurgence and the Idiom of Urbanisation', *Planning Theory* 8, 1: 76–87.

Roy, Ananya 2016, 'Class Politics in the (Re-)Making of Space: Displacing the Urban Poor in Kolkata, India', *Human Geography* 9, 3: 43–62.

Ruddick, Sue, Linda Peake, Gökbörü S. Tanyldiz, and Darren Patrick 2018, 'Planetary Urbanisation: An Urban Theory for our Time?' *Environment and Planning D* 36, 3: 387–404.

Ryerson, Stanley 1983, *Unequal Union*, Toronto: Progress Books.

Sabeg, Yazid 2012, 'Avec la rénovation urbaine, on refait du ghetto, mais en plus propre', [interview], *Le Monde*, 17 March.

Saberi, Parastou 2017a, *The 'Paris Problem' in Toronto: The State, Space and the Political Fear of 'the Immigrant'*, PhD Dissertation, Faculty of Environmental Studies, York University.

Saberi, Parastou 2017b, 'Humanising Pacification: On the Role of Urbanism in French Colonial Pacification Strategies', in *Destroy, Build, Secure: Readings on Pacification*, edited by Tyler Wall, Parastou Saberi, and Will Jackson, Ottawa: Red Quill Books.

Saberi, Parastou 2017c, 'Toronto and the "Paris Problem": Community Policing in "Immigrant Neighbourhoods"', *Race and Class* 59, 2: 49–69.

Saberi, Parastou 2019, 'Preventing Radicalisation in European Cities: An Urban Geopolitical Question', *Political Geography* 74, October: 1–10.

Sacriste, Fabien 2012, 'Surveiller et moderniser. Les camps de "regroupement" de ruraux pendant la guerre d'indépendence algérienne', *Métropolitiques*, 15 February.

Sadler, Simon 1999, *The Situationist City*, Cambridge, MA: MIT Press.

Said, Edward 1979, *Orientalism*, New York: Vintage.

Said, Edward 1999, 'Travelling Theory Reconsidered', in *Rethinking Fanon: The Continuing Dialogue*, edited by Nigel Gibson, New York: Humanity.

Said, Edward 2000, *Reflections on Exile*, Cambridge: Cambridge University Press.

Said, Edward 2003, 'Orientalism 25 Years Later: Worldly Humanism vs. the Empire-builders', *Counterpunch*, 5 August, http://www.counterpunch.org/2003/08/05/orientalism/

Sala Pala, Valérie 2013, *Discriminations Ethniques: Les politiques du logement social en France et au Royaume-Uni*, Rennes: Presses Universitaires de Rennes.

Samara, Tony Roshan, Shenjing He, and Guo Chen (eds) 2013, *Locating Right to the City in the Global South*, London: Routledge.

Sanderson, Frances, and Heather Howard-Bobiwash (eds) 1997, *The Meeting Place*, Toronto: Native Canadian Centre.

Sandford, Mark 2006, *Qallunaat! Why White People Are Funny*, Montreal: National Film Board.

Santos, Milton 1971, *Les villes du tiers-monde*, Paris: Génin.

Santos, Milton 1974, 'Geography, Marxism and Underdevelopment', *Antipode* 6, 3: 1–9.

Santos, Milton 1975, *The Shared Space: The Two Circuits of the Urban Economy in Underdeveloped Countries*, London and New York: Methuen.

Santos, Milton 1977, 'Society and Space: Social Formation as Theory and Method', *Antipode* 9, 1: 3–13.

Sarkar, Sumit 2000, 'The Decline of the Subaltern in *Subaltern Studies*', in *Mapping Subaltern Studies and the Postcolonial*, edited by Vinayak Chaturvedi, London: Verso.

Sarkar, Sumit 2002, *Beyond Nationalist Frames: Postmodernism, Hindu Fundamentalism, History*, Bloomington: Indiana University Press.

Sartre, Jean-Paul 2001a, 'Colonialism is a System', in *Colonialism and Neocolonialism*, translated by Azzedine Haddour, Steve Brewer, and Terry McWilliams, London: Routledge.

Sartre, Jean-Paul 2001b, 'The Sleepwalkers', in *Colonialism and Neocolonialism*, translated by Azzedine Haddour, Steve Brewer, and Terry McWilliams, London: Routledge.

Sartre, Jean-Paul 2004 [1960], *Critique of Dialectical Reason, Volume One*, translated by Alan Sheridan-Smith, London.

Sassen, Saskia 1988, *The Mobility of Labour and Capital*, Cambridge: Cambridge University Press.

Sassen, Saskia 1991, *The Global City: New York, London, Tokyo*, Princeton: Princeton University Press.

Sayad, Abdelmalek 1991, *L'immigration ou les paradoxes de l'alterité*, Paris: Editions Universitaires.

Sayad, Abdelmalek 1995, *Un Nanterre algérien, terre de bidonvilles*, Paris: Autrement.

Sayad, Abdelmalek 1999, *La Double Absence*, Paris: Seuil.

Schmid, Christian 2003, 'Raum und Regulation. Henri Lefebvre und der Regulationsansatz', in *Fit für den Postfordismus? Theoretisch-politische Perspektiven des Regulationsansatzes*, edited by Ulrich Brand and Werner Raza, Münster: Westfälisches Dampfboot.

Schmid, Christian 2005, *Stadt, Raum und Gesellschaft: Henri Lefebvre und die Theorie der Produktion des Raumes*, München: Franz Steiner.

Schmid, Christian 2006, 'Theory', in *Switzerland: An Urban Portrait. Book 1: An Introduction*, edited by Rolf Diener, Jacques Herzog, Marcel Meili, Philippe de Meuron, and Christian Schmid, Basel: Birkhäuser.

Schmid, Christian 2012, 'Henri Lefebvre, the Right to the City and the New Metropolitan Mainstream', in *Cities for People, Not for Profit: Critical Urban Theory and the Right to the City*, edited by Neil Brenner, Peter Marcuse, and Margit Mayer, New York: Routledge.

Schmid, Christian 2015, 'Specificity and Urbanisation', in *The Inevitable Specificity of Cities*, edited by ETH Studio Basel, Basel: Birkhäuser.

Schmid, Christian 2018, 'Journeys through Planetary Urbanisation: Decentring Perspectives on the Urban', *Environment and Planning D* 36, 3: 591–610.

Schmidt, Hajo 1990, *Sozialphilosphie des Krieges*, Essen: Klartext.

Schmidt, Nelly 2005, *L'abolition de l'esclavage. Cinq siècles de combat*, Paris: Fayard.

Schmidt, Nelly 2009, *La France a-t-elle aboli l'esclavage? Guadeloupe, Martinique, Guyane 1830–1935*, Paris: Perrin.

Schnepel, Ellen M. 1998, 'The Language Question in Guadeloupe: From the Early Chroniclers to the Post-War Generation', *Plantation Society in the Americas* 5, 1: 60–94.

Schrader, Stuart 2018 'Henri Lefebvre, Mao Zedong, and the Global Urban Concept', *Global Urban History*, 1 May, https://globalurbanhistory.com/2018/05/01/henri-lefeb vre-mao-zedong-and-the-global-urban-concept/

Scott, David 2010, 'Antinomies of Slavery, Enlightenment, and Universal History', *Small Axe* 14, 3: 152–62.

Seabrook, Jeremy 1996, *In the Cities of the South*, London: Verso.

Sears, Alan 2017, 'Body Politics: The Social Reproduction of Sexualities', in *Social Repro-*

duction Theory: Remapping Class, Recentring Oppression, edited by Tithi Bhattachar-ya, London: Pluto.

Sekyi-Otu, Ato 2018, *Left Universalism, Africa-Centric Essays*, London: Routledge.

Sekyi-Otu, Ato 2011, 'Fanon and the Possibility of Postcolonial Critical Imagination', in *Living Fanon*, edited by Nigel Gibson, New York: Palgrave.

Sekyi-Otu, Ato 1996, *Fanon's Dialectic of Experience*, Cambridge, MA: Harvard University Press.

Sevilla-Buitrago, Álavaro 2014, 'Urbs in Rure', in *Implosion/ Explosion*, edited by Neil Brenner, Berlin: Jovis.

Sexton, Jared 2016, 'Afropessimism: The Unclear Word', *Rhizomes* 29.

Shariati, Sara 2016, 'Fanon, Shariati et la question de la religion: cinquante ans après', *Politique Africaine* 143: 59–72.

Sharpley-Whiting, Denean T. 1996, 'Anti-Black Femininity and Mixed-Race Identity: Engaging Fanon to Reread Capécia', in *Fanon: Critical Reader*, edited by Lewis Gordon, Denean Sharpley-Whiting, and R.T. White, London: Blackwell.

Sharpley-Whiting, Denean T. 1999, 'Fanon's Feminist Consciousness and Algerian Women's Liberation: Colonialism, Nationalism and Fundamentalism', in *Rethinking Fanon: The Continuing Dialogue*, edited by Nigel Gibson, New York: Humanity.

Sharpley-Whiting, Denean T. 2002, *Negritude Women*, Minneapolis: University of Minnesota Press.

Sharpley-Whiting, Denean T. 2003, '*Tropiques* and Suzanne Césaire: The Expanse of Negritude and Surrealism', in *Race and Racism in Continental Philosophy*, edited by Robert Bernasconi and Sybil Cook, Bloomington: Indiana University Press.

Sheppard, Eric, Vinay Gidwani, Michael Goldman, Helga Leitner, Ananya Roy, and Anant Maringanti 2015, 'Introduction: Urban Revolutions in the Age of Global Urbanism', *Urban Studies* 51, 11: 1947–61.

Shih, Shu-mei 2013, 'Comparison as Relation', in *Comparison: Theories, Approaches, Uses*, edited by Rita Felski and Susan Stanford Friedman, Baltimore: Johns Hopkins University Press.

Shipley, Tyler 2020, *Canada in the World: Settler Colonialism and the Colonial Imagination*, Winnipeg and Halifax: Fernwood.

Simon, Catherine 2009, *Algérie, les années pieds-rouges (1962–1969)*, Paris: La Découverte.

Simon, David 1992, *Cities, Capital, and Development: African Cities in the World Economy*, London: Belhaven.

Simon, Patrick 2003, 'Le logement social en France et la gestion des "populations à risques"', *Homme et Migration* 1246: 76–91.

Simone, AbdouMaliq 2010, *City Life from Jakarta to Dakar: Movements at the Crossroads*, New York: Routledge.

Simpson, Audra 2014, *Mohawk Interruptus*, Durham, NC: Duke University Press.

Simpson, Audra 2016, 'The State is a Man: Theresa Spence, Loretta Saunders, and the Gender of Settler Sovereignty', *Theory and Event* 19, 4.

Simpson, Audra, and Andrea Smith 2014, 'Introduction', in *Theorising Native Studies*, edited by Audra Simpson and Andrea Smith, Durham, NC: Duke University Press.

Simpson, Leanne Betasamosake 2011, *Dancing on Our Turtle's Back*, Winnipeg: Arbeiter Ring Publishing.

Simpson, Leanne Betasamosake 2017, *As We Have Always Done*, Minneapolis: University of Minnesota Press.

Situationist International 1981a [1966], 'Address to Revolutionaries of Algeria and of All Countries', in *Situationist International Anthology*, edited by Ken Knabb, Berkeley: Bureau of Public Secrets.

Situationist International 1981b [1966], 'The Class Struggles in Algeria', in *Situationist International Anthology*, edited by Ken Knabb, Berkeley: Bureau of Public Secrets.

Smith, Adrian A. 2019, 'Towards a Critique of "Socio-Legality" in Settler Capitalist Canada', in *Change and Continuity: Canadian Political Economy in the New Millennium*, edited by Mark Thomas, Leah Vosko, Carlo Fanelli, and Olena Lyubchenko, Montreal and Kingston: McGill and Queen's University Press.

Smith, David A. 1996, *Third World Cities in Global Perspective: The Political Economy of Uneven Urbanisation*, Boulder: Westview.

Smith, Dorothy 1987, *The World as Everyday Problematic: A Feminist Sociology*, Toronto: University of Toronto Press.

Smith, Michael Peter, and Joe Feagin 1987, *The Capitalist City*, Oxford: Basil Blackwell.

Smith, Neil 1984, *Uneven Development: Nature, Capital and the Production of Space*, London: Basil Blackwell.

Smith, Neil 1991, 'Afterword: The Beginning of Geography', in *Uneven Development*, second edition, Oxford: Basil Blackwell.

Smith, Neil 1993, 'Homeless/Global: Scaling Places', in *Mapping the Futures*, edited by J. Bird et al., London: Routledge.

Smith, Neil 1996, *The New Urban Frontier: Gentrification and the Revanchist City*, London: Routledge.

Smith, Neil 2003, *American Empire: Roosevelt's Geographer and the Prelude to Globalisation*, Berkeley: University of California Press.

Smith, Neil 2005, *The Endgame of Globalisation*, New York: Routledge.

Soja, Edward 1980, 'The Socio-Spatial Dialectic', *Annals of the Association of American Geographers* 70: 207–25.

Soja, Edward 1989, *Postmodern Geographies: The Reassertion of Space in Critical Social Theory*, London: Verso.

Soja, Edward 1996, *Thirdspace*, Oxford: Blackwell.

Sotiris, Panagiotis 2017, 'From the Nation to the People of a Potential New Historical Bloc: Rethinking Popular Sovereignty through Gramsci', *International Gramsci Journal* 2, 2: 52–88.

Southall, Aidan 1998, *The City in Time and Space*, Cambridge: Cambridge University Press

Sparke, Matthew 2003, 'American Empire and Globalisation: Postcolonial Speculations on Neocolonial Enframing', *Singapore Journal of Tropical Geography* 24, 3: 373–89.

Spire, Alexis 2005, 'L'héritage du passé colonial', in *Etrangers à la carte: l'adminstration de l'immigration en France (1945–1975)*, Paris: Grasset.

Spivak, Gayatri Chakravorty 1998, 'Translator's Preface', in Jacques Derrida, *Of Grammatology*, corrected edition, Baltimore: Johns Hopkins University Press.

Spivak, Gayatri Chakravorty 1990, *The Postcolonial Critic: Interviews, Strategies, Dialogues*, edited by Sarah Harasym, New York: Routledge.

Standing Rock Sioux Tribe 2016, 'Standing Rock Sioux Tribe's Statement on US Army Corps of Engineers Decision to Not Grant Easement', http://standwithstandingrock.net/standing-rock-sioux-tribes-statement-u-s-army-corps-engineers-decision-not-grant-easement/ 4 December, accessed on 10 December 2016.

Stanek, Łukasz 2011, *Henri Lefebvre on Space: Architecture, Urban Research, and the Production of Theory*, Minneapolis: University of Minnesota Press.

Stanek, Łukasz 2014, 'Introduction: A Manuscript found in Saragossa: Toward an Architecture', in Henri Lefebvre, *Toward an Architecture of Enjoyment*, Minnesota: University of Minnesota Press.

Stanger-Ross, Jordan 2008, 'Municipal Colonialism in Vancouver', *Canadian Historical Review* 89, 4: 541–80.

Starblanket, Gina, and Dallas Hunt 2020, 'Indigenous Communities and Covid-19', *The Globe and Mail*, 27 March.

Stasiulis, Daiva, and Rhada Jhappan 1995, 'The Fractured Politics of a Settler Society', in *Unsettling Settler Societies*, edited by Daiva Stasiulis and Nira Yuval-Davis, London: Sage.

Stephanson, Anders 2010, 'The Philosopher's Island', *New Left Review* 61: 197–210.

Stevenson, Winona 1999, 'Colonialism and First Nations Women in Canada', in *Scratching the Surface*, edited by Ena Dua and Angela Roberston, Toronto: Women's Press.

Stora, Benjamin 1992, *Les immigrés algériens en France: une histoire politique*, Paris: Fayard.

Stora, Benjamin 2004, *Histoire de l'Algérie coloniale (1830–1954)*, Paris: La Découverte.

Stovall, Tyler 1996, *Paris Noir: African Americans in the City of Light*, Boston: Houghton Mifflin.

Stovall, Tyler 2003, 'From Red Belt to Black Belt: Race, Class and Urban Marginality in Twentieth-Century Paris', in *The Color of Liberty: Histories of Race in France*, edited by Sue Peabody and Tyler Stovall, Durham, NC: Duke University Press.

Streule, Monika 2018, *Ethnografie Urbaner Territorien: Metropolitane Urbanisierungs-prozesse von Mexico-Stadt*, Münster: Westfälisches Dampfboot.

Streule, Monika, Ozam Karaman, Linsay Sawyer, and Christian Schmid 2020, 'Popular Urbanisation: Conceptualising Urbanisation Processes Beyond Informality', *International Journal of Urban and Regional Research* online.

Taalba, Farid n.d., 'Emeutes à Barbès en 1955: Chronique d'une vieille habitude', http://fsqp.fr/IMG/pdf/BARBES_1955.pdf last accessed 17 December 2014.

Tafuri, Manfredo 1976, *Architecture and Utopia: Design and Capitalist Development*, translated by Barbara Luigia La Penta, Cambridge, MA: MIT Press.

Talaga, Tanya, 2017, *Seven Fallen Feathers: Racism, Death and Hard Truths in a Northern City*, Toronto: Anansi Press.

Tang, Wing-Shing 2014, 'Where Lefebvre Meets the East Nowadays: Urbanisation in Hong-Kong', in *Urban Revolution Now*, edited by Ákos Moravánsky, Christian Schmid, and Łukasz Stanek, Farnham: Ashgate.

Tanter, Annick, and Jean-Claude Toubon 1999, 'Mixité sociale et politique de peuplement', *Sociétés contemporaines* 33–4: 59–87.

Taylor, Keeanga-Yamahtta 2016, *From #Blacklivesmatter to Black Liberation*, Chicago: Haymarket.

Taylor, Keeanga-Yamahtta 2019, 'Black Feminism and the Combahee River Collective', *Monthly Review* 70, 8: 20–8.

Terral, Roméo, and Mario Sélise 2018, 'Dynamiques urbaines communes et spécificités des villes des Antilles françaises (Guadeloupe, Martinique) des origines de la colonisation (1635) à nos jours', *Etudes caribéennes* 39–40.

Tessier, Pascale 2016, 'Sartrouville: Le quartier des Indes repensé par Bouygues Immobilier et Logement français', *Le Moniteur*, 26 February.

Tevanian, Pierre 2003, *Le ministère de la peur: réflexions sur le nouvel ordre sécuritaire*, Paris: L'esprit frappeur.

Tevanian, Pierre 2012, *Dévoilements: les dessous d'une obsession française*, Paris: Libertalia.

Thapar, Romila 2003, *The Penguin History of Early India*, Delhi: Oxford.

Thomas, Deborah 2004, *Modern Blackness: Nationalism, Globalisation, and the Politics of Culture in Jamaica*, Durham, NC: Duke University Press.

Thomas, Greg 2018a, 'Afro-Blue Notes: The Death of Afro-Pessimism', *Theory and Event* 21, 1: 282–317.

Thomas, Greg 2018b, 'Wynter with Fanon in the FLN: The "Rights of Peoples" Against the Monohumanism of Man', *American Quarterly* 70, 4: 857–65.

Thomas, Peter 2017, 'The Plural Temporalities of Hegemony', *Rethinking Marxism* 29, 2: 281–302.

Thomas-Müller, Clayton n.d., 'Just Environmentalism? An Interview with Clayton Thomas-Müller', *Upping the Anti*, available at: http://uppingtheanti.org accessed in May 2016.

Thörn, Håkan, Margit Mayer, and Catharina Thörn 2017, 'Re-thinking Urban Social Movements, "Riots" and Uprisings: An Introduction', in *Urban Uprisings: Challenging Neoliberal Urbanism in Europe*, edited by Margit Mayer, Catharina Thörn, and Håkan Thörn, London: Palgrave.

Timberlake, Michael (ed.) 1985, *Urbanisation in the World Economy*, Orlando: Academic Press.

Tissot, Sylvie 2005, 'Une discussion informelle? Usages du concept de mixité sociale dans la gestion des attributions du logement HLM', *Actes de la recherche en sciences sociales* 159: 54–69.

Tissot, Sylvie 2007a, *L'Etat et les quartiers: genèse d'une catégorie de l'action publique*, Paris: Seuil.

Tissot, Sylvie 2007b, 'The Role of Race and Class in Urban Marginality', *City*.

Tobias, John 1991 [1976], 'Protection, Civilisation, Assimilation', in *Sweet Promises*, edited by J.R. Miller, Toronto: University of Toronto Press.

Toews, Owen 2018, *Stolen City: Racial Capitalism and the Making of Winnipeg*, Winnipeg: ARP.

Tomba, Massimiliano 2013, *Marx's Temporalities*, translated by Peter D. Thomas and Sara R. Farris, Leiden: Brill.

Tombazos, Stavros 2014, *Time in Marx: The Categories of Time in Marx's Capital*, Chicago: Haymarket.

Tomiak, Julie 2011, 'Indigeneity and the City', in *Lumpencity*, edited by Markus Kip, Alan Bourke, and Tia Dafnos, Ottawa: Red Quill, pp. 163–91.

Tomiak, Julie 2016, 'Unsettling Ottawa', *Canadian Journal of Urban Research* 25, 1: 8–21.

Tomiak, Julie 2017, 'Contesting the Settler City', *Antipode* 49, 4: 928–45.

Tomiak, Julie 2019, 'Contested Entitlement', in *Settler City Limits: Indigenous Resurgence and Colonial Violence in the Urban Prairie West*, edited by Heather Dorries, Robert Henry, David Hugill, Tyler McCreary, and Julie Tomiak, Winnipeg: University of Manitoba Press.

Tomich, Dale W. 1979, 'The Dialectic of Colonialism and Culture: The Origins of the Negritude of Aimé Césaire', *Review* 2, 3: 351–85.

Tomich, Dale W. 2004, *Through the Prism of Slavery: Labour, Capital and the World Economy*, Lanham: Rowman and Littlefield.

Tomich, Dale W. 2016 [1990], *Slavery in the Circuit of Sugar: Martinique and the World Economy*, second edition, New York: SUNY Press.

Tournon, Mariana 2018, 'Du redressement économique au projet urbain. Gestion financière des HLM et genèse de la rénovation urbaine (1980–2000)', *Métropolitiques*, 19 March, http://www.metropolitiques.eu/Du-redressement-economique-au-projet-urbain-Gestionfinanciere-des-HLM-et.html

Traboulsi, Fawwaz 2008, 'Orientalising the Orientals: The Other Message of Edward Said', in *Waiting for the Barbarians: A Tribute to Edward Said*, edited by Müge Gürsoy Sökmen and Basak Ertür, London: Verso.

Tranb, Jérôme 2005, 'La rénovation urbaine, ou comment en finir avec les quartiers d'habitat social', *Esprit* 311: 36–44.

Trebitsch, Michel 2002, 'The Moment of Radical Critique', Preface to Henri Lefebvre, *Critique of Everyday Life*, Volume 2, London: Verso.

Trouillot, Michel-Rolph 1998, 'Culture of the Edges: Creolisation in the Plantation Context', *Plantation Society in the Americas* 5, 1: 8–28.

Tuck Eve, and Wayne Yang, 2012 'Decolonisation is Not a Metaphor', *Decolonisation: Indigeneity, Education and Society* 1, 1: 1–40.

Turner, Lou 1996, 'On the Difference between the Hegelian and Fanonian Dialectic of Lordship and Bondage', in *Fanon: A Critical Reader*, edited by Lewis Gordon, Denean Sharpley-Whiting, R.T. White, London: Blackwell.

Turner, Lou 1999, 'Fanon and the FLN: Dialectics of Organisation and the Algerian Revolution', in *Rethinking Fanon: The Continuing Dialogue*, edited by Nigel Gibson, Amherst, NY: Humanity Books.

Turner, Lou 2001, 'Marginal Note on Minority Questions in the Thought of Frantz Fanon', *Philosophia Africana* 4, 2: 37–46.

Turner, Lou 2003, 'Fanon Reading (W)right, the (W)right Reading of Fanon: Race, Modernity, and the Fate of Humanism', in *Race and Racism in Continental Philosophy*, edited by Robert Bernasconi with Sybil Cook, Bloomington: Indiana University Press.

Tyner, James A. 2007, 'Urban Revolutions and the Spaces of Black Radicalism', in *Black Geographies and the Politics of Place*, edited by Katherine McKittrick and Clyde Woods, Toronto: Between the Lines.

Tyner, James A. 2006, '"Defend the Ghetto": Space and the Urban Politics of the Black Panther Party', *Annals of the Association of American Geographers* 96, 1: 105–18.

Unist'ot'en n.d., available at http://unistoten.camp/ accessed in June 2016.

United Nations 2018, *World Urbanisation Prospects* https://population.un.org/wup/

Urban Studies 2015, 'Urban Revolutions in the Age of Global Urbanism', special issue, 52, 11.

Van Nostrand, John 2014, 'If We Build It, They Will Stay', *Walrus*, September 34–9.

Vasudevan, Alexander 2017, *The Autonomous City: A History of Urban Squatting*, London: Verso.

Vergès, Françoise 1997, 'Creole Skin, Black Mask: Fanon and Disavowal', *Critical Inquiry* 23, 3: 578–95.

Vergès, Françoise 2017, 'Racial Capitalocene', in *Futures of Black Radicalism*, edited by Gaye Theresa Johnson and Alex Lubin, London: Verso.

Viau, Roland 2012, 'L'esprit des lieux', *Histoire de Montréal et de sa région 1*, edited by Dany Fougères, Québec: Presses de l'Université Laval.

Viet, Vincent 1999, 'Les politiques du logement des immigrés (1945–1990)', *Vingtième Siècle* 64: 91–104.

Viviano, Michel 2005, 'Le financement de la politique de rénovation urbaine', *Revue du Trésor* 85, 2: 75–9.

Voldman, Danièle 2015, 'Les métamorphoses de l'habitat populaire: La genèse des grands ensembles', in *En finir avec les banlieues? Le désenchantment de la politique de la ville*, edited by Thomas Kirszbaum, Paris: L'Aube.

Wachsmuth, David 2014, 'City as Ideology', in *Implosions/Explosions*, edited by Neil Brenner, Berlin: Jovis.

Wacquant, Loïc 1999, *Les prisons de la misère*, Paris: Raisons d'Agir.

Wacquant, Loïc 2008, *Urban Outcasts: A Comparative Sociology of Advanced Marginality*, Cambridge: Polity.

Wainstein, Liza, and Xuefei Ren, 2009, 'The Changing Right to the City: Urban Renewal and Housing Rights in Globalising Shanghai and Mumbai', *City and Community* 8, 4: 407–31.

Wajeman, Lise 2017, 'Frantz Fanon par Raphaël Confiant, ou l'extension du domaine de la créolité', *Médiapart.fr*, 15 June.

Walcott, Rinaldo 2006, 'Black Men in Frocks: Sexing Race in a Gay Ghetto (Toronto)', in *Claiming Space: Racialisation in Canadian Cities*, edited by Cheryl Teelucksingh, Waterloo: Wilfried Laurier University Press.

Walcott, Rinaldo 2015, 'Genres of Human: Multiculturalism, Cosmo-Politics, and the Caribbean Basin', in *Sylvia Wynter: On Being Human as Praxis*, edited by Katherine McKittrick, Durham, NC: Duke University Press.

Walcott, Rinaldo 2016, *Queer Returns: Essays on Multiculturalism, Diaspora, and Black Studies*, London: Insomniac Press.

Walker, Ryan, Ted Jojola, and David Natcher (eds) 2013, *Reclaiming Indigenous Planning*, Montreal and Kingston: McGill-Queen's University Press.

Walker, Richard 1981, 'A Theory of Suburbanisation: Capitalism and the Construction of Urban Space in the United States', in *Urbanisation and Urban Planning in Capitalist Society*, edited by Michael Dear and Allen Scott, London and New York: Methuen.

Wallerstein, Immanuel 1997, 'Eurocentrism and its Avatars: The Dilemmas of Social Science', *New Left Review* 226: 93–107.

Wallerstein, Immanuel 2009, 'Reading Fanon in the 21st Century', *New Left Review* 57.

Walton, John 1994, *Free Markets and Food Riots: The Politics of Global Adjustment*, Cambridge, MA: Blackwell.

Ware, Syrus Marcus, and Giselle Dias (Niigaanii Zhaawshko Giizhigokwe) 2020, 'Towards Black and Indigenous Futures on Turtle Island: A Conversation', in Rodney Diverlus, Sandy Hudson, and Syrus Marcus Ware, *Until We Are Free: Reflections on Black Lives Matter in Canada*, Regina: University of Regina Press.

Warf, Barney, and Santa Arias (eds) 2009, *The Spatial Turn: Interdisciplinary Perspectives*, London: Routledge.

Watkins, Mel (ed.) 1977, *Dene Nation*, Toronto: University of Toronto Press.

Watts, Julia H. 1998, 'An Interview with Raphaël Confiant', *Plantation Society in the Americas* 5, 1: 41–59.

Weate, James 2001, 'Fanon, Merleau-Ponty, and the Difference of Phenomenology', in *Race*, edited by Robert Bernasconi, Oxford: Blackwell.

Webber, Jeffrey 2011, *Red October*, Leiden: Brill.

Whitehead, Judith 2010, *Development and Dispossession in the Narmada Valley*, New Delhi: Pearson.

Whitehead, Mark 2014, *Environmental Transformations: A Geography of the Anthropocene*, London: Routledge.

Wilder, Gary 2003a, 'Panafricanism and the Republican Sphere', in *The Color of Liberty: Histories of Race in France*, edited by Sue Peabody and Tyler Stovall, Durham, NC: Duke University Press.

Wilder, Gary 2003b, 'Unthinking French History: Colonial Studies Beyond National Identity', in *After the Imperial Turn: Thinking with and through the Nation*, edited by Antoinette Burton, Durham, NC: Duke University Press.

Wilder, Gary 2004, 'Race, Reason, Impasse: Césaire, Fanon and the Legacy of Emancipation', *Radical History Review* 90: 31–61.

Wilder, Gary 2008, 'Untimely Vision: Aimé Césaire, Decolonisation, Utopia', *Public Culture* 21, 1: 102–40.

Wilder, Gary 2009a, 'Aimé Césaire: contra commeration', *African and Black Diaspora: An International Journal* 2, 1: 121–3.

Wilder, Gary 2009b, 'Thinking with Aimé Césaire', in *The Work of Man Has Only Just Begun* https://cesairelegacies.cdrs.columbia.edu/political-legacy/thinking-with-aime-cesaire/

Wilder, Gary 2015, *Freedom Time: Negritude and Decolonisation and the Future of the World*, Durham, NC: Duke University Press.

Williams, Raymond 1973, *The Country and the City*, Oxford: Oxford University Press.

Wilson, Elizabeth 1991, *The Sphynx in the City: Urban Life, the Control of Disorder and Women*, London: Virago.

Wilson, Japhy 2011, 'Notes on the Rural City: Henri Lefebvre and the Transformation of Everyday Life in Chiapas, Mexico', *Environment and Planning D: Society and Space* 29: 993–1009.

Wilson, Japhy, and Manuel Bayòn 2017, 'Fantastic Materialisations: Interoceanic Infrastructures in the Ecuadorian Amazon', *Environment and Planning D: Society and Space* 35, 5: 836–54.

Withold de Wenden, Catherine, and Rémy Leveau 2001, *La beurgeoisie: Les trois âges de la vie associative issue de l'immigration*, Paris: Babélio.

Wolch, Jennifer, and Michael Dear 1989, *The Power of Geography: How Territory Shapes Social Life*, Boston: Unwin Hyman.

Wolf, Eric 1969, *Peasant Wars of the 20th Century*, New York: Harper and Row.

Wolfe, Patrick 2001, 'Land, Labour and Difference: Elementary Structures of Race', *The American Historical Review* 106, 3: 866–905.

Wolfe, Patrick 2006, 'Settler Colonialism and the Elimination of the Native', *Journal of Genocide Research* 8, 4: 387–409.

Wolfe, Patrick 2013, 'The Settler Colonial Complex: An Introduction', *American Indian Culture and Research Journal* 37, 2: 1–22.

Wood, Ellen Meiksins 2003, *Empire of Capital*, London: Verso.

Wotherspoon, Terry, and Vic Satzewich 2000, *First Nations*, Regina: Canadian Plains Research Center.

Wright, Gwendolyn 1991, *The Politics of Design in French Colonial Urbanism*, Chicago: University of Chicago Press.

Wynter, Sylvia 1973, 'Creole Criticism – A Critique', *New World Journal* 4: 12–36.

Wynter, Sylvia 1989, 'Beyond the World of Man: Glissant and the Discourse of the Anti-lles', *World Literature Today* 63, 4: 637–48.

Wynter, Sylvia 2000, 'The Re-enchantment of Humanism: An Interview with Sylvia Winter', Interview by David Scott, *Small Axe* 8: 119–207.

Wynter, Sylvia 2003, 'Unsettling the Coloniality of Being/Power/Truth/Freedom: Towards the Human, After Man. Its Overrepresentation – An Argument', CR: *The Centennial Review* 3, 3: 257–337.

Wynter, Sylvia, and Katherine McKittrick 2015, 'Unparalleled Catastrophe for Our Species? Or: To Give Humanness a Different Future: Conversation', in *Sylvia Wynter on Being Human as Praxis*, edited by Katherine McKittrick, Durham, NC: Duke University Press.

Yellowhead Institute 2019, *Land Back, A Yellowhead Institute Red Paper*, Toronto: Yellowhead Institute.

Yellowhead Institute 2020, 'Covid-19 and Indigenous Communities: Information and Resources', https://yellowheadinstitute.org/covid19/

Yiftachel, Oren 2009, 'Critical Theory and "Gray Space": Mobilisation of the Colonised', *City* 13, 2: 246–63.

Yinka Dene Alliance n.d., available at http://yinkadene.ca accessed in May 2016.

Young, Robert 2001, *Postcolonialism: An Historical Introduction*, Oxford: Blackwell.

Yvelines en luttes 2007, www.yvelines-en-lutte.info/spip.php?article66 27 January, accessed 1 May 2010.

Zalik, Anna 2016, 'Duty to Consult or License to Operate?' in *First World Petro-Politics*, edited by Laurie Adkin, Toronto: University of Toronto Press.

Zappi, Sylvia 2015, 'Au Val-Fourré, une mixité sociale mais pas ethnique', *Le Monde*, 1 April.

Zeilig, Leo 2016, *Frantz Fanon, the Militant Philosopher of Third World Revolution*, London and New York: I.B. Tauris.

Zerrouky, Madjid 2020, 'Coronavirus: en Algérie, l'épidémie sert la répression', *Le Monde*, 16 April.

Zobel, Joseph 1976, *La Rue Cases-Nègres*, Dakar and Paris: Présence Africaine.

Zouligha 1999, 'Challenging the Social Order: Women's Liberation in Contemporary Algeria', in *Rethinking Fanon: The Continuing Dialogue*, edited by Nigel Gibson, New York: Humanity.

Index

www.ingramcontent.com/pod-product-compliance
Lightning Source LLC
Chambersburg PA
CBHW070611030426
42337CB00020B/3755